A Practical Guide to Teaching Art and Design in the Secondary School

A Practical Guide to Teaching Art and Design in the Secondary School bridges the gap between key themes in Art and Design education theory, professional practice and the classroom. This practical and accessible book introduces methods for the delivery of engaging Art and Design lessons that safely and meaningfully address the current key issues in the subject.

Each chapter includes tasks to support trainee and early career teachers in implementing, reviewing and adapting their teaching. Chapters cover a range of core approaches to the curriculum such as powerful knowledge for the Art and Design teacher, the place of Art History in the curriculum and critical thinking in Art and Design learning. In addition, emerging cultural and political issues (such as decolonising the Art and Design curriculum, gender and sexuality, anti-ablism, sustainability and well-being) are explored in ways designed to guide teachers towards applying their own unique teaching style.

Linking directly to the planning and delivery of the subject in Key Stages 3, 4 and 5, the book is divided into three sections:

- Imaginative Curiosity for the Art and Design Teacher
- Epistemological Curiosity for Teachers and Learners
- Critical Curiosity in the Art and Design Classroom

Designed to be used independently or alongside the essential textbook *Learning to Teach Art and Design in the Secondary School*, this book is packed with practical strategies, teaching ideas and activities in every chapter. The book provides everything trainee and early career teachers need to reflect on and develop their teaching practice, helping them to plan lessons across the subject in a variety of teaching situations.

Andy Ash is an Associate Professor at UCL IOE. His expertise and research include Art Education, Contemporary Art, Galleries & Museums, Teaching & Learning, Visual Art Practice as Research and Initial Teacher Education. He is the President (elect) of NSEAD and InSEA Chair for the European Regional Council.

Peter Carr is a past PGCE Subject Leader Art and Design at Birmingham City University. Prior to working in Initial Teacher Training, he taught in secondary schools and in FE. He is engaged in research on pupils' affective perceptions of school design.

Routledge Teaching Guides

Series Editors: Susan Capel and Marilyn Leask

Other titles in the series:

A Practical Guide to Teaching Design and Technology in the Secondary School
Edited by Gwyneth Owen-Jackson

A Practical Guide to Teaching History in the Secondary School
Edited by Martin Hunt

A Practical Guide to Teaching Citizenship in the Secondary School
Edited by Liam Gearon

A Practical Guide to Teaching ICT in the Secondary School
Edited by Steve Kennewell, Andrew Connell, Anthony Edwards, Michael Hammond and Cathy Wickens

A Practical Guide to Teaching Computing and ICT in the Secondary School
Andrew Connell and Anthony Edwards with Alison Hramiak, Gavin Rhodes and Neil Stanley

A Practical Guide to Teaching Mathematics in the Secondary School, 2nd Edition
Edited by Clare Lee and Robert Ward-Penny

A Practical Guide to Teaching Physical Education in the Secondary School, 3rd Edition
Edited by Susan Capel, Joanne Cliffe and Julia Lawrence

A Practical Guide to Teaching English in the Secondary School, 2nd Edition
Annabel Watson and Ruth Newman

A Practical Guide to Teaching Music in the Secondary School, 2nd Edition
Edited by Carolyn Cooke and Chris Philpott

A Practical Guide to Teaching Science in the Secondary School, 2nd Edition
Douglas P. Newton

A Practical Guide to Teaching Foreign Languages in the Secondary School, 3rd Edition
Edited by Norbert Pachler & Ana Redondo

A Practical Guide to Teaching Art and Design in the Secondary School
Edited by Andy Ash & Peter Carr

These Practical Guides have been designed as companions to **Learning to Teach X Subject in the Secondary School**. For information on the Routledge Teaching Guides series please visit our website at www.routledge.com/education.

A Practical Guide to Teaching Art and Design in the Secondary School

Edited by
Andy Ash
and
Peter Carr

Routledge
Taylor & Francis Group

LONDON AND NEW YORK

Designed cover image: © Lisa Dynan

First edition published 2024
by Routledge
4 Park Square, Milton Park, Abingdon, Oxon, OX14 4RN

and by Routledge
605 Third Avenue, New York, NY 10158

Routledge is an imprint of the Taylor & Francis Group, an informa business

© 2024 selection and editorial matter, Andy Ash and Peter Carr; individual chapters, the contributors

The right of Andy Ash and Peter Carr to be identified as the authors of the editorial material, and of the authors for their individual chapters, has been asserted in accordance with sections 77 and 78 of the Copyright, Designs and Patents Act 1988.

All rights reserved. No part of this book may be reprinted or reproduced or utilized in any form or by any electronic, mechanical, or other means, now known or hereafter invented, including photocopying and recording, or in any information storage or retrieval system, without permission in writing from the publishers.

Trademark notice: Product or corporate names may be trademarks or registered trademarks, and are used only for identification and explanation without intent to infringe.

British Library Cataloguing-in-Publication Data
A catalogue record for this book is available from the British Library

Library of Congress Cataloging-in-Publication Data
Names: Ash, Andy, 1965– editor. | Carr, Peter, 1956– editor.
Title: A practical guide to teaching art and design in the
secondary school / Andy Ash and Peter Carr.
Description: Abingdon, Oxon: Routledge, 2024. |
Series: Routledge teaching guides |
Includes bibliographical references and index.
Identifiers: LCCN 2023050236 (print) | LCCN 2023050237 (ebook) |
ISBN 9781032455310 (hardback) | ISBN 9781032455303 (paperback) |
ISBN 9781003377429 (ebook)
Subjects: LCSH: Art—Study and teaching (Secondary) |
Design—Study and teaching (Secondary)
Classification: LCC N363 .P73 2024 (print) | LCC N363 (ebook) |
DDC 707.1/2—dc23/eng/20240126
LC record available at https://lccn.loc.gov/2023050236
LC ebook record available at https://lccn.loc.gov/2023050237

ISBN: 978-1-032-45531-0 (hbk)
ISBN: 978-1-032-45530-3 (pbk)
ISBN: 978-1-003-37742-9 (ebk)

DOI: 10.4324/9781003377429

Typeset in Palatino
by codeMantra

Contents

Foreword

This timely book draws upon the experiences of the very best of contemporary art and design education practitioners; the emphasis here is on *practitioners*. Practice, in all its manifestations, is at its heart. Art teachers are often asked the question 'do you have time to do your own work?' to which one might reply 'this *is* my own work', that is, being a professional art teacher, not an artist who happened to teach. Many art teachers never stop doing their own artwork and sometimes work alongside their pupils and students, but the divide between practice as a teacher and practice as an artist is ever-present. Contemporary art and design education has gone a long way towards removing that divide, with the practice of art-making becoming embedded into the practice of art and design teaching; there are books on artist-teacher practice, and higher degree courses offering courses for artist-teachers. In addition, studio art and design practice as a research method has gained a significant foothold, and there is a growing awareness that art-making, in all of its manifestations, is not a 'below the wrist' activity, but essentially involves cognition and can be a particular way of knowing.

There are some subtle and not-so subtle distinctions between the various school subject areas referred to in this book. 'The Arts' for example, usually covers dance, drama, music and visual art which in the UK schools sometimes comes under the umbrella of 'Expressive Arts'. 'Craft' has disappeared from the UK curriculum in terms of its use as a subject title, having previously been aligned with both 'Art' and 'Design'; in the latter case for some years there was a school subject called CDT – 'Craft, Design and Technology' but that particular nomenclature has fallen out of favour. We are however seeing the beginnings of a revival of a concern for craft skills. Contemporary fine art practice, outside of schooling, is wide-ranging and can cover all aspects of expressive arts, craft and, to some extent, design. 'Design' is for the most part coupled with 'Technology' and is often a very different subject from the 'Design' as practised by 'Art & Design' teachers. 'Design' as a school subject has had a chequered history and, despite efforts on the part of some academics and (perhaps misguided) government policy, it has not really delivered in terms of meaningful learning experiences for young people; the late Fraser Smith, who formerly mentored the editors, often referred to 'Design' as being 'epistemologically slippery', while 'art-making' as a human phenomenon is a paradigm example of a contested concept.

A preferred term, one that covers the art, craft and design practices from around the globe from pre-history to the present is 'creating aesthetic significance' – but this is too much of a mouthful for a school timetable. *Art & design education* is an academic area that is distinct from both art and education and can be deemed to be an epistemological entity, in that it has its own literature, knowledge base and practices; it differs from, but is a part of and informed by both subject areas. Like art, it is contested and fluid in terms of people's understanding; like general education, art and design education moves with the times and reflects society's values.

Art & design education has huge potential to lead the way, doing more that reflecting cultural norms, but showing a way forward for general education with pioneering and challenging practice – this is reflected in Ash and Carr's choice of authors and topics. It is implicit in the practices described in *A Practical Guide to Teaching Art and Design in the Secondary School* that contemporary practice should inform what we can call, as a form of shorthand, 'Art & Design'; this subject title can include for example, performance, digital technology and craft skills – it is this flexibility and diversity that enriches the subject and helps prevent orthodoxies from creeping in and settling. Challenging orthodoxies has almost become an orthodoxy in itself, but it is born out of curiosity – a desire to enquire further and ask questions – such as 'why is this done this way?' and 'what is the purpose of...?'. It is curiosity that underpins this book's three sections: 'Imaginative Curiosity, Epistemological Curiosity and Critical Curiosity'. Each section offers insights into how art and design teacher practice can move forward in a practical way that reflects the lives of the learners in their charge.

Ultimately, we need to return to the question 'what are schools for?'. A cynical reply might be to stop adolescents roaming the streets or, more commonly, to provide a knowledgeable workforce. However, knowledge, especially school knowledge, is not enough – we need to generate and promote *practical sagacity*. Art & design teachers, through their practice and their practical engagement with various materials and media, can facilitate wisdom amongst their learners. Practical imaginative activity is not confined to art & design of course, but all subject areas could be enhanced through adopting some of the practices that are commonly associated with art & design and which are highlighted in this innovative publication.

Richard Hickman
Emeritus Professor, University of Cambridge

List of Contributors

Andy Ash is an Artist, Researcher and Educator. He is an Associate Professor at UCL IOE and has worked in four Russell Group Universities. His expertise and research include Art Education, Contemporary Art, Galleries & Museums, Teaching & Learning, Visual Art Practice as Research, and Initial Teacher Education. He is the President (elect) of NSEAD and InSEA Chair for the European Regional Council. Andy exhibits his artwork globally.

Fiona Byrne is a second-level Technology Teacher with experience in design and technology curriculum development. She was a Technology Subject Advisor with Junior Cycle for Teachers, a Department of Education support service and has worked with The Big Idea, a second-level creative education programme. Fiona studied Industrial Design and completed an education research masters in NCAD.

Peter Carr taught Art and Design in London for 17 years before moving into teacher training at Middlesex University and Birmingham City University where he became PGCE Secondary Subject Leader for Art and Design. His research interests are in the design of educational space and the application of radical geography theory to children's and young people's agency in learning environments.

Emma Creighton is a Lecturer in design at the National College of Art and Design (NCAD), Dublin where she teaches across undergraduate and postgraduate programmes in product and interaction design. Her ongoing research focuses on the transformative role that design and technology can play in shaping learning experiences, spaces and tools, specifically within the areas of education and healthcare.

Stephanie Cubbin is an Artist-teacher at the St Marylebone School, London where she is the Head of the Art Department. Stephanie also works with other Art Departments in a consultancy role, supporting middle leadership in their curriculum development and result improvement. Stephanie is an experienced Awarding Body Moderator, still teaches in all key stages and maintains an arts practice.

Mousumi De, PhD, is an Assistant Professor, Curriculum and Instruction at the School of Education, University of Redlands, United States. Her background involves using visual arts, media and new media technologies for multicultural and peace education, social justice education, conflict transformation and social development of minority, marginalized and indigenous communities.

Jo Fursman is an Artist, Researcher and Educator employing lens-based practice to critically explore the distinct fields of the photographic image, art practice and pedagogy to examine the contemporary appearances of school. This practice emerged through a PhD in which young people participated in the research by reflecting on their school environment with digital cameras. Fursman is the subject leader for PGCE Art and Design at Birmingham City University and has worked in Secondary, Further and Higher Education since 2005. Fursman has taught on the Artist-Teacher Scheme, BA and MA Art and Education Practices and in Primary Initial Teacher Education.

Ged Gast is a freelance art and design and school improvement specialist, working in creativity, visual literacy, digital literacy, critical thinking, SMSC and pedagogies for improving learning. He is a member of NSEAD Executive and is a NSEAD Past President. He is a patron of Art History in Schools and was formerly an Ofsted Inspector from 1992 until 2014. He is PQSI qualified.

Will Grant is a Senior Lecture in Art and Design Education at the School of Education and Childhood, University of the West of England, Bristol. He is interested in the cultural friction between standardized models of schooling and the authentic character of artistic practice and in particular, as leader of a PGCE programme, how this friction might be navigated by student teachers.

Gary Granville is an Emeritus Professor of Education at the National College of Art and Design (NCAD), Dublin. In recent years, he has chaired national development groups for second-level art and design in Irish post-primary schools. His research and professional activities include arts education and creativity, curriculum and assessment policy and educational evaluation.

Michele Gregson is a General Secretary and CEO of the National Society for Education in Art and Design. After working for many years as an art teacher, head of department and school leader, she joined Kent County Council's Advisory Service for Schools as Adviser for Art and Design, for all Kent schools. She worked as an independent arts consultant, before taking office at NSEAD.

Rebecca Heaton is an Assistant Professor in Visual and Performing Arts at the National Institute of Education (NIE), Nanyang Technological University (NTU) in Singapore. Rebecca disseminates research and art practice internationally concerning cognition, art, technology and education. She has held teaching and advisory positions in Schools, Higher Education Institutes and with Curriculum Development organisations in the United Kingdom and abroad.

Dr Sandra Hiett is a Senior Lecturer in Art and Design Education at Liverpool Hope University where she leads the PGCE Art and Design course and supervises doctoral students within the School of Education. In addition, Sandra is a freelance researcher with a focus on cultural education and arts education for social justice.

Dr Tabitha V.P. Millett is an Assistant Professor and Course Leader of the Art and Design PGCE at Cambridge University. She researches in the areas of queer theory, new materialism and art education. Tabitha has taught Art and Design in a number of London schools and continues to develop her own artistic practice.

Tabitha is also Director of Queering the Art Classroom, a small non-profit organisation working with the National Trust, Fitzwilliam and Kettle's yard to exhibit school students' artwork and create workshops on gender and sexuality. Tabitha has held exhibitions at the National Trust, Dean Street Soho, The Oxford International Women's Festival, Brick Lane, Roman Road, King's college Cambridge, Maze gallery and Hackney Road.

Bayley Morris is a Doctoral Candidate in Education at Birmingham City University, where she has taught on the PGCE Secondary Art and Design course. Her research entangles and deterritorializes contemporary art and education to imagine new pedagogical possibilities. She has previously been a Teacher of Art in Secondary schools.

Henrietta Patience is a Lecturer in Art and Design Education teaching on the both the PGCE Secondary and Primary programmes at Goldsmiths University. Henrietta has taught Art and Design and Film Studies in South East London secondary schools for the last 23 years and continues to support curriculum development in schools. Her research interests are in inclusion, aspiration towards creative pathways and sustainability.

Claire Penketh is an Associate Professor, the Head of Disability Studies and a core member of the Centre for Culture and Disability Studies at Liverpool Hope University. She is author of *A Clumsy Encounter: Drawing and Dyspraxia* (Sense, 2011) and is the co-editor of *Disability, Avoidance and the Academy* with her colleague Professor David Bolt (Routledge, 2016).

Andrea Pratt has worked in the education sector for 25 years and is currently the Deputy Programme Leader for Initial Teacher Education for Secondary Programmes and Subject Leader for Art and Design at Liverpool John Moores University. Her educational research interests are transforming teaching through evidence informed practice and examining the role of early career teacher research.

Ângela Saldanha coordinates community arts projects in the Portuguese Visual Arts Teachers' Association, APECV. She coordinated the APECV team in the European Commission-funded Horizon 2020 project titled *AMASS: 'Action on the Margin: Arts as Social Sculpture'* and InSEA Europe team in the EU Project Narcissus Meets Pandora.

Dr Marquard Smith is the Programme Leader, MA Museums & Galleries in Education at UCL Institute of Education, Deputy Director (Collaborations & Partnerships) at LAHP, Professor of Artistic Research at Vilnius Academy of Arts, Lithuania, and Editor-in-Chief, Journal of Visual Culture.

Kate Thackara has been the Head of Art at Lady Margaret School in South West London since 2016. She is also one of the founding collaborators of the Artisteacher network, set up in 2019 with Andy Ash and Henry Ward with the Freelands Foundation as a space to support and inform art educators' professional and personal artistic and teaching practices.

Teresa Torres de Eça is a Coordinator of the Portuguese Research Group Arts Community and Education *(GriArCE)*. She was the President of the International Society for Education Through Art *(InSEA)* during 2014–2017 and Chair of the World Alliance for Arts Education *(WAAE)* during 2023.

Ernst Wagner studied at the Art Academy in Munich (painting, sculpture and art education). He did his PhD in art history and philosophy. Today he researches and teaches mainly in international networks, based at the University of Erlangen-Nuremberg, where he coordinates the European section of the trans-continental project 'Exploring Visual Cultures' (www.explore-vc.org). His main areas of interest include art education and sustainable development (in a broad sense), international and transcultural pedagogy. He has published more than 300 book chapters and books.

Neil Walton is a Lecturer in the Educational Studies Department at Goldsmiths UoL. He has published on the journal Block, on theorist Anton Ehrenzweig and on the National Arts Education Archive (NAEA). He has worked with artist Cathie Pilkington on the exhibitions 'The Ancestors' at the Royal Academy of Arts and 'The Covering' at Karsten Schubert. Neil is a Trustee of the Association for Art History (AHA), a former co-editor of the International Journal of Art and Design Education (IJADE) and a Visiting Professor at the Royal Academy Schools. His current work includes developing a historicist pedagogy of Art and Design and examining how Brandom's inferentialism can inform art education.

Carol Wild currently leads the Secondary Art and Design PGCE at the Institute of Education, UCL. Her research interests include the classroom as an aesthetic phenomenon, speculative and arts-based research methods in education, the histories of the art and design education, neoliberal art education policy and feminist models for creative pedagogy.

Marlene Wylie is a Creative Education Consultant, RSA Fellow and President of NSEAD. Marlene is a member of the NSEAD Anti-Racist Art Education Action group, speaking to the critical issue of anti-racism and through her lived experi-ence. Marlene has taught art, craft and design in London primary and secondary schools for over 25 years. She has delivered whole school training from EYFS to secondary, and to trainee teachers on ITT programmes. Marlene is currently the Visualise Project Visualising Inclusive Practice Lead for the Runnymede Trust, which aims to deliver the first major research commission into access to the vis-ual arts for Black, Asian and minority ethnic students.

Introduction: 'A Curriculum of Curiosity & Hope'

Andy Ash and Peter Carr

In 2016, the Tate Modern advertised the opening of its new extension with the slogan 'Art Changes: We Change'. The intention and vision behind the campaign was to redefine the museum after the first 16 years of its operation, 'placing artists and their art at its centre while fully integrating the display, *learning* and social functions of the museum, and strengthening links between the museum, its community and the city' (nparadoxa, 2016). These were admirable and for the most part welcome objectives. However, the opening of the extension was met with controversy and demonstrations with concerns expressed about the lack of representation in the selection of the artists. It was thought that the changes didn't go far enough in reflecting contemporary society. Furthermore, the big focus on putting learning or education at the core of the museum with the new 'Tate Exchange' education spaces being housed in the extension, whilst initially very successful, was abandoned just five years later in 2021. This once dedicated, forward-looking, educational space for debate, reflection upon contemporary topics and ideas, designed to encourage audiences to get actively involved, think through doing and make a difference to their communities, is no longer a dedicated education space. So, it would seem that in this case as far as change and education go, the vision was short lived.

It therefore seems timely, with the DfE, Ofsted, subject associations and the awarding bodies all reviewing the school curricula, and with schools responding to the many changes in society and culture post the pandemic, to reflect again on the slogan 'Art Changes: We Change' and apply it to Art and Design education by thinking about art classrooms, art teaching and the learning that this brings about. In doing this, we have to ask ourselves, have those of us involved in Art and Design education changed in line with the recent radical changes in society and the economy; does our subject truly reflect contemporary society?; and is current Art and Design education preparing pupils for the 21st century as dramatically as Tate Modern attempted to do, at least initially, in 2016? We would suggest that it has not changed as much as it could have done, and, as at the Tate Exchange, the hoped-for ideals have become side-lined with in many cases Art and Design teachers continuing to tread a well-established and traditional path.

There are many reasons for this inertia that exists in some parts of the teaching of our subject just as there are in other aspects of cultural and professional life.

DOI: 10.4324/9781003281399-1

This being the case, the chapters in this book are written with the specific intention of upholding *better practice* and challenging the well-trodden and less creative aspects of secondary school Art and Design education. They do this by presenting practical ideas for re-routing and developing classroom practice to fully prepare this generation's pupils to better meet the challenges of the future. Furthermore, the chapters in this book are designed to enable training teachers, Early Career Teachers and established art teachers alike to reflect on the decisions they make for the curriculum and to consider plotting their own more informed course through an engagement with the complex landscape of contemporary issues related to Art and Design. The book aims to give art teachers agency and hope – agency to generate and deliver a relevant Art and Design curriculum, and the hope to feel suitably empowered to make decisions that will be meaningful for whatever educational context they are working in. The book points to ways in which Art and Design teachers can step off a rigid track of orthodoxy and develop their knowledge and understanding by exploring the more open terrain of the many possible Art and Design curriculums and pedagogies that are available to the committed art teacher.

Those entering the teaching profession often report that the initial training year was one of the most difficult things they have ever done. It challenges many personal understandings and is physically and emotionally demanding for a start. Yet they also acknowledge that it taught them more than just about teaching and learning in schools. They say that it also taught them more than they thought it would about the subject matter they thought they knew so well. Whilst this journey often asks difficult questions of them about the beliefs, values and understandings about themselves and their field of art or design, it also helps them make sense of their personal experience of Art and Design education. It sometimes, less positively, also presented them with an orthodoxy of practice (Addison and Burgess, 2003), with an approach to art that can feel out-dated and distant if their Higher Education or professional practice included more contemporary, post-modern, post-industrial, post-colonial and critically engaged practice. For those who have recently graduated, 'school art' (Efland, 1976) often appears unrelated to their contemporary understanding and philosophies about the subject matter they care so much about. For these trainee teachers, having to reinforce entrenched orthodoxies and teach for making in a 'school art' style is at odds with their beliefs, creating fundamental tensions for them from the start. On the other hand, the chapters in this book acknowledge that for some other trainee Art and Design teachers, an orthodox 'school art' curriculum and pedagogy may provide a welcome certainty by mirroring the school experience they remember from their schooling, and by appearing to anchor their practice securely in current school demands. For these trainees, a 'school art' approach, as defined by Efland, may provide some certainty but it is questionable if it will properly support them in developing the 21st century curriculum that their pupils need. It is one of the aims of this book to support all trainee Art and Design trainee teachers in navigating their way to their own professionally meaningful ways of teaching a viable curriculum for the 21st century.

Whichever approach they adopt in their training year, trainees who attend an academically rigorous training course that referenced a wide range of Art and Design and education practices, say that the year was possibly the most enjoyable thing they have ever done. It challenged and supported them in articulating positions, using research to inform practice, and developing an individual professional language that fully expresses their developing beliefs and insights. They welcomed the opportunity it offered them to become a part of a community of Art and Design teachers that mutually guides and supports its diverse members.

The editors of this book, Andy Ash and Peter Carr, first met on their PGCE course at Reading University; Andy came to the course from an artist in industry residency at a foundry in Derbyshire, and Peter from independent fine art practice. We have remained in contact throughout our PGCE teaching careers. Upon editing this book, it was interesting for us to think about those early days and the influence of our PGCE tutor, (Ian) Fraser Smith. Fraser Smith was a ceramic artist, who continued to practice, exhibit (with the London Potters) and share his making while teaching. He modelled for us an artist teacher practice method (Sayer, 2019), where one started the journey of learning by deconstructing one's Art and Design experience, by critically engaging with new insights and building and moving your teaching on from a position of strength, i.e. from your specialism. All of this was underpinned by a position of embracing difference, whether race, gender, class, sexual orientation etc., whilst encouraging us to engage with different types of Art and Design practice. Fraser gave us the confidence 'to be', to be the art teacher you wanted to be, to build upon your specialism and develop your practice for you and your learners. It was normal in the context of Fraser Smith's teaching to talk about identity, our experiences and values, and how to work with the context and community we were teaching in. This enabled a range of approaches and a range of different teaching paths to be pursued, something that we feel remains valuable for trainee teachers to do today.

Alongside his teaching on the Reading University PGCE course, Fraser Smith was writing in the 1980s about his outlook on the Art and Design education of his time. In one article, he created a typology in which he plotted the different types of Art and Design teachers that he observed in schools and the professional and philosophical tensions that existed when they articulated their values, curriculum content and the beliefs that drove their teaching. Fraser Smith framed the Art and Design teachers of his time in terms of models or stereotypes, which 'may simultaneously explain observed differences within the group as a whole and highlight problems of value in art teaching' (Smith, 1980, p. 144). His models or stereotypes were:

From the 1960s:

- Free Expressives;
- Basic Designers;

From the 1980s:

- High Priests – art historians or Fine Art Connoisseurs;
    - Magicians – Herbert Read fans, art as magic and mystery;
    - Mystics – art is personal, art is unteachable, it's about talent and giftedness;

- Technocrats – diametrically in opposition to the High Priests;
    - Engineers – tinkerers of the structure of education/curriculum/syllabus, offering blueprints to be taught – often HoD/F;
    - Designers – unsure about design education in Art and Design but committed to the 'material circus' or 'crafts cycle';

- Social Workers – see themselves as true inheritors of Herbert Read's position on aesthetic education as corrective forces and way forward for society;
- Anomics – lack of any coherence or belief or value with respect to art education – alienated from the field, therefore tending to attack everything;
- Pedagogues – multi-dimensionality in their set of views and values, art education can make sense of many disciplines, philosophy, psychology and sociology.

In the article, Smith makes it clear that the reason why the art teachers of his time frequently encountered difficulty in evaluating what they were doing educationally – why they struggled to articulate the values, the content and the beliefs that drove their teaching was because their stereotypical thinking made it 'not that simple' (Smith, 1980) for them. He concluded that it could have been their closely held values and beliefs that, although held in good faith, were sometimes creating educational blind spots for them that held them back from progressing the Art and Design education of their pupils. We think this is still an issue for some Art and Design teachers today. They may attempt to resolve this at least superficially by adopting a well-tried and relatively easy-to-facilitate 'school art' curriculum if they encounter this in their training. This can appear to allow them to sidestep the difficulties to be found in translating their previously held professional values into a set of educational values that match in vibrancy and purpose the art or design values that they joined their training course with. It is one of the key aims of this book to support Art and Design teachers in the transition of their artistic or design-erly values and beliefs into a personally crafted set of practical principles for their teaching that will help them to avoid simply relying on the default orthodoxy and the making of 'school art'.

Fraser Smith was writing in the 1980s and the references he makes relate to the research and practice at that point in the history of Art and Design education. Others since then have provided overviews of the differing approaches that Art and Design teachers can take. A more recent analysis that can help make sense of the positions the new Art and Design teacher may first see in today's classrooms is the typology given by Addison and Burgess (Addison and Burgess, 2007), rendered here in Task 1.1.

Task 1.1 Typology of Approaches

Upon entering the Art and Design department, see if you can identify the type of approaches, values and beliefs that the teachers are committed to and are communicating to learners. How can you identify the positions they take on the landscape of Art and Design education? Look at the SoW and projects, what do they privilege, what is being covered and what is not? How do the art teachers describe themselves, also what is the label over the door – is it the art dept, Art and Design studio, visual arts dept, expressive art dept, design dept, visual communication dept etc. – language is key to helping understand how they position and see themselves. Use the Addison & Burgess list to identify the 'continuing approaches within the art and design curriculum (11–18)' (Addison and Burgess, 2007) in relation to your dept. This should help you make sense of why you feel at home or not in the Art and Design curriculum of your school:

1. Perceptualist: mimetic procedures, a search for the 'absolute copy' reduction to appearance (Clement, 1993);
2. Formalist: a reduction to the visual elements, exercise driven, representational and/or abstract (Palmer, 1989);
3. Expressive: intuitive making through affective and /or material exploration: privileging the essential and individual (Watkin, 1974);
4. Genre-based: preconceived types perpetuated by teacher expertise and the imitation of exemplars, the successful work of past students, e.g. still life, life drawing, landscape, CD covers, ceramic figures;
5. Pastiche: the imitation of canonic exemplars, occasionally assimilating the post-modern practice of parody (SCAA1996 now QCA);
6. Technical: the development of a succession of discrete technical skills: drawing followed by printmaking, followed by batik etc.;
7. Object based: response to common – sometimes themed, often spectacular – artefacts in the form of a big still life/installation, e.g. natural and made forms; a multicultural potpourri (Taylor and Taylor, 1990)
8. Critical and contextual: an investigation of art as a means of social and cultural production privileging cognitive and analytical procedures (Field, 1970; Dyson, 1989; Taylor, 1989)
9. Issue-based: an integration of the personal with the social, political and moral through responses to current and contentious issues (Kennedy, 1995a)
10. Postmodern: promoting plural perspectives and approaches and embracing the new technologies (Efland et al., 1996; Swift and Steers, 1999)

Most departments will not use one approach exclusively, they may use combinations, but there may be a dominating position. Which ones seem to dominate in your dept and what are the consequences of this approach for the pupils? These can be positive or negative in your view.

Metaphors are helpful in the context of reflecting on the Art and Design teacher's lot, as they convey vivid imagery that can transcend literal meanings and create images that are easier to understand and respond to than literal language. As Art and Design teachers, this way of thinking is well understood, we often use metaphorical language to activate the imagination to convey emotions and understandings. The organisational theorist Gareth Morgan (Morgan, 2006) uses metaphors to help organisations, managers and individuals find appropriate ways of seeing, understanding and shaping situations. Morgan contends that individuals can become trapped by constructions of reality that give an imperfect grasp of the world. He outlines how it is possible to become trapped by favoured ways of thinking, and how these can prevent us from exploring new things and reaching new heights. Morgan says that individuals can be unaware that they are in what he refers to as a 'psychic prison' (Morgan, 2006) as their way of thinking feels to them like a normative practice that cannot be altered; a story that can often be reflected in Art and Design classrooms. Morgan offers the 'ART' approach as a way of breaking free from his 'psychic prison'. Task 1.2 enables you to apply Morgan's ART approach to your own position in Art and Design education.

Task 1.2 The ART Approach to Breaking from the Psychic Prison

We can start to change if we start to take control of our thought life. Are those norms and thoughts serving you at the present moment of where you are at in your approach to the teaching of Art and Design and where you want to be in the future? If the answer is 'no' then maybe it is time to change. Unhelpful thoughts can keep us in the psychic prison, so how can we rewire the unhelpful thoughts. We can start with self-reflection:

- **Acknowledge** that your current thoughts maybe unhelpful and may not be serving you;
- **Replace or reframe** those thoughts;
- **Take action** reframed thoughts should manifest in different courses of action (Consult, 2016).

There are many voices at present in the field of Art and Design education; politicians, Ofsted, awarding bodies, MAT's etc., all attempting to influence the agenda and trying to shape the field. We feel it is time that Art and Design teachers take back the initiative and take action to reframe their curriculums in line with the values that they work out for themselves and their subject. What better way is there than to start with your personal observations, knowledge and concerns about the subject and reflect upon the possibility of changing the education paradigm (Robinson, 2010), to start to orientate oneself in the field, to get one's bearings and then start to plot your own path.

As PGCE tutors, we see how Art and Design teachers have had to adapt and change their practice within the education policy landscape that has become well-established in recent decades. It is understandable that the pressures, restrictions and audit culture, driven by neo-liberal government agendas of controlling the education sector and 'steering centrally' (Ball, 2007) has had an impact. We have seen the results of this in a daily pragmaticism, the surrendering to the dominant policy discourse and a playing of the game of chasing statistical validation rather than teaching meaningfully while feeling unable to challenge the dominant discourse. This is the 'set up to fail syndrome' (Manzoni and Barsoux, 1998) that describes a dynamic in which colleagues and staff members perceived to be out of line with the general policy discourse live down to the low expectations their managers have for them. We hope that this book can create a dialogue for change and empower Art and Design teachers through curiosity about different ways to teach, challenge the status quo and start on a more transformative journey.

This book is rooted in practice for the classrooms and comes from the many Art and Design classrooms that we have experienced regionally, nationally and internationally, listening to art teachers, watching art teachers, continually engaging in dialogue and inquiring in many different conversations about the context and content of their curriculum and pedagogy. We are persistently challenged and inspired by the teachers we work with and so are highly respectful of the insights, the 'common sense' that we encounter whilst also being clear that:

> ...in order to get beyond 'common sense' you had to use it. Just as it is unacceptable to advocate an educational practice that is satisfied with rotating on

the axis of 'common sense', so neither is an educational practice acceptable that sets at naught the 'knowledge of living experience' and simply starts out with the educator's systematic cognition'.

(Freire, 2004)

This book starts with the Art and Design teacher's 'here and now', we know that to move forward we must work with practice and the practical. We want this text to respect and enable Art and Design teachers, to build upon present practice, the 'here and now' and make accessible potential points for change:

> …you never get *there* by starting from *there*, you get *there* by starting from some *here*. This means, ultimately, that the educator must not be ignorant of, under-estimate, or reject any of the 'knowledge of living experience with which edu-cans come to school.

(Freire, 2004)

This book sets out to support Art and Design teachers in developing a positive, forward-looking curriculum of *hope* that will enable them to develop their educational language; to build upon the concrete realities of teaching, to develop a practical language that we hope will allow Art and Design teachers to return to their classrooms, their practical contexts, to design a new curriculum of hope for their learners. When we talk about hope we don't think of it as simply something that you want to happen, but hope can also be used as a verb that means to 'strive for a wish…'. Hope is more than a feel-good emotion, it is an action-orientated strength involving agency, motivation and confidence that goals can be reached. Hope is a belief that our futures can be better than our past, and that we have a role to play in the making of that future into a reality. We hope that this book may enable effective pathways to be devised in order to drive towards that desired future.

The book has been devised around three themes to support your learning journey; Imaginative Curiosity, Epistemological Curiosity and Critical Curiosity. We hope to develop a *curious* mind, the chapters use inquiry-based learning and tasks that engage and ask questions about the Art and Design teacher's world. We feel the book will bridge the *here* to the *there*, allowing the reader to investigate the different themes in the chapters and be excited by the new or possibly unexpected terrain the authors map out within the landscape of Art and Design education. Learning begins with the curiosity to know, and our hope is we can develop an active inquisitiveness in the Art and Design teacher about the possibilities for their curriculum and the way that they will teach it.

The first theme is explored in 'Part 1: Imaginative Curiosity for the Art & Design teacher'. In this section the authors invite the reader to make a start on their journey, to begin playing with familiar aspects of their knowledge of lived experience. The reader will combine previous knowledge with observations and experimentation, ask what is going on here, and unpack how practice works and the principles that follow from it. The reader will use their ingenuity to practice and consider what needs to be done to get a desired result. The second section is 'Part 2: Epistemological Curiosity for Teachers and Learners' (Freire, 2005). 'Epistemological' refers to a desire for knowledge that motivates individuals to learn new ideas, eliminate gaps and solve intellectual problems. It is an opportunity to know more about Art and Design education, go deeper into and become more of an expert in practice. The third and final section is 'Part 3: Critical Curiosity in the Art & Design Classroom'. If Imaginative Curiosity begins and motivates the act of discovering how something works and if Epistemological Curiosity signifies methods and principles for probing more deeply into how something works, then Critical Curiosity is the curiosity that encourages the learner to seek alternative and more culturally relevant methodologies for Art and Design teaching. In fact, to be critical or to critique a concept or a practice means to conduct a detailed analysis and assessment of it, which in the case of Art and Design education enables the teacher to look at the concept or practice from multiple angles in order to gain a full picture of it, and gain an understanding of that 'something' that Ebrace refers to (Ebrace, 2010).

These three sections together offer a discoverable landscape or topology of Art and Design education through which the reader can pick their own routeway. They can use their own judgement to find a pathway in the chapters of the book that is relevant to the stage of training or early career teaching that they are in, and the teaching contexts within which they are operating. Whatever pathway the reader takes through the chapters, and whatever their hoped-for ideals for themselves and their learners, the reader should be able to move from their own 'here' through curiosity to a meaningful and effective 'there' for their learners.

In the chapters 'Remapping the Curriculum: a landscape designed for the future' and 'The Big Landscape', Ash & Gast signpost the start and the end of the parameters of the book. By giving an outline in 'Remapping the Curriculum' of how the many versions of the Art and Design curriculum that are in place have been arrived at, Ash and Gast give a 'here' of the curriculum as it is in many schools. In 'The Big Landscape', they point the way to the future pathways that are available for the Art and Design teacher as they grow in independence and as their professionalism deepens.

In 'Part 1: Imaginative Curiosity for the Art and Design Teacher', the chapters examine some fundamental aspects of the pedagogy of the subject in ways that demonstrate that these parts of your pedagogy can and should be the site of your curiosity about how your teaching works; and how these aspects of your teaching need not be the simple, standardised, unexamined basics of your lessons. On the contrary, chapters such as Heaton's and Pratt's offer creative approaches to every aspect of Art and Design teaching, including to the principles of enduring Art teaching practice such as modelling and demonstrating, and how to curate what is known about cognition in secondary age pupils as a vehicle for your creative teaching. Cubbin looks at coursework as a collaborative process in which teachers and learners access the core democratic principles of learning in Art and Design, which chimes with Thackara's account of 'artistic behaviour' for both teachers and learners. Wild takes up Efland's theme of 'school art' and challenges the binary opposition to this of apparently more contemporary approaches that Wild contends has become embedded in the literature. Wild looks for authenticity in the teaching of Art and Design and suggests that, through a clear-headed and unencumbered practice in today's schools, art teachers can discover in their teaching a professional authenticity whatever their approach to 'school art'. Gregson remembers that the well-being of teachers is as crucial as that of their learners and indicates practical approaches towards this that will enhance learning in Art and Design and potentially enrich the whole school community.

In 'Part 2: Epistemological Curiosity for Teachers and Learners', the chapters move on to an examination of how the theoretical underpinnings of the subject can be brought alive in practical ways. The focus of this part of the book is on the area of overlap between contemporary theoretical issues in society and in Art and Design education. The chapters focus on how current Art and Design education thinking is engaging with societal issues that are currently of concern to educators and theorists in the field of young peoples' social development. Walton demonstrates how the art historical elements of Art and Design need not be constrained by what may appear to be the de-facto universalising chronological implications of the National curriculum but can be made inclusive and pluralistic through practical activities that are meaningful to learners. Fursman and Torres de Eça & Saldanha look at lens-based practice from the perspective of educational and social theory about young peoples' approaches to the camera and social media. Both chapters draw on photography within education as a theoretical field that demonstrates how practitioners use camera technologies to explore both a trainee teacher's 'teacherly' self and a young person's ways of self-representation. Both chapters place photography as a key literacy of its own in the education space and the visual, media and legal worlds of digital networking. In these chapters, the digital era is the starting point for a critical pedagogy approach to the skills that teachers and their learners must develop intelligently to equip them for the 21st century.

Granville, Byrne and Creighton explore designerly thinking theory as a basis for the cultivation of divergent and original practical activity in the classroom, and Ash and Smith argue for learners in Art and Design to become curator-practitioners in collaborative activities that indicate ways in which they can be made responsible for organising and presenting their work, and that of others, as an integral aspect of learning. Grant makes an ethical case for a critical Art and Design education. He looks at the environmental, economic and social justice issues that preoccupy many educators, teachers, trainee teachers and school pupils, looking at practical ways that these can brought to the Art classroom. In Morris, open-endedness and surprise are advocated for, especially at Key Stage 3. Morris's aim is to look at practical ways of bringing a different pedagogy to your classroom other than the skills-based, prescriptive orthodoxies and recurring phenomena.

The chapters in 'Part 3: Critical Curiosity in the Art and Design Classroom', provide authoritative ways of building engaging and exciting Art and Design lessons around some key areas of contemporary critical thinking as these emerge into life issues for young people and the whole of society. The chapters in this section address some of the most difficult and contentious issues in society, looking at how these can be approached safely and constructively in Art and Design lessons. The authors in this section of the book take on the issues uncompromisingly with a commitment to linking learning in Art and Design to some key areas of society that are being actively addressed in other areas of the secondary curriculum. These authors believe that the Art and Design curriculum should be as curious and alive to current critical issues as these other subject areas are. They do this with a strong sense of responsibility to young peoples' progress towards citizenship, aligning this with an equal sense of responsibility to the development of the Art and Design curriculum. Wylie addresses the current colonial and Euro-centric educational landscape through a powerful personal history in education as both learner and teacher. Millett proposes practical ways that support Art and Design teachers to queer their classrooms, using discussion and activities that centre on helping pupils to a definition of queer and what it means to learn in a queer curriculum and pedagogy. Penketh & Hiett offer perspectives from disability studies to introduce and explore an anti-ableist approach towards art education, challenging the limitations that can arise from presumptions about what bodies and minds can be and do. All of these chapters address issues relating to the lived experience of our diverse student groups and engender open experimental art practice in the fullest spirit of Art and Design learning and teaching. Patience offers practical ways for Art Departments to be more environmentally conscious and promote ecological knowledge and skills while De's & Wagner's goal of promoting peace through Art and Design education will support art teachers in the development of pedagogies that address issues of peace and peacebuilding. All of the chapters in this section of the book underline the role that Art and Design can play in promoting learners' agency alongside the benefits to their thinking in other areas of the curriculum and in their life after school.

BIBLIOGRAPHY

Addison, N. and L. Burgess (2003). Challenging orthodoxies through partnership: PGCE students as agents of change. *Issues in Art and Design Teaching*. N. Addison and L. Burgess. London, Routledge Falmer: 158–165.

Addison, N. and L. Burgess (2007). Introduction. *Learning to Teach Art and Design in the Secondary School: A Companion to School Experience*. N. Addison and L. Burgess. London, Routledge Falmer.

Ball, S. J. (2007). *Education plc: Understanding Private Sector Participation in Public Sector Education*. New York, Routledge.

Consult, C. (2016) Psychic prisons and personal change. *Consult Change Ltd.* https://change-consult.com/psychic-prisons-and-personal-change/ Accessed 22nd December 2022.

Ebrace. (2010). What is ingenious, epistemological and critical curiosity? *Uncategorised* https://actionsupport.wordpress.com/2010/08/27/what-is-ingenious-episte mological-and-critical-curiosity/ Accessed 23rd December 2022.

Efland, A. (1976). In the school arts' style; a functional analysis. *Studies in Art Education* **17**(2): 37–44.

Freire, P. (2004). *Pedagogy of Hope: Reliving Pedagogy of the Oppressed*. London, Continuum.

Freire, P. (2005). *Pedagogy of the Oppressed*. New York, Continuum.

Manzoni, J.-F. and J.-L. Barsoux (1998). The set-up-to-fail syndrome. *Harvard Business Review: Managerial Behaviour*.

Morgan, G. (2006). *Images of Organizations*. Thousand Oaks, CA, Sage.

nparadoxa. (2016). Art changes, we change – Women artist in the new tate modern. *International Feminist Art Journal, Polenics/Contestations* Vol. 38 https://npara-doxa.wordpress.com/2016/06/16/art-changes-we-change-women-artists-in-th e-new-tate-modern/ Accessed 22nd December 2022.

Robinson, K. (2010). *Changing Education Paradigms*. R. Animate. TED Talk.

Sayer, E. (2019). The artist teacher. *Oxford Research Encyclopedia of Education*: 35.

Smith, F. (1980). Art. *Values and Evaluation in Education*. F. W. Straughan, J. London, Harper & Row **1**: 143–168.

PART 1

IMAGINATIVE CURIOSITY FOR THE ART AND DESIGN TEACHER

Chapter 1

Remapping the Curriculum: A Landscape Designed for the Future: Part 1. What Has Shaped the Art and Design Curriculum to be the Way It Is?

Ged Gast and Andy Ash

INTRODUCTION

This chapter explains the purpose of a curriculum for a school and for an Art and Design department. We will focus upon the compulsory element of a secondary pupil's Art and Design education and investigate their entitlement at Key stage 3 (KS3, ie: 11–14 years old). Through a series of questions and explanatory responses, we explore the various perspectives Art and Design departments can consider when designing a curriculum. We set this exploration in the context of the last 50+ years of UK education and Art and Design subject development, supported by examples of visual models of the conceptual frameworks for our subject that theorists have produced during that time.

We question what is meant and understood by the scope of art, craft and design (ACD) education, the relevance of a concept of this as an entitlement, and whether we continue to believe that these three words are fit for purpose as a definition of our subject in a post-modern world. We question whether there might be a better contemporary definition of the scope of the subject, considering what might be lost and what could be gained for contemporary graduates entering the teaching profession as teachers of Art and Design.

OBJECTIVES:

At the end of this chapter, you should be able to:

- Use your understanding of the history and development of the Art and Design curriculum to clarify how you will determine your own curriculum values and content priorities;
- Determine how you will address the teaching of creative thinking and learning;
- Redefine the scope of your curriculum and set this within the context of your national, regional or school curriculum.

DOI: 10.4324/9781003377429-3

WHAT IS THE PURPOSE OF A CURRICULUM AND WHY DO WE NEED ONE?

The word *Curriculum* is from New Latin (a post-medieval form of Latin used mainly in churches and schools), which means 'a course of study.' It shares its ultimate root in classical Latin, where it meant 'running' or 'course' (as in 'race course'), with other words in English such as *corridor*, *courier*, and *currency*, all coming from the Latin *currere* 'to run' (Merriam Webster 2022).

It would be easy to suggest therefore that the sole purpose of the curriculum is to set out what will be taught in a course of study. In the context of a contemporary UK secondary school subject, this is in the form of Programmes of Study, Schemes (or Units) of Work and lesson plans. These set out how students will learn, make expected progress and achieve planned outcomes across either a whole key stage (educational stage), a module of work or just one lesson. These structures for learning are essential, but without some deeper thinking about the purpose of education, in our case Art and Design education, do not fully define curriculum purposes, which, as we shall see, have always evolved with greater expectations for breadth and depth of entitlement than simply the transfer of knowledge. We might also suggest that an Art and Design curriculum should include reference to how the content will be taught (subject specific pedagogy) and contextualised by the core principles, values and the ethos of the curriculum, including the values of national and local policy and of the individual teacher.

A well-considered curriculum will articulate the subject's purpose, guiding you in making informed context-specific decisions. It is a statement which reassures both students and the school community of the value of what will be learned.

THE HISTORY OF ART & DESIGN EDUCATION OVER THE LAST 50+ YEARS AND THE PRESENT CURRICULUM

What we now consider to be the totality of a school curriculum was based on curricula and subject choices originally defined in 1904 (Chitty 2008). This first truly 'National Curriculum' was formulated from an amalgam of the traditional grammar school experience and the 1902 Education Act, known as the 'Balfour Act' and the 1904 Board of Education Regulations for Secondary Schools, which prescribed the subject based syllabus for pupils of 13+ (Aldrich 1988). In this curriculum, students would have taken lessons in English, geography, history, arithmetic, writing, drawing and physical exercise, with provision for activity to develop accuracy of observation and skill of hand (within drawing) and for singing. Interestingly, the term 'Art' doesn't appear at that time, but 'drawing' features in the preparatory curricula and 'manual instruction' for boys (the use of the ordinary tools for handicrafts in wood or iron) and practical course of 'housewifery' for girls (cookery, laundry work, dairy work or needlework).

Local Education Authorities (LEAs) were first established by the 1902 Act, to replace School Boards and create a system of largely standardised secondary education moving for the first time towards a concept of an entitlement curriculum. This remained in place for over 40 years until the rise in social optimism post the Second World War that was prompted by, among other political initiatives, the 1944 Education (Butler) Act. This resulted in an expanded state-funded primary and secondary education system and significant County School building programmes. LEAs were charged with the provision of schooling, preparing children for matriculation (progression), with employment skills or beginning professional advancement through examinations. The curriculum at this time was aligned with career pathways, defined by the selective tripartite school system of Secondary Technical, Secondary Modern and Grammar schools, (the latter receiving the higher percentage of local funding).

The 1944 Act's vision for equality of opportunity through the education system eventually led to the introduction of Comprehensive schools by a Labour Government in 1976, extending aspiration for education-driven social mobility. The Comprehensive concept of 'levelling up' was to be achieved by the absorption of all three of the selective school types created by the Butler Act into a single 'comprehensive' school type. This however was seen by some as being undermined by the retention in some LEAs of Grammar schools and other local selective systems. At the time and since then, some commentators, sociologists and education historians have taken this trajectory of secondary education in the mid-20th century as a contributing factor to the creation of a new elite, as identified by Michael Young in his 1958 book *The Rise of Meritocracy.* This can be seen alongside developments more recently, where the arts in state provision have been reduced largely in response to financial cuts yet remain stable within the independent sector.

It was in the mid-20th century when an Art, or Art and Craft curriculum, alongside other arts and technical subjects up to Ordinary (O) and Advanced (A) Level General Certificate of Education (GCE) examinations began to be introduced, as a part of the increasing opportunity and 'valuing all abilities and skills' agenda of the time. The subject curriculum was defined by the examination specifications and in the early secondary years, by the need to bridge transition from primary experience to secondary schooling, thereby preparing students to be able to self-select their examination subject courses of choice.

Task 1.1 Review Two Differing Historical Approaches

Watch the following two videos from the 1960s:

1. *For Whom the Bell Rings – School Life in 1965.* https://www.youtube.com/watch?v=-tFh1wyJtaE
2. *Looking at Britain* (1962). https://player.bfi.org.uk/free/film/watch-comprehensive-school-1962-online

Video 1 is filmed in Urmston Grammar School for Boys where we see several clips from art lessons featuring lower school lino and mono-print activities (see Figure 1.1), or an examination group where students are engaged independently in drawing (Figure 1.2), large observation landscape paintings, representational and abstract sculpture and construction.

The illustrations below are examples from the National Art Archive and provide additional typical curriculum outcomes for consideration. They reinforce the objectives of 'accuracy of observation and skill of hand' identified earlier.

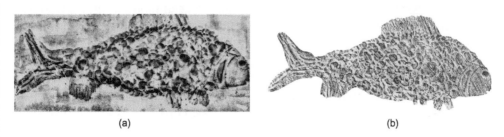

(a)   (b)

Figure 1.1 Typical mono-print from the 1950s (NAEA BHLSPD-7-1 and BHLSPD-7-1-2).

Figure 1.2 NAEA Large scale colour chalk drawings Hatfield School 19?

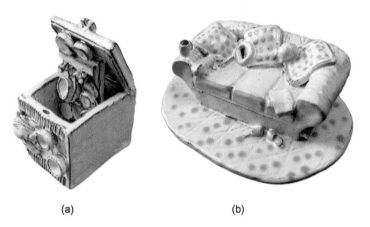

Figure 1.3 Ceramic pieces (NAEA SW-SC-07 and SW-SC-11 19?).

Video 2 is made at Holland Park Comprehensive School, which gives us a window into an art curriculum that incorporates a breadth of art and craft learning processes and diverse media. It features a lower school thematic painting project on 'fear', a pottery lesson and lower school figurative clay sculptures, with pupils engaged in glazing and kiln unloading activities. An examination group is shown wood carving into balsa-wood blocks, directly from life as a student reclines in a pose with a musical instrument. The video shows a wide breadth of opportunity for pupils including applied vocational courses in craft, industry or commerce, leading to practical career pathways (Figure 1.3).

Compare the two videos and the different schools' approaches/activities/possibilities. How would you describe the two art curriculums and the student experiences? Thinking about your own curriculum offering what would you be able to provide and deliver in comparison? What would you struggle to deliver and why?

The 1970s and 1980s were the periods of intense constructive debate in Art and Design. This was viewed positively by art teachers of the time, who were increasingly defining the breadth of the subject as ACD, and considered themselves to be trusted to innovate with teaching approaches and explore how best to organise the curriculum. This included introducing new materials and processes without fear of judgement or sanction, other than through their exam results. Local Authorities funded the appointment of local Art Advisers who ran wide-ranging Continuing Professional Development (CPD) programmes and often funded the purchase of

Figure 1.4 Hatfield School-08, Hatfield School-04, Hatfield School-05 CSE & O level examples (NAEA).

specialist ceramics and darkroom equipment, textiles and printing facilities for schools, supported with specialist training and guidance. Some LEAs and boroughs even had specialist Teachers' Centres! These actions drove the curriculum expansion in ACD, requiring parallel developments in subject leadership, curriculum innovation and organisation. This was the period that saw the switch from two-tier O Level GCE and Certificate of Secondary Education (CSE) (Figure 1.4) examinations at age 16 to the new General Certificate of Secondary Education (GCSE) examination.

These developments were supported locally by the growing network of specialist subject advisers and nationally by the work of the Art and Design teachers' professional society, the National Society for Education in Art and Design (NSEAD), this organisation's research journal IJADE, and other publications and guidance. Teachers positively recall the work of Maurice Barrett (the 1980s Art Adviser for the London Borough of Redbridge) as helping them visually conceptualise ways in which they might redefine the totality of their curriculum. Barrett published coherent conceptual frameworks for the subject, supported by easy to assimilate conceptual diagrams (Barrett 1979) (see Figures 1.5–1.7).

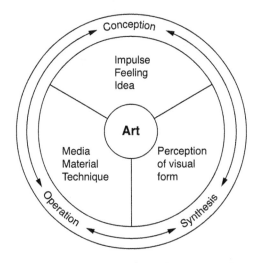

Figure 1.5 Maurice Barrett 'The nature of art'.

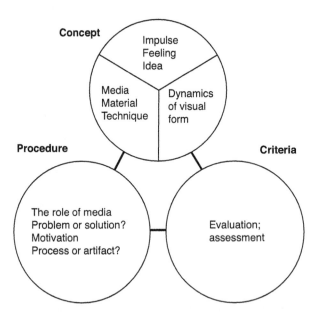

Figure 1.6 Maurice Barrett 'The process model'.

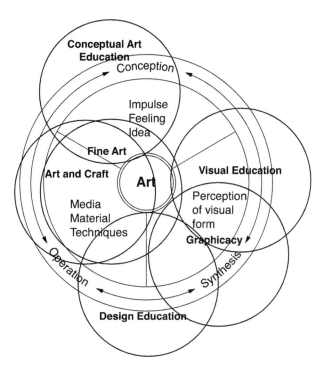

Figure 1.7 Maurice Barrett 'The rationales of art education'.

Setting out a process model for an art syllabus (curriculum), Barrett makes the case for a syllabus of activities 'worthwhile in themselves rather than as a means towards objectives'. He suggests;

> Art is not a body of knowledge, a skill, a set of rules, a process. The sum of all our visual knowledge is not only what we know, but the way we know it. It is the commitment to this idea which forms the crucial concern in art.
>
> (Barrett 1979)

Barrett makes a case for art as a process and not an artefact, planning learning through the Conceptual, Operational and Synthetic dimensions, using 'media to organise our subjective experiences in visual form'. A syllabus of 'inherent worth' developing the senses, but also impulses, feelings and ideas, concerned with the relationship between inner reality, sensory experience and environment (see Figures 1.5 and 1.6). In his diagram (Figure 1.7), he sets out a 'conceptual or art-based rationale', proposing a syllabus of six main strategies each supported by distinct rationales, sharing common aims, but operating in different ways to bring together a complex but stimulating range of experiences, developing skills and techniques and offering some choice to the student. Barrett gives structure and rationale to the more experiential and diagnostic curriculum of the time, defining a broader entitlement aspiration and setting out a three element framework for all teaching:

1. personal and conceptual (interest and curiosity, emotional/personal meaning driven response)
2. technical (organisation and use of materials and processes to develop skills)
3. visual elements (visual perception and formal understanding)

Task 1.2 Review Barrett's Approach and Make a Diagram of Your Own Rationale

Using Barrett's 'rationale' and 'process models' (Figures 1.6 and 1.7) and his three element framework for teaching, consider how different or similar these concepts are from the curriculum models you find in your current placement or early career teacher setting. Question whether Barrett's approaches would make any difference if applied to a curriculum of today.

Make a diagram of your own conceptual or art-based rationale for Art and Design (ACD) education using your present practice as its basis.

This exciting and dynamic period of innovation was followed by the phased introduction of a National Curriculum for England from 1988 to 1992 by the National Curriculum Council, and the creation of the Office for Standards in Education (Ofsted) in 1992 and the resulting introduction of a national/regional school inspection programme, with broadly similar developments in Northern Ireland and Wales. Art and music were the last National Curriculum subjects implemented, following a model of statutory orders of Attainment Targets and Programmes of Study, coming closer again to the definition of an entitlement curriculum, defined and supported by non-statutory guidance, to model best practice. Now, over 30 years later Ofsted HMI continued to make a strong connection between curriculum and progression in their publications following the removal of Levels for Assessment in England in 2014, using the phrase 'the curriculum is the progression model', as was originally proposed by Michael Fordham and Christine Counsell to resolve the challenge of making expected progress without teaching to an assessment. The concept of a curriculum which is not a list of learning but which models the progress expected, has revitalised an understanding of the importance of the curriculum, as explained by Fordham in his 'Clio et cetera' blog (Fordham, 2020). In comparison, Scotland's separate education system mirrored some of these developments with their 'Curriculum for Excellence' promoting ACD within the Expressive Arts area contributing to a broader aspiration including curriculum subjects, attributes, skills and knowledge.

The introduction of a National Curriculum in the 1980s was viewed as the solution to the variability of the state system where 'children of different abilities were achieving widely different standards depending on what part of the country they lived in' (Brighouse and Waters 2022). Brighouse and Waters' analysis goes on to suggest that this was 'the wrong solution to the right problem' as they detail the reasons for the controversy surrounding its development and subsequent revisions by numerous Secretaries of State for Education, seeking to re-shape the curriculum to address rising expectations and a rapidly changing society. Brighouse and Waters conclude that;

> …the curriculum on its own will never be the solution because it never stands alone. It always influences, or is influenced by, factors such as pedagogy, leadership, qualifications, testing, parental engagement and pupil disposition to learning.
>
> (Brighouse and Waters 2022)

Although the focus of this chapter is curriculum, in line with Brighouse and Waters, we emphasise the interconnectedness of this with pedagogical approaches, societal aspiration and support for the arts. However, the discussion of leadership, testing and student attitudes requires a different forum.

In 1986, Robert Clement (Art Adviser for Devon) published *The Art Teacher's Handbook* for primary and secondary teachers. Considered a landmark publication at the time, it successfully challenged and exposed societal misconceptions about the value of ACD, presenting the subject as the equal of others, raising teacher expectations of equal standing in preparation for a National Curriculum.

Clement's Handbook clarifies the purpose and structure for an art curriculum, including a conceptual framework for Art Education, that just a few years later he used to inform his drafting of the first English National Curriculum for Art, published in 1991 (Figure 1.8).

This resulted in two Attainment Targets for the subject.

AT1: Investigating and Making
AT2: Knowledge and Understanding

It is surely to the advantage of every secondary Art and Design department to draft a curriculum which sets out the totality of the learning experience to be gained in the subject, over a defined key stage or number of years. This experience can be divided in several ways to help sequence the planning and usefully define blocks of experience into terms, years, key stage/phase or for different ability groups or areas of subject experience e.g. 2D, 3D, Graphic, Print, digital or textile media, critical/contextual, practical etc. This approach should define what teachers plan to teach, but it must also specify how they intend to teach it. In a subject like Art and Design, we must consider how areas of knowledge including process, experiential, theoretical and conceptual knowledge will be set within relevant contexts, which could have an impact on the way these things are taught. At no point should this approach be seen as confining or restricting modification, review and redefinition. In the next section, we will set out the scope of a subject curriculum for Art and Design.

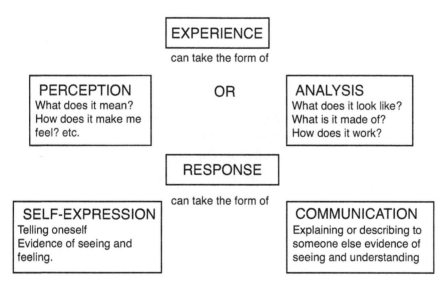

Figure 1.8 A Framework for Art Education, Clement R. 1986.

WHAT IS THE BEST WAY TO ORGANISE OR STRUCTURE AN ART CURRICULUM? DO VISUAL MODELS HELP OUR UNDERSTANDING?

The sequencing of learning can be arranged in a number of different ways to ensure the learning experiences are coherent and over time promote increasing depth and challenge (complexity) so the learner can make progress. The sequence is often determined by different forms of knowledge in Art and Design (e.g. procedural, technical, material or experiential) to ensure students gain concepts in a particular order that build both depth and breadth of understanding and enable new skills to be gained or previous skills extended or refined. Specifically in Art and Design, the way that we sequence the building of knowledge and skills in each concept is essential in promoting creativity. Students need to acquire forms of knowledge in ways that enable them to make personal choices, act with increasing confidence, developing resilience and independence across time so that they can form original thoughts and ideas, applying their knowledge, skills and understanding to realise their intended goals and outcomes. Across the first phase of secondary education we are seeking to build this capacity in preparation for the greater independence and personal originality expected at GCSE.

Task 1.3 The Conceptual Framework of the National Curriculum

This Conceptual Framework sets out a visual description of the organisation of the 'principle elements'. Figure 1.9 is a diagram of the 2014 English National curriculum for Art and Design as an example. A visual representation can be a powerful tool in providing a singular visual mnemonic that summarises the complexity of curriculum process and vision with curriculum elements and any holistic intentions. Teachers might want to reflect on and consider developing their own for students, or modifying the conceptual framework shown here to produce a version that captures the essential elements and components of their own subject curriculum. Share it with students, ask for feedback. Does this make sense to them? Is this how they see and experience art in the department? How does this drawing reference the earlier Task 1.2 reflecting on Barrett's model or his framework for teaching?

Figure 1.9 Principle elements of the English National Curriculum.
Dan China and NSEAD 2015.

HOW DO WE BALANCE THE CHALLENGE OF TRADITION AND CREATIVE EXPRESSION WHEN DRAFTING A CURRICULUM?

The approaches to organising subject content described above are well understood and have shaped our curriculum priorities over the decades. However, in the 2020s and beyond, there is a group of new issues relating to what might be defined as 'context' in education that require acknowledgement and possibly incorporation into any revised curriculum going forward.

In parallel to having a clear understanding of the organisation, sequencing and teaching of knowledge and skills as these have been defined across the later 20th century, you might consider organising some learning through what we have become used to thinking of as curriculum 'aspects' i.e. equality and diversity, literacy and numeracy, career opportunities, life-long learning or the benefits of including contemporary expectations for learning in areas such as:

- a decolonised curriculum to support understandings of cultural diversity and anti-racist learning;
- equality and anti-ableism;
- promoting a growth mindset or positive mental health and wellbeing classroom approach to teaching and learning;
- sustainability and understanding the climate crisis.

While some or all of these issues might engender debate about their place in the curriculum, it is important to recognise that the 21st century issues must shape the curriculum and consequently redefine the ways in which creative learning methodologies and current debates on what social 'values' should be are communicated through content and contexts as a part of teaching and learning. Multi-Academy Trusts are not statutorily required to follow the National Curriculum in England, so it is in the hands of the leaders and teachers in the academies in these trusts to select those agendas they wish to support, promote, and expect their subject leaders to determine those most relevant to their curriculum.

Additionally, we suggest that the evolution of the subject is now being transformed by new teachers beginning careers with a background less strictly defined by a tri-partite ACD division. In keeping with the expansion of the creative, media and design industries and the breadth of design-related careers, higher education colleges of Art and Design have expanded their design course provision, with a consequent reduction in craft and even fine-art provision. Many university courses have embraced transdisciplinary and interdisciplinary approaches to course content and as a consequence are engaging graduates in a more contemporary understanding of creativity across the visual arts.

Many recent graduates view the tri-partite model as unfamiliar and redundant, and on entering secondary education as teachers feel restricted in their teaching by historic false barriers. This has been perceived as an issue for those graduating without an experience in the three historical areas of ACD, whose interests may lie in conceptual modes of expression including e.g. photography, video and installation. The traditional skillset or fundamental handcraft experiences as makers or fine artists may not apply to them. However, this group are still faced with a requirement as teachers to prepare their students for examinations that remain rooted in convention and traditional skills. This remains the expectation in all the awarding body Art and Design specifications, causing us to question whether our Art and Design qualifications at Key stages 4 and 5 are preparing students for the

21st century, or are they still rooted in a late 20th century model? It could be said that art changes, artists and art teachers change, but Art and Design as it is taught in schools does not.

The present orthodoxies of Art and Design education for the pre-examination secondary age curriculum can be characterised as typically the teaching of the visual elements (formalism), with skills and techniques centred around drawing and painting, typically followed by more limited 3D or print and textile experience, an emphasis on sketchbook practice and little meaningful acknowledgement of design. This is a challenge for new ACD teachers in their creation of a purposeful and relevant curriculum that they can believe in. These pressures appear to have led to many teachers putting aside their motivation for change, instead widely accepting models of study typified by projects in which a selected fine-art artist/movement/genre focus, e.g. Cubism, Pointillism, 'Aboriginal art' or 'African masks" is followed by a practical sketchbook task often 'in the style of', before engaging in practical making activities involving the learning of a technique and the practising of manual skills. For many new teachers, such a singular approach will place limits on critical and creative thinking, imagination and originality, as well as the drive to experiment, discover and investigate the world by doing.

Such approaches also do little to address gendered perceptions of learning needs and preferences, favouring those who enjoy sketchbook working and careful planning to a 'template' design; to say nothing of upholding an ingrained colonialist approach to world cultures. It can also unthinkingly elevate western historical traditions as the key cultural source for imagery, relegating other traditions to the study of folk art, symbols, pattern and decoration. This curriculum model limits space for contemporary issue or theme-based study of diverse Art and Design forms that would encourage critical thinking and more individualised responses.

In order to overcome this problem, we argue that Art and Design teachers should be pursuing a more contemporary, inclusive and nuanced curriculum which addresses a broad context of contemporary issues of e.g. the environment, sustainability, equity, wider definitions of British ethnicities and the wider culture. Society is no longer engaged in binary conversations regarding gender, race, western and non-western traditions, contemporary and historical forms. The purpose of ACD must be to focus on the needs of 21st century students, including all ethnicities, genders, abilities, those with specific learning needs or disabilities and who have English as an additional language. This will provide a meaningful grounding in ACD at KS3, both for those intending to pursue pathways to vocational careers and academic routes into higher education, and those who are not.

Research confirms that the inclusive qualities of ACD education make the subject powerful in enabling personal statements and the expression of ideas and in establishing creative independence (see resources The benefits of Art, Craft and Design education in schools: A Rapid Evidence Review. Thomson P. & Moly, L.). ACD should not be seen as a subject that is somehow therapeutic or as an option choice for those with less academic ability in other subjects. We know that ACD practice can be highly demanding, as creative expression requires a spread and balance of both academic and practical expertise. At best, the breadth of the subject is only limited by the creative opportunities and choices students make, the specialist qualifications available and the career directions graduates might take. This makes it a more embodied and inclusive, nuanced hybrid of a subject, requiring teachers to explore different ways in which they can structure and model inquiry and creative realisation.

Task 1.4 Auditing Your Skills and Your Pupils' Needs

Find out about your students:

1. Complete a survey of your students. Ask them simple questions about what they like to do in art and what they dislike doing. What do they think are the important issues in society now? What are the issues that they would like art to help them explore? Do pupils understand your vision of the subject? Ask them to try to express what they think the value and purpose of art in the school is?

2. In Art and Design, it is highly desirable to establish a subject baseline on standards on entry to the school, to maintain an annual review of experience and ability. Use the Y7 Baseline Thinking in Art and Design by Gast G. (2016) NSEAD (see resources) to see if you can audit your present practice and establish clear evidence to work with. How can you use this to help develop a profile for students on skills, knowledge and understanding? Use the template offered to consider how you might assess progress and monitor needs.

3. At the same time, you might record and analyse so called 'soft' skills, learning habits and behaviours to profile the learning needs and thereby modify their curriculum. See the resources for further definition of these characteristics which are evident in the '10 Lessons the Arts Teach' (Eisner 2002).

SUMMARY

The intention of this chapter is to give a background to some of the questions trainee and early career teachers ask about the curriculum they find in place in their settings. The objectives have been to encourage trainee and subject practitioners to examine their current approaches, to make better sense of the framework they are working in and to empower them to navigate their own path, so that they can design their own course with greater relevance to the context of their school and the future lives of the students that they are teaching.

The journey of art as a subject, from the beginning of the last century up to the present day, has been transformative, making Art and Design education one of the great success stories of the UK education, contributing to UK creative industries being 'Celebrated As An International Success Story' (Council 2021). Within the career lifetime of the authors, teaching in Art and Design from the 1990s to the present day can be seen as an ever increasing tension between the dominant approaches of 'ideas and concepts' in opposition to 'techniques and skills'. Unfortunately, in an environment based on high-stakes testing, this tension can pull teachers back towards a low-risk reliance on honing 'technique and skills' in the pursuit of guaranteed results and performance measures. In the final chapter of this book, we go on to suggest that a negative consequence of this tension is not inevitable as we set out what we refer to as the NSEAD 'Big Landscape' of Art and Design education. The final chapter goes on to provide guidance that will inform your means to navigate this more varied, challenging and ultimately more rewarding landscape of opportunities and possibilities.

RESOURCES

Elliot Eisner (2002). Ten Lessons the Arts Teach. https://www.arteducators.org/advocacy-policy/articles/116-10-lessons-the-arts-teach

Gast, G. (2016). Year 7 Baseline Thinking in Art and Design by NSEAD. https://www.nsead.org//files/f75b88ee0e38b1951b294cba55cdac59.pdf

Thomson, P. and Maloy, L. (2022). The Benefits of Art, Craft and Design Education in Schools, A Rapid Evidence Review. https://www.nsead.org/files/6f85ab858 7bc53ce653702da1cc15690.pdf

BIBLIOGRAPHY

Aldrich, R. (1988). The National Curriculum: An historical perspective. *The National Curriculum*. D. Lawton and C. Chitty. London, Institute of Education, University of London. **33**: 21–33.

Barrett, M. (1979). *Art Education: A Strategy for Course Sesign*. London, Heinemann Educational Books.

Brighouse, T. and Waters, M. (2022). *About Our Schools: Improving on Previous Best*. Carmarthen, Crown House Publishing.

Chitty, C. (2008). The UK National Curriculum: An historical perspective. *Forum*. **50**(3): 5.

Council, C. I. (2021, February 2021). UK Creative Industries Celebrated as Global Success. From https://www.thecreativeindustries.co.uk/site-content/uk-creative-overview-news-and-views-news-uk-creative-industries-celebrated-as-global-success.

Eisner, E. W. (2002). *The Arts and the Creation of Mind*. New Haven, Yale University Press.

Fordham, M. (2020) *Clio et cetera*. What did I mean by 'the curriculum is the progression model'? from online blog https://clioetcetera.com/2020/02/08/what-did-i-mean-by-the-curriculum-is-the-progression-model/ (Accessed: 27 December 2023).

Merriam Webster, (2022) Dictionary, https://www.merriam-webster.com/dictionary/curriculum (Accessed: 8 August 2022).

Chapter 2 Strategies to Mobilise Cognition in Secondary Art and Design

Rebecca Heaton

INTRODUCTION

This chapter introduces you to the concept of cognition in Secondary Art and Design. You will engage with the theoretical and practical relevance of cognition and its association with art and education in teaching, research, policy and practice. You will see how cognition, as knowledge, develops across psychological, physical and virtual spaces in Secondary Art and Design and you will engage with cases and activities to explore cognitive concepts and practices. Strategies to access, understand, use and progress cognition will be discussed, trialled and reflected on to build your disposition as a cognitive curator. This disposition is relevant to the Secondary Art educator because you have responsibility for identifying, monitoring and developing learner cognition. You therefore need to begin to understand how your own cognition develops to understand how another's does.

This chapter will guide you to think about personal cognitive capacities (what you know about cognition), competencies (your ability to engage with or learn about cognition) and dispositions (your beliefs, attitudes and acts to use cognition) and those of learners to ensure the Secondary Art and Design provision you offer is conducive to a life-long learning. Many cognitive forms exist in education; meta-cognition, situated cognition, mis-cognition and trans-cognition for example. This chapter will help unpick these concepts, so cognition becomes a term and practice that you are confident to engage with and defend when considering learner provision. As art educators you will be asked in school to discuss pupil progress and assessment, understanding cognition will enable you to do this confidently because you will be able to vocalize and exemplify how and where learners are enhancing cognition in academic, affective, conceptual and expressive means. You will also be able to connect theory and practice to support and deepen your justifications of knowledge gains and pursuits.

DOI: 10.4324/9781003377429-4

OBJECTIVES:

At the end of this chapter, you should be able to:

- Understand the relevance, meaning and purpose of cognition in Secondary Art and Design;
- Be aware of strategies to mobilize cognition in Secondary Art and Design;
- Know how to develop personal and learner cognition.

PART 1: DEVELOP AN UNDERSTANDING OF COGNITION

What Is Cognition?

Cognition is present in all aspects of life and learning. In neuroscience, cognition is the output of the brain's cerebral cortex (Mason, 2011, p.284). Many art educators already provide deep cognitive experiences for learners knowingly and unknowingly. So, when I discuss cognition in Art and Design, I do not present it as a new concept but one which needs considering, accessing and reflecting on to enhance learning and practice. Cognition is an Art and Design concept that acts like a foundational thread. It is always present in experiences as our subject evolves because it is central to human experience and can exist peripherally or be mobilized as educators choose. In this section, to help you understand cognition, theoretical perspectives, frameworks to assist engagement and practice alignments are discussed to bring the concept to life.

Theory demonstrates that cognition is unique to individuals occurring consciously and subconsciously (Sullivan, 2005; Tavin, 2010). It involves mapping, connections, inquiry, making and reflecting (Cunliffe, 1999; Gnezda, 2011; Vitulli, Giles & Shaw, 2014), which are all teaching and learning approaches, and as such is complex. Cognition evolves with environments, times and people (Heaton, 2021) and is a means to learn. In Art and Design, cognition connects psychology, cognitive science, art, technology and history as examples and is generated through experiences across disciplines. Cognition is not just relevant to art and design. It is a concept that helps connect educational and lived experiences because it involves 'the mind, body and situational context' (Critchfield, 2014). Cognition is an embodied experience (Heaton, 2021) just like art. Cognition research in Art and Design suggests that it can infiltrate change (Biesta, 2017; Heaton, 2018a,b). For example, engagement with it may alter opinions or values, pedagogy or artistic practice or move one's ideas, thoughts or actions in new directions. Based on this idea, cognitive engagement becomes advantageous to your professional development. Engaging with cognitive theory and practice could also position you as a change-maker (Rivers, Nie & Armellini, 2015; Heaton & Crumpler, 2017), someone who uses and develops moral and socially just principles to incite change (Caldwell, Whewell, Bracey, Heaton, Crawford & Shelley, 2021). Being aware of cognition is therefore valuable to you, to leaners and society.

With many theoretical definitions of cognition in Art and Design, see Figure 2.1, it can be difficult to understand. Scholars like Elliott Eisner (1986, 1994, 2002), Michael Parsons (1998), Charles Dorn (1999), Arthur Efland (2002), Graham Sullivan (2001, 2005), Kevin Tavin (2010) and Nicole Gnezda (2011) forged space for cognitive study in Art and Design. They conceived the concept largely as conscious and unconscious entities and connections of our mind, thoughts, actions and experiences.

In research with artist teachers (Heaton, 2021), I suggested that cognition can be defined in relation to four components: knowledge, process, interdisciplinarity

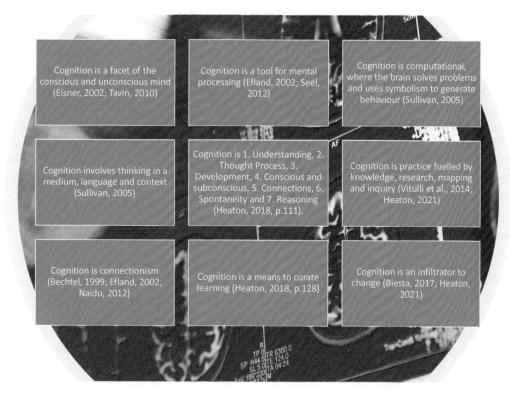

Figure 2.1 Definitions of cognition (Rebecca Heaton, 2021).

and embodiment. I now explain these components and contextualize them in Secondary Art and Design scenarios.

Knowledge

To create knowledge, we map and connect ideas and experiences, we engage, in living inquiry (Marshall, 2019) an ongoing journey of coming to know. Through this journey we create and encounter knowledge in many guises. For example, we may learn about knowledge concepts like metacognition (Fahey & Cronen, 2016); thinking about thinking, or cultural cognition (Seel, 2012); thinking about how beliefs, values, social circumstances or environments shape knowing. We may think about our artist, educator or learner dispositions and create knowledge by building cognitive connections in view of these (Sullivan, 2005; Heaton & Chan, 2022a). Or we may, as suggested in *Purposes of Art Education* (Heaton & Hickman, 2020), build knowledge in view of perceptions, like our aesthetic perception, or in relation to cultural heritage. These are examples of how cognition as knowledge can be defined in Art and Design and there are others. What is important is that when we consider knowledge, we possess a unique connectome, the neural brain network that shapes who we are (Naidu, 2012), which contributes to how we define, understand and experience knowledge or cognition.

For the secondary educator trying to define cognition, you need to understand that definitions of cognition can be individual, socially constructed, accepted and contested (Heaton, 2018). It is important that Art and Design learners engage with their understanding of cognition and/or knowledge. Cognition being the act or result of a cognate process and knowledge being a known or learnt entity. Engagement is important so that learners have clarity about what knowledge and cognition are in their discipline, this will help them better document and defend learning taking place. If art educators do not clearly understand cognition, or knowledge, they may not recognize construction through perceptive or minute processes like the imitative, anticipative, experimental, temporal or bodily experiences (Ojala, 2013) that occur daily in learning. They may also not recognize knowledge as implicit and explicit or its creation through joining perceptive, representative or productive experiences (Mottram & Whale, 2001). It is therefore essential as an art educator that you develop an understanding of cognition and knowledge formation. You are not expected to be an expert, but you should be open to growing a repertoire of ways in which cognition and knowledge can be defined and understood, so that you can identify success in the evolving identities, knowledge pursuits and practices of learners.

Process

Cognition in Art and Design can be a psychologic, physical and digital process (Heaton & Chan, 2023a). Cognition can be defined as mind orientated and mindful. For example, where links form mentally between people, products and experiences to know or show awareness of feelings and senses which shape knowing (Efland, 2002; Seel, 2012). Turner (2006) wrote about the creation of knowing in Art and Design as a process where the mind blends artistic elements through cognitive operations. An example of cognitive engagement could involve an imaginative pursuit which Efland (2002) suggests is a significant contributor to Art and Design because the imagination facilitates conscious exploration of the mind's processes and products (Hickman & Heaton, 2020). If you reflect on how frequently learners engage with their imagination in Art and Design, in expressive drawing, in generating the virtual, when solving problems or in creative pursuits as simple examples, then Art and Design's process of cognitive exploration becomes central to the everyday. But how do we comprehend such cognitive processes and model or explain them to Secondary learners in an accessible way?

First, we must recognize Art and Design as a cognate knowledge acquiring process (Heaton, 2021) and then we can encourage awareness of knowledge relationships that can form between us, Art and Design experiences and lives. This knowledge acquisition process needs to be progressive and practiced in varied ways. Sometimes it is appropriate to create first and let knowledge develop naturally or through making, at other times we may engage in practices like focused engagement or reflection to facilitate this pursuit with a specific purpose. This chapter offers several ideas, like playing, taking risks, experimenting, framework alignment and interdisciplinary connection to acquire knowledge. When creating knowledge and developing cognition in Art and Design you need to be prepared for knowledge formation in many ways and at different speeds and junctures. Heaton and Hickman (2020, p.7) discuss how the process of art engagement, such as experiencing an artist's work, can help learners build emotional intelligence, ambiguity and an openness towards alternative world engagements.

The artwork, 'Anywhen,' by Philippe Parreno (2016) installed in the Tate Modern Turbine Hall (https://www.youtube.com/watch?v=M1RWxQaM5mc) exemplifies art's importance as a cognitive process. The artwork brought the space alive like a theatre, the work played with objects, sound, light, movement and technology to depict art and life changing and responding to one another. Moving speakers and panels lower and retreat from the ceiling, lights pulse through the hall. Planes, inflatable fish and the sounds of football matches intermittently interject the space whilst audience and algorithms control the ever-changing immersive experience. The change depicted in, through and on reflection of this artwork is a cognitive knowledge gaining process, for the artist, audience and I. The artist may learn cognitively about how people interact with the work, the audience gain cognate and affective responses in and from the work and I through reflection cognitively formulate ideas and connections to art practices, pedagogy and research endeavours. In essence, as 'art changes: we change' – this was the motto depicted on the front of the Tate Modern Building when this exhibition took place. The motto is still prevalent today, through art's processes cognition alters, art also changes in response to cognition. In art learning, whether experiencing it (reacting), making (or researching), reviewing (or reflecting) or enacting (or responding) a connectionist or sometimes spiraled (Heaton & Hickman, 2016) model of cognition develops.

Interdisciplinarity

Phillipe Parreno's work, discussed above, is interdisciplinary, his work plays with mediums and concepts that intersect art with technology, science and psychology. Learning pursuits in art and design, where art mediums, concepts, subjects, people and cultures connect, collide and/or repel provide spaces to learn about, use, build and project interdisciplinary cognition (Heaton, 2021); cognition formed through interdisciplinary endeavours or in facilitation of them. In interdisciplinarity (Petrie, 1992; Darts, 2011; Song, 2012; Klaassen, 2018), mindsets or methods from two or more educational concepts, methods or practices fuse to generate cognition through dialogue. The idea of dialoguing between disciplines to know has been extended into transdisciplinarity, where discipline-specific concepts are decoupled creating new possibilities for exploring phenomenon (Burnard, Grey & Pallawi, 2021). Interdisciplinarity and transdisciplinarity are cognitive processes, they are, and use, cognition to know and understand.

In Art and Design, learners often engage with interdisciplinary and transdisciplinary cognition. For example, when making art learners may research how different disciplines approach or express a concept or idea and dissect these through making. At other times, learners may use skills from one discipline, like technology, and apply them in another like exhibiting film. An alternative may involve dissection, like taking technology, codes or algorithms apart and rebuilding to generate new digital art forms. Through these interdisciplinary and transdisciplinary endeavours, cognition moves between people, spaces, and objects and between human and non-human resources. In these transactions, it can be difficult for educators, and learners, to track cognitive exchanges (Heaton, 2023). Sometimes this is where knowing becomes lost, or cognition becomes too complex to follow. Not being able to track or justify cognition, or knowledge transfer, challenges Art and Design, providing one reason why our subject's academic credibility is marginalized.

Therefore, when planning or engaging interdisciplinary or transdisciplinary opportunities to build cognition, we should try to foresee, track and reflect on how cognitive learning occurred. This is not easy and there is no definitive way to do this. But with practice, forming, documenting and reflecting on cognitive connections, through drawing, journaling, photography, voice overs, blogging or film for example can make cognition more visible, which can consequently help strengthen Art and Design's cognitive contribution and influence. The documentary processes suggested are familiar practices many Art and Design educators and learners engage in. What we perhaps don't do though is look or respond to these with a cognitive or connectionist eye to observe and engage with **how** knowledge forms.

The case study above exemplifies how interdisciplinary cognition could manifest in Art and Design.

CASE STUDY: A STEAM EXPERIENCE

A class of year 8 learners in the UK visited the Design Museum Exhibition, Waste Age: What can design do? https://designmuseum.org/exhibitions/waste-age-what-can-design-do# to fulfil the KS3 Art National Curriculum Aim: to know about great artists, craft makers and designers, and understand the historical and cultural development of their artforms (DfE, 2013, p.1).

Whilst visiting the exhibition, the learners were asked in small groups to select an artwork of interest and consider how the artwork connected to learning in other disciplines: Science, Technology, Engineering and/or Maths (STEAM). Whilst in the gallery, the learners were given iPads to research the artwork and artist of their choice, to further understand the ideas and issues behind the artist's work. The learners were then tasked with creating a Pod Cast Episode about their chosen artwork, its history, its relationship with contemporary living and interdisciplinary connection. Back at school each group's episode was shared with the class to communicate their learning on a shared, but closed to the school, digital platform (the school intranet).

One group explored the artwork of Ghanaian artist Ibrahim Mahama (https://www.youtube.com/watch?v=jyFQ69cbm2s) who created an installation of electronic screens as a statement about Agbogbloshie, the world's largest e-waste dump in Accra Ghana. Many issues are associated with this dump besides its growing scale, toxic e-waste is burned to extract metals which cause damage to locals and workers, device hacking occurs and illegal transportation of e-waste from the West is sent to this site. In learning about this artist and his work the learners made associations to environmental science learning, about the impact of their and society's technologic consumption, about geographical understanding, the engineering of products and the cost and transportation of goods for discard and decomposition.

Through art engagement the students developed their cognitive knowledge in different curriculum disciplines, STEAM learning (Colucci-Gray, Burnard, Cooke, Davies, Gray & Trowsdale, 2016). Their knowledge and research in Art and Design opened cognitive connections to other learning areas, and audio recording/ Podcasting provided a space for exploring, questioning, reflecting on and sharing cognitive knowledge. Through cognitive learning connections a dialogic learning space (Wegerif, 2013) was created, because current and culturally relevant themes of interest were opened (environmentalism, technologic impact, cultural change and ethics, as examples) that learners could explore further.

Through engagement in interdisciplinary experiences, or STEAM education as an example, learners can also see how education, learning and the cognition are processes that work more efficiently when learning connections occur. Connecting is one step in the pursuit of being a curator of cognition. Elaine Perignat and Jen Katz-Buonincontro (2019) documented that the success of STEAM education concerns how it is implemented and how much self-efficacy and autonomy are given to learners to forge new understandings. This is likely true for other interdisciplinary or integrated Art and Design experiences, because when we are engaged in creative acts, or making, our creative dispositions and mind habits are used to a greater extent. It has however been recognized that a problem with STEAM experiences is a lack of Art and Design outcomes (Perignat & Katz-Buonincontro, 2019). So, to change this we need to make art in the process of, in response to and as a documentation of interdisciplinary and STEAM educational experiences. Doing so will not only show what interdisciplinary or STEAM experiences offer learners, endeavours will also show the cognitive contribution art makes in and beyond educational systems.

Embodiment

As mentioned, cognition in Art and Design is embodied (Ash, 2019; Heaton, 2021) involving mind, body and contextual interaction. It can also be a process of becoming where we learn and unlearn (Payne, 2020). Gulliksen (2017, p.8) in research about the importance of making proposed that 'all cognition is embodied in the sense that the input and output is the result of mind-body interaction.' Embodied cognition (Wilson & Golonka, 2013) is a term, but it has been identified as unnecessary (Gulliksen, 2017) if all cognition is embodied. So why is considering embodied cognition relevant to Secondary Art and Design? Well, when you engage in Art and Design you encounter a relational way of knowing (Powell & Lajevic, 2011). By experimenting with aesthetics, visual culture and the self you experience sensationalism and become affected by and towards mind, body and context experiences of self and other (Duncum, 2005). It is therefore important for teachers and learners to understand that in Art and Design engagements there is a larger embodied and cognitive process of knowing at play, between perceptions, actions, encounters, feelings and real-world interactions.

Mathewson Mitchell (2015) when examining practice in Secondary Art and Design recognized there is a gap concerning educator knowledge at a theoretical level and knowing about enactment at a classroom level. By becoming knowledgeable about cognition, and its constitution as embodiment, you can gain knowledge about how to teach Art and Design, whilst recognizing embodiment as a cognitive component in student learning and practice. For example, you could look out for how the mind or body enables and constrains possibilities (for concept development, research, making, participation, collaboration or reflection) in your learner's processes, artworks or actions (Schatzki, 1996). Such recognition would help defend the teaching practices you have used to engender learner cognition whilst showing your learner's and subject's cognitive potential.

Now you have considered how cognition can be knowledge, process, interdisciplinarity and embodiment it would be timely to reflect on personal understandings and considerations of cognition in your current practice. You may find there are several things that you already do in your Art and Design provision to engage you and your learner's cognition. If there are not, then now is an opportunity to think about what you can do to enhance cognition.

Task 2.1 Reflect on Your Understanding of Cognition

(a) Create four drawings which represent your understanding of cognition as knowledge, process, interdisciplinarity and embodiment;

(b) Underneath list things that you do, or aspire to do, in your art and design practice that facilitate engagement with cognition.

For example:

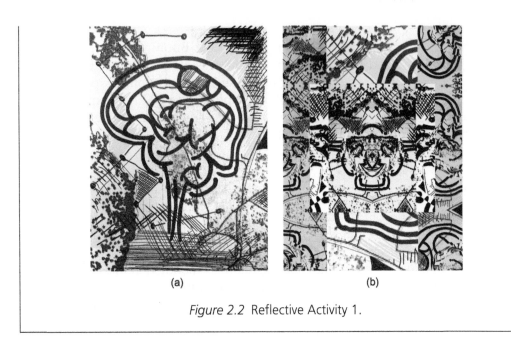

(a) (b)

Figure 2.2 Reflective Activity 1.

The important message that can be derived from considering theory and practice is that cognition is continuously at play in all Art and Design experiences. Our challenge as educators is acknowledging, identifying and giving purposeful recognition to cognition to enhance learners' teaching, learning and life experiences beyond formal encounters.

PART 2: THE RELEVANCE OF COGNITION TO SECONDARY ART AND DESIGN

Cognition is central to education, not just Secondary Art and Design, because it uses and explores beliefs, actions, perceptions and experience (Davis & Sumara, 1997; Gardenfors & Johansson, 2005; Heaton, 2021). When humans interact with stimuli in life, learning takes place (Meltzoff, Kuhl, Movellan & Sejnowski, 2009). World engagement, dialoguing (Biesta, 2017), finding and forming new ways of interpreting, interacting, representing and questioning is the essence of Art and Design (Hickman, 2010; Heaton & Hickman, 2016). As the editor of *Studies in Art Education* recently alluded experiencing Art and Design, its pursuits, and challenges in physical, intellectual and affective ways, is learning (O'Donoghue, 2021). In Art and Design, learners need encouragement to bring their life stimuli and travels into artistic pursuits, so they develop cognition and social and environmental learning.

When cognition is considered in education this can occur in isolated or integrated ways, such as individually in one's perceptions, thoughts and behaviours, or at a group or systems level like in collaborative experiences or policy, like curriculums. In learning science research (Jamaludin, Loong & Xuan, 2019) and artist teacher education (Heaton, 2018), teachers have commented that learning about cognition and its science have opened depth and possibilities for personal and student learning. In Art and Design, studies concerning cognition and learning science are still slight, but are needed to decolonize art practice and curriculums, to reduce subject marginalization and to demonstrate that Art and Design learning is as beneficial to human development, particularly in its cognitive capacity, as learning in other subjects (Heaton, 2021). So, in secondary Art and Design where can cognition be found?

PART 3.1: IDENTIFYING AND APPLYING COGNITION

To identify and apply cognition it is useful to be knowledgeable about the concept. Hopefully, now you have engaged with Part One of this chapter, you have insight into how cognition is defined theoretically and how it has practice relevance. In Art and Design, cognition can be situated, affected by time pressures, inclusive of perception and action and used to engage with the world on and offline (Gulliksen, 2017). Because cognition involves all mental processes it is considered at work in all art engagements: perceiving, making, analysing, reflecting etc. This section consequently focuses on strategies that can be used to help identify cognition and applies it to learners. To complement the approaches discussed, you can also observe, document, analyse and reflect on (through photos, film, voice recordings, sketchbooks or blogs for example) cognition occurring in personal and learner's Art and Design experiences. Whether they involve making, conversations or daily life experiences etc. Doing so will bring knowledge creation forward in thoughts and practices and cognitive choices and decisions.

Models and Frameworks

Mark Selkrig and colleagues (2020) working at several Australian universities recently wrote about an L-PEC model (Learning, pedagogy, environment, community dynamics) for effective and quality teaching and learning in Art and Design (with a focus on teacher education), see Figure 2.3. The model is an underlying philosophy for generating a professional learning dialogue in Art and Design. But it can also act as a useful tool to consider where cognitive learning, or learning in general, be identified or applied, in Secondary Art and Design provision and learner or educator practice.

If you look at the L-PEC model closely, you will likely see practices and strategies that you use to teach. If we focus on the component 'Learning', you probably get learners to act and feel like artists, to explore artistic materials, to look, listen, work individually and collectively to learn, to create knowledge and to build cognitive understanding. The model demonstrates 'connectionism' and 'mapping' as forms of cognitive learning widely recognized in Art and Design scholarship (Cunliffe, 1999; Vitulli, Giles & Shaw, 2014). If learners, and educators, are given opportunities to map learning (or as I say curate cognition (Heaton, 2021; Heaton & Chan, 2022b), then they can build complex and deep webs of knowledge. Knowledge webs can help us track, reflect, grow and locate learning and its challenges. They can also help us see avenues for learning development, not thought of previously.

Research has communicated the effects of knowledge maps on concept acquisition and retention in Art and Design (Vitulli, Giles & Shaw, 2014) highlighting that they can help learners process information especially when learners create them. In Secondary Art and Design, we have numerous possibilities for creating knowledge maps, and this is where learner and educator creativity can come forward. Learners could use sketchbook or portfolio work to map knowledge, they could use blogs or podcasts to showcase knowledge links. This practice could occur at set intervention points or be encouraged by the teacher, as a standalone activity or as a live, travelling or reflexive learning pursuit. Cunliffe (1999) cautioned that if learners do not have opportunities to form cognitive maps in Art and Design, they may become lost in the process of learning. What the L-PEC model, see Figure 2.3, for Art and Design teaching and learning can assist with is helping educators and learners to see potential domains and connections to explore for cognitive learning. The model could be used alone or with curriculum documentation, planning

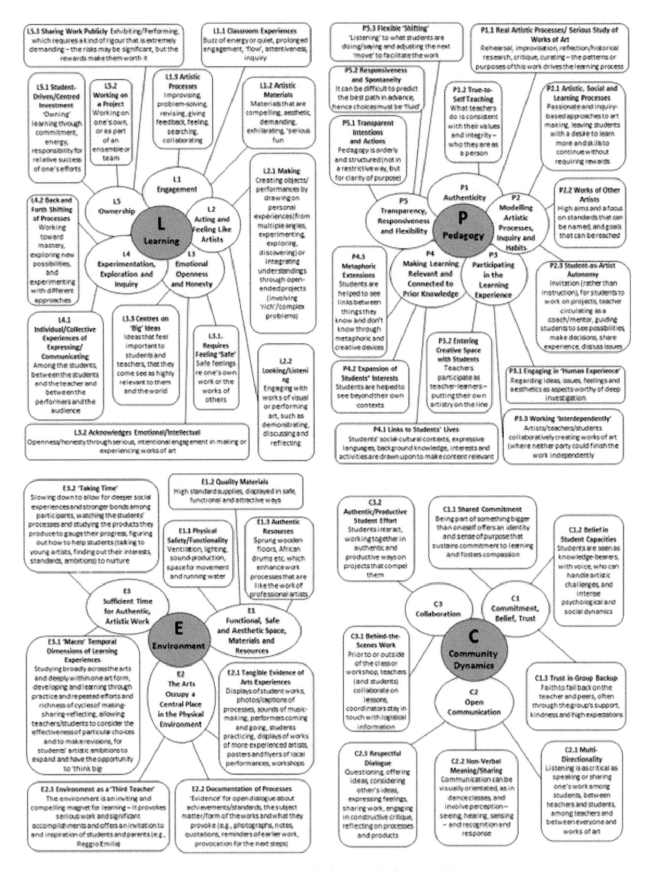

Figure 2.3 L-PEC elements and sub elements (Selkrig, Wright, Hannigan, Burke, & Grenfell, 2020, p.5).

materials or artwork or experiences to help open or track cognitive learning dialogues. The model is not shared as a device that you must use as a Secondary Art and Design educator, it is presented as a guiding tool to explore, facilitate and stretch dialogues about cognitive learning. It may be used individually to learn or reflect, or with subject teams to review provision.

As mentioned, in Art and Design cognition can present in and between psychologic, physical and virtual spaces so it is beneficial to have several strategies for identification and application. Bloom's taxonomy (Bloom, 1956), which considers cognitive thinking development from lower to higher order skills, and Bloom's digital taxonomy (Churches, 2008), which utilizes tools and technology to facilitate learning with an emphasis on collaboration, can also act as tools to identify and guide cognitive mapping or curation in Art and Design. In considering Bloom's digital taxonomy, Churches (2008, p.2) identified that 'it is the quality of the action or process that defines the cognitive level, rather than the action or process alone' (Churches, 2008, p.2). This means that it is not enough for educators and learners to just use a desired digital tool (e.g., Padlet), act (e.g., coding) or cognitive strategy (e.g., analysing or creating) to show cognition. They need to do so with breadth, depth, exploration and reflection to achieve development and quality in their cognitive competencies, this too applies to cognitive pursuits in Art and Design which use these learning means.

Cognition in Secondary Art and Design will present digitally in ways like blogging, wiki editing, through social media, video-calls and blended learning as examples. As changes in digital education occur, like using Artificial Intelligence, Virtual Reality and extended reality (XR) technology to provide immersive, adaptive and personalized learning experiences, educators will be required to consider how cognition is developing in these domains. It is therefore important that technology is integrated through Art and Design practice as it is in our connectivity orientated lives, and that the cognitive learning that occurs in it is given credit. Being aware of and using technologic learning models, like updates to Bloom's digital taxonomy (Ray, 2021), can therefore help us to critique, maintain relevance and draw relationships in cognate and technologic pursuits. The text *Pedagogy for Technology Education in Secondary Schools* (Williams & Barlex, 2020) may also act as a useful guide for integrating cognitively rich technologic learning pursuits. The National Society for Education in Art and Design also provides Digital Media advice and resources on their website: https://www.nsead.org/resources/digital-media/ to support technologic provision in Art and Design.

Hopefully you see that cognition can connect with many commonly used theoretical models and frameworks in education. A set of models and tools specifically designed to develop thinking and cognition in Art and Design are those produced by Harvard Project Zero: http://www.pz.harvard.edu/thinking-routines. Project Zero is a research centre of the Harvard Graduate School of Education in the United States founded in 1967 by philosopher Nelson Goodman and it investigates human potential through learning, thinking, creativity and ethics as examples. If you engage with the website, you will be introduced to resources and strategies that you can apply in your provision to elicit learner thinking. The resources should help you to expand your repertoire of how to enact cognition (Figure 2.4).

In the above task, you connected cognitive, psychologic thought with learner's visual outputs. When learners engage in artistic experiences, they connect psychologic (cognate) and physical/virtual worlds. In this process, they learn and develop cognition, but to understand this process further in Art and Design one could consider the Studio Habits of Mind (Hetland, Winner, Veenema & Sheridan, 2007, 2015). In this, eight cognitive dispositions: Develop craft, engage and persist, envision, express, observe, reflect, stretch and explore and understand art worlds,

Figure 2.4 Reflective Activity 2.

can be used to engender, connect and generate thinking and learning in Art and Design. The Studio Habits of Mind are accessible to learners and educators and can be taught about to demonstrate how cognitive thinking can occur. For example, very simply if we consider image five (Figure 2.4), learners have documented patterns found in their environments – the learners have *observed* their worlds to *express* observations in drawn outputs. They have moved between at least two habits of mind and their physical and psychologic worlds.

In image two (Figure 2.4), learners have again *observed* their environments, this time architecture, but they have had to *develop* their drawing and collage crafts, *stretching* their explorations to *express* ideas visually. More connections have occurred between mind habits, students could even build from or extend their ideas into digital or virtual artworks. The point is that the cognitive dispositions in the habits of mind model can provide an anchor or viewing platform to consider cognitive learning from. These can be used by educators and learners as tools to voice, reflect on, plan for or stretch expressions of cognitive thinking.

Other scholars (Hetland, Cajolet & Music, 2010; Heaton & Edwards, 2017; Heaton, 2021) have also shown how cognitive dispositions can be used to monitor cognitive developments and understandings. As people engage in mind habits, connections are formed, mapped, experimented with and applied to create complex cognitive knowledge webs. In each disposition, an understanding of depth can be developed, so the framework can be used at different Art and Design phases: primary, secondary, etc. For example, if the disposition *developing craft* is considered it can be applied to many art mediums and each has a progressive model of concepts, skills and practices. So, as in other aspects of Art and Design, when the development of cognitive dispositions and understanding are considered, one needs to ensure such concepts and practices are introduced with relevance and progression.

In Secondary Art and Design, as an example one may introduce each cognitive disposition individually, so learners understand it. It could then be linked to different experiences encountered across Art and Design like in a range of media, individually or collaboratively, or beyond the classroom in museum, gallery or outdoor contexts. A next step may be to link dispositions, to give learners ownership to explore or communicate about the dispositions or links and after use them in interdisciplinary or intercultural scenarios. The intention is to build a progressive understanding of the cognitive dispositions for Art and Design experiences, so that learners develop a personal repertoire of and autonomy for cognitive strategies which can be used later in experiences in and beyond the classroom.

In the Upper Secondary Art Education Curriculum in Singapore (MOE, 2018, p.21) a learning model is adopted, as advocated by Fisher and Frey (2013), to encourage student self-directed learning (SDL) where teachers support and release learning responsibility to students over time. Release can be achieved by teachers through designing effective learning environments, which could be those opening dialogue about cognition. Learners are afforded opportunities to understand their learning requirements, they are encouraged to set goals and targets and choose resources and learning strategies whilst evaluating learning outcomes. By using cognition to start discovering and teaching about learning connections (whether through framework consideration, questioning or dialogue as examples), students can build SDL knowledge and competencies.

Questioning and Dialogue

With cognition linked to the way learning connections are formed, it is important to consider how questioning and dialogue can be developed to enhance cognition. In this section, I propose several resources you could engage with to enhance your questioning and dialogue strategies.

David Bell (2011) produced an influential research paper about conversational paths in learning in, through and about art. The paper involves an Early Childhood setting in New Zealand, but it communicates a message relevant to all Art and Design disciplines. He articulates that when dialoguing and conversing about art, questions may be categorized into seven forms: looking questions, descriptive questions about perceptions, questions which analyse, narrative questions, those which explore contexts, doing questions and those which evaluate. He models in an empirical way how a dialogue involving these questions may unfold. Engaging with this conversation could help you identify how questions initiate learning connections that present as dialogue whilst demonstrating cognition between learners, educators and peers.

Secondary Art and Design dialogues will take many forms (physical, virtual etc.) and will likely be more complex. Bell's work communicates a clear model though that can act as starting point to critic and develop dialogic engagement in Art and Design provision. His work is insightful because it shares how engagement with art objects can facilitate learning connections, a central element of cognition, and he voices this can occur when connecting to prior experiences involving family, personal encounters, community or cultural experiences. He also reiterates, how establishing learning habits, as a form of SDL discussed above, encourages life-long learning dispositions.

Another resource art educators should engage with is Ged Gast's, an Art and Design consultant and ex-Ofsted inspector, Effective Questioning and Classroom Talk document (2022). This resource presents ideas and strategies for initiating and maintaining dialogue in Art and Design provision. Each idea can be used by educators to enhance questions and conversations whilst encouraging and supporting learners to access higher order thinking. If you are short of time but want to experiment pedagogically, ensure progressive dialogue and build cognate connections then access this document – the pdf link is in the reference list.

Another strategy to facilitate cognition may seem counter to facilitating questioning and dialogue, but it is necessary for educators to consider or be reminded of. Cognition and cognitive exchanges can reside intra-mentally in the mind (Peacock & Cowan, 2017). Intra-mental cognitive practices are a retreat – space afforded to regulate and probe the self. In relation to cognition in Art and Design, it is important that learners are given time to take a break, to step away and pause in their cognitive processing to use and enhance it at another time. This could be as simple as pausing to allow a learner time to respond. Or as prevalent as engaging in another unrelated activity to engender a break from knowledge pursuits before reengaging and progressing cognitive or artistic knowledge. Allowing space to pause, can be challenging in a time pressured and results driven discipline like education, but this action is in the best interest of developing effective educator and learner cognition.

Shared in this section are a few strategies for thinking about, initiating and applying cognition in Art and Design, there are many others. Individuals will craft cognition in personal ways aligned to their connectome (Naidu, 2012). But educators can design opportunities to progress cognition, they can also facilitate learners to own their cognitive development through identification, analysis tracking and curation.

PART 3.2: DEVELOP AN UNDERSTANDING OF COGNITION

Several strategies can be used to develop an understanding of cognition in Art and Design, like valuing voice and dialogue, the ones suggested in this section build on strategies presented earlier. The emphasis though is on development. To begin, engage in the task below:

Task 2.2 How Does Cognition Develop in Secondary Art and Design? Connect Theory and Practice

There are several theories about how cognition develops in Art and Design, using the table below engage with the theory and write a list of practices that you use or know about that demonstrate or use the theory suggested. Connecting theory and practice will help you visualize how cognition is active in art experiences. It may also make you aware of provision to further enhance learner cognitive experiences. Link to ideas presented in this chapter for assistance (Figure 2.5).

Cognitive development theories in Art and Design			
Cognition is built in socio-cultural spaces (Eisner 1994; Jagdoninski and Wallin, 2013).	Cognition is developed through analytical thinking and visual processing (Perkins, 1992)	Cognitive intelligence can be progressed through the process and products of art (Eisner 1986; Dorn, 1993; Efland, 2002).	Cognitive competencies develop when learners engage in meaningful art practices (Parsons, 2005)
Practice examples of cognitive development in art and design			
Consider, where and how you create or use social or cultural environments in learning provision? •	*Consider, where you create opportunities for learners to be analytical? How do your learners process their ideas?*	*Consider, how learners show cognitive intelligence (evidence of thinking) in artistic processes or products?*	*Consider, what is a meaningful art practice? What practices do you encourage that facilitate engagement with meaning?*

Figure 2.5 Reflective Activity 3.

In the above task, you were required to be analytical about pedagogy and learning approaches. Through engagement you have used and developed your cognition to review Art and Design practice. Self or learner-initiated acts like this can help create a learning ethos that fosters growth, reflection and cognitive development, because voice is afforded (Heaton, 2021).

Gaining confidence to voice cognition, verbally, visually, digitally or performatively can be challenging. It can cause vulnerability, so sharing needs supporting. There are many ways to afford voice in Art and Design, I am sure you can think of a few, such as through dialogue, exhibitions, presentations and gestures. These expressions can be subtle, overt and unspoken (McNiff, 2008; Rose, 2012). Voice can also be explored from lenses like the personal, theoretical, cognitive or analytical (Chase, 2005; Heaton, 2018). Voice affordance can open cognate discussions about sustainable and intercultural factors influencing change in Art and Design (Heaton & Crumpler, 2017; Heaton & Chan, 2022a). To develop personal and learner cognition you should therefore seek opportunities to develop and empower voices in provision.

As indicated earlier, cognition and cognitive movement in Art and Design occurs in and between psychologic, physical and virtual spaces (Heaton & Chan, 2022a,b). Rupert Wegerif, a Cambridge University scholar, also recognizes cognitive movement occurs through and for dialogue (Wegerif, 2019) and creates collective intelligence (Wegerif, 2021). In a task conducted with trainee visual art teachers I became aware of how technologic tools connect and develop learner cognition across domains. For example, learners explored their initial understandings of creativity on a shared Miro Board whilst engaging in virtual learning, see Figure 2.6.

What evolved on screen when learners interacted was a live dialogue and engagement of cognition. Learners connected psychologic thoughts, with those on the virtual screen through physical engagement. They also actively engaged with each other, linking and commenting on other's ideas through the virtual platform to develop, question, challenge and extend the cognition of others concerning

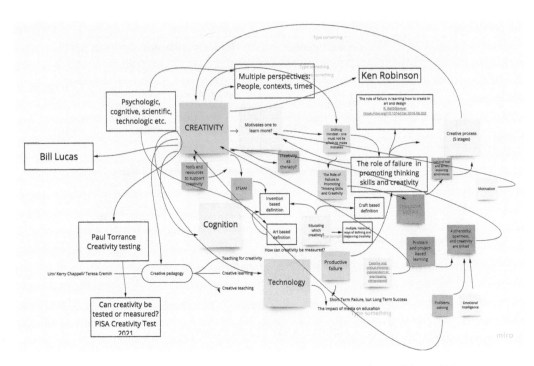

Figure 2.6 A Miro Board investigating the concept of creativity, 2021.

creativity. It was a joy to watch this active learning and cognitive process. You may have also noticed in Figure 2.6 that the connections formed resemble a side profile of a human head, this was not intentional to my knowledge and was only a visual observation noticed on reflection. But one I see as fitting to the cognitive learning experience that unfolded. Through this experience, I became aware that how one selects, interacts and organizes tools, content and pedagogy with learners changes the way cognition is used and curated. As educators, we therefore need to be mindful of how our decisions and actions concerning cognition influence learners. Virtual collaborative platforms for Art and Design often provide space and opportunities for learners to connect cognitive, visual and life interpretations and experiences. I am sure if you conducted virtual art experiences during the pandemic you saw learners use personal contexts and environments in cognitive and creative endeavours, perhaps more than when lessons occurred in school.

As I close this chapter, now may be a good time to review how your understanding of cognition has developed. Consider writing some notes prior to reading the final section.

PART 3.3: REFLECT ON THE VALUE OF COGNITION

A text edited by Kevin Tavin, Gila Kolb and Juuso Tervo (2021) suggests we now practice Art and Design in a Post-Digital, Post-Internet phase meaning that digital and virtual engagements are normal parts of existence. In this text, a comment was made that 'cognition takes a back seat, as the time-based material field provides the impulses and signals of transmission through the materialization of digital data' (Tavin, Kolb & Tervo, 2021, p.2). However, through active creation of digital data, as I indicated in the Miro Board example, cognition appears fully activated; learners are thinking, engaging in real time, participating in dialogic creation and are owning the production of digital spaces and signals. In education, cognition therefore cannot be peripheral. Now more than ever, particularly with developments in neuro-education, we need to recognize the contribution cognition can make to developments in Art and Design learning.

As educators, you can raise cognition's profile in Secondary Art and Design by nurturing cognitive dispositions in learners. You can model and identify how cognition fuels and develops learning; you can also show how understanding cognition can cause one to adapt, respond and change. If we look to changes in technology and contemporary art, they often advance faster than in education. We therefore need to work on ensuring educational factors in our control, like our use of Art and Design pedagogies, develop with societal advances. However, we need to do this with caution and relevance, as sometimes change can be fleeting or unnecessary. According to Rousell and Fell (2018), in the artistic processes of contemporary art cognitive exchanges locate and are important to facilitate cognitive development and educational progression.

SUMMARY

Remember, cognition is unique to individuals and their experiences. As an educator you therefore need to develop an autonomous disposition for cognitive progression yourself and with your learners. If you both own your cognitive concepts, understandings and practices, then you should be able to develop the cognitive connections and opportunities you create so learning develops and responds to changing times and experiences.

You will become a cognitive curator (Heaton & Chan, 2022a) and an educator able to identify, scaffold, facilitate and reflect on cognition to ensure that the Secondary Art and Design provision you offer is challenging, relevant and up to date. An important message to remember, is that cognition is not separate from one's bodily (creative or making) experiences, our thoughts and actions initiate happenings (Gulliksen, 2017; Heaton, 2021). How you understand, develop, implement and explore cognition will influence the way cognition is understood and used in Art and Design learning in future. In your emergent role as a cognitive curator, you will be able to review your and other's cognition in line with curriculum progression in educational, creative and cultural worlds. You can use knowledge developed in this chapter to facilitate your journey to engage with cognition. Try out, develop and research strategies for understanding cognition and be open to cognitive travel as art, education and its allied disciplines, like neuroscience and technology, progress.

RESOURCES

Eisner, E. (2004) *The arts and the creation of mind,* New Haven, CT: Yale University Press.
Read this seminal text to find out more about art's connection with psychologic processes and cognition. If you wish to enhance student thinking, engage with or develop your approaches to assessment or explore new directions for facilitating art learning then this text will help you. It may be nearly twenty years old, but it is a fundamental read which many developments in Art and Design have connected to.
https://youtu.be/1D69mKyndEY
Watch this 2 minute film clip: New Studies Link the Arts to Crucial Cognitive Skills to gain a quick insight into why cognition has relevance in Art and Design. Learn about cognitive studies and consider how you can enhance cognitive provision.
http://www.pz.harvard.edu/topics

The Harvard Project Zero Website will help you to explore resources, projects and topics relevant to Art and Design such as the subject topic: Cognition, thinking and understanding. It will inform you about current events, tools and research and offers practical advice about how to develop teaching in the classroom, such as how to hone questions to facilitate cognition.

https://www.nie.edu.sg/our-people/academic-groups/visual-and-performing-arts/care

The National Institute of Education, Singapore, Centre for Arts Research in Education Website invites you to access information about projects, events and resources concerning current and historic issues in Art and Design. Engagement with these resources will help develop your Art and Design teaching, learning and knowledge opening you to a global community of art educators.

BIBLIOGRAPHY

Ash, A. (2019) 'The unfamiliar grey matter(s): Talking brains', *Finnish Studies in Art Education Journal*, 2, 1–22.

Bechtel, W. (1991) 'Connectionism and the philosophy of mind: An overview', *Studies in Cognitive Systems*, 9, 30–59.

Bell, D. (2011) 'Seven ways to talk about art', *International Journal of Art and Design Education*, 7(1), 41–54.

Biesta, G. (2017) *Letting art teach: Art education beyond Joseph Beuys*, Arnhem: ArtEZ Press.

Bloom, B. S. (1956) *Taxonomy of educational objectives, Handbook I: The cognitive domain*, New York: David McKay Co Inc.

Burnard, P., Colucci-Gray, L. and Sinha, P. (2021) 'Transdisciplinarity: Letting arts and science teach together', *Curric Perspect*, 41, 113–118. DOI: 10.1007/s41297-020-00128-y

Caldwell, H., Heaton, R. and Whewell, E. (2020) 'The impact of visual posts on creative thinking and knowledge building in an online community of educators', *Thinking Skills and Creativity*, 36, 1–24.

Caldwell, H., Whewell, E., Bracey, P., Heaton, R., Crawford, H. and Shelley, C. (2021) 'Teaching on insecure foundations? Pre-service teachers in England's perceptions of the wider curriculum subjects in primary schools', *Cambridge Journal of Education*, 51(2), 231–246. DOI: 10.1080/0305764X.2020.1819202

Chase, S. (2005) 'Narrative inquiry: Multiple lenses, approaches, voices', In Denzin, N. and Lincoln, Y. (Eds.) *The Handbook of qualitative research* (pp. 651–679), Thousand Oaks, CA: Sage.

Churches, A. (2008) *Bloom's digital taxonomy*, viewed 21 April 2022 from http://burtonslifelearning.pbworks.com/w/file/fetch/26327358/BloomDigitalTaxonomy2001.pdf

Colucci-Gray, L., Burnard, P., Cooke, C., Davies, R., Gray, D. and Trowsdale, J. (2016) *Reviewing the potential and challenges of developing STEAM education through creative pedagogies for 21st century learning: How can school curricula be broadened towards a more responsive, dynamic and inclusive form of education?*, viewed 21 April 2022 from https://www.bera.ac.uk/wp-content/uploads/2017/11/100-160-BERA-Research-Commission-Report-STEAM.pdf

Critchfield, T. (2014) 'Prospective cognition in education and enculturation: an overview', *Journal of Cognitive Education and Psychology*, 13(2), 139–146.

Cunliffe, L. (1999) 'Learning how to learn, art education and the "background"', *Journal of Art and Design Education*, 18(1), 115–121.

Darts, D. (2011) 'Invisible Culture: Taking art education to the streets', *Art Education*, 49–53.

Davis, B. and Sumara, D. (1997) 'Cognition, complexity, and teacher education', *Harvard Educational Review*, 67(1), 105–125.

DfE (Department for Education). (2013) *Art and design programme of study, Key Stage 3, National Curriculum England*, viewed 21 April 22 from https://assets.publishing.service.gov.uk/government/uploads/system/uploads/attachment_data/file/239062/SECONDARY_national_curriculum_-_Art_and_design.pdf

Dorn, C. M. (1999) *Mind in art: Cognitive foundations in art education*, New York: Routledge.

Duncum, P. (2005) Visual culture and an aesthetics of embodiment. *International Journal of Education through Art*, 1(1), 9–20. DOI: 10.1386/etar.1.1.9/1

Efland, A. (2002) *Art and cognition*, New York: Teachers College Press.

Eisner, E. (1986) 'The role of the arts in cognition and curriculum', *Journal of Art and Design Education*, 5(1), 57–67.

Eisner, E. (1994) *Cognition and curriculum reconsidered* (2nd ed.), New York: Teachers College Press.

Eisner, E. (2002) *The arts and the creation of mind*, New Haven, CT: Yale University Press.

Fahey, P. and Cronen, L. (2016) 'Digital portfolios in action: Acknowledging student voice and metacognitive understanding in art', *The Clearing House: A Journal of Educational Strategies, Issues and Ideas*, 89(4–5), 135–143.

Fisher, D. and Frey, N. (2013) Gradual Release of Responsibility Instructional Framework. Alexandria, VA: ASCD.

Gardenfors, P. and Johansson, P. (Eds.) (2005) *Cognition, education, and communication technology*, London: Lawrence Erlbaum.

Gast, G. (2022) *Effective questioning and classroom talk*, viewed 21 April 2022 from https://www.liberty.k12.ga.us/pdf/TandL/Effective_Questioning_Talk.pdf

Gnezda, N. (2011) 'Cognition and emotions in the creative process', *Art Education*, 64(1), 47–52.

Gulliksen, M. (2017) 'Making matters? Unpacking the role of practical aesthetic making activities in the general education through the theoretical lens of embodied learning', *Cogent Education*, 4(1). DOI: 10.1080/2331186X.2017.1415108

Heaton, R. (2018) *Autoethnography to artography: An exhibition of cognition in artist teacher practice*, PhD thesis, University of Cambridge, United Kingdom, viewed from DOI: 10.17863/CAM.33324

Heaton, R. (2018b) 'Artist teacher cognition: connecting 'self' with 'other.'' *Australian Journal of Art Education*, 39(1), 139–145. Visual essay.

Heaton, R. (2021) 'Cognition in art education', *British Educational Research Journal*, 47(5), 1323–1339. DOI: 10.1002/berj.3728

Heaton, R. (2023). Curating cognition in the teaching-research-practice nexus of higher degree art education. *Research in Education*. DOI: 10.1177/003452372312130

Heaton, R. and Chan, S. (2022a) 'A visual inquiry: Artist teacher perceptions of art education provision in Singapore', *Studies in Art Education*. DOI: 10.1080/00393541.2022.2050988

Heaton, R. and Chan, S. (2022b) *Managing cognitive dissonance in art teacher education* [Unpublished Manuscript], Visual and Performing Arts, National Institute of Education, Nanyang Technological University.

Heaton, R. and Chan, S. (2023a). 'Managing cognitive dissonance in art education', *Cambridge Journal of Education*, 1–21. DOI: 10.1080/0305764X.2023.2175789

Heaton, R. and Crumpler, A. (2017) 'Sharing mindfulness: A moral practice for artist teachers', *International Journal of Education & the Arts*, 18(26), 1–20.

Heaton, R. and Edwards, J. (2017) 'Art'. In Caldwell, H. and Cullingford-Ague, S. (Eds.) *Technology for SEND in Primary Schools* (pp. 119–137), London: Sage.

Heaton, R. and Hickman, R. (2020, October 27) 'Purposes of arts education', In *Oxford research encyclopedia of education*, Oxford: Oxford University Press. DOI: 10.1093/acrefore/9780190264093.013.390

Hetland, L., Cajolet, S. and Music, L. (2010) 'Documentation in the visual arts: embedding a common language from research'. *Theory into Practice*, 49(1), 53–63. DOI: 10.1080/00405840903436079

Hetland, L., Winner, E., Veenema, S. and Sheridan, K. (2007) *Studio thinking: The real benefits of visual arts education*, New York: Teachers College Press.

Hetland, L., Winner, E., Veenema, S. and Sheridan, K. (2015) *Studio thinking 2: The real benefits of visual arts education*, New York: Teachers College Press.

Hickman, R. (2010) *Why we make art—And why it is taught* (2nd ed.), Bristol: Intellect.

Hickman, R. and Heaton, R. (2016) 'Visual art', In Wyse, D., Hayward, L. and Pandya, J. (Eds.) *The SAGE Handbook of curriculum, pedagogy and assessment: Two volume set* (pp. 342–358), London: SAGE.

Jamaludin, A., Loong, D. and Xuan, L. (2019) 'Developments in educational neuroscience: Implications for the *art* and *science* of learning', *Learning: Research and Practice*, 5(2), 201–213. DOI: 10.1080/23735082.2019.1684991

Klaassen, R. (2018) 'Interdisciplinary education: A case study', *European Journal of Engineering Education*, 43(6), 842–859. DOI: 10.1080/03043797.2018.1442417

Marshall, J. (2019) 'Art inquiry: Creative inquiry for integration and metacognition', In Costes-Onishi, P. (Ed.) *Artistic thinking in the schools* (pp. 87–106), Springer: Singapore. DOI: 10.1007/978-981-13-8993-1_5

Mason, P. (2011) *Medical neurobiology*, Oxford, New York: Oxford University Press. DOI: 10.1093/med/9780195339970.001.0001

Mathewson Mitchell, D. (2015) 'Examining practice in secondary visual arts education', International Journal of Education & the Arts, 16(17), 1–16.

McNiff, S. (2008). 'Art-based research', In Knowles, G. and Cole, A. (Eds.) *Handbook of the arts in qualitative research* (pp. 29–40), Thousand Oaks, CA: Sage.

Meltzoff, A. N., Kuhl, P. K., Movellan, J. and Sejnowski, T. J. (2009) 'Foundations for a new science of learning', *Science*, 325(5938), 284–288.

Ministry of Education. (2018) *Art syllabus: Upper secondary normal (technical) course*, viewed 21 April 2022 from https://www.moe.gov.sg/-/media/files/secondary/syllabuses-nt/arts-ed/2019_nt_art_syllabus.ashx?la=en&hash=1E934925217CD0CC8C9CFF13ECE09E96DA817037

Mottram, J. and Whale, G. (2001) 'New knowledge and new technology: Restructuring fine art education', *Journal of Visual Art Practice*, 1(2), 98–110. DOI: 10.1386/jvap.1.2.98

Naidu, S. (2012) 'Connectionism', *Distance Education*, 33(3), 291–294.

O'Donoghue, D. (2021) 'Traveling in, with, and away from art education', *Studies in Art Education*, 62(3), 203–208. DOI: 10.1080/00393541.2021.1954424

Ojala, M. (2013) 'Constructing knowledge through perceptual processes in making craft-art', *Techne Series A*, 20(3), 62–75.

Parreno (2016) The artwork, 'Anywhen,' by Philippe Parreno (2016) installed in the Tate Modern Turbine Hall (https://www.youtube.com/watch?v=M1RWxQaM5mc)

Parsons, M. (1998) 'Integrated curriculum and our paradigm of cognition in the arts'. *Studies in Art Education*, 39(2), 103–116.

Payne, R. (2020) 'The shock of the new', *International Journal of Art and Design Education*, 39(4), 724–738.

Peacock, S. and Cowan, J. (2017) 'Retreats for intramental thinking in collaborative onlinelearning',*ReflectivePractice*,18(1),1–13.DOI:10.1080/14623943.2016.1206876

Perignat, E. and Katz-Buonincontro, J. (2019) 'STEAM in practice and research: An integrated literature review', *Thinking Skills and Creativity*, 31, 31–43. DOI: 10.1016/j.tsc.2018.10.002

Petrie, H. G. (1992) 'Interdisciplinary education: Are we faced with insurmountable opportunities?', *Review of Research in Education*, 18, 299–333.

Powell, K. and Lajevic, L. (2011) 'Emergent places in preservice art teaching: Lived curriculum, relationality and embodied knowledge', *Studies in Art Education*, 53 (1), 35–52. DOI: 10.1080/00393541.2011.11518851

Ray, K. (2021) *Updating blooms digital taxonomy for digital learning*, viewed 21 April 2022 from https://www.techlearning.com/news/updating-blooms-taxonomy-for-digital-learning

Rivers, B., Nie, M. and Armellini, A. (2015) 'University teachers' conceptions of 'changemaker': A starting point for embedding social innovation in learning and teaching', *Education and Training*, 57(5). DOI: 10.1108/ET-07-2014-0078

Rose, G. (2012) *Visual methodologies* (3rd ed.), London: Sage.

Rousell, D. and Fell, F (2018) 'Becoming a work of art: collaboration, materiality and posthumanism in visual arts education'. *International Journal of Education through Art*, 14(1), 91–110.

Schatzki, T. R. (1996) *Social practices: A Wittgensteinian approach to human activity and the social*, Cambridge: Cambridge University Press.

Seel, N. (Ed.) (2012) *Encyclopedia of the sciences of learning*, New York: Springer.

Selkrig, M., Wright, S., Hannigan, S., Burke, G. and Grenfell, J. (2020) 'Art educators' professional learning: Reflecting together to consider ontologies of quality in our praxis', *Teaching in Higher Education*, 1–15. DOI: 10.1080/13562517.2020.1729724

Song, Y. (2012) 'Educating for peace: a case study of a constructivist approach to understanding peace through artistic expression'. *Creative Education*, 3(1), 79–83. DOI: 10.4236/ce.2012.31013

Sullivan, G. (2001) 'Artistic thinking as transcognitive practice'. *Visual Arts Research*, 27, 2–12.

Sullivan, G. (2005) *Art practice as research*, London: Sage.

Tavin, K. (2010) 'Six acts of mis-cognition: Implications for art education', *Studies in Art Education*, 52(1), 55–68.

Tavin, K., Kolb, G. and Tervo, J. (Eds.) (2021). *Post digital, post-internet art and education*, Palgrave Macmillan. https://link.springer.com/book/10.1007/978-3-030-73770-2

Turner, M. (Ed.) (2006) *The artful mind: cognitive science and the riddle of human creativity*. Oxford: Oxford University Press.

Vitulli, P., Giles, R. and Shaw, E. (2014) 'The effects of knowledge maps on acquisition of retention on visual arts concepts in teacher education', *Educational Research International*. DOI: 10.1155/2014/902810

Wegerif, R. (2013) *Dialogic: Education for the Internet age*, London: Routledge.

Wegerif, R. (2019) *Dialogic education*, Oxford Research Encyclopedias. Available at https://oxfordre.com/view/10.1093/acrefore/9780190264093.001.0001/acrefore-9780190264093-e-396 (Accessed: 21 April 2022).

Wegerif, R. (2021) *Designing education for collective intelligence: A research agenda,* viewed 21 April 22 from: https://www.rupertwegerif.name/blog/designing-education-for-collective-intelligence-a-research-agenda

Williams, P. J. and Barlex, D. (2020) *Pedagogy for technology education in secondary schools: Research informed perspectives for classroom,* Cham: Springer.

Wilson, A. and Golonka, S. (2013) 'Embodied cognition is not what you think it is', *Frontiers in Psychology,* 4. DOI: 10.3389/fpsyg.2013.00058

Chapter 3

Transforming Teaching: Demonstration, Modelling and the Art of Instruction

Andrea Pratt

INTRODUCTION

In this chapter, you will learn about modelling and demonstration and the fundamental principle of the quality of instruction to support pupil learning in Art and Design. You will reflect on the reciprocal relationship between theory and practice when demonstrating, modelling and employing instruction in the Art and Design classroom. This chapter recognises that there is a benefit to practice if informed by an understanding and application of high-quality research (Ofsted, 2019). Research and practice should inform your own critical thinking and reflection on 'what works' (*the approach*), 'why it works' *(the evidence)* and for 'whom it works' *(the context)*. The purpose of this chapter is to consider that effective demonstration and modelling as a teaching approach must be planned well and can take many forms. Through this chapter, you will acquire an understanding of these teaching approaches enabling you to plan and teach effectively centring around sound instructional practices.

OBJECTIVES:

By the end of this chapter, you should be able to:

- *Develop* your understanding of modelling, demonstration and instructional practice in Art and Design teaching to support effective learning;
- *Select* the appropriate approaches for teaching in the Art and Design classroom;
- *Reflect* on your own practice and teaching skills to inform targets for your development.

TEACHING APPROACHES

The role of pedagogy (teaching approaches) in Art and Design emerges from a rich history of research that informs how we teach today (Dewey, 1916; Piaget, 1936; Lowenfeld and Brittain, 1982; Gardner, 1988; Eisner, 2002). The transformative nature of Art and Design education is rooted in historical theoretical principles and in more recent perspectives on the practical nature of inquiry and art functioning

DOI: 10.4324/9781003377429-5

through experience (Adams, 2013). We need to ensure that we use appropriate teaching approaches and methods rooted in theory to ensure pupils can produce creative work, develop proficiency, evaluate, analyse and know about the historical, cultural and contemporary development of art forms and practice. Doing this will support you to 'translate your practice in art, craft and design into pedagogy' (Addison and Burgess, 2014, p.3).

Task 3.1 Your Own Way of Learning and Approaches to Teaching Art and Design

Reflecting on your own learning of a process:

- Think about a practical lesson you have experienced as a learner in which you were taught how to do a practical process.
- What teaching approach was used that enabled you to learn this new skill, what did the teacher do that made the difference, why was this successful?
- What was an approach that was less successful?

Further reading: The didactic vs heuristic continuum, Addison and Burgess (2014) table 3.1.1, pp. 23–24. This highlights the different approaches for teaching art and design and for what purpose and is a useful reference.

THE ROLE OF KNOWLEDGE

As a student teacher, you bring a wealth of subject knowledge within your field of Art and Design. You now need to consider what role this knowledge plays in your training to teach, and why this training is not just about your subject knowledge in Art and Design.

Education theorist L.S. Shulman first introduced the principle of thinking beyond subject matter when teaching and defined this as 'pedagogical content knowledge (PCK)' which he described as 'powerful analogies, illustrations, examples, explanations and demonstrations' (Shulman, 1986, p.9). For Shulman, PCK is about the teacher making the subject clear to others by having these kinds of pedagogical approaches to hand in the classroom. The stages of any sequence of learning should be taught in a way that your pupils can understand, with new ideas being linked to pupils existing knowledge. The theoretical framework of PCK was considered further by Grossman (1989) who presented it in three stages. Firstly, there is **general pedagogical knowledge**, the theories linked to generic teaching and learning. For example, theories about classroom management and how children learn. Secondly, there is **subject content knowledge,** which Shulman defines as ideas, facts, and concepts. Ofsted suggested three domains of knowledge for our subject. '**Practical knowledge** (linked to technical proficiency), **theoretical knowledge** which is the cultural and contextual content that pupils learn about artists and artwork and **disciplinary knowledge** which is what pupils learn about how art is studied, discussed and judged' (Ofsted, 2023), Finally returning to Schulman there is **pedagogical context knowledge,** the principles and techniques of teaching and supporting procedural knowledge in the context of the individuals in your school (Grossman, 1990). Here we can see that the literature establishes that subject content and pedagogy are different but are inextricably linked. Additionally, the conditions in which your pupils will be learning is an essential conversation you will be having with expert

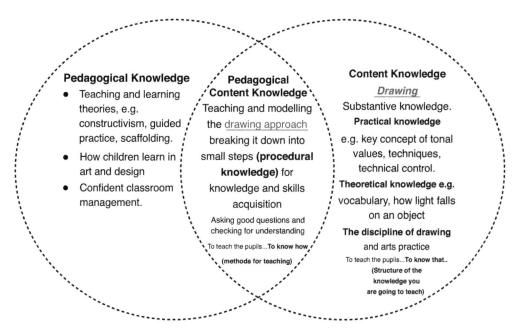

Figure 3.1 Example of PCK in context adapted from Shulman (1986) for a tonal drawing lesson.

practitioners in your context during your training. For example, how to introduce new learning before introducing more complex ideas, related to the ages and stages of individual pupils' development in a particular topic.

To consider this body of theory in practice we also need to ensure we mitigate against pupils just *'doing art.'* For example, in a lesson on tonal drawing, you must ensure you focus your planning on what you want the pupils to *learn,* for example, *'to use tone to create depth or contrast in drawing'* rather than what you want them to simply *do*, for example, *'pupils will shade using tone'*. In this case, it is important that you are aware that you are teaching children the foundation knowledge, in a sequence, and teaching the essential elements of using tone as building blocks for understanding meaning when drawing, (not simply to reproduce a surface representation in a drawing). While we as teachers may have the knowledge of the concept of tone (how we describe light falling on an object), it is also imperative to consider how that knowledge becomes part of our teaching (Grossman, 2018). Here is an example of PCK theory in practice for a tonal drawing activity (Figure 3.1):

HOW CHILDREN LEARN IN ART CRAFT AND DESIGN

Learning how children learn in art, craft and design requires you to explore theoretical perspectives, evidence, your own practice and that of others. Learning in Art and Design is effective when it is taught through a carefully sequenced curriculum and is how children 'get better' at Art and Design (Ofsted, 2023). Within this, modelling and demonstration play an essential role. These methods have links to the work of Vygotsky and the related principle/theory of constructivism, which hypothesises that learners actively construct knowledge for themselves socially in the school environment (Vygotsky, 1978). Effective teaching is 'much more than face to face interaction or the simple transmission of prescribed knowledge and skills' (Daniels, 2001, p.2). Learning is defined in social constructivist theory as leading to the 'transformation of socially constructed knowledge into that which is individually owned by the learner' (Verenikina, 2008, p.161). This is another important theoretical foundation on which to build when teaching Art and Design, shifting your practice from a teacher led, didactic approach to finding the balance that encourages pupil-centred learning appropriate to Art and Design (Addison and Burgess, 2014, pp.23–24).

SCAFFOLDING LEARNING

For all pupils, new knowledge needs to be taught, (direct instruction) rather than pupils finding things out for themselves from the start which is not supported by research (Kirschner, 2006). Direct instruction when associated with demonstration and modelling is aligned with the theory of scaffolding by providing structures that support the learning process (Bruner, 1977; Vygotsky, 1978). A useful visual metaphor for this is the creation of a temporary scaffold to support learning. This support is relevant while students acquire skills, develop practice and achieve proficiency. For example, the use of an underlying grid to support the construction of a drawing when learning about proportion. The grid can be removed when understanding is secure, as the learning has taken place and the skills become more natural to the learner.

> Guides, scaffolds and worked examples can help pupils apply new ideas, but should be gradually removed as pupil expertise increases.
>
> (CCF, 2019, p.16)

When pupils learn well, this information is retrieved from memory as the pupil knows more and can remember more about proportion and can apply this to their work. Scaffolds of course can also be reintroduced at any stage to aid learning if required. As teachers we need to ensure we consider the individual carefully, teaching new content and skill to ensure the learning is within reach rather than too difficult or demotivating (Vygotsky, 1978).

Task 3.2 Reflecting on Learning

- Can you think of an example in your own learning of a practical aspect of Art and Design that was perhaps just out of reach and what your teacher may have provided to bridge the gap in your learning?
- This is an example of your teacher implementing theory in their practice.

You should now be concluding that an understanding of theory and research in your initial teacher education is vital in developing your knowledge of teaching and learning. This understanding should emerge through your effective practice, observing pupils constructing their learning in your lessons coupled with your responses in the classroom while the pupils are working, therefore putting your pedagogic subject knowledge into practice. The research presented in the 'What makes great teaching' report suggests that promoting learning in the classroom requires teachers to have confidence in their ability to know the *how and why of teaching* (Coe et al., 2014).

THE ART OF THE TEACHER DEMONSTRATION

The teaching approach of demonstration is (as stated previously) aligned with direct instruction (DfES, 2004) for the introduction of a new concept, material or process in Art and Design. This step-by-step approach is highly valued by art teachers, along with the showing of a worked example and a progressive series of examples and 'in many instances, [the demonstration of] the aesthetic ideas and creative possibilities underlying the artistic activity that emerge during [the] demonstration and the dialogue that accompanies it' (Burton, 2001, p.137). This highlights the importance of explaining when demonstrating. Planning a teaching demonstration requires rehearsal in the early stages of training which can happen before teaching takes place, for example, with a peer group. This is referred to by Grossman as 'approximations in practice' (Grossman, 2018), in which both process and thought are rehearsed.

Demonstration artistically, by the teacher, allows students to relate to what is being practically demonstrated, and to then respond to this in their own work. The demonstration could be of a method or process, for example, in monoprinting, where to start on the page, how to roll out the ink, the amount of the ink on the printing plate and the visual and manual process of making the print. It is essential when demonstrating in this way to clarify for yourself the teaching points that will make the students' work successful, and to explain these steps in your practical demonstration. While demonstrating, dialogue and questioning support how you check for pupil understanding, requiring structured questions to evaluate prior knowledge (known as 'retrieval practice'). It is also important to highlight potential misconceptions, in printmaking, for example, these could be with positive and negative space or the reversing of images or letters. Through rehearsal, you can anticipate what knowledge or skills may be more difficult to convey and can clarify terminology appropriate to the age of the learners and the stage of their learning and what adaptations you can make to secure a deeper understanding for the pupils.

Task 3.3 Planning a Demonstration

Think of a practical lesson you will teach and a demonstration that is required within the lesson:

- Discuss with an expert practitioner/mentor the important teaching points and dialogue required when explaining a particular process.
- Note as part of your planning, the key learning and steps.
- Practice and set up a demonstration area to ensure you have all the equipment to hand.

After the demonstration, discuss with your mentor if the foundation knowledge from the demonstration was secure for the learners and deconstruct what went well and aspects to develop in your teaching.

A level of discernment needs to be considered in planning your demonstration. Discuss the learning intentions for the lesson with a mentor to help you ascertain when a demonstration is appropriate in the lesson. Additionally, time needs to be given for consideration of the length of your demonstrations, one that takes too long will lead to pupils losing interest and potential opportunities for disengagement.

Demonstrations need practice and careful preparation with a sound knowledge of the process or subject content. Hattie considers the effectiveness of demonstration in his influential 'Visible Learning' (Hattie, 2009). Hattie states that it is important to consider the learning that has taken place prior to the demonstration. Imagine, for example, watching an artist painting a portrait without any explanation of the formative process or the complex decisions of colour mixing. What key knowledge needs to be isolated and learned? Where would you start in sequencing this learning as the teacher?

It can also be important in demonstration to demonstrate the wrong way to approach the learning by making the same errors as pupils often do (Hughes, 2009). Additionally, encouraging pupils to share what they might not understand fully ensures that your teaching will address any potential misconceptions and clarify key learning points. Sometimes we can utilise the 'spot demo' which requires skill to determine the suitable time in the lesson to undertake this (McLain et al., 2013). This could be a result of discerning the need to clarify or reteach an aspect of the lesson; however, it is important to allow for pupils to practise crucial components of these techniques (Ofsted, 2023) which in turn would lead to more independence.

There is however the necessity in demonstrations to strive for high expectations through the 'use of well-judged examples and demonstrations with good opportunities to refer to professional work' (Ofsted, 2012, p.18). However, for more able pupils' discussions about unresolved (unfinished examples) work can be pedagogically beneficial (Ofsted, 2023).

Task 3.4 Key Subject Knowledge for Beginning Teachers

- A **hue** is a pigment/pure colour.
- A **tint** is a pure pigment with white added.
- A **shade** is a pigment with black added.
- A **tone** is a pigment with grey added.

Teaching a Lesson about Colour: Tints and Shades

In an example lesson, let's break down the learning.

- What is a tint or shade in painting? (This is **what** pupils are learning) (Figure 3.2)
- Pupils will then use tints and shades when mixing paint colours in the lesson (this is **how** pupils are learning – application of skills)
- To extend our range of colours that we use in painting (this is **why** we are learning) (Figure 3.3)

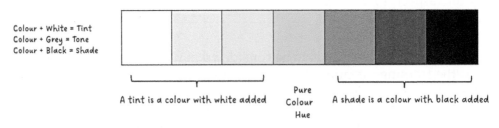

Colour + White = Tint
Colour + Grey = Tone
Colour + Black = Shade

A tint is a colour with white added   Pure Colour Hue   A shade is a colour with black added

Figure 3.2 What *pupils are learning.*

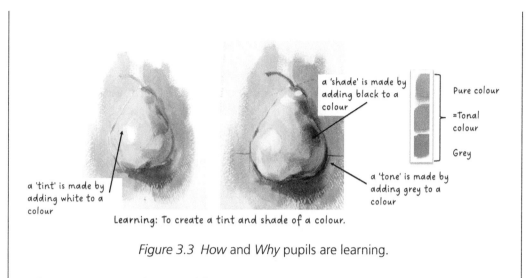

Learning: To create a tint and shade of a colour.

Figure 3.3 How and Why pupils are learning.

What Demonstration Could Be Done to Support the Learning in the Lesson?

- Taking learning further: To extend the palette of painting by creating tone with a colour or hue by adding grey.

MOVING FORWARD WITH MODELLING TO ENCOURAGE THINKING

Having considered that demonstration is an accepted pedagogical approach in practical subjects (McLain et al., 2014), it is important to also take into account that the demonstration of a method can lead to knowledge not being taught or being lost if it is not reinforced by additional methods. It is possible for pupils to become dependent and simply imitative of the examples they have been shown (Addison and Burgess, 2014). It is here that modelling as an approach needs to be considered in addition to demonstration because of the added richness it brings to teaching in Art and Design;

> The demonstrator will, of course, demonstrate more than how to perform a task. The demonstrator will also model what he or she knows, and the level of skills and safe practice attained.
>
> (Petrina, 2007, p.14)

So, what is the difference between demonstration and modelling? Modelling is an extension of demonstration (DfE, 2004) and as such is a process that is highly effective for the learning of knowledge and skills (Bandura, 1986). Modelling is defined as 'an active process, not merely the provision of an example. It involves the teacher as the 'expert', demonstrating how to do something and making explicit the thinking involved.' (DfES, 2004, p.3) A more recent definition is, 'an instructional strategy in which the teacher demonstrates a new concept or approach to learning and students learn by observing' (Salisu and Ransom, 2014, p.54). A demonstration is a practical teaching process (concise and short in time), whereas modelling can be attributed to both task *(practical teaching, e.g., methods and processes)* and metacognitive modelling *(theoretical teaching and thinking, e.g., analysing and evaluating the work of others or decision making).*

Task 3.5 Observation of Expert Practitioners: Modelling

- During your observation of a lesson, focus on when modelling takes place as a teaching approach.
- How did the teacher's modelling keep the pupils' attention and make explicit the thinking and decisions needed during the task?
- What was effective about the approach and how could this inform your teaching?
- List three things that you can take forward when modelling in your lessons.

Modelling as an approach encourages a narrative of the thinking required in learning and makes this explicit to pupils (Duplass, 2006). The process being 'how to begin…how to select…how to organise…protocols, and how to end' (DfES, 2004, p.16). For example, to develop the *learning* in the skills (not simply the *doing* of them) would instil in the students the confidence to take a process forward and remember more of it long term. In a dynamic model of educational effectiveness teaching by modelling is valued as it encourages problem solving and develops strategies in the learners (Creemers and Kyriakides, 2011). Table 3.1 is a useful research-informed reference for the beginning teacher as to the benefits of effective modelling.

After considering the above, we now consider a contextual example of modelling for a drawing technique. In the modelling during the lesson, you would unpack or deconstruct the drawing approach to articulate the thinking behind the decisions made when drawing. Consider tonal shading, the analysis of how light falls on the object, how the light and dark areas appear on the object and how you would explain this through dialogue and explanations appropriate to the age and stage of the pupils. Ofsted's Research Review for Art and Design (Ofsted, 2023), states that modelling work effectively with clear explanations and connections will support long term learning when approached effectively. Having time to practice coupled with effective instruction are also highlighted as an effective approach (Figure 3.4).

Duplass asks us to consider when teaching, the 'thinking out loud' of a process and how this can help pupils to develop skill and confidence in developing their own responses, suggesting that this will make explicit for them the links to the

Table 3.1 *Effective modelling in lessons (DfES, 2004, p.3)*

When effective modelling is a regular feature of lessons:

- the work pupils produce is more likely to achieve the standard required by the teacher;
- teachers see work meeting reasonable standards and their expectations of pupils rise accordingly;
- pupils are able to make use of the processes, skills, conventions and procedures that have been developed and consolidated in previous years;
- pupils are generally on-task, engaged and motivated;
- pupils are better able to work independently of the teacher, being clear about the skills they need to use and what a good, finished product should look like;
- pupils feel they have the knowledge and skills to accomplish tasks to a good standard;
- pupils feel they have succeeded, and this results in improved confidence.

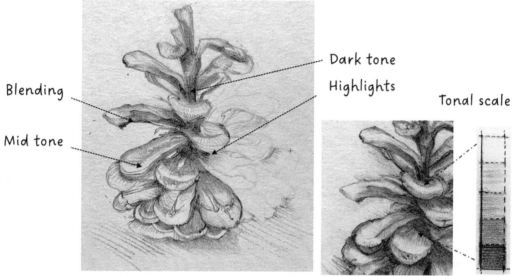

Learning: Shading is a technique used in art to represent light and dark. In this example pencil is used to create a tonal drawing. Shading creates depth, shape and communicates form.

Figure 3.4 Worked example of shading as a process and terminology.

process and will support a meaningful dialogue about making sense of the process and its application (Duplass, 2006, p.205) a view also supported by Rosenshine (2012). Dialogue and terminology need to be planned to maintain pupil engagement while modelling and having pre-prepared questions can help to develop a more student-centred or interactive approach as well as 'in the moment' (Ofsted, 2023) questioning. When using modelling as a scaffolding technique, teachers must consider the students' position in the learning process, including their prior learning (Bruner, 1977). Questions about what pupils already know play an important role in this process.

Alexander presents a useful framework to consider when asking questions that has been adapted in this case to include content knowledge (Alexander et al., 2022). This could extend your visual modelling further and create/plan a meaningful dialogue with your pupils as you develop your teaching repertoire (Table 3.2).

Salisu and Ransom advocate the model of the apprenticeship. This involves firstly modelling in which the learners observe the modelling and the explanations involved. Secondly, scaffolding, in which support is provided while the learner

Table 3.2 Modelling good questions

Ask a Well-Structured Question	Expectations for the Response	Constructivist Conversation
• What are harmonious colours? *(Pupils will have learned in a previous lesson what harmonious colours are)*	• Colour/s that sit beside each other on the colour wheel • A colour that works well with another	• Pupils share ideas • Pupils can identify harmonious colours, e.g., in their work or the work of others • Terminology is discussed, e.g., that harmonious colours are aesthetically pleasing and why.

Adapted from Alexander et al. (2022).

carries out the activity. Thirdly comes the concept of fading; in which there is a measured withdrawal of support and finally comes coaching, which requires encouragement and feedback (Salisu and Ransom, 2014). In your practice, you may see more and earlier 'fading' with older pupils as teachers encourage pupils to work with more independence.

There are several strategies you can use for effective modelling, 'prepare the lesson well, take into account pupils' prior knowledge and experience, try to maintain the view of the class, maintain the pace, repeat the modelling and establish rules' (DfES, 2004, p.4). Modelling in practice can be live (in class modelling) or pre-prepared, for example, worked examples, associated with the teaching of skills (Mujis and Reynolds, 2017). Mujis and Reynolds also state that modelling is more effective than using verbal explanations alone. Worked examples demonstrate what success looks like. However, for this to be an effective strategy modelling needs to be followed by practice (learner centred). This relates well to how expert practitioners formatively assess pupil practice and provide appropriate feedback that is essential in monitoring learning and progress.

What is also important to consider is using modelling to address misconceptions or aspects of teaching that are perhaps unclear or complex, possible pitfalls and corrections that may be needed, and finally the possible hazards to avoid (DfES, 2004). Anticipation of what pupils may find difficult, or the effects of a misconception carried into finished artwork, needs to be thought about in advance of any teaching. Through considered planning and your own immersion in the practical process, you can put yourself in the shoes of a pupil and anticipate what they may find difficult. Deconstructing the intuitive skills or tacit knowledge (Schindler, 2015), you have developed as an artist and making the implicit nature of creating artworks explicit in the process of teaching, you can support working memory, long-term memory, and retention of knowledge in your pupils. Rosenshine states that highly effective teachers, teaching through principles of instruction present:

> new materials in manageable amounts, modelling, guiding students, helping students when they made errors and providing for sufficient practice and review.

> (Rosenshine, 2012, p.12)

SUMMARY

This chapter concludes that demonstration, modelling and the art of instruction play a vital role in Art and Design teaching and can take many forms. We have learned that '…modelling helps pupils understand new processes and ideas, good models make abstract ideas concrete and accessible' (CCF, 2019, p.16). Through principles of instruction (Rosenshine, 2012), worked examples and thinking out loud, the teacher can effectively support pupil learning and the steps involved in it. Modelling is a significant and important approach in making our own thinking visible. Through this, we 'assist students in learning not simply "that" but also "how to" as these terms refer to a range of cognitive processes, skills, and dispositions' (Stickler, 2016, p.1).

This chapter positioned demonstration and modelling as effective teaching methods, informed by research and practice. As reflective practice becomes part of your teacher identity, reflect regularly on what works, why and for whom. As your confidence grows over time, you will establish a more intuitive and responsive approach to individuals (Atkinson and Claxton, 2000) building on your own emerging practice and knowledge of your pupils and can teach more 'in the moment' (Ofsted, 2023).

Modelling in Art and Design requires an artistic and thoughtful approach, balanced with skill to ensure that the implicit and tacit knowledge of the discipline becomes explicit in your teaching. Modelling allows for growth of both the teacher and the learner. So, model well, with clear aims, effective resources and well-chosen examples; think out loud with clear age-appropriate vocabulary and literacy strategies and explore and stretch pupil thinking to encourage metacognitive and self-regulatory responses. Watch your pupils grow as artists, allowing time for pupil practice to lead to increased proficiency and independence in the subject.

BIBLIOGRAPHY

Adams, E. (2013) *Drawing to Learn, Learning to Draw.* [online] Available at: https://www.nsead.org/files/f7246b7608216d52696dc3ed81256213.pdf [Accessed 22.10.22].

Addison, N. and Burgess, L. (2014) *Learning to Teach Art and Design in the Secondary Classroom: Second Edition: A Companion to School Experience.* Abingdon: Routledge.

Alexander, K., Gonzalez, C. H., Vermette, P. J. and Di Marco, S. (2022) Questions in secondary classrooms: Toward a theory of questioning. *Theory and Research in Education*, 20(1), 5–25.

Atkinson, T. A. and Claxton, G. L. (2000) *The Intuitive Practitioner: On the Value of Not Always Knowing What One Is Doing.* Buckingham, Open University Press.

Bandura, A. (1977) *Social Learning Theory Bandura Social Learning Theory.* [online] Learning Theories. Available at: https://www.learning-theories.com/social-learning-theory-bandura.html [Accessed 22.10.22].

Bandura, A. (1986) *Social Foundations of Thought and Action: A Social Cognitive.* Englewood Cliffs, NJ: Prentice Hall.

Bruner, J. S. (1977) *The Process of Education.* Cambridge, MA: Harvard University Press.

Burton, D. (2001) How do we teach? Results of a national survey of instruction in secondary art education. *Studies in Art Education*, 42(2), 131–145.

CCF. (2019) *The Initial Teacher Training (ITT) Core Content Framework.* [online] Available at: https://assets.publishing.service.gov.uk/government/uploads/system/uploads/attachment_data/file/974307/ITT_core_content_framework_.pdf [Accessed 22.10.22].

Coe, R., Aloisi, C., Higgins, S. and Major, L. M (2014) *What Makes Great Teaching?* [online] Available at: https://www.suttontrust.com/wp-content/uploads/2014/10/What-Makes-Great-Teaching-REPORT.pdf [Accessed 25.10.22].

Creemers, B. P. and Kyriakides, L. (2011) *Improving Quality in Education: Dynamic Approaches to School Improvement.* New York: Routledge, Taylor & Francis Group.

Daniels, H. (2001) *Vygotsky and Pedagogy.* New York: Routledge/Falmer.

Department for Education. (2013) *National Curriculum: Art and Design Programmes of Study: Key Stage 3.*

Dewey, J. (1916) *Democracy and Education.* New York: Macmillan.

DfES. (2004) *Pedagogy and Practice: Teaching and Learning in Secondary Schools Unit 6: Modelling.* Norwich: HMSO. Available at http://webarchive.nationalarchives.gov.uk [Accessed 22.10.22].

Duplass, J. (2006) *Middle and High School Teaching: Methods, Standards, and Best Practices.* Boston, MA: Houghton Mifflin Company.

Eisner, E. W. (2002) *The Arts and the Creation of Mind.* New Haven, CT: Yale University Press.

Gardner, H. (1988) Toward more effective arts education. *Journal of Aesthetic Education,* 22(1), 157–167.

Grossman, P. L. (1990) *The Making of a Teacher. Teacher Knowledge and Teacher Education.* New York: Columbia University, Teachers College Press.

Grossman, P. L. (2018) *Teaching Core Practices in Teacher Education.* New York: Harvard Education Press.

Grossman, P., Wilson, S. M. and Shulman, L. (1989) Teachers of substance: Subject matter knowledge for teaching. In Reynolds, M. (Ed.), *Knowledge Base for the Beginning Teacher* (pp. 23–36). New York: Pergamon Press.

Hattie, J. (2009) *Visible Learning: A Synthesis of Over 800 Meta-Analyses Relating to Achievement.* New York. Routledge.

Hattie, J. (2015) *Visible Learning.* Available at: https://www.visiblelearningplus. com/content/faq *Worked examples* [Accessed 22.10.22].

Hughes, M. (2009) Demonstration and its implications for design based craftwork. *Studies in Design Education Craft & Technology,* [S.l.], 14(1). ISSN 0305 766. Available at: https://ojs.lboro.ac.uk/SDEC/article/view/1034 [Accessed 22.10.22].

Jay, J. K. and Johnson, K. L. (2002) Capturing complexity: A typology of reflective practice for teacher education. *Teacher and Teacher Education,* 18, 73–75.

Kirschner, P., Sweller, J and Clark, R (2006) Why Minimal Guidance During Instruction Does Not Work: An Analysis of the Failure of Constructivist, Discovery, Problem-Based, Experiential, and Inquiry-Based Teaching. *Educational Psychologist,* 41, 75–86.

Lowenfeld, V. and Brittain, W. L. (1982) *Creative and Mental Growth.* New York: Macmillan.

McLain, M., Pratt, A. and Bell, D. (2013) *Show-How Know-How: Part 1 Theory and Practice for Demonstrating in Design and Technology.* D&T Practice, 3/2013. Wellesbourne: Design and Technology Education.

McLain, M., Pratt, A. and Bell, D. (2014) *Show-How Know-How: Part 2 Theory and Practice for Demonstrating in Design and Technology.* [PDF] D&T Practice/1: 2014, p. 34. Available at: https://repository.edgehill.ac.uk/6575/1/Show_How_Part_2.pdf [Accessed 02.10.22].

Mujis, D. and Reynolds, D. (2017) *Effective Teaching: Evidence and Practice* (5th edition). London: SAGE Publications Ltd.

Ofsted. (2012) *Art, Craft and Design Education: Making a Mark.* Gov.uk. https://assets.publishing.service.gov.uk/government/uploads/system/uploads/attachment_data/file/413330/Making_a_mark_-_art_craft_and_design_education_2008-11.pdf [Accessed 22.10.22]

Ofsted. (2019) *Education Inspection Framework: Overview of Research.* [Online] https://assets.publishing.service.gov.uk/government/uploads/system/uploads/attachment_data/file/963625/Research_for_EIF_framework_updated_references_22_Feb_2021.pdf [Accessed 25.10.2022].

Ofsted. (2023) Curriculum Research Reviews Series: Art and Design. Available at: https://www.gov.uk/government/publications/research-review-series-art-and-design/research-review-series-art-and-design [Accessed 16.03.23].

Petrina, S. (2007) *Advanced Teaching Methods for the Technology Classroom.* London: Information Science Publishing.

Piaget, J. (1936) *Origins of Intelligence in the Child.* London: Routledge.

Quigley, A. and Coleman, R. (2019) Improving Literacy in Secondary Schools. Guidance Report. *Education Endowment Foundation.*

Rosenshine, B. V. (1983) Teaching functions in instructional programs. *The Elementary School Journal,* 83, 335–351.

Rosenshine, B. V. (2012) Principles of Instruction: Research-Based Strategies That All Teachers Should Know. *American Educator*, Spring 2012. Available at: https://www.aft.org/sites/default/files/periodicals/Rosenshine.pdf [Accessed 22.10.22].

Salisu, A. and Ransom, E. (2014) The role of modeling towards impacting quality education. *International Letters of Social and Humanistic Sciences*, 32, 54–61

Schindler, J. (2015) Expertise and tacit knowledge in artistic and design processes: results of an ethnographic study. *Journal of Research Practice*, 11, 1–22.

Shulman, L. S. (1986) Those who understand: Knowledge growth in teaching. *Educational Researcher*, 15(2), 4–14.

Verenikina, I. (2008) Scaffolding and learning: Its role in nurturing new learners. In Kell, P., Vialle, W., Konza, D. and Vogl, G. (Eds.), *Learning and the Learner: Exploring Learning for New Times* (236p). University of Wollongong. https://ro.uow.edu.au/cgi/viewcontent.cgi?article=1043&context=edupapers

Vygotsky, L. S. (1978) *Mind in Society: The Development of Higher Psychological Processes* (Cole, M., John-Steiner, V., Scribner, S. and Souberman, E., Eds.). Cambridge, MA: Harvard University Press.

Chapter 4

Is 'School Art' Always a Bad Thing? 'Powerful Knowledge' for the Trainee Art Teacher

Carol Wild

INTRODUCTION

After 46 years, Arthur Efland's 1976 'The School Art Style: A Functional Analysis' remains one of the journal *Studies in Art Education's* top ten most cited papers. The interest in the paper largely stems from its status as the first to theorise a particular phenomenon, that of 'School Art', as something separate from, and out-of-step with, art in the world outside the classroom, apparently framing School Art in negative terms. I first heard School Art referred to during my teacher training, completed at Homerton College, with Richard Hickman, in the late 1990s. One of the citations of 'The School Art Style' is Hickman's (2001) paper describing what he found on arriving at Homerton: a department physically full of 'School Art cliches'. This, he explains, necessitated a large-scale clear-out – something I remember he was in the middle of doing when I arrived for my interview just a few days after he had started the role. Twenty-five years later the evidence I see when visiting schools suggests that we (collectively as teachers and teacher educators in the subject) are no closer to metaphorically clearing out the clutter of School Art than Hickman was then. Faced with this apparent failure, Efland's text is interesting to return to for the insight it can bring to new teachers. I 'return' to it here in three ways: through a thematic analysis of texts that cite Efland's analysis, a close reading of Efland's original paper, and through Bernstein's theory of the pedagogic device.

OBJECTIVES:

By the end of this chapter, you should be able to:

- Identify features of School Art in your context and understand how these are enabled;
- Discuss the difference between the manifest and latent functions of art and design education;
- Understand how connecting School Art practices to contexts beyond school develops their educative potential.

DOI: 10.4324/9781003377429-6

THEMATIC REVIEW

By cross-referencing the list of citations of Efland's paper provided by the *Studies for Art Education* website with Google Scholar, and searches of individual art education-related journal archives, I identified approximately 450 texts. To ensure relevance, I discounted citations in online masters and PhD submissions, those not written in English and those focused solely on the Child Art movement pre-1976. The themes I developed from the literature are discussed below. They do not offer a definitive definition of School Art because, as the literature shows, School Art is not *one* thing but a relationship of things. I agree with Smith that Efland's use of the word 'style' is misleading. Smith suggests instead, the word 'syndrome' may be more appropriate than 'style' for referring to School Art's 'constellation of problems' (1989, p.95). The themes I present below can therefore be understood in this light. I wonder if you recognise any of them within your own school context?

THEME 1: CLUTTER AND CHANGE

Just a year after Efland's paper, Field (1977) refers to School Art's out-of-date practices as 'like bits of driftwood left by the tide' (p.5) and Wieder (1977) discusses it in the context of art education requiring some 'house-cleaning'. The themes of clutter and clearing-out continue to appear periodically throughout the School Art literature, recurring most recently in Hickman (2001) and Pistolesi (2001). The clutter of School Art must be cleared out to make space for the new, it is cast as 'out of date' on two fronts: with the contemporary popular culture of students (Wilson and Wilson 1977; Nadaner 1985; Kuhn and Hutchen 1986; Thompson 1987; Anderson 1994; Smith 1995; Check 2000; Hickman 2001; Darts 2008; Haanstra et al. 2008; Buffington 2014) and with contemporary art and design practice (Wieder 1977; Maitland-Gholson 1986; Jeffers and Parth 1996; Anderson and Milbrandt 1998; Pistolesi 2001; Darts 2000; Pistolesi 2007).

Alongside clutter therefore is the theme of change or, more significantly, the teacher as change-maker, charged in the 1980s with changing art education (Thompson 1987), in the 1990s with changing, through contemporary arts practice, the school more generally (Anderson and Milbrandt 1998) and by the 2000s with changing society itself (Pistolesi 2007; Darts 2008). A sub-theme of this is the *new teacher* as changemaker (Thompson 1987; Anderson and Milbrandt 1998). This is a narrative that I (Wild 2011) and Hanawalt (2018) and Hanawalt and Hofsess (2020) question, observing that new teachers are often not the change-makers their training tasks them with being, adopting instead the orthodox School Art practices of more experienced colleagues.

THEME 2: TEACHER COMPLACENCY

Teacher complacency is therefore an additional theme (Day and DiBlasio 1983; Anderson 1992), described as an 'abdication of responsibility' (Koroscik 1982) as 'educational malpractice' (Thompson 1987, p.18), and requiring little 'cognitive strain' from students (Anderson and Milbrandt 1998; Pistolesi 2007). It can result in apparently lazy practices, such as the 'multi-cultural' project of homogenous 'African' outcomes (Smith 1989). The judgement by those observing new teachers in school can be scathing, lessons are described as 'tepid' (Thompson 1987), 'boring' Stokrocki (1988) and revealing something 'seriously wrong with education' (Check 2000).

THEME 3: COMPROMISE AND CONDITIONING

Pariser cautions that 'Art teachers are, after all in a difficult position' (1981, p.89) and that School Art is the inevitable compromise. Compromise appears in the 1980s, in largely practical terms, being the fault of centralised school budgets, leading to decreasing funds and restricted time allocation for art (Jagodzinski and Palmer 1984; Hamblen 1988). From the late 1980s, standardised assessment criteria are said to encourage a 'look', so that even if resources were available certain practices would still prevail (Hamblen 1987; Hickman 1990), an incentivisation increased by externally imposed accountability measures in the 2000s (Wild 2011; Hanawalt 2018; Hanawalt and Hofsess 2020). But the incentivisation towards the compromise of School Art also comes from within the school. It is the tacit internalisation of School Art (understood as a shared cultural practice) that leads to belonging of the professional community (Atkinson 2006; Wild 2011; Hanawalt 2018). To reject it is to risk not belonging. It is possible therefore to be unconsciously dependent on School Art as an identifying condition whilst being consciously aware that it compromises, or even *censors*, what Art and Design education might be and become.

THEME 4: CENSORSHIP

First mentioned by Field, who notes that 'anything taboo in middle-class morality has generally been taboo in the artroom also' (1977, p.5), the avoidance of controversy, if not outright censorship, in favour of therapeutic objectives is a consistent complaint (Diblasio 1983; Jeffers and Parth 1996; Anderson and Milbrandt 1998; Hathaway 2009). Post 2001 this is expressed more urgently, with the avoidance of social and political issues seen as an abdication of political or democratic responsibility (Pistolesi 2007; Darts 2000, 2008; Duncum 2009). Reflective of contemporary art as a social practice, there is a concurrent call for democratic and social constructivist theories of learning which position the teacher as a facilitator and co-learner with their students, in contrast to School Art which is seen to be teacher-directed (Hathaway 2009; Gude 2013; Hathaway 2013; Gates 2016; Park 2019).

THEME 5: FORMALISM

The above calls for more critical content and pedagogy appear in the literature as a rejection of the formalist concerns of modernism. Early citations were critical of School Art for embracing the myth of spontaneous, untutored, childhood creativity, a modernist trend itself (Diblasio 1983; Wieder 1977; Wilson and Wilson 1977; Koroscik 1982). A swing away from this through Basic Design in the UK and Discipline Based Art Education in the United States meant that by the 1990s, a different School Art was dominant, criticised for little connection to children's lives (Hamblen 1988; Heard 1988; Smith 1995). Described as 'mastering the elements and principles of design and the manipulation of media' (Anderson and Milbrant 1998, p.14), this form of School Art has been at the heart of all four iterations of the National curriculum for England (and Wales) since 1992 (Wild 2022). The calls for contemporisation in the 2000s and 2010s were not simply about making space for a bit of contemporary art, but about transforming School Art from its formalist foundations.

THEME 6: THEORETICAL INCOHERENCE

Rather than contemporary practices replacing formalist School Art though, the literature suggests they sit side-by-side in the twenty-first century art room. Buffington (2014) observes a lesson in which the teacher begins a class with a challenging debate about power and race, through the contemporary work of artist Kehinde Wiley but then requires the students to complete a 'safe' task more indicative of School Art, choosing half a face from a magazine, and copying it 'realistically'. In Downing and Watson's (2004) *School Art: What's in it?* 'traditional' schools prioritise a modernist canon, the formal elements and material manipulation but so do the 'contemporary art' schools, where more 'innovative' approaches are apparently built on top of a School Art foundation of colour wheels and tonal ladders.

Responding to calls for postmodern arts practices to be embraced in the classroom, Rayment discerns a difference between the desire of the 'art education establishment' (of researchers and teacher educators) for a theoretically coherent rationale for art and design in school and the pragmatic approach of teachers to find 'what works' for them in the classroom, 'tempered by practical considerations', whether it is theoretically coherent or not (Rayment 2001, p.116). The accusation that School Art is a reductive and formulaic (rather than authentic), distortion of 'real' practice is a constant complaint even before the twenty-first century (Field 1977; Clarke and Zimmerman 1978; Jagodzinski and Palmer 1984; Nadaner 1985; Kuhn and Hutchen 1986; Smith 1995; Pistolesi 2007; Gude 2013; Hanawalt 2018).

My recent research suggests that confusion continues. Exploring the trend for a knowledge-rich curriculum I observed that in knowledge-rich contexts, the clutter of formalism appears to be enjoying a resurgence, but combined with a new kind of School Art, the adoption of hyperreal painting and drawing practices utilising high-quality printouts of digital images which may reflect (although superficially) pressing social and political themes, such as the climate crisis, racism or mental health care that both teachers and students care about deeply (Wild 2022).

IT TAKES AN EARTHQUAKE

Pistolesi, based in California, asks whether in the contemporary context, 'Because it really does mean now that anything can be art does that mean that anything can be art education?' and ponders whether art and design teachers should ignore postmodern practices and 'fearful of throwing the Bauhaus out with the bath water, continue to doggedly teach the elements and principles?' (Pistolesi 2001, p.12). How does he report that he released himself and his student teachers from this dilemma?

It took an earthquake.

An actual earthquake that caused the destruction of the buildings he and his trainee teacher students were based in, the loss of all their resources, their furniture and work already in progress. Forced to improvise in conditions when even finding a chair to sit on from the rubble was a challenge their first post-earthquake project was inspired by their lack of seating. It took the literal destruction of art education, to, as he describes, 'lift the very great weight' (ibid. p.17).

This points to a feature of School Art implied by Smith's suggestion of the word 'syndrome' rather than 'style' (1985, p.95). A 'syndrome' is often identifiable in one's DNA, passed down through one's genetic heritage. If it is part of who we are, then it cannot easily be cleared out or replaced. If School Art is a 'syndrome', then, it is not something separate to art and design education – it *is* art education. How do you, as a new teacher, escape the orthodoxy of School Art therefore? – short of blowing up your school and teaching in its rubble, you can't.

Task 4.1 Defining learning in Art and Design for yourself

- What do you think is meant by 'little cognitive strain'? Can you think of examples of projects in school that put 'little cognitive strain' on students? To what extent do you think this is justified?
- What do you think must be included in the curriculum for what happens in the classroom to be recognised as art and design education?
- Are there contemporary issues that art and design educators have a political and moral responsibility to connect to in the classroom? Do you see this happening?

A CLOSE READING OF 'SCHOOL ART: A FUNCTIONAL ANALYSIS'

...we have been fooling ourselves all along. We have been trying to change school art when we should have been trying to change the school!

(Efland 1976, p.41)

Despite much of Efland's paper apparently criticising the content and pedagogy of elementary art education, his is not a pedagogical study. The theoretical context is that of *functional analysis,* a sociological method developed by Robert Merton and cited by Efland. Functional analysis, as Efland explains, proposes that institutional practices have 'manifest' (explicit) functions, and 'latent' (implicit) functions that support the overall coherence of the institution. Efland draws on two related studies about the functions of schooling, Illich's *Deschooling Society* and Gintis' *After Deschooling.* He takes from Illich that the manifest function of school is the 'cognitive development' of students, whereas its 'latent' function is the socialisation of 'the individual into accepting authority' (p.40). Gintis' contribution is that School is manifestly a pillar of democratic society, but latently related to the 'modern corporation' requiring compliant subordination (ibid. p.41). Efland describes this in colonialist terms, noting the presence of the 'School Art style' in countries such as Ghana as supporting cultural compliance. Being framed within the apparently benign context of elementary schooling (the middle primary years) kind of masks, these more radical lines of inquiry.

MANIFEST AND LATENT FUNCTIONS OF ART EDUCATION

Efland's analysis asks how School Art serves the manifest and latent functions of school by exploring whether it has developmental or socialising outcomes. He observes that art in the elementary school does not serve its manifest educative (developmental) aims very well. He lists three manifest aims for art education: transmitting a cultural heritage (p.38), teaching children 'about art in the world beyond school' (p.39) and 'helping children become more human through art' (p.40). He observes that the products of School Art bear little relation to cultural narratives or practice outside school and are anti-developmental in their lack of intellectual challenge and aversion to critique or instruction. Creative development is undermined by discouraging children from making connections with their own imaginative worlds or the visual culture within which they live. Thus, he proposes that these manifest functions mask an alternative latent function, in which School Art serves a purpose for the wider function of schooling, rather than for the individual child.

Efland argues that School Art firstly provides individualised outcomes that have the 'look of humanistic learning' (p.41) in support of the manifest function that school develops the individual, but secondly 'minimizes the psychological cost of institutional repression' through offering a therapeutic release (p.37) from the latent function of school towards compliant socialisation. These functions, he continues, are symbolic rather than actual as teachers must carefully control students' work so that it achieves the right look and good teachers 'will be able to turn on the creativity and turn it off again in time to clean up and get the children back to math and reading' (p.41). The 'therapy' of art education is therefore only partial, providing, as Efland describes 'time off for good behaviour' (p.40).

Efland cautions that blaming School Art on the individual teacher is unfair, like 'blaming the crime on the victim' (p.40) but what do you as an art and design teacher do therefore, other than wait for the ideal school to materialise? You might be waiting a very long time (if the last 46 years are anything to go by). Efland's final paragraphs include two points that are easy to pass over. He ponders whether School Art is so easily perpetuated in schools because its formulaic, anti-intellectual guise does not really require trained specialists to teach it (p.43) but also acknowledges that contemporary art does 'find its way into the classroom, harbouring the illusion that the curriculum is changing' (Efland 1976, p.143). I will return to these points after discussion the sociological perspective provided by Bernstein.

Task 4.2 Observing the symbolic and actual value placed on learning in Art and Design in your school

- Observe how images of and products of Art and Design are displayed around your school, on your school website and in school promotional material. What symbolic value do images of children being 'creative' have for your school community? Do these images reflect actual value placed on your subject through resourcing, curriculum time and so on?

BERNSTEIN'S PEDAGOGIC DEVICE

Bernstein engages in sociological analysis concerned more with structure than function. His premise is that sociological work in the field of education tends to pathologise relations, to identify 'syndromes' as I have done with 'School Art' above. He argues that, in focusing on school as a 'pathological' device, such studies neglect to examine the structure that creates or enables the syndrome, (Bernstein 2000, p.29); this enabling structure he calls the pedagogic device.

Two texts offer a substantive exposition of the pedagogical device (Bernstein 1990, 2000), from these I provide a condensed summary: The device is composed of three interacting fields: the field of production, the field of recontextualisation and the field of reproduction. Knowledge created in the productive field of research (the university) is selectively appropriated by agents of the official recontextualising field (government education departments and associated organisations) and the pedagogic recontextualising field (university education departments and specialised educational media) for relocation, refocusing and reproduction in school. This process separates knowledge from its social and power relations and is a site of struggle involving the 'play of ideology' (1990, p.180), no matter whether 'the dominant principles of a given society celebrate capitalist, collective, or dictatorship ideologies' (1990, p.194). The struggle of recontextualisation functions to make the knowledge to be transmitted 'safe', ensuring it serves rather than undermines the interests of the powerful (1990, p.192), separating it from its initial meaning and redirecting it to stand for something other than itself.

This *de*contextualisation, *re*location, *re*focusing and making safe, therefore, transforms and distorts the knowledge so that it 'may not obviously correspond to the 'original' knowledge it derives from' and 'may not appear to be 'authentic' (Wild 2022, p.86). Significantly, it is not just some knowledge that goes through this process in school but *all* knowledge. Whenever you plan a lesson, scheme of work or curriculum map, you participate in the recontextualising struggle that turns art and design into *School Art*. That is what art and design teachers do. From Bernstein's model of the pedagogic device, it is possible to argue that there is not and never will be an idealised form of authentic 'real' art and design education somewhere, where all evidence of School Art clutter is erased. If this does exist – *it is not in a school.*

THE PEDAGOGIC DEVICE AND CHANGE

The pedagogic device is not however a static model but a process of change. Bernstein explores the gradual efforts of government to change the orientation of the pedagogic device (e.g. reducing the powers of the 'pedagogic recontextualisation field' of teacher education) and notes the increasingly strong alignment of the device with economic aims. His later work observed that 'market relevance is becoming the key orientating criterion' of the pedagogic device (2000, p.103), a significant aspect of this orientation being to smooth the movement of knowledge so that it can 'flow like money' (ibid.) through removing it from its connection to individuals:

> …divorced from persons… literally dehumanised. Once knowledge is separated from inwardness, from commitments, from personal dedication, from the deep structure of the self, then people may be moved about, substituted for each other and excluded from the market.

> (ibid. p.103)

This, I suggest, marks a change from Efland's framing of the functions of schooling. Whereas Efland's text suggested the latent function of school was socialisation to the relational structures of the corporation (being a skilled compliant worker, although still potentially a 'dedicated' one), Bernstein's analysis suggests that schooling socialises young people to the needs of the market (being an easily detachable, repackaged, modifiable resource).

The use of the word 'dehumanised' by Bernstein is of note in relation to Efland's claim that School Art's latent function is to have the 'look of humanistic learning'. I have speculated elsewhere that the humanistic function of School Art may be waning (Wild 2022, p.102). To illustrate this we can look at Efland's 1976 statement that 'A class where everyone draws the same view of the same leaf… would not be tolerated as an accepted practice today' (p.41) and compare it to work in some art departments today where a whole class does copy the same image (of a leaf, a fir cone, a bottle, a collection of sweets etc.) at the same time, in the same way.

It is perhaps also possible to argue that the continuing dominance of formalism in school supports Bernstein's observation that the pedagogised knowledge that serves the economic function of school is divorced from individuals; art knowledge repackaged in small objective chunks that require nothing of the self-invested in them (ibid.).

I am speculating and being deliberately provocative, but it is important to emphasise that from Bernstein's perspective the idea of any kind of knowledge being 'foundational' (such as the formal elements) is not a logical, objective fact inherent to a discipline, but a social compromise created by the pedagogic device that regulates who gets access to what knowledge, when and in what form. What the changes noted above do show is that through the pedagogic device School Art does change just not necessarily in ways that make it more authentically art.

Task 4.3 The Pedagogic Device – learning or schooling?

- In what ways do you perceive that Art and Design is 'made safe' in a school context?

BERNSTEIN, EFLAND AND THE INDIVIDUAL TEACHER

In Bernstein's exposition and in Efland's analysis the individual teacher is passive, Efland exonerating the teacher of any blame for School Art and Bernstein declaring that the 'transmitter' (the teacher) 'may find themselves unable or unwilling to reproduce the expected code of transmission' (1990, p.190). Both leave the teacher with the choice to either reproduce School Art, or walk away. I am neither a sociologist nor a structuralist, and I am aware that in recontextualising Efland and Bernstein for what is essentially an educational text I may well be refocusing their thinking in ways that distort to support a particular view, but I do find in their work alternative strategies for action.

BE A SPECIALIST

Efland concluded that School Art is more easily enabled when the art teacher is not a specialist. Why is specialist knowledge so powerful? From Bernstein's perspective, specialist knowledge is closer to the field of production than that of reproduction, making it easier to recognise when knowledge is recontextualised in ways that distort and instrumentalise for latent purposes. For example, it is possible to imagine Kehinde Wiley's work, as mentioned in Buffington's (2014) paper being repurposed in the classroom to teach about proportion, colour and pattern (formalist concerns) with very little attention given to the history and politics of representation that his work explores. Someone who was a 'specialist' in Wiley's work, or created work exploring a similar theme themselves, may be less inclined to instrumentalise his work in such a way. Specialist knowledge is also attached to individuals who have a relationship with that knowledge, making it more difficult for it to be detached, and redirected to serve the latent interests of the school.

A strategy for being an active participant in the creation of School Art, rather than simply a passive transmitter is therefore to embrace being a specialist, to get close to the field of production through being a producer as well as a reproducer of knowledge, through practicing, in your own way, as an artist, designer, maker or art historian. In this way, you will have your own resources that enable you to participate meaningfully in the process of recontextualisation. This is something different from engaging in art activity for your own therapeutic benefit (although this is a good thing too), art activity that requires little 'cognitive strain' on your part is not the same as active engagement in the production of new knowledge.

CONSIDER THE 'YET TO BE THOUGHT'

Bernstein suggests that there are limitations to the effectiveness of the pedagogic device. He describes three kinds of knowledge, the thinkable, the unthinkable and the unthought. The 'thinkable' is what is distributed in schools by teachers, the knowledge that has already been recontextualised and made safe for reproduction in school and become tried and tested in successfully producing desired results. The 'unthinkable' is new knowledge in creation, yet to be recontextualised and made safe. It is produced in such places as universities but also, in the context of art and design, by those currently practicing in the field. Bernstein continues:

> It is not possible to control the thinkable without the shadow of the 'unthinkable. The principles which are reproduced carry orders of possibility other than the set to be reproduced.

> (Bernstein 1990, p.180)

And Bernstein notes, between the 'unthinkable' and the 'thinkable' is the 'yet to be thought' (1990, p.173).

These are rather abstract concepts, but I am interested in what these might mean, in practice, for the teacher in the classroom. I will suggest just one possibility through an activity that takes its starting point a classic piece of School Art clutter that features several times in the School Art literature, the colour wheel. To create space for the 'unthinkable' and the 'unthought' is to engage with the question of what more there is to know about it and particularly, whether, having been made 'safe' through recontextualisation, there is any way to reinject some danger, not by reversing the process to recover a presumed original authentic context, but by making it into something new that engages creatively with the world as it is now.

These questions of reconnection to the world are ones that I do see teachers in school asking – sometimes producing incoherent projects that appear to engage with the unthinkable before retreating into safe 'thinkable' practice, but sometimes not. Such an approach turns on its head an observation that Efland makes, that the contemporary does find its way into the classroom in ways 'harboring the illusion that the curriculum is changing' (Efland 1976, p.143). I wonder if the opposite might be true, that under the guise of School Art, more radical ideas do slip through.

Task 4.4 What more is there to know about colour?

Brief: Respond to the question *What more is there to know about colour?* by planning and teaching one lesson (or a series of lessons) around the theme of colour that either builds on and extends an existing lesson taught within your school or introduces a completely new lesson.

   Rationale: Colour is a common foundational concept that retains a central place in secondary school art and design at Key Stage 3. It is frequently the focus of the first lessons that student teachers are tentatively given to plan and teach themselves. The teaching of colour at Key Stage 3 is often connected to the practice of colour mixing through the creation of a colour wheel and building understanding of what are commonly called harmonious and complimentary colours. Thus the concept is often engaged with in formalist terms with no further applied or expressive objectives, no exploration of the relationship of colour and pigment to the natural, social, economic and political world that young people inhabit and no introduction to colour in art and design outside of a Modernist canon.

Things to consider: What else might a colour wheel do other than introduce students to a reductive version of colour theory often disconnected from the actual process of producing a meaningful work? What might it have to say about colonialism through considering the socio-economic relations of the manufacturing of colour, or about the climate crisis through visualising how the palette of the natural world might change as a result of extreme weather patterns? How might the colour wheel be rethought as something other than it has previously been in school?

SUMMARY

After almost 50 years, the longevity of Efland's paper emphasises that School Art is here to stay and cannot be cleared out, it is part of art and design education's DNA. As a teacher of art and design, your job is not to eradicate it or to pretend it does not exist but to be realistic and honest about the 'constellation of problems' you encounter in your particular context and the compromises you make because of them. You might find yourself in a department where you have no choice about what to teach or may be in a brand new school where, despite the new start, external assessment and exam criteria incentivise a particular approach (Hamblen 1987; Hickman 1990; Wild 2011; Hanawalt 2018), leading to compromises. There are strategies you can take though to try to heal the 'gaping wound' (Smith 1989) between School Art and art as it is practiced outside of school. You can build your specialist knowledge and find ways to stay close to the production of new art and design practice and understanding, and you can seek to reconnect the clutter of School Art to contexts outside of school, to issues pertinent to your students' lives, to ask what else it might be and become. This will be the work of a life-time, and will sometimes be a struggle - so pace yourself, there is a lot of clutter, and more yet to come.

This chapter *is not* a demand for immaculately maintained, theoretically coherent art and design education but is an acknowledgement of the 'lived in' classroom, in which the clutter of School Art is life. As a new teacher you may notice the clutter but as you become accustomed to your teaching environment you may cease to notice it and the ways in which your teaching separates art from contexts outside of school. Some housekeeping of your curriculum now and then to remind yourself of this is vital but as the well-known fridge magnet says, 'Only dull women have tidy houses!'. If you devote your energies to specialist activities and connecting to contexts and issues outside the classroom through making art, participating in artist networks, pursuing further study, reading about art and art theory, visiting galleries, listening to art podcasts etc. then the clutter will take care of itself, and a little bit of School Art here and there will just make your classroom feel lived in.

Task 4.5 Some questions to guide your School Art housekeeping

- What does this do for my department / school community?
- To what extent is this a compromise?
- To what extent does it ask my students to think hard?
- Would I save this in an earthquake?
- What from a contemporary context can I pair this with?
- Will it bring joy (thank you Marie Kondo)?

RESOURCES

For a more detailed exposition of the benefits of specialist artist-teacher practice for the classroom see:

Wild, C. (2022) *Artist-Teacher Practice and the Expectation of an Aesthetic Life Creative Being in the Neoliberal Classroom Routledge Research in Arts Education*. Routledge: London and New York

For an interesting take on why the 'formal elements' are not 'foundational' see:

Walton, N. (2020) 'There are no formal elements'. In Addison, N. & Burgess, L. *Debates in Art and Design Education*, 72-82. Routledge: London and New York.

BIBLIOGRAPHY

Anderson, T. (1992) 'Premises, Promises, and a Piece of Pie: A Social Analysis of Art in General Education', *Journal of Social Theory in Art Education*, 12(1), 34–52.

Anderson, T. (1994) 'The International Baccalaureate Model of Content-Based Art Education', *Art Education*, 47(2), 19–24. DOI: 10.1080/00043125.1994.11652260

Anderson, T., & Milbrandt, M. (1998) 'Authentic Instruction in Art: Why and How to Dump the School Art Style', *Visual Arts Research*, 24(1), 13–20. http://www.jstor.org/stable/20715931

Atkinson, D. (2006) 'School Art Education: Mourning the Past and Opening a Future', *International Journal of Art & Design Education*, 25(1), 16–27. DOI: 10.1111/j.1476-8070.2006.00465.x

Bernstein, B. (1990) *The Structuring of Pedagogic Discourse* (2003 Edition). Florence: Taylor & Francis Group. Available from: ProQuest Ebook Central.

Bernstein, B. (2000) *Pedagogy, Symbolic Control, and Identity* (Revised Edition). Oxford, England: Rowman & Littlefield Publishers.

Buffington, M. L. (2014) 'Power Play: Rethinking Roles in the Art Classroom', *Art Education*, 67(4), 6–12. DOI: 10.1080/00043125.2014.11519277

Check, E. (2000) 'Caught Between Control and Creativity: Boredom Strikes the Art Room', In Fehr, E. D. *Real World Readings in Art Education: Things Your Professors Never Told You*, pp. 137–145. Routledge: New York and London.

Clark, G. A. & Zimmerman, E. (1978). 'A Walk in the Right Direction: A Model for Visual Arts Education', *Studies in Art Education*, 19(2), 34–49. DOI: 10.2307/1319823

Darts, D. (2000) 'Art Education for a Change: Contemporary Issues and the Visual Arts', *Art Education*, 59(5), 6–12. DOI: 10.1080/00043125.2005.11651605

Darts, D. (2008) 'The Art of Culture War: (Un)Popular Culture, Freedom of Expression, and Art Education', *Studies in Art Education*, 49(2), 103–121. DOI: 10.1080/00393541.2008.11518729

Day, M. & DiBlasio, M. (1983) 'Contributions of Research to the Teaching of Art', *Studies in Art Education*, 24(3), 169–176. DOI: 10.1080/00393541.1983.11650339

DiBlasio, M. K. (1983). 'The Troublesome Concept of Child Art: A Threefold Analysis', *Journal of Aesthetic Education*, 17(3), 71–84. DOI: 10.2307/3332410

Downing, D. & Watson, R. (2004) *School Art: What's in It?: Exploring Visual Arts in Secondary Schools*. London: National Foundation for Educational Research.

Duncum, P. (2009) 'Toward a Playful Pedagogy: Popular Culture and the Pleasures of Transgression', *Studies in Art Education*, 50(3), 232–244. DOI: 10.1080/00393541.2009.1151877

Efland, A. (1976) 'The School Art Style: A Functional Analysis', *Studies in Art Education*, 17(2), 37–44. DOI: 10.1080/00393541.1976.11649921

Field, D. (1977) 'Recent Developments and Emerging Problems in English Art Education', *Art Education*, 30(8), 5–8. DOI: 10.1080/00043125.1977.11652826

Gates, L. (2016) 'Rethinking Art Education Practice One Choice at a Time', *Art Education*, 69(2), 14–19. DOI: 10.1080/00043125.2016.1141646

Gude, O. (2013) 'New School Art Styles: The Project of Art Education', *Art Education*, 66(1), 6–15, DOI: 10.1080/00043125.2013.11519203

Haanstra, F., van Strien, E. & Wagenaar, H. (2008) 'Teachers' and Students' Perceptions of Good Art Lessons and Good Art Teaching', *International Journal of Education Through Art*, 4(1), 45–55. DOI: 10.1386/eta.4.1.45_1

Hamblen, K. (1987) 'What General Education Can Tell Us about Evaluation in Art', *Studies in Art Education*, 28(4), 246–250. DOI: 10.1080/00393541.1987.11650575

Hamblen, K. (1988) 'What Does DBAE Teach?', *Art Education*, 41(2), 23–36. DOI: 10.1080/00043125.1988.11651381

Hanawalt, C. (2018) 'School Art in an Era of Accountability and Compliance: New Art Teachers and the Complex Relations of Public Schools', *Studies in Art Education*, 59(2), 90–105. DOI: 10.1080/00393541.2018.1440151

Hanawalt, C. & Hofsess, B. (2020) 'Holding Paradox: Activating the Generative (Im)possibility of Art Education Through Provocative Acts of Mentoring with Beginning Art Teachers', *Studies in Art Education*, 61(1), 24–45. DOI: 10.1080/00393541.2019.1700068

Hathaway, N. (2009) 'Teaching for Artistic Behaviour: Fostering Creative Possibility', In Hafenstein, N., Haines, K. and Cramond, B. *Perspectives in Gifted Education: Creativity*. Perspectives in Gifted Education. 5. Institute for the Development of Gifted Education, Ricks Center for Gifted Children, University of Denver. https://digitalcommons.du.edu/perspectivesingifteded/5

Hathaway, N. (2013) 'Smoke and Mirrors: Art Teacher as Magician', *Art Education*, 66(3), 9–15. DOI: 10.1080/00043125.2013.11519218

Heard, D. (1988) 'Children's Drawing Styles', *Studies in Art Education*, 29(4), 222–231. DOI: 10.1080/00393541.1988.11650688

Hickman, R. (1990) 'Reflections upon Aspects of Art Education in Singapore', *Singapore Journal of Education*, 11(1), 82–87. DOI: 10.1080/02188799008547717

Hickman, R. (2001) 'Art Rooms and Art Teaching', *Art Education*, 54(1), 6–11. DOI: 10.1080/00043125.2001.11653426

Jagodzinski, J. & Palmer, M. (1984) 'Reflections on the New Elementary Art Curriculum for Alberta', *Art Education*, 37(5), 9–11. DOI: 10.1080/00043125.1984.11654186

Jeffers, C. & Parth, P. (1996) 'Relating Controversial Contemporary Art and School Art: A Problem-Position', *Studies in Art Education*, 38(1), 2133. DOI: 10.1080/00393541.1996.11649988

Koroscik, J. S. (1982) 'Art Education: Another Prospective', *Childhood Education*, 59(2), 116–119. DOI: 10.1080/00094056.1982.10520560

Kuhn, M. & Hutchens, J. (1986) 'Facilitating Educational Access to Social Networks for the Arts', *Art Education*, 39(4), 37–40. DOI: 10.1080/00043125.1986.11649767

Maitland-Gholson, J. (1986) 'Theory, Practice, Teacher Preparation, and Discipline-Based Art Education', *Visual Arts Research*, 12(2), 26–33. http://www.jstor.org/stable/20715624

Nadaner, D. (1985) 'Responding to the Image World: A Proposal for Art Curricula', *Art Education*, 38(1), 9–12. DOI: 10.1080/00043125.1985.11649651

Park, H. (2019) 'Painting "Out of the Lines": The Aesthetics of Politics and Politics of Aesthetics in Children's Art'. *Visual Arts Research*, 45(2), 66–79. DOI: 10.5406/visuartsrese.45.2.0066

Pariser, D. A. (1981). 'Linear Lessons in a Centrifugal Environment: An Ethnographic Sketch of an Art Teaching Experience', *Review of Research in Visual Arts Education*, 7(1), 81–90. http://www.jstor.org/stable/20715314

Pistolesi, E. (2001) 'Good Art Education is Good Art,' *Art Education*, 54(5), 11–17. DOI: 10.1080/00043125.2001.11653462

Pistolesi, E. (2007) 'Art Education in the Age of Guantanamo', *Art Education*, 60(5), 20–24. DOI: 10.1080/00043125.2007.11651120

Rayment, T. (2001). 'School Art in the United Kingdom: Postmodernism or Pragmatism?', *Journal of Aesthetic Education*, 35(2), 113–117. DOI: 10.2307/3333678

Smith, P. (1989). 'Reflections on "The School Arts Style"', *Visual Arts Research*, 15(1), 95–100. http://www.jstor.org/stable/20715696

Smith, P. (1995) 'Art and Irrelevance', *Studies in Art Education*, 36(2), 123–125. DOI: 10.1080/00393541.1995.11649971

Stokrocki, M. (1988) 'Teaching Preadolescents During a Nine-Week Sequence: The Negotiator Approach', *Studies in Art Education*, 30(1), 39–46. DOI: 10.1080/00393541.1988.11650700

Thompson, C. (1987) 'Experience and Reflection: An Existential-Phenomenological Perspective on the Education of Art Teachers', *Visual Arts Research*, 13(1), 14–35. http://www.jstor.org/stable/20715636

Wieder, C. (1977) 'Three Decades of Research on Child Art: A Survey and a Critique', *Art Education*, 30(2), 4–11. DOI: 10.1080/00043125.1977.11649883

Wild, C. (2011) 'Making Creative Spaces: The Art and Design Classroom as a Site of Performativity', *International Journal of Art & Design Education*, 30, 423–432. DOI: 10.1111/j.1476-8070.2011.01722.x

Wild, C. (2022) *Artist-Teacher Practice and the Expectation of an Aesthetic Life Creative Being in the Neoliberal Classroom*. Routledge Research in Arts Education.

Wilson, B. & Wilson, M. (1977) 'An Iconoclastic View of the Imagery Sources in the Drawings of Young People', *Art Education*, 30(1), 4–11. DOI: 10.1080/00043125.1977.11649876

Chapter 5

The Art of Managing Coursework in Art and Design

Stephanie Cubbin

INTRODUCTION

> The arts teach children that in complex forms of problem-solving, purposes are seldom fixed but change with circumstance and opportunity. Learning in the arts requires the ABILITY and a WILLINGNESS to surrender to the unanticipated possibilities of the work as it unfolds.
>
> (Eisner, 2002)

Elliot Eisner's words act as a reminder that Art and Design teachers have the opportunity to plan and teach without knowing what the outcome of the students' work is going to be. Art and Design teachers are flexible and responsive and draw on many approaches to support their students. John Dewey's (1934) and Paulo Freire's (1970) progressive and democratic thinking about pedagogical systems, and their ideas about the teacher and the student developing together with the teacher as facilitator, will have been touched on in your Initial Teacher Training. In this chapter, we will discuss how the classroom philosophies of these two key figures have helped to create the educational environment in which today's students in Art and Design can successfully manage coursework as a feature of their development.

Using Dewey (1934), Eisner (2002), Reeve, Bolt and Kai (1999) as well as current Awarding Body specifications, we are going to explore some of the possibilities that lie within the concepts of personalisation of learning and coursework portfolios. The chapter will help you identify principles that can guide your planning in Key Stages 4 and 5; and finally, we will consider how you might provide early opportunities in your Key Stage 3 planning that will prepare your students for independence in their learning at General Certificate of Secondary Education (GCSE).

OBJECTIVES:

By the end of this chapter, you should be able to:

- Articulate and understand your own creative process in relation to students' learning for Key Stages 4 and 5 examination Assessment Objectives (AOs);

DOI: 10.4324/9781003377429-7

- Identify principles that can guide your planning in Key stages 4 and 5;
- Consider how you might provide early opportunities in your Key stage 3 planning that will prepare your students for their later independent learning.

CONCEPTS OF PERSONALISING LEARNING AND COURSEWORK PORTFOLIOS AT KEY STAGES 4 AND 5

There are different pedagogical approaches to teaching coursework subjects. At one end of the spectrum is direct control by the teacher, referred to as 'didactic' by Kai, Bolt and Reeve (1999). In this approach, which is not a preferred method by many Art and Design teachers, every student is using the same resource with the same materials. Reeve, Bolt and Kai's research observed the learning of students who were being taught 'didactically' which they referred to as 'controlling students';

> Situationally pressured teachers talked more, communicated with "should" statements, used frequent praise and criticism, asked controlling questions, stated deadlines, and generally created an atmosphere characterized by pressure. What these behaviours have in common is the teacher's emphasis on directing students towards a right answer.
>
> (Reeve, Bolt & Kai, 1999, pp. 547–548)

There may appear to be benefits to the 'controlling students' approach, at least in the short term for the teacher. It can appear to reduce teacher's workload, increase simplicity in lesson planning, reduce reliance on the students to complete homework and offer more control over coursework outcomes. Behaviour may superficially appear to be more easily managed, and the teaching methods can be adapted to suit delivery by a non-subject specialist teacher. However, it would probably be agreed by most teachers of Art and Design that this is not the pedagogical approach that is most desirable or beneficial for students' learning in our subject.

Throughout the field of art education, you will find teachers of Art and Design that combine their teaching practice with their own artistic practice, where the distinctive qualities of both merge and the pedagogical spaces they embody become democratic and allow for the students they teach to also feel like artists. In the 'Artist teacher: A Philosophy for Creating and Teaching', Daichendt (2010) argues that the 'actions, philosophies, and contexts we work within as artists inform much of what we know and teach.'

Alternatively, a situation where students are working more independently on their own projects is what Reeve, Bolt and Kai refer to as the 'autonomy-supportive approach' (Reeve, Bolt & Kai, 1999, pp. 547–548). This relates to a pedagogical approach in which the teacher is more of a facilitator. There will of course be moments in this methodology that require the teacher to demonstrate to the whole class a technique or material, but the sources of inspiration for students will be more personalised. For this approach to work, students must be grounded in the techniques appropriate to this method. We are going to focus on this pedagogical approach and look at the preparation and planning, the support structures and classroom management that will enable this to be successful.

Throughout this chapter, I will be referring specifically to GCSE Art and Design specifications, but I write with all coursework specifications in mind. To help you develop your own concepts of the autonomy supportive approach, we should begin with some self-reflection. As an Art and Design specialist, you will have come from a background in which *process* is fundamental. In helping you to understand the processes that you will come to expect the young people you teach to be using in their Art and Design coursework, it is important to look at how you develop ideas in your own practice. This will be the case even if you come from an art history background because you are entering a profession in which the practical exploration of Art and Design materials is at the forefront. At this point, it is important to think about the different aspects of your own art educational experiences.

Task 5.1 Reflecting on Your Own Creative Process

Articulating and understanding your own process as an artist, designer or art historian is the starting point for rooting your ideas about pedagogy. Use this space to reflect on the kinds of *process* you use in your own creative practice in your field of art or design:

In Key Stage 4, you are going to teach a course that encourages your students to explore a range of experiences and ideas that meet the GCSE AOs, either all together in one unit of work or separately. The work in GCSE modules is planned by the teachers with a full two-year course in mind. The work is assessed holistically at the end of the course. This is usually done by the teachers scrutinising samples of the best work which has been selected as best fit evidence of each student's progress. The teachers make judgements against the AOs that are set by the Awarding Body. Until the mid-1990s, there were many Examination Boards, which were often regionally based. At this time, many of these regional Exam Boards merged their academic and vocational offer in line with the introduction of GCSE examinations for students at age 16. There was also some merging of Exam Boards into a smaller number of these, along with a change in their corporate structure to become Awarding Bodies. Today there are five Awarding Bodies offering GCSE specifications in the UK. These are the Assessment and Qualifications Alliance, Oxford, Cambridge and RSA, Pearson/Edexcel, Welsh Joint Education Committee and Council for Curriculum, Examinations and Assessment. Each Awarding Body offers slightly different course recommendations and materials. All Awarding Bodies are overseen by the national regulatory body for qualifications, the Office of Qualifications and Examinations Regulation (Ofqual). This body determines the fundamental content of the GCSE and regulates the assessment of courses to ensure uniformity for GCSE and A Level specification across the Awarding Bodies. Schools and Subject Leaders in schools can select the GCSE specifications the AOs of which best meet the needs of their students.

Here is an example of a GCSE Assessment Grid for Art and Design, showing the four AOs and the six levels of attainment that students can achieve (Figure 5.1).

For the purpose of this chapter, I will use the Edexcel/Pearson specification as an example. It is important that you read through the specification that your Art Department is using. You should make notes about its core underlying principles and the expectations that it has for the successful provision of learning at GCSE level. In the Edexcel specification, there are two elements for Art and Design GCSE. These are the Personal Portfolio, which is assessed at 60% of the final grade, and the Externally Set Assignment (ESA) which is assessed at 40% of the final grade.

| Centre number: | | Title: | | Candidate name: | |
| Areas of study: | | Subject code: | | Candidate number: | |

GCSE assessment grid – you should use this assessment grid to assess all student work for both components and all titles

Assessment Objectives	0	Level 1 LIMITED ABILITY — Insufficient knowledge, understanding and skills; minimal evidence of, and lack of structure in, the development and recording of ideas			Level 2 BASIC ABILITY — Some knowledge, understanding and skills demonstrated but they are simplistic and deliberate; some structure and repetition in the development and recording of ideas			Level 3 EMERGING COMPETENT ABILITY — Knowledge, understanding and skills are generally adequate but safe			Level 4 COMPETENT AND CONSISTENT ABILITY — Knowledge, understanding and skills are secure and cohesive throughout			Level 5 CONFIDENT AND ASSURED ABILITY — Knowledge, understanding and skills are effective and focused throughout			Level 6 EXCEPTIONAL ABILITY — Knowledge, understanding and skills are in-depth, perceptive and accomplished throughout			
Evidence meets requirements		Just	Mostly	Fully	Just	Mostly	Fully	Just	Mostly	Fully	Just	Mostly	Fully	Just	Mostly	Fully	Just	Mostly	Fully
AO1 Develop ideas through investigations, demonstrating critical understanding of sources	0 (No rewardable material)	1	2	3	4	5	6	7	8	9	10	11	12	13	14	15	16	17	18 (AO1 mark)
AO2 Refine work by exploring ideas, selecting and experimenting with appropriate media, materials, techniques and processes	0 (No rewardable material)	1	2	3	4	5	6	7	8	9	10	11	12	13	14	15	16	17	18 (AO2 mark)
AO3 Record ideas, observations and insights relevant to intentions as work progresses	0 (No rewardable material)	1	2	3	4	5	6	7	8	9	10	11	12	13	14	15	16	17	18 (AO3 mark)
AO4 Present a personal and meaningful response that realises intentions and demonstrates understanding of visual language	0 (No rewardable material)	1	2	3	4	5	6	7	8	9	10	11	12	13	14	15	16	17	18 (AO4 mark)

Recording of marks for all GCSE work

Component	AO1 mark: indicate a mark out of 18	AO2 mark: indicate a mark out of 18	AO3 mark: indicate a mark out of 18	AO4 mark: indicate a mark out of 18	Total marks out of 72 for each component
Component 1 Personal Portfolio	AO1 mark	AO2 mark	AO3 mark	AO4 mark	Total COMPONENT 1
Component 2 Externally Set Assignment	AO1 mark	AO2 mark	AO3 mark	AO4 mark	Total COMPONENT 2

Figure 5.1 GCSE Assessment Grid for Art and Design, Edexcel 2022. GCSE, General Certificate of Secondary Education. (https://qualifications.pearson.com/content/dam/pdf/GCSE/Art%20and%20Design/2016/teaching-and-learning-materials/art-and-design-assessment-grid.pdf)

The ESA is released to Art Departments in January of the second year and many schools choose to provide students with eight weeks in which to complete the preparatory work for the final Timed Test of ten hours. In this, the students complete a personal outcome relating to the preparatory work that they have been developing over the preceding eight weeks.

How each department organises the teaching approaches and sequences of learning in the coursework and ESA is entirely up to them. However, they must ensure that there are sufficient opportunities for the students to meet the AOs to the best of their ability. You can see from the AOs that the specification focuses heavily on the process of making artwork, with three quarters of the marks in the assessment going to the preparatory work. AO1, AO2 and AO3 are all holistically working towards a personal outcome AO4.

Dewey grounds us in understanding that the process is the most important aspect of the creative journey, and this is mirrored in the specifications for both GCSE and A level Art and Design. The key is for students to develop a pathway from idea to outcome. Many departments prefer to manage this pathway by directing students through specific tasks. You may have seen visual or textual spider diagrams made in class where the title of a unit is divided up by the students into different ideas, concepts and options that they could take in their exploration of the title.

The reader should be carried forward, not merely or chiefly by the mechanical impulse of curiosity, not by a restless desire to arrive at the final solution, but by the pleasurable activity of the journey itself.

(Dewey, 1934, p.4)

Returning to the Eisner's quote in the opening of this chapter, in Art and Design teaching, what the student outcome will be is a wonderful process of discovery together. Eisner also believed that the study of Art and Design was important to a student's cognitive development. Dewey stated that everyone has the capabilities of being an artist, and that the process of making art, exploring and experimenting is transformative. In 'Art as Experience', Dewey emphasises that art is a fundamental part of our human existence.

By valuing all forms of the visual, Dewey says that we are only able to experience existence fully and that we should acknowledge the connection between the aesthetic and the everyday experience. His emphasis on the process of making art and the emotional response to this experience remains a driving influence in Art and Design education today.

> The intelligent mechanic engaged in his job, interested in doing well and finding satisfaction in his handiwork, caring for his materials and tools with genuine affection, is artistically engaged.
>
> (Dewey, 1934, p.4)

There are recommended course structures on the website of each of the awarding bodies that can help plan, but there are no prerequisites and I have found the courses to be open and free to interpretation. Your department will have chosen a methodology that suits their students, the time allocated to the subject and the expectations of coursework. Your department may have decided to use the first year of the GCSE course to develop skills and plan a series of workshops to hone specific skills such drawing and painting, sculpture, photography or textiles. These will have been chosen because of the specific skill set of the teachers in the department, the resources available or even the time given for lessons or preparation. Alternatively, the department may choose to offer the development of the skills through set projects. At this point, we look back at the reflections of our own practice and in the following tasks, we will compare these with the GCSE specifications that the schools that you are teaching in are using.

Task 5.2 Aligning Your Own Creative Process with the Structuring of Learning

Write a short reflection here on how your department structures the GCSE course. Note in particular how the Year 10 units prepare students for Year 11.

Reflect here on if you think that this structure is in line with your own creative process as you have outlined this in Task 5.1. If it is not, consider whether you will adapt your approach to meet the existing structure, or if you would like to bring an aspect of your own creative process to the way you would like teach your GCSE students.

One of the benefits of a flexible structure is that you can align the course to a process that an artist might follow. I have found it beneficial for students to know that the four AOs of GCSE Art and Design have a fundamental relationship to the way that many artists work. This links the classroom and the wider professional world for the students. Although not everything in the classroom can mirror the artist's or designer's studio, when artists and designers talk about their process, they emphasise the importance of thinking/making as concurrent acts. While the documentation of this process is less important in the professional studio because the artist or designer has developed a high level of embedded skill that they do not need to consciously refer to, it is vital that the novice artist/designer on a GCSE examination course consciously develops this skill. To this end, AO1 requires students to, "Develop ideas through investigations, demonstrating critical understanding of sources", and AO3 requires, "Record ideas, observations and insights relevant to intentions as work progresses". These AOs direct students to the understanding that their choices need qualifying. For example, a student might choose to make a wire drawing, choosing florist's wire for the material. The wire they have chosen is malleable and easier to shape with its soft structure, and their written explanation shows their understanding of the material and that they have applied this knowledge to their own personal work. (GCSE Pearson Edexcel Level 1/Level 2 GCSE (9-1) in Art and Design). The student who can justify these choices will be on the way to a good GCSE grade and to an embedded understanding of how to manage the creative process in their later career, whether this is in the creative industries or not.

PLANNING FOR INDEPENDENCE

Creating a safety net for students who are struggling with organisation, independence or motivation is important as a facilitating teacher. It is important to plan your course with this in mind.

In this chapter, the focus is on the 'supporting autonomy' teacher who finds ways to ensure students have ownership over the direction and subject matter of the work. Instead of planning for uniform tasks, they plan for a process that would enable the students to find their own tasks. This creates the opportunity to write personal and meaningful annotations on the choices made and the materials chosen, reflecting on the relevance and success of the ideas and materials. Student ownership is key to examination coursework, not least because the specification asks for students to make independent choices 'Acquire and develop technical skills through working with a broad range of media, materials, techniques, processes and technologies with purpose and intent' (GCSE Pearson Edexcel Level 1/Level 2 GCSE (9-1) in Art and Design).

To plan and prepare a GCSE coursework unit, the teacher may create a project title and demonstrate five exemplar ways in which a project might develop. A previous GCSE title such as 'Barriers' could be developed by the teacher into concepts for the students to explore such as 'physical barriers', 'human barriers' and 'geographical barriers', and all these choices will have related artists that the teacher will have researched as potential inspiration for the students' own work. You might have made a presentation of slides or a hard copy sheet that they can hold on to and keep for their own reference at any time. Art Department VL platforms and blogs can also contain links to relevant artists' work. The key is that the students can make their choices and add their own inspiration to start their project.

Some students can struggle with the organisational skills that a coursework subject demands and the Art and Design teacher can mitigate against these problems through planning ways that will initially support their students' organisational abilities and then enable them to do this for themselves. One of the challenges for both teacher and student is the reliance on the students to research independently. As an alternative, there could be a resource box for each of the five ways the project can develop. The resource box will have a range of artists' images, magazine images, photographs and postcards and would be an exciting place to go to. The student could still make choices, own the project, and be inspired to work independently while meeting the teacher's expectations.

The Rhizome model in education is a variety of pedagogical practices informed by the work of Gilles Deleuze and Félix Guattari. In this model, the Rhizome is presented like a complex mind map in which aspects of knowledge and context interweave (Deleuze & Guttari, 1987, pp. 1–26). The teacher can plan a series of actions not unlike a transport network that one can jump on or off at any point. Often imagery associated with Rhizomatic learning is visually connected to imagery of building synapses in the brain.

> The rhizome operates by variation, expansion, conquest, capture, offshoots. Unlike the graphic arts, drawing, or photography, unlike tracings, the rhizome pertains to a map that must be produced, constructed, a map that is always detachable, connectable, reversible, modifiable, and has multiple entryways and exits and its own lines of flight.
>
> (Deleuze & Guttari, 1987, pp. 1–26)

This is a theory that lends itself to a democratic approach as the direction of study can be determined and driven by the interests of the student. Such models have been seen in Mathematics in which complex concepts are designed as pathways that interconnect and are not designed within timed and teacher directed schemes of work. Whilst uniformity is not the aim, having a clear set of interconnected requirements gives the students something to start from. These set of building blocks or processes can be used in any order.

> The work undertaken for this component should be seen as part of a substantive project(s), rather than a series of disjointed tasks, and work should evidence all the Assessment Objectives holistically.
>
> (GCSE Pearson Edexcel Level 1/Level 2 GCSE (9-1) in Art and Design)

Task 5.3 Adapting Units of Work to Meet Pupil Needs and Demonstrate Progression

Select an existing GCSE Unit of Work that your department is currently teaching. Consider how you might be able to adapt it to a more Rhizomic structure that could allow the students to meet the AOs in an order that meets their learning needs while still demonstrating progression through the Unit of Work.

This is one example of a planning for process schedule which students are given at the beginning of a unit. This could apply to a GCSE or A Level coursework unit or an External Set Assignment (ESA) unit. Students can see how their work leads to the next stage of the process and builds up to an outcome.

Week of (3 Lessons)	Class Task	In Sketchbook	HW Reminders
	Introduce the unit Find 5–8 Images in relation to own theme and print out ready for presenting onto 3 × A4 sheets.	3 × pages of collecting or key artist you are interested in and collected images.	Print images for next lesson.

(Continued)

81

Week of (3 Lessons)	Class Task	In Sketchbook	HW Reminders
	One artist study of your own choosing whose technique you want to learn from. Tutorials this week to determine theme and initial photography	A4 Artist copy and 2 × pages of 5–8 initial photographs. Continue working on artist pages if not finished.	Finish artist pages to high standard.
	Responses to photos, use the material that seems most appropriate to the artist research.	2 responses which will be recorded onto A4 pages. (Painting, drawing, sculpture, collage)	Finish response to photos pages to high standard.
	Responses to photos, use the material that seems most appropriate to the artist research.	2 responses which will be recorded onto A4 pages. (Painting, drawing, sculpture, collage)	Finish response to photos pages to high standard.
	Using print to develop ideas, using engraving, lino, tetra Pak or another printing method, start thinking composition	A couple of pages of printing worked into, discussing compositional ideas and how they might develop into a final piece.	
Half Term	**HW to Finish off Anything That Needs Completing**		**HW to Finish Off Anything That Needs Completing**
	Think about artist technique and style, and working from your own photography to start working out compositions for your final piece	Development piece, could be a painting, print, drawing or photo of a maquette, presented into book with artist reference and annotation	Go through book and continue working on any unfished work.
	Think about artist technique and style, and working from your own photography to start working out compositions for your final piece	Development piece, could be a painting, print, drawing or photo of a maquette, presented into book with artist reference and annotation	
	Final planning and prep for final piece	Final plan, with artist references and final photographic resources. All ideas documented on one page.	Go through book and make sure all work for this project is completed and finished for hand in date.
	Preparing materials, surfaces, underpainting, preparing printing plates, or making armatures		
	Final pieces days	Photo of final piece in book	Evaluation of creative process

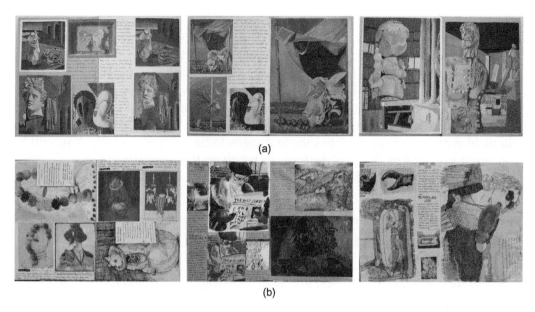

(a)

(b)

Figure 5.2 Two different GCSE students' approaches to coursework. 5.2a shows a row of images of one student's approach to a GCSE coursework theme, and 5.2b shows a row of images of a different student's approach to the same coursework theme. GCSE, General Certificate of Secondary Education.

The visuals in Figure 5.2 show two different students' approaches to the process table above. I like to think of this process list as the starting point, the students will diverge from this in their own self-directed way. They will progress through their own lines of enquiry based on the artists' work that has inspired them. I would expect students to tailor the process list to their own artistic journey. For example, a student has chosen to work with sculpture, using plaster casting, latex casting, 3D textiles and ceramics to explore the body. This student would not find printing particularly useful in their journey and would replace this with another task. This conversation would happen in a tutorial, in the classroom, whilst others are working on their own developments. The document is lengthened or shortened depending on the time scales of the unit, it is personalised by teachers for students and sometimes by the students when discussing their unit with their teacher. There is a flexibility needed which is guided by the Rhizome theory that allows entry and exit at various points.

The AOs for GCSE and A Level are similar building blocks which can be used for the students to progress though or measure success against. There is no prerequisite for the order of which the objectives are handled by teacher or student.

HOW WE CAN PREPARE STUDENTS IN KEY STAGE 3 FOR INDEPENDENCE

When we plan for students' progression, it is essential to have in mind the skills that will be needed in the next stage of their education. For Y10 students to work with some independence in Key Stage 4, they need to have been prepared to work in this way in Key Stage 3. The joy that teaching brings is particularly high when students make or create something that they did not expect they were capable of. The teacher's high expectations and ability to 'lift the lid' on a wealth of subject knowledge for students through their subject knowledge and pedagogic skill is the way to bring this about.

Think about your A Level students and your expectations of them. Consider how you can apply these to your KS3 teaching. Your A Level students can articulate their process and critically review their own work and underpin their ideas with excellent research from a wide range of sources including live ones. If we are preparing Key Stage 3 students for GCSE and beyond, they should be given the opportunity to demonstrate progress towards the same skills. The students develop confidence and responsibility for their own decision making and can articulate why they have selected these images to be in their projects. You will be planning for your Key Stage 3 students to be given the opportunity to make their own connections, which will prepare them for their Key Stages 4 and 5 work.

Task 5.4 Auditing for Independent Learning in Key Stage 3

Audit here by year group the opportunities there are in your school for students in KS3 Art and Design to practice the independent self-directed behaviours needed in KS4

- Yr7
- Yr8
- Yr9

All teachers know that students need to feel success in order to remain motivated, yet often Year 7 students arrive in secondary school already believing that they either can or cannot 'do art' due to preconceived ideas. The Art and Design teachers' first job is to widen the experience of Art and Design and build in opportunities for students to succeed from the start, even those who at first have the preconceived idea that they cannot 'do art'. Some Art and Design teachers consider it essential at the start of Yr7 to give students the challenge of attempting to achieve well in the orthodoxies of representational drawing. However, I would challenge this approach. Teachers break down their pedagogic language for teaching, so why not do the same thing for a key concept like drawing? Expecting Key Stage 3 pupils to tackle every aspect of this fundamental feature of Art and Design practice will in most cases be too demanding, especially the representation of objects in three dimensions which is what many students will regard as good drawing. Instead, I advocate for a broader approach in which students follow the teacher's own skill set in image making, whatever this may be. They spend time building a language of the fundamentals of the teacher's artistic language whatever this is, and when this is mastered, they tackle the more advanced aspects of representation in this field. This enables the students to grow in confidence as they achieve success in small chunks without immediately giving up having taken on too much.

As an example of practice, students in each year group in KS3 could have an annual independent project. They are given a theme related to the projects in the year, and a series of tasks. Students decide which practical tasks they will achieve in lessons, and which for homework. The tasks include artist research with responses, photographs, drawings and paintings from life or photos, and then some developmental ideas towards an outcome. The outcome idea is developed from their own work, which can be completed in exam-style lessons. If students do not have the capacity to bring in their own resources, or engage with the unit, it can be adapted to meet their needs. In this way, students achieve the outcomes of the independent project and learn about their own motivation, character and organisational skills.

The shift in language in schools and inspectorates from differentiation to adaptive teaching is useful to reference here, with teachers required to adapt their teaching to make it appropriate for everyone in their classroom, making learning inclusive. Understanding each child in the classroom is key to this, in combination with assessment and personal feedback. In the Educational Endowment Foundation Blog, Kirsten Mould, a behaviour specialist, writes about how 'adjusting, adapting and assessing is crucial to the progress of all individuals.' One small way to include adaptive teaching in Art and Design is to discuss and unpick with students some recent individual written feedback. Next, encouraging the students to make notes and targets for themselves, and setting a classroom task for the students to improve a piece of work of their choice from the feedback. This strategy helps the students understand how to use their feedback to make improvements in their work and encourages the use of assessment to feed into their own learning.

SUMMARY

In this chapter, the references to Reeve, Bolt and Kai's research offered the concept of supporting autonomy, and Dewey and Freire's more democratic educational theories continue to act as building blocks for classroom practice. Eisner and Dewey both encourage the student's experiential and personal connection to the work and point out how this can fundamentally shift the working practices in the classroom. Whilst it may seem that the facilitator's workload and planning is more time consuming, it is important to point out that over time, your own time-saving strategies and shifts in classroom practice make the difference negligible. Once the processes have been established, the art rooms become a deeply collaborative creative space in which both the teacher and the student develop as artists. There can be the same ethos of shared experimentation that is found in the higher levels of Art and Design education, for example in a fine art or design department in a university. Students will be always trying something new, explaining what they find out, giving and taking from each other, encouraging a constant flow of thoughts and play, a buzz of ideas.

RESOURCES

View these Awarding Body websites to see and download their GCSE Art and Design specifications:
https://ccea.org.uk
https://ocr.org.uk
https://www.aqa.org.uk
https://www.wjec.co.uk

BIBLIOGRAPHY

Daichendt. (2010) *Artist Teacher: A Philosophy for Creating and Teaching*. University of Chicago Press.
Deleuze, G. & Guattari, F. (1987) *A Thousand Plateaus*. Minneapolis: University of Minnesota Press.
Dewey, J. (1934) *Art as Experience*. New York: Pedigree.

Eisner, E. W. (2002) 'What can education learn from the arts about the practice of education?', *Journal of Curriculum and Supervision*, 18(1): 4–16. Fall 2002.

Freire, P. (1970). *Pedagogy of the Oppressed*. New York: Continuum.

Jensen, F. E. (2015). *The Teenage Brain*. London: Harper Thorsons.

Mould, K. (2021) *EEF Blog: Assess, Adjust, Adapt – What Does Adaptive Teaching Mean to You* https://educationendowmentfoundation.org.uk/news/eef-blog-assess-adjust -adapt-what-does-adaptive-teaching-mean-to-you

Pearson Education Limited, *Specification, GCSE Pearson Edexcel Level 1/Level 2 GCSE (9-1) in Art and Design,* London, 2015.Reeve, J., Bolt, E. & Cai, Y. (1999) 'Autonomy-supportive teachers: How they teach and motivate students', *Journal of Educational Psychology*, 91(3): 537–548.

Chapter 6

Facilitating Artistic Behaviours in the Classroom

Kate Thackara

INTRODUCTION

The great thing about artistic practice is that it is a reflective process grounded in problem solving, criticality, lateral thinking and the ability to generate, explore and apply ideas and knowledge. This array of characteristics means that the good artist strives to never stop learning. The National Curriculum for Art and Design (DfE 2013) stresses that learning in Art and Design should equip students with the skills to experiment, invent and create, which are fundamental thinking skills for the artist.

Much has been written about students' learning in 'Art and Design' and how it can be negatively affected if the teaching is preoccupied with the mastery of practical skills without much critical engagement (Addison and Burgess 2003; Bieste 2017). Furthermore, learning to teach Art and Design may be centred solely around the explication of the trainee art teacher's concrete knowledge and skills, again without much critical engagement in the subject. This focus on handing down a limited set of practical skills is normative in the sense that it concretises a specific idea of what is good or correct in the teaching and learning of Art and Design, rather than allowing for a more formative focus, one which encourages the trainee art teacher to explore, expand and develop their own ideas about the teaching of the subject. A deeper exploration of the artistic process itself, and the artistic behaviours required to facilitate this process, is the most positive approach to take in the classroom for both teacher and student. It is these artistic behaviours that prepare the trainee for the implementation of the implicit skills required when working artistically with a group of young people in a classroom, where, when teaching is at its best, nothing can be assumed or predicted, but anything can happen.

I will argue that instilling artistic behaviours in the classroom is vital in order to ensure meaningful progress for your students beyond the predetermined and planned. Dennis Atkinson's ideas on pedagogy of the event (2009) or pedagogy against the state (2011) are well worth investigating in this context. Atkinson highlights the importance of facilitating but not controlling the outcomes of learning:

> A flexible teaching-learning space that attempts to accommodate unpredictable or unexpected directions in learning encourages learners to take risks in

their practice, by implication, suggests that teachers themselves are also taking risks in that they have to be able to 'let things happen'; they have to be able to facilitate these learning pathways without a clear sense of outcome.

(Atkinson 2009)

This chapter will explore how to effectively facilitate artistic behaviours in the classroom by building a community of practice (Lave and Wenger 1991) where both the teacher and the students have the space to learn together. These ideas can be placed within what Vygotsky (2004) calls a social constructivist approach to pedagogy, where knowledge is constructed through social interaction, conversation and shared experience.

OBJECTIVES:

By the end of this chapter you should be able to:

- Articulate the characteristics and skills that support artistic behaviour in the context of Art and Design teaching and learning;
- Consider learning as a social and collaborative experience;
- Develop strategies and activities to enhance and support artistic behaviour in the classroom as part of a community of practice;
- Equip students with a set of metacognitive skills to support their artistic practice.

THE ARTIST TEACHER AND THE ARTIST STUDENT

The relationship between Artistic and Teaching practice in Art and Design education can be a significant discourse for art educators (Ward 2005; Wild 2022). Many refer to themselves as artist teachers, where their identity as an artist is key to their art practice and their teaching, whilst others see being the teacher as key and their art practice less important or even separate to the teaching role. Other teachers may be on a sliding scale between these two positions. You may be reflecting on your own position within this duality as you train to teach. Furthermore, what does it mean to be a school student, a learner, who is pursuing an artistic practice in an educational setting, should they perhaps be referred to as an 'artist student'? (Vygotsky 2004). By asking this question I am highlighting that to be artistic in the classroom is to have a sometimes-problematic duality, for both educators and learners. It is good to start by unpacking these dualities together, in order to understand and critically reflect on what it means to be a part of your classroom community.

To be an artist student requires risk taking, resilience, and the confidence to make mistakes, whilst simultaneously adhering to the rules, objectives and assessment systems of the school. Similarly, as an artist teacher, you may find it conflicting to try to balance your own views of the values of artistic practice within systems of behaviour and classroom management, data deadlines, department expectations and the wider school ethos.

A student's social and cultural background, life experience and education will also affect how they engage with the idea of the 'artist'. Students may consider being an artist as a highly privileged vocation that involves isolation, working alone in a big studio, or might have an awareness of traditions other than those that the student has familiarity with. To some, the idea of an 'artist' may seem idyllic, and to others an absurdity. Students may know an artist or individual working in the creative industries and as a result have a broader and more realistic understanding of what this means. It is important to facilitate students' ability to see beyond the stereotypes and preconceptions, in order to develop a clear and comprehensive understanding of what it means to be an artist. It is also integral that they see their art education as about a set of hugely diverse transferable skills that can be applied to any range of creative or other future ambitions that they may have.

The activity below sets up an opportunity to have an open conversation about what it means to navigate these complex identities. The activity is a chance for you and your students to reflect criticality on what they are learning, and why they are learning it. It also draws on the parallels between artist teachers and artist students and therefore can build bonds between you and your students in a shared endeavour.

Task 6.1 Explore the Duality of the Artist Student Experience

With your students, make a table with two columns, one titled 'Artist', and one titled 'Student' Ask the class to fill in each column, first the student, and then the artist, with the behaviours, skills and activities they associate with each. You may also complete your own table, 'replacing student' with 'teacher'.

Once everyone has had a chance to reflect and fill in the table, ask for verbal contributions to the group and use this time to discuss and reflect on the similarities and differences between these two identities. You can then also present your own table, connecting your own identity with your students.

Some questions to consider:

- What do we consider to be the main characteristics of an artist? How far do what the students have put in the 'Artist' column challenge these assumptions?;
- Where do the same behaviours, skills and activities cross both artist and student columns? What does this tell us?;
- Are there similarities and differences between students in art lessons and art teachers? What characteristics and skills do we share?

This final question is particularly significant, as it draws similarities and parallels between your own experience as an artist teacher and your students. As Paolo Freire, critical pedagogue and author of Pedagogy of the Oppressed highlights, 'Education must begin with the solution of the teacher-student contradiction, by reconciling the poles of the contradiction so that both are simultaneously teachers and students' (1970, p72). A sense of oppression and control is an experience that can be shared between all working in an educational setting, particularly schools, and exploring shared behaviours and qualities can help us look beyond these limitations and towards empathy, understanding and a motivation to transform existing educational orthodoxies. From this point, there can be a formative focus on how to thrive as both an artist and a student/teacher in the classroom.

Having unpacked these complex identities, it is also valuable to break down for your students what all the different types of artistic practice can be and the range of career opportunities there are in the creative industries, from painter, photographer, project manager, art director to graphic designer, stylist, set designer etc.

Doing this can open up ideas of what learning in Art and Design in the classroom can lead to in the future and furthermore highlight the transferable skills Art and Design can provide beyond just careers in creative industries. No matter what students' ambitions might be, the artistic behaviours learnt in the classroom can support their development as critical and innovative thinkers, problem solvers and socially engaged agents for change. It is important that they are aware of the value of these experiences.

THE CLASSROOM AS A COMMUNITY OF PRACTICE

Exploring what it means to be artistic with your classroom community is a great way of co-constructing an identity that can engage, enthuse and inspire your students and yourself through shared experience (Vygotsky 2004; Page 2012). A community of practice is a social classroom practice where students learn through participating and contributing to the community rather than receiving knowledge by replicating it through instruction (Lave and Wenger 1991). As a teacher, you are responsible for your classroom community and therefore need to be sensitive and responsive to the individual and the group dynamics in order to facilitate a productive, creative and positive environment, where students can actively explore artistic behaviour.

Students need ample opportunity to discuss and develop a range of creative and cognitive skills, in a multimodal environment where they can ultimately discover the value of participation through meaningful interactions with the teachers and peers. Developing a community of practice to facilitate a pedagogy of the event (Atkinson 2009) helps to build bonds, promotes empathy and respect and breaks down the teacher student hierarchy towards a more collaborative and co-constructed interaction.

Facilitating a dynamic space where meaningful, discursive and social interactions can take place requires an investment in the time needed to gain an understanding of the individuals who make up your classroom community. A good place to start in gaining an understanding of the individuals in your classroom and the dynamics between them is a critical awareness of the physical space in which you work, as part of your lesson planning. Seating plans are integral to effective classroom and behaviour management, considering educational needs, vulnerabilities and social dynamics. The following activity takes the concept of a seating plan a step further. It encourages you to consider the seating plan as a map of social interactions, in order to explore the ways you can facilitate dynamic and effective interactions between your students. Regularly changing room layouts, if possible, and moving seating plans around means students do not get bored and have more opportunity to socialise with their peers.

Task 6.2 Mapping Learning and Reflecting Visually

Make a map of your Learning Community:

> Draw out the classroom space, and draft three different layouts. Consider how these could be moved around to change where students face, who they can communicate with, and how they might move around the room;

Consider interesting student dynamics you might have not done before but that might offer positive improvements to learning. Think about students' individual needs and how their placement in the room is supported or hindered;

Draw some movements and interactions onto the seating plan, where you could move around in order to enhance the social dynamism of the room.

After a lesson that is particularly fruitful or effective, use this mapping activity to reflectively visualise the interactions between the students and yourself, and to remind yourself for future lessons how to build on these dynamics.

THE LEARNING CURRICULUM

Atkinson describes a learning curriculum as the structure and content of curriculum and pedagogy being viewed from the perspective of learners, stating that if the pedagogical encounter begins from the question, 'who are you?' then a different relation seems to emerge and it is possible to turn this question into, 'How does the other learn?' (Atkinson 2009). It is important that students have the opportunity to actively contribute to the lesson they take part in with a sense of responsibility and visibility, so that they feel respected, valued and are therefore more likely to be engaged. As a teacher, this means reflecting on your lesson objectives and wider pedagogical aims, and considering what a range of students are benefitting from your lessons. I recommend looking at your scheme of work, syllabus and curriculum from a broader perspective, beyond the implicit knowledge and concrete artistic outcomes. For example, consider at what point there is opportunity for collaboration with peers, critiques of work and time and space within your planning that prioritises student autonomy and independence.

Your interactions with students and classes may run over a term, a year and you may even teach some students over a number of years. Therefore, developing a learning curriculum can be thought of as a slow process within a slow institution. Doing this will enable you to focus on the long-term learning and development of students' deeper artistic behaviours rather than simply their art making skills. It is important to first ground your lessons in clear structures and scaffolding, and then over time more autonomy can be provided. This could include more open-ended experiential learning (Kolb 1984), meaning to learn by doing and then reflecting, where the outcome is responsive to students' ideas and interpretations. It could also include collaborative making, where students work together towards a collective aim.

Metacognitive activities such as making an Artist Student Manifesto Figure 6.1 are a good way of modelling artistic behaviours before any practical activities happen. Metacognition can be defined as the process of understanding one's own knowledge; essentially learning about your own learning behaviours. For example, in this context the students have the opportunity to critically reflect on how and why they are learning about artistic practice. Students are therefore applying artistic behaviours to practical skills rather than uncritically engaging with an activity.

Task 6.3 Creating Learning Objectives with Your Pupils

Discuss with the students what a learning objective is, and that this can include behaviours, social values and shared experiences as well as developing a technical skill.

Questions could include:

What skills would you like to develop this year in Art and Design? This could be specific materials and processes;

What behaviours and attributes does an artist student need? This could include resilience, determination, independence, criticality etc.;

What are our aims and ambitions in Art and Design? This could include some phrases or mottos that the students could remember;

Key words, phrases, aims and rules can be drawn out on a large piece of paper and displayed in the classroom to reference in future lessons;

Figure 6.1 Y7 Artistudent Word Bank Manifesto in the front of their sketchbook, listing key characteristics and attributes required of an artist student. Lady Margaret School 2021.

This returns us to Atkinson's essential point about the importance of 'real learning; where 'the self is erased through risk to reform according to a new set of ontological coordinates' (Atkinson 2009). Being open minded and responsive to the range of ways students in your classroom may learn, and to include them in the process of developing artistic behaviour requires careful consideration, but also a confidence to take risks and explore the unknown in these 'magic moments' (Harding 2005) (Figure 6.1).

No matter what age group or Key stage you are working with, when moving on once having established what your students' artistic behaviours are going to be, you can establish your community of practice by implementing what I have called a series of 'Process Workshops'. These can be one-off lessons in which students explore a certain practical way of making, or a certain cognitive approach to making. The workshops are intensive, social, collaborative and explorative and can be pitched as a moment for students to really take risks, make mistakes and learn from the activity rather than focusing on a predetermined outcome.

This activity is called 'Follow the Recipe!'. It is a fun and accessible way to explore the journey from declarative and procedural knowledge, meaning knowing how to do something in an objective way, to embodied knowledge, meaning to learn through the body itself in a more emotive and intimate way. It is a way to discuss the balance between learning a specific skill as a group and finding one's own individual voice within that skill.

Task 6.4 Making 'Recipes for Learning' for Individual Lessons

Follow the recipe!

- In preparation for this activity, write a clear and focused set of recipe style instructions that take a student through the process of making a piece of art. You can format this set of instructions however you like, and in accordance with your scheme of work, process or materials you are exploring. (Below is an example recipe that will facilitate the exploration of drawing.)
- When in the workshop, clearly explain the task at hand, and firstly discuss the similarities between cooking from a recipe book and making a piece of art in school.
- Give students ample time and independence to complete the recipe. Try to give them as little guidance as possible, so that they are working with full autonomy.
- Once complete, bring the outcomes together and lead a group crit. Ensure students give focused feedback to each other and reflect on the similarities and differences between the outcomes.

The following questions could help guide this discussion.

- What are your first impressions of the artworks we have all made?
- What are the similarities and differences between the artworks? Has anything surprised you?
- Did you enjoy following the recipe? Why? Why not?
- What aspect of the works do you think have been successful/unsuccessful?
- What do these artworks tell us about following a set of instructions when making art?
- Is it artistic to follow a recipe?

What thoughts on making art would you take from this workshop and consider for future lessons?

Example Recipe:

Ingredients

Make one fantastic artwork prep time: 15 minutes
Pens, pencils, paints, paper and scissors
To season: some creativity, and anything else you would like to make art with.

1. To prepare your ingredients, please make the worst possible drawing you can imagine on a piece of A4 paper, the worse the better? You have one minute to do.
2. Once you are happy the drawing is truly awful, scrunch up the paper in an aggressive manner, into an angry ball and place it in front of you, you now have your initial art mix to work from.
3. Do a three-minute continuous line drawing of your paper ball on a new piece of A3 paper, making sure to be big, bold and fill the page.
4. Rotate the paper around so your drawing is upside down and do another three-minute continuous line drawing using a different medium, but this time draw your own hand. Allow the drawing to fill the page and overlap.
5. Spend five minutes adding some tonal shading to some areas of your drawing, remember to be super technical, to tick those boxes and jump through those hoops!
6. Look around the room for an interesting face, and spend ten minutes doing a beautiful observational drawing of someone's portrait, this is an important filling that showcases your sense of proportion and perspective, tasty!
7. Fill in as much negative space as possible for one minute… don't overdo it or the artwork will curdle.
8. Write a range of words that relate to your year so far as an artist student, write the words in a way that reflects the mood and emotion of those words, you have 90 seconds to do this or it risks becoming contrived.
9. Time to mix and shape. Make three cuts into your paper and manipulate your work into an abstract 3D form, consider how it looks from all angles.
10. Season for taste! Look at the artwork, spend five minutes refining, adding some extra spice and vibrancy to any bland or boring areas.
11. And your art is ready to serve to the hungry audience.

This activity is metacognitive in the sense that students will understand how they learnt to make their artwork and are able to critically reflect on the benefits and shortcomings of this didactic approach. It also tests their resilience and builds confidence in becoming more independent and original in their approach to making, rather than focusing on reproducing a predetermined outcome. They will also see that even if they are all following the same instructions, their outcomes can be significantly different, and that this is an artistic quality to be embraced (Figure 6.2).

Devising activities like this within your longer-term planning ensures you are allocating sufficient time to promote artistic behaviour in your lessons. Other activities could include:

- Making work collaboratively as a group, to explore ownership, team work, and sharing skills and ideas;

Figure 6.2 Y10 artist students making an artwork with the 'Follow the recipe activity'. Students wear chefs' hats to enter role play and feel less self-conscious. Lady Margaret School, 2022.

- Performance/spoken word art opens up discussion about the importance of language in art, whether performance can be considered art, and whether art has to have a tangible product;
- Instant exhibition, where students must use a set of objects/materials/artworks and curate/present within a specific space. They could use lighting and arrange the space in a certain way to consider how someone would view and experience the art. Discuss how the atmosphere, scale and composition of an exhibition affect the work for the viewer.

OTHER COMMUNITIES OF PRACTICE

As well as working with students in the classroom, it is good to also explore other communities of practice that are available. An important one of these is other artist teachers, either in your department, people you are training to teach with or teachers in other schools. It is anomalous that teaching is a highly social practice that can also feel isolating at times. This being the case, networking with likeminded creative educators from a range of backgrounds and settings will broaden your own understanding, provide a supportive outlet and enable you to develop your professional and personal artistic practices in whatever form they may take. There are already a number of groups, forums and networks that run which are worth exploring.

For example, the Artisteacher Network, set up two years ago by myself, Andy Ash and the Freelands Foundation, is a regular discussion forum that meets both online and in-person to support art teachers and educators. The Network was formed in response to a need for a long-lasting and dynamic social space where artists and educators could continue to develop their practices and work with others in an expanded community of practice, beyond Initial Teacher Education or other post graduate study. As Dr Esther Sayers points out in her paper on the artist teachers taking part in postgraduate study, 'teachers' personal development as artists can have a directly beneficial impact on their effectiveness as teachers, and, as a result, on their students' learning and creativity' (2006, p8). Through the facilitation of reflective activities and networking opportunities, the Network

Figure 6.3 Artisteacher Network Session, collecting thoughts in relation to artist teacher practice as part of the MAKE exhibition at the Freelands Foundation, September 2022.

provides this same experience, artist teachers from a range of school and community contexts are encouraged to critically engage with their practices and explore the principles of teaching as artistic practice, share projects as well as work collaboratively to develop new ideas. There is always value in teachers' continued learning (Figure 6.3).

SUMMARY

An ability to facilitate artistic behaviours in the classroom allows for real learning where students and teachers are visible, heard and valued. It enhances the excitement, surprise and rewards of lessons for all who are contributing. The activities provided in this chapter will support you in continuing to take risks and challenge yourself as an artist teacher, reflecting on your own artistic behaviours and reminding you that your own learning is paramount to your wellbeing and development. It takes confidence, experience, and time, it will be a career-long process of your own learning, and should be embraced and enjoyed as such.

The realities of implementing the ideas above are of course dependent on the type of institution you work in, the resources and time available to you, the dynamic you have with colleagues, your head of department and senior leadership colleagues. Whatever your professional circumstances, I suggest that you approach the development of your teaching practice slowly, taking pride in the micro events, and noticing and acknowledging the small magic moments in every lesson. This will help you to sustain good practice. Utilising school websites, social media and networks of art educators to share what is happening within your classroom communities will make your students and you active and relevant contributors to the wider Art and Design education community. Most importantly, embracing your artistic behaviours as artist teachers and artist students can be great fun.

RESOURCES

Carney, P. (2021). *Art & Design Curriculum - What's Right and Wrong with the Current Model* [Online video]. Available from: https://www.youtube.com/watch?v=RhzMdF7IdGU (Accessed: December 6th 2021).

The Freelands Foundation: https://freelandsfoundation.co.uk/education/artisteacher

BIBLIOGRAPHY

Addison, N. and Burgess, L. (2003) *Issues in Art and Design Teaching.* London and New York: Routledge.

Allen, F. (2011) *Documents of Contemporary Art: Education.* London: Whitechapel Gallery; Cambridge: MIT Press.

Atkinson, D. (2009). *Pedagogy of the Event.* Available from: https://www.kettlesyard.co.uk/events/symposium-on-not-knowing-how-artists-think/ (Accessed December 6th 2021).

Bieste, G (2017) *Letting Art Teach.* Arnhem, Netherlands. ArtEZ Press.

Bourriaud, N. (2002). *Relational Aesthetics.* Dijon: Les Presses du réel.

Department for Education. (2013) *National Curriculum in England: Art and Design Programmes of Study.* Available from: https://www.gov.uk/government/publications/national-curriculum-in-england-art-and-desi gn-programmes-of-study (Accessed 14th April 2022).

Freire, P. (1970). *Pedagogy of the Oppressed.* New York: Seabury Press.

Harding, A. (2005) *Magic Moments: Collaboration Between Artists and Young People.* London: Black Dog.

Kolb, D. A. (1984). *Experiential Learning: Experience as the Source of Learning and Development.* Englewood Cliffs, NJ: Prentice-Hall.

Lave, J. and Wenger, E. (1991) 'Legitimate peripheral participation in communities of practice' in *Situated Learning: Legitimate Peripheral Participation.* Cambridge: Cambridge University Press, pp. 89–119.

Page, T. (2012) 'A Shared Place of Discovery and Creativity: Practices of Contemporary Art and Design Pedagogy.' *International Journal of Art & Design Education* Issue 31, pp. 67–77.

Schon, D. A. (2008) *Reflective Practitioner How Professionals Think In Action.* New York: Basic Books.

Vygotsky, L. S. (2004) 'Imagination and Creativity in Childhood.' *Journal of Russian and East European Psychology,* 42(1), pp. 7–97.

Ward, H. (2005) 'Championing Contemporary Practice in the Secondary Classroom' in Atkinson, D. and Steers, J. *Social & Critical Practices in Art Education.* Stoke on trent: Trentham Books.

Wild, C. (2022) *Artist-Teacher Practice and the Expectation of an Aesthetic Life.* London: Routledge.

Chapter 7

Well-Being in the Art Classroom: For Teachers *and* Learners

Michele Gregson

INTRODUCTION

'Art Saves Lives' says artist Bob and Roberta Smith. And perhaps we can go further: art *teachers* make lives – and schools – better. Why is it that school Art and Design departments are such lunchtime havens for students? For many, it is the place where they feel most understood and at ease.

Mental health and emotional well-being are a vital part of public health policy, and the work that schools do. Schools have a significant role in supporting mental health and well-being by developing approaches tailored to their pupils' needs. In this chapter, we will explore the unique contribution of Art and Design.

Education can bring pressures – but should also be where young people can develop the attributes, dispositions, and behaviours that help them cope with the challenges they face. When well-being is actively planned for, we may also see a profound effect on learning, deeper engagement with the subject, and positive benefits that reach across the school community (Smith, 2013) (Figure 7.1).

Figure 7.1 Art Saves Lives, © Bob and Roberta Smith, 2022.

DOI: 10.4324/9781003377429-9

In nurturing a learning environment for well-being, we can create the conditions for better relationships in the classroom. This requires opportunities for reflection and expression, developing positive behaviours for learning and personal development, health, and well-being. We can achieve this by ensuring that the scope, breadth, and design of the curriculum fully reflect the interests and lived experiences of our learners. We can work with pupils to organise learning (and the learning environment) so that they make independent choices and take responsibility for their work. We can engage our whole school community, celebrating and learning from the process and production of art that has meaning and value. And in the process, we must be mindful of our own health and well-being – because any environment for well-being must also consider the needs of the teacher.

OBJECTIVES:

By the end of this chapter you should be able to:

- Understand how actively planning for well-being enhances learning in art and design and enriches the whole school community.
- Explore how you might organise the curriculum to promote well-being.
- Identify the conditions for well-being in your learning environment for you and your learners (Figure 7.2).

WAYS TO WELL-BEING IN THE ART AND DESIGN CLASSROOM

Figure 7.2 Art is for Health and Wellbeing NSEAD advocacy postcard © NSEAD.

DEFINING WELL-BEING

What do we understand by the term 'well-being'? There are many interpretations and models of wellness, and it can be characterised in many ways. The Foresight Mental Capital and Wellbeing Project offer a helpful definition of mental wellbeing:

> … (a) dynamic state, in which the individual can develop their potential, work productively and creatively, build strong and positive relationships with others, and contribute to their community. It is enhanced when an individual can fulfil their personal and social goals and achieve a sense of purpose in society.
>
> (The Government Office for Science, 2008, p. 10)

WELL-BEING AND THE NATIONAL CURRICULUM

Under the Childrens Act of 2004, the welfare of pupils is a responsibility for local authorities. School inspection frameworks for the UK-maintained schools look at pupils' wider development, requiring schools to develop confidence and resilience, to enhance pupils' spiritual, moral, and social cultural learning and ensure an inclusive environment that meets the needs of all pupils. The National curriculum in each of the four UK nations set expectations for pupils' personal development and positive contribution to civic society. In Northern Ireland and England, the emphasis is on developing skills for success in work and life, while the Scottish Curriculum for Excellence (CfE) focuses on the fundamental capacities that children need to flourish. Health and well-being are recognised as being particularly important:

> We know that physical, social, emotional, and economic well-being have a significant impact on children and young people's success in school and beyond school. We also know that aspects of these factors are significant barriers to learning and achievement for a large proportion of our learners.
>
> (Education Scotland, 2015, p. 5)

The new Curriculum for Wales promotes individual and *national* well-being. Schools and practitioners must organise learning that puts learner needs at the heart of curriculum design. Whilst there is a difference in emphasis and focus across the four nations, responsibility and opportunity for well-being and personal development are woven through every subject and are the responsibility of all staff.

How do you approach this responsibility as a teacher of Art and Design? There is a compelling evidence base that engagement with the arts can improve our physical and mental well-being (Thomson & Malloy, 2022). During the Covid 19 pandemic, researchers found that arts engagement helped people use certain psychological strategies for coping and emotion regulation:

> The arts were found to facilitate relaxation, escapism, mood, confidence, positivity and a sense of connection, and to reduce loneliness, worries and negative emotions.
>
> (Bradbury, Warran, Mak & Fancourt, 2021, p. 2)

Furthermore, the arts can create opportunities for people to learn from and about each other and the world, with wider community benefits and pro-social behaviours (Andrews, Bunting, Corrie & Fox, 2017). And, importantly, it is recognised that creative approaches to teaching and learning can raise standards, in our subject and across the curriculum. An Ofsted survey to investigate creative approaches to learning reported:

> Schools in challenging circumstances…showed the greatest improvements in pupils' ability to draw discerningly on a range of data and work collaboratively to solve problems; their reading and writing; their speaking and listening; and their personal development.
>
> (Ofsted, 2010, p. 4)

WELL-BEING AND CURRICULUM INTENTION

If you want to teach for well-being, consider how opportunities within art, craft, and design foster the attitudes, dispositions, and behaviours that are directly related to social and emotional well-being. Consider *what* you are teaching and *why*.

Art and Design touches all areas of our lives, every day. But what is important in the lives of your learners? Are they learning about and making art that is relevant to them – their cultural heritage, their lived experience, and their aspirations for the future? Art and Design education is about much more than securing knowledge that can be harnessed for the creative and knowledge economies. There is a deep connection between knowledge production and social action – between what your pupils learn and how and why they learn it (Graham, Graziano & Kelly, 2016).

Task 7.1 Observation Activity: Qualities of Learning in Art and Design That Support Well-Being

Think about how you might use your findings from this task in your planning for teaching.

1. Over a term, identify lessons and activities with a specific learning focus from the table in Figure 7.3. Observe your pupils and make a note of what you see.
2. Which qualities of art learning seem to contribute most to the well-being of your pupils? Can you find ways to extend these activities for deeper engagement?

PRACTICAL APPROACHES TO TEACHING FOR WELL-BEING

A useful starting point for thinking about practical approaches to well-being in the school context is the 'Five Ways' framework (Figure 7.4), a set of evidence-based public mental health messages aimed at improving the mental health and well-being of the whole population. They were developed by the New Economics Foundation in 2008 and have been widely adopted and adapted by health and local authorities throughout the UK (Aked, Marks, Corden & Thompson, 2008). The Five Ways model is often adapted to reflect local priorities. For example, Kent County Council introduced a sixth way to well-being, 'Care for the Planet,' influenced by discussions with young people. A first step in planning for well-being in your classroom could be to agree some well-being principles with your pupils.

Quality of art learning	Activity	Class	Observations
Close observation and analysis of what is seen and experienced			
Creative thinking and innovation			
Experimentation and thinking with and through materials, concepts and visual elements			
Critical reflection and external awareness			
Communication of ideas and intentions			
Collaboration with others			
Multiplicity of perspectives and potential solutions			
Making qualitative judgements and choices			

Figure 7.3 Qualities of learning observational log.

Figure 7.4 Five Ways to Well-being © Isobel McFarlane.

Task 7.2 Pupil Discussion: Agree Principles for Well-Being

This activity is a good way to get to know more about a new class:

1. Arrange your classroom so that the pupils are sat in a circle. You should remain on the outside of the circle and take the role of 'host' for the discussion.
2. Choose an artwork that addresses themes of well-being (you might use the image by Bob and Roberta Smith 'Art Saves Lives')
3. Read out the Five Ways statements and ask the students to consider each one in relation to the artwork.

    *   Connect with other people.
    *   Be physically active.
    *   Keep learning new things.
    *   Be mindful and pay attention to the moment.
    *   Give to others.

4. Ask the students to make statements in response to the work. Write them down on a large sheet of paper or board. Choose one of the statements for discussion.
5. Ask your pupils to suggest other well-being ways that could be added. (e.g. Care for the planet).
6. Pupils can present their 'ways to well-being' as a graphic for display.

APPLYING THE FIVE WAYS TO LEARNING IN ART AND DESIGN

Having established what is meaningful in terms of curriculum content, how will you organise your learning spaces and teaching and learning so that they actively promote well-being? You can use the framework to map approaches to learning and identify strategies to create the conditions for well-being. The following sections set out the 'Five Ways' framework in the context of Art and Design education and consider how you might apply them in your planning.

Connect

As the teacher you are the prime point of connection in your classroom. Well-being begins with you and your relationship with your learners. Making and sharing art can be an exposing process and is one that many people shy away from. The professional practice of artists, makers, and designers is rarely solitary and provides a model of how professional relationships depend on empathy. Think about how you can organise working in groups where students need to work together to co-construct or find design solutions. This could be in short, open-ended make and build activities exploring the quality of materials or responding to a given stimulus, or longer, structured projects working in response to a brief, requiring students to act as design teams.

Every lesson can include moments of dialogic activity, with shared conversations to explore the meaning of what is being made and the work of others. Well-structured group critique, inquiry conversations, and reflection create spaces where positive experiences can be shared, and supportive peer learning relationships can be developed. These activities build resilience and team skills that will equip your young artists to refine and improve their work, with deeper learning and better outcomes. Can you create a cycle of empathy in your classroom where everyone (you included) feels heard and understood? Be alert and question your assumptions about the 'difficult' group or the disengaged pupil. Consider what you know about them, and what more you need to learn.

Be Active

Making is a physical activity. It is an interaction of the whole body with the brain and can be deeply rewarding on a physical and emotional level. It stimulates and stretches visual and tactile senses. The development of hand-eye co-ordination, fine and gross motor skills, strength, and flexibility are intrinsic (Crafts Council, 2021). The greater the range of materials, processes, and skills your students explore, the greater the range of physical engagement – from tightly controlled, fine-grained work through to physically strenuous activities manipulating and shaping materials, tools, and equipment. Plan for activity that allows large-scale work, 'messy' materials that test dexterity and co-ordination, as well as those that need precision and patience (Figure 7.5).

In an Art and Design classroom, the management and organisation of the space, equipment, and materials is a prime consideration. Think about the way that your pupils physically occupy the space, how they move around, how they access what they need. Their physical relationship to the space is key to the smooth and efficient management of activities, but also to their independence, and taking responsibility. In so many areas of school life, pupils are sedentary and passive, following

Figure 7.5 'Tree of life,' Faith Bebbington, co-created with Nottingham High School, 2021.

direct instruction about when and where they can move. Managed well, your classroom can offer much more freedom and purposeful movement.

As you plan for an active classroom environment, consider the needs of your learners. Have you organised the learning space so that it is inclusive and accessible to all? Is your classroom an efficient space that functions as a practical studio for multiple users? Universal Design for Learning (UDL) is a framework to improve and optimise teaching and learning for all people based on scientific insights into how humans learn. You can use UDL principles to support your planning for a classroom space that allows free movement and independence. A stress-free, efficient art room will contribute to everyone's well-being – including yours.

Task 7.3 Audit Your Teaching Space

You should look for ways of integrating the outcome of this task into your planning for teaching in any space.

Think of an Art and Design teaching space that you know well. Draw a plan view of the room. Include the position and dimensions of tables, screen and projector, display areas, circulation space, and the position of the places where tools, equipment, and materials can be accessed.

Make notes on your drawing about the accessibility of your space, with these three UDL principles in mind:

- how learners will engage with the lesson.
- how information is presented to learners.
- how learners are expected to act strategically & express themselves.

1. Does the space provide options that can help all learners:

    - take part in activity that requires them to do, listen, speak, and move? (e.g. tables and benches at the right height, clear lines of sight, space to work, good acoustics).
    - understand and use resources regardless of their experiences, knowledge, language skills, or current concentration level? (e.g. how materials and equipment are labelled, organised, and accessed).
    - move safely in the space as they need (e.g. hazards minimised, clear routes, and routines).
    - be efficient and comfortable as they work (e.g. clear access routes and routines for collection and return of materials, space, and process-specific workstations).

2. Is the arrangement of furniture, etc. flexible enough to be changed to support diverse access needs according to the activity you have planned? (e.g. furniture and screens, fixed or movable).
3. What improvements and adaptations can you make?

Learn New Skills

Skills are at the heart of learning in Art and Design. They include: problem solving, creating, envisaging, imagining, speculating, visioning, realising, investigating, exploring, experimenting, and making (Gast, 2021). Alongside these subject-specific skills, learners develop the intrinsic 'soft' skills of expression, self-awareness, self-esteem, resilience, inclusion, confidence, and peer engagement. All skills make a huge contribution to pupils' personal development. It is also the experience of success, and visible progress that is itself so rewarding. When we apply ourselves to practice skills and become adept, we feel a sense of purpose and achievement that boosts our self-confidence and self-esteem. It is a positive aspect of learning in our subject.

Be explicit in your planning to name the skills being developed in each activity and ensure that pupils are given enough opportunities to practice, consolidate, and extend. Allow sufficient time and pace to acquire a skill through repetition and by revisiting it in a variety of activities.

But, beware. 'Success' is often defined in terms of visible outcomes – the 'final piece,' produced for summative assessment. Certainly, your pupils may have very fixed ideas of what 'good' looks like. If the focus is exclusively on outcomes, with a rigid standard of value, many pupils will feel disheartened and disengaged. The opposite of well-being! It is important to ensure that *process* has at least as much value in your classroom as finished products. Help your pupils name their skills and recognise their own progress. Use a range of strategies to support pupils to evaluate their skills development through feedback and give regular praise in a variety of ways.

Take Notice

Many schools incorporate mindfulness activity into the school day. Paying more attention to the present moment can improve your mental well-being. This includes your thoughts and feelings, your body, and the world around you. The engagement of both physical and cognitive senses through engagement with art, craft, and design can be a way for pupils to 'be in the moment.' One way this can happen is by creating space for deep, immersive making. When a 'flow' state is achieved, with an intense focus and concentration on the task in hand, physiological changes take place too. 'Flow' is strongly associated with well-being, being productive and motivated, and is closely related to mindfulness (Nakamura & Csiksentmihalyi, 2002). This can be difficult to achieve in school settings, with the day chopped up into timetable chunks. But if you can name moments when your pupils can really immerse themselves in a task, in a calm environment, then that 'flow' state can be possible.

What do you need to do to create an atmosphere of calm?

- Allow time for uninterrupted activity. It might be as little as five minutes; it is about full focus during the time available.
- Reduce noise in the space – make these 'no talking' times (including you), use calming music, visual rather than verbal prompts.
- Choose a task where pupils have established a good skill base – this is a time to consolidate rather than introduce new learning. The level of difficulty needs to be not so easy that it is tedious, but not so challenging that it is stressful.
- Make this 'low stakes' activity – not for assessment or display but all about process and consolidation of learning (be clear in your lesson planning that this is the learning intention).

Activity might be making, engaging with materials, or focused looking taking a mindful approach to looking at and thinking about artworks.

Task 7.4 Slow Looking Meditation

This activity is based on the National Gallery series of 5 minute 'slow looking' exercises and is one that you can build into your planning for teaching (https://www.nationalgallery.org.uk).

1. Choose an artwork for the group to focus on. You might do this in the classroom on a smart board or projector, or in a gallery or museum, in front of the actual artwork.
2. Introduce the activity. Ask your pupils to get comfortable, to sit up with their feet planted on the floor, to focus on the soles of their feet, and to be aware of the sensations in the soles of their feet. Then, take their attention to the contact of their body pressed into the seat of their chair, notice the air around them. Is it warm or cold?
3. Finally, take three deep breaths, breathing in for a count of six, then out for a count of six.
4. Turning attention to the artwork, ask pupils to imagine themselves in the world of this artwork. Take time to look carefully and slowly at the work, guide your pupils through the work, dwelling on the details, inviting them to imagine the sensations and feelings suggested in the artwork.
5. Make space for silent reflection.

You can guide your class through a slow looking mediation yourself, looking at an artwork related to your scheme of work – or play one of the National Gallery films and enjoy a mindful moment alongside your pupils.

Giving to Others

Engaging in the arts can foster empathy and kindness, and act as a catalyst to unlock individual and societal wellness, creating the conditions for kindness to grow (Broadwood, Bunting, Andrews, Abrams & Van de Vyver, 2012). In a school community, the Art and Design department can be a dynamic focus for community celebration, and shared values. There are so many opportunities to engage the people in your school community with all the good things that you do. Here are a few ideas:

• Work in partnership with local cultural organisations in participatory projects that benefit your pupils and their community.
• Celebrate the work that you do through exhibitions and displays in your classroom, your department, the school and beyond. Don't just share the finished artworks, think about how you can make the process visible. Working walls in public spaces, pupil presentations, and sketchbook displays are some of the ways you might do this.
• Invite parents, carers, and other teachers to get involved in workshops led by your pupils.
• Collaborate with local businesses to develop live briefs for your pupils to work on, connecting through a designer-client dynamic.

By being outward facing you can make the case for the value of the subject. Your pupils benefit from a stronger, more connected community that they are actively contributing to as young artists. This is a powerful thing to be part of.

A HEALTH WARNING

Wherever and whoever you may be teaching, you can be confident that Art and Design is a subject that can make a positive contribution to your pupils' well-being. But it is important to note – teaching for well-being is different from art therapy, which is an area of highly specialist activity. It is **not** within the scope of the art teacher to provide therapeutic activity (even if you have qualifications or experience in counselling). This is not your job! Art therapy is a form of psychotherapy that uses art media as its primary mode of expression and communication. It should only be conducted by those with specialist qualifications and suitable clinical experience. Therapeutic activity takes place in a confidential setting with all the necessary safeguards in place. In this context, art is used as a medium to address emotional issues which may be confusing and distressing. Unlike the art teacher, the art therapist is not concerned with developing art skills. Emotionally beneficial as an art lesson may be, it is not the place for therapeutic psychological help or professional counselling.

Making artwork can be a safe space in which to examine our feelings and share that with others, something exemplified in the Photography Movement's Show and Tell project. However, the very personal and self-reflective nature of learning in Art and Design may well lead to confusing or distressing emotions for some pupils. Make sure that you understand the safeguarding procedures in your school and know what to do if a pupil discloses something that might be a welfare concern. This might be things that they say, behaviours that you observe or images that they collect or make. If you have a concern, pass it on to your safeguarding lead (Figure 7.6).

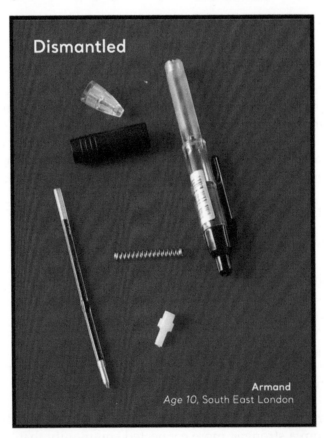

Figure 7.6 Dismantled (2020) by Armand Holland; For the 'How are you feeling?' Show and Tell project.

YOUR WELL-BEING

Your well-being is important. Your behaviour sets the tone for everything that happens in your classroom. You hold the space, you model empathy. You are the host of the haven! Don't underestimate how important it is for you to attend to your own needs if you are going to support the well-being of your pupils.

There is increasing awareness of the impact of work-related stress. Teaching can be hard. There may be times when you feel stressed, overloaded, and undervalued. What are the conditions that you need to flourish? How can you be mindful of your own needs, and resilience?

- Celebrate your subject and the work that you do. Be an advocate for art, craft, and design education, and challenge those who do not recognise the value of the subject. There are many advocacy resources available to help you make the case.
- Know your rights in the workplace. Dedicated teachers always give 'above and beyond,' but you should set boundaries, be informed and confident to challenge unreasonable expectations.
- Be inspired by your pupils and the work that you do together. Let their success bolster your sense of achievement and satisfaction.
- Take strength from your professional learning community. Connect with other art educators for support and to share good practice.
- Check in with colleagues, see how they are doing, and encourage a culture of kindness and care in your workplace.
- Practice what you preach – if engaging with art is good for your pupils, it is good for you too. Don't lose sight of your own interests and practice. Make time to engage with art, craft, and design on your own terms.
- Make time for play.
- Keep learning, engage, and connect. Be kind to yourself.

SUMMARY

We can foster well-being in Art and Design education if we design that experience with the aim of providing an enabling environment for learning. It is important that what pupils learn about and the way they learn is by consent. If it has no relevance to their needs and interests, they are unlikely to thrive, either as artists or as citizens. Art and Design education is an opportunity for every child to make sense of the world and their experience of it. If we organise learning so that opportunities for well-being are clearly identified and integral to our curriculum aims, we can support pupils to achieve their potential as young artists actively connected to each other and their community through their practice.

Teaching for well-being does not aim to create a therapeutic service. It is about being alive to the unique power of our subject and maximising the inherent well-being benefits. And we can model wellness by being empathetic teachers, taking time to nurture our own creativity, mindful of our own well-being. What is good for your pupils is also good for you. Take time to check in on your own feelings, ensure that you are heard and understood in your workplace, and take pride in the unique difference that you make to your pupils, your school, and society.

RESOURCES

https://artuk.org/learn/learning-resources/wellbeing-resources Art UK have gathered a selection of learning resources from museums, galleries, and art collections around the UK, which can be used in both classroom and home learning settings, to improve and increase awareness of young people's wellbeing.

AD Magazine Published by the National Society for Education in Art and Design. *AD* is NSEAD's magazine for members and anyone with an interest in art education. *AD* is 34 pages of key art, craft and design information, inspiration, ideas, and resources. Published three times a year, free to members and available to purchase.

https://www.mentalhealthatwork.org.uk A helpful set of resources from MIND to support employers and employees promote good mental health in the workplace.

https://www.nsead.org/ The official website of the National Society for Education in Art and Design. Hundreds of resources to inspire best practice, support your advocacy and keep you connected with the art education community.

BIBLIOGRAPHY

Aked, J., Marks, N., Cordon, C. and Thompson, S. (2008) *Five ways to wellbeing: A report presented to the Foresight Project on communicating the evidence base for improving people's well-being*, London: New Economics Foundation.

Andrews, T., Bunting, C., Corri, T. and Fox, S. (2017) *Changing the world through arts and kindness*, Canterbury: People United Publishing.

APPG on Arts, Health, and Wellbeing. (2017) Inquiry report creative health: The arts for health and wellbeing, 2nd edition, viewed 30 August 2022 from https://www.culturehealthandwellbeing.org.uk/appg-inquiry/Publications/Creative_Health_Inquiry_Report_2017_-_Second_Edition.pdf

Bradbury, A., Warran, K., Mak, H. W. and Fancourt, D. (2021) The role of the arts during the COVID-19 pandemic, viewed 14 September 2022 from https://www.artscouncil.org.uk/sites/default/files/download-file/UCL_Role_of_the_Arts_during_COVID_13012022_0.pdf

Bradshaw, C. (2022) Make it routine to prevent workplace stress, ACAS blog viewed 30 August 2022 from https://www.acas.org.uk/make-it-routine-to-prevent-work-related-stress

Broadwood, J., Bunting, C., Andrews, T., Abrams, D. and Van de Vyver, J. (2012) *Arts & kindness*, Canterbury: People United Publishing.

CAST. (2018) Universal design for learning guidelines version 2, viewed 12 September 2022 from http://udlguidelines.cast.org

Crafts Council. (2021) Reasons craft is good for your mental health, viewed 23 August 2022 from https://www.craftscouncil.org.uk/stories/4-reasons-craft-good-your-mental-health

DFE (Department for Education). (2014) Statutory Guidance National Curriculum in England: Framework for key stages 1 to 4, p. 5, viewed 10 September 2002 from https://www.gov.uk/government/publications/national-curriculum-in-england-framework-for-key-stages-1-to-4/the-national-curriculum-in-england-framework-for-key-stages-1-to-4

DFE (Department for Education). (2018) Mental health and behaviour in schools, viewed 11 September 2022 from https://assets.publishing.service.gov.uk/government/uploads/system/uploads/attachment_data/file/1069687/Mental_health_and_behaviour_in_schools.pdf

Education Scotland. (2015) How good is our school?, 4th edition, viewed 10 September 2022 from https://education.gov.scot/nih/Documents/Frameworks_SelfEvaluation/FRWK2_NIHeditHGIOS/FRWK2_HGIOS4.pdf

Education Scotland. (2019) Curriculum for excellence, viewed 10 September 2022 from https://education.gov.scot/documents/All-experiencesoutcomes18.pdf

Estyn. (2022) What we inspect, viewed 10 September 2022 from https://www.estyn. gov.wales/system/files/2022-09/What%20we%20inspect%20-%202022_0.pdf

Gast, G. (2021) 3Rs Webinar – Life after lockdown: Support notes for art and design, mental health and wellbeing – Part 1, viewed 30 August 2022 from https://lifeafterlockdownproject.com/3rs-webinar-life-after-lockdown-support-notes-for-art-design-mental-health-and-wellbeing-part-1/

Hiett, S. (2022) Towards anti-ableist pedagogies, *AD Magazine*, 35, 28–29.

Graham, J., Graziano, V. and Kelly, S. (2016) The educational turn in art: Rewriting the hidden curriculum, *Performance Research*, 21(6), 29–35.

Nakamura, J. and Csiksentmihalyi, M. (2002) Chapter 7, The concept of flow, In *Handbook of positive psychology,* pp. 95–96, Oxford: OUP.

NSEAD. (2021) Introduction to the ARAEA checklists, viewed 11 September 2022 from https://www.nsead.org/resources/anti-racist-art-education/

NSEAD. (2022) Introducing sensitive subjects into the art, craft and design curriculum toolkit, viewed 20 March from https://www.nsead.org/trade-union/introducing-sensitive-topics-into-the-art-craft-and-design-curriculum-toolkit/

Ofsted. (2003) Expecting the unexpected, developing creativity in primary and secondary schools HMI 1612, viewed 30 August from https://dera.ioe. ac.uk/4766/1/Expecting_the_unexpected_(PDF_format).pdf

Ofsted. (2010) Learning: Creative approaches that raise standards HMI: 080266, viewed 30 August 2022 from https://dera.ioe.ac.uk/1093/1/Learning%20creative%20approaches%20that%20raise%20standards.pdf

Ofsted. (2022) School inspection handbook, viewed 2 September 2022 from https://www.gov.uk/government/publications/school-inspection-handbook-eif/school-inspection-handbook

Ofsted. (2023) Research review series: Art and design, viewed 20 March 2023 from https://www.gov.uk/government/publications/research-review-series-art-and-design/research-review-series-art-and-design#contents

Public Health England. (2016) Arts for health and wellbeing: A framework for evaluation, viewed 30 August 2022 from https://assets.publishing.service.gov. uk/government/uploads/system/uploads/attachment_data/file/765496/PHE_Arts_and_Health_Evaluation_FINAL.pdf

Smith, D. (2013) An independent report for the Welsh Government into Arts in Education in the Schools of Wales, pp. 15–23, viewed 11 September from https://gov.wales/sites/default/files/publications/2018-04/independent-report-for-the-welsh-government-into-arts-in-education-in-the-schools-of-wales_0.pdf

The Government Office for Science. (2008) *Foresight mental capital and wellbeing project: Final project report.* (Foresight). London: The Government Office for Science.

The National Archives. (2004) Children Act 2004, viewed 11 September 2022 from https://www.legislation.gov.uk/ukpga/2004/31/section/10

Thomson, P. and Malloy, L. (2022) The benefits of art, craft and design education in schools a rapid evidence review, viewed 10 August 2022 from https://www. nsead.org/files/6f85ab8587bc53ce653702da1cc15690.pdf

Welsh Government. (2021) Curriculum for Wales, viewed 10 September 2022 from https://hwb.gov.wales/curriculum-for-wales

PART 2

EPISTEMOLOGICAL CURIOSITY FOR TEACHERS AND LEARNERS

Chapter 8

Creativity, Designerly Thinking and the Wicked Problems of Life

Gary Granville, Emma Creighton and Fiona Byrne

INTRODUCTION

Our school systems can justifiably claim many accomplishments but, despite noble aspirations, it is difficult to include the cultivation of creativity among them. Yet, across the globe, the promotion of creativity is consistently seen as one of the most desirable aims of contemporary education (OECD, 2019).

Schools are almost entirely constructed on the basis of habit – habits of mind, of practices and of cultural assumptions that shape everyone involved, including teachers, pupils and parents. Schools, for the most part, foster a culture of conformist thinking: conformity with norms, with the conventions and rhythms of school life and of course with the rubrics of examinations and assessments. Not only are there 'right' answers to most school questions, there are 'right' ways of addressing those questions, of going about the daily routines of school life (Biesta, 2016; James et al., 2019; Robinson, 2011; Robinson and Aronica, 2015). Not much room for creativity there!

Even in Art and Design, we struggle to identify true pathways to creativity. Designerly[1] thinking and practice, however, does provide a form of scaffolding and practice that allows the learner to find and express their own creativity. This can be applied across the entire curriculum as an approach to teaching and learning. But it has its most natural and productive home in the space of Art and Design. Just as the term 'painterly' indicates a fine artist with the capacity to explore and express their identity through the medium of paint, so the term 'designerly' captures the importance of immersion within the discipline and methodologies of design.

The Art and Design classroom is the richest soil for planting the seeds of designerly thinking. The art room is the site of most divergent practice in many students' experience of schooling. So, as a teacher of Art and Design, you have a wonderful opportunity to develop both your own confidence and that of your students in exploring new ways of working.

This chapter aims to help you to develop an enhanced role for design within your teaching and to promote design education in the school curriculum generally.

DOI: 10.4324/9781003377429-11

OBJECTIVES:

By the end of this chapter you should be able to:

- Describe the process of designerly thinking and practice;
- Demonstrate how design can be incorporated in Art and Design teaching and learning;
- Describe the broad curriculum and educational qualities that designerly thinking can foster;
- Identify the cross-cutting educational benefits (key skills; 21st century skills) that design education can achieve with young people;
- Promote the role of Art and Design and of designerly thinking in broader educational policy and in the school setting and beyond.

AMBIGUITY AND RISK IN ART AND DESIGN

Despite its title, Art and Design in school has always tended to be more about art than design. Fine art – painting and drawing in particular – usually dominates the teaching and learning of the subject in schools. Curriculum specifications, examination syllabi and school customs always tend to focus on the fine art element of the subject.

There are many reasons for this which cannot be addressed here, but you can address this in your art room should you wish to. Learning through design addresses so much more than the technical skills of compositional aesthetics and functional impact: it incorporates the capacity to identify and analyse issues and problems, to empathise with the concerns and perspectives of others, to collaborate in addressing common concerns – and perhaps most significantly, to use both success and failure as positive elements of learning.

The fear of failure is endemic in our education systems. The high stakes attached to examinations and qualifications in terms of selection, of entry to higher education and employment, and of social status all have the effect of directing the energies and attention of teachers, students, parents and others onto the achievement of these predefined outcomes, the 'right answers'. A designerly approach to teaching and learning, however, reshapes the concept of failure into an essential component of learning. Within the design process, 'failure' is reframed and seen not as a terminal defeat but as a positive component of creative learning and as a platform for further and deeper engagement.

There is an 'uncertainty principle' underpinning Art and Design education and practice that incorporates both ambiguity and risk. Perhaps this shared characteristic also includes a crucial point of distinction and complementarity between Art and Design. Risk carries a level of understanding of likely outcomes of an action, and by inference a rationale for selection of appropriate action. Ambiguity on the other hand is a more literally uncertain process, with outcomes likely to be entirely unpredictable. While constructive engagement with both concepts is inherent to both Art and Design education, in the case of the latter, there is an ultimate solution sought. The design process looks to a final resolution which can be tested against reality: a solution or range of solutions that 'work' and can be demonstrated to do so. By contrast, art practice tends to be more at ease with ambiguity itself as a desirable process and outcome. Art studio thinking encourages the unplanned and sometimes accidental discovery of patterns and indeed will frequently produce work which is ambiguous in its final form: the work is open to the interpretation of the viewer as much as to the intention of the artist. Of course, examination criteria and school routines have tended to place greater emphasis on the 'product' of visual art education – the finished artwork which becomes the focus of assessment and judgement. This internal contradiction is at the heart of what is sometimes disparagingly referred to as 'school art' to distinguish it from actual art practice.

There is a distinction but not a conflict between Art and Design as components of the single school subject, Art and Design. The final outcome of a design process is nearly always subject to assessment against the criteria of effectiveness and efficiency, of form and function. The traditional truism that 'form follows function' in designing and making has been developed to include a greater emphasis not just on aesthetic qualities and elegance, but on cultural, social, personal and environmental factors in design. Nevertheless, the requirements of functionality remain a predominant criterion in designing.

Task 8.1 The Art Room as Design Studio

The environment plays a significant role in learning. With very simple adaptation, the classroom can be configured to support a designerly mode of working.

- Create designated areas within the classroom for different activities. For example, you might create an area for general design work such as sketching and another for making. Design often involves collaboration, so it works well to group tables together. To facilitate making, materials and tools should be made easily accessible.
- Whether working individually or in groups, students should have access to a vertical work surface for displaying material from their research, idea exploration and the development of the final outcome. This could be a wall, flip chart or large sheets of paper or card which can be stored away between classes. Working in this way the learners become immersed in their learning.
- A positive and collaborative atmosphere can be created by supporting open communication between learners. When working individually or in groups, students benefit from sharing, discussing, critiquing and negotiating ideas and opinions. You should provide opportunities for sharing work and receiving feedback throughout the duration of a project (Figure 8.1).

Figure 8.1 The art room as a design studio.

Engagement with social and environmental issues is a shared concern of both contemporary design and contemporary visual arts. Socially Engaged Art, participatory practice and relational aesthetics are forms of art practice that involve the artist in collaborative work with non-artists, with outcomes frequently expressed in forms far removed from the traditional studio/gallery format. Similarly, designers today are as much concerned with inter-personal processes and dynamics, with ethical production and with sustainable development as they are with commercial artefacts. For you as an Art and Design teacher, the opportunity to invite your students to engage with an issue of a social, environmental or ethical nature can open up pathways of relevance to both fine Art and Design practice.

Task 8.2 Designerly Tools and Techniques

You might consider adapting for the classroom, some simple tools and techniques that designers use in practice. For instance –

An empathy map helps to clarify the needs of the notional person or group for whom the design task is intended. On a large sheet, students place the person at the centre of the page and then create four segments, labelled 'says', 'does', 'thinks' and 'feels'. The students can place their findings from research in the appropriate area.

A problem statement requires the student to complete a short paragraph to capture their problem using guiding sentence stems;

> Our …(product/service etc.) helps … (user, society, environment etc.) who want to …. (jobs or tasks to be done), by … (verb eg. reducing/avoiding & user pain), and (verb e.g. increasing/enabling & user gain), unlike … (competing designs).

This strategy provides a framework for students to reference if they experience difficulty in generating ideas or validating their thinking and design decisions at the prototyping or delivery stages.

Students might like to generate an I wonder statement – "I wonder could we help our user to feel more/less …so that they can …?" This strategy can be used as a quick fire technique at the start of a class to create a culture of sharing raw, unpolished ideas where there is an open feedback loop at the concept stage of ideation.

Hoffman Davis (2008) gives a concise summation of the unique features of an arts education. These have particular resonance when applied to a successful Art and Design classroom. She identifies five key features, each with their own personal and social dimensions. In the Art and Design classroom, the student is engaged with a tangible product, a task or problem that they are endeavouring to resolve through the application of their own imagination and agency. As well as the knowledge and skills associated with the discipline, that work has an essential emotional component, through expression (this is how I feel) and empathy (this is how you feel). Art and Design work is always ambiguous, risky, tentative and provisional: the work should foster interpretation (what I think matters) and respect (what you think matters). The work practice is process-oriented, always open to the possibility of changes of direction on foot of new ideas or random accidents: it relies on skills of inquiry (what do I want to do?) and reflection (how am I doing?). Finally, it is concerned with connection – connecting with people across time and place, fostering qualities of engagement (I care about what I'm doing) and responsibility (I care about others).

Design practice in an arts setting relates to each of these criteria, most notably in its emphasis on engaging with others, on the necessity for empathy and collaboration. Teaching and learning in Art and Design provides opportunities that cannot be replicated in other subjects. As an Art and Design teacher you can help young people to find their own avenue to expression and empathy through some simple exposure to design experiences.

DESIGNERLY THINKING AND PRACTICE

Victor Papanek, one of the earliest advocates of design as an underlying matrix of life, famously proclaimed that

> Design is composing an epic poem, executing a mural, painting a masterpiece, writing a concerto; design is also about cleaning and reorganizing a desk drawer, pulling an impacted tooth, baking an apple pie, choosing sides for a back-lot baseball game, and educating a child.
>
> (1971: 3)

In curriculum terms, however, design has tended to have a more reductive role, often as little more than ornamentation or superficial enhancement of visual art work (Granville, 2019; Murray-Tiedge, 2015) or focused predominantly on technical procedures and finished artefacts (Kimbell and Stables, 2008).

Designerly thinking is an approach to issues, problems and situations that fosters innovative and novel solutions. It is a process that tries to overcome bias, prejudice and conventional norms in addressing various situations, ranging from mundane, everyday tasks to profound and challenging problems.

Task 8.3 Understand a Problem

At the planning stage of a project, introducing a social issue to frame the learning presents an opportunity for students to immerse themselves in the design process. Integrating a series of research, analysis and investigation strategies at the start of the project will support students to work collaboratively to gain a deeper understanding of the issue. Students can then move to co-creating a refined design brief which resonates with them and their context. Engaging with strategies like *Cause and Effect* diagrams, *The Five Whys* investigative questioning and *Concept Mapping* all support students to understand the parameters of an issue and the constraints.

A complex problem like Food Poverty might become more tangible and relatable to a student's context through a project brief like 'Design a solution to support families, shops or restaurants in your local area to reduce food waste'. Actively involving students in the co-creation of a brief supports autonomy, agency and motivation as they progress an idea from concept to realisation.

Designerly thinking is essentially concerned with 'wicked' problems – situations that are difficult to resolve due to the incomplete, conflicting or inconsistent nature of the information and data available (Buchanan, 1992; Cross, 2001). This type of thinking develops the capacity to select the most appropriate response, while recognising the provisional nature of most solutions. In formal logic, this is termed abductive reasoning (reaching a viable conclusion based on incomplete data) as distinct from deductive (reaching a definitive conclusion based on proof) or inductive reasoning (a probable solution based on limited but consistent evidence). In life, the wicked problems give us the greatest challenges but our traditional schooling does not equip us well to address them. Designerly thinking offers us a means to address them confidently.

Expressing opinions, thinking aloud and listening to the views of others are educational processes frequently encountered in the exchanges that occur when students are discussing the qualities and features of art work of their own, of fellow students or of established artists. They are also features of designerly thinking. Your role as art teacher and facilitator, providing support and scaffolding to each student, is crucial in the process.

While there is no single model for designerly thinking, there are a number of key components that apply to any process involving this approach. These components consist of:

- the identification and analysis of the various dimensions of the problem (sensemaking);
- the identification of a wide range of possible responses and solutions (ideation);
- the crystallisation around optimal solutions; and
- the testing and evaluation of prototype solutions.

In addressing a design problem, you should enable students to work through these stages in a more or less sequential manner. This approach shares two key elements with other important and influential models of design education: the iterative nature of the stages of evolution, involving review, revision and reflection, and the collaborative nature of the exercises. Group activity, teamwork and shared thinking are distinguishing characteristics of the process. In that respect, design education is different from most of the secondary school curriculum where individualized learning remains the dominant mode.

However, reducing design to staged steps in a process could result in very crude applications. Recognising this, Kimbell and Stables (2008) depict the design process as dynamic, as activity moving between thought and action, mind and hand. Design is seen as an interactive process driven by the development of the idea, with initial hazy conceptions developing through a range of sub-processes, which are not prescribed in advance but are instead led by or defined by the task and the idea itself – finding out new information, making decisions, articulating the form of the idea and so on.

Task 8.4 Designerly Enquiry

It is important to introduce the concept of doing research in design, to explain what it is, and why it is important in design. Within design, research is more than gathering information and inspiration, it involves people, and it is action oriented.

Here are some suggested methods of research:

- *Observation and field research* involves studying people, objects or environments. Observations are carried out 'in the wild' that is in a natural context. Data is captured in the form of handwritten notes, sketches and where possible photographs or video.
- Interviews involve collecting data from people who have knowledge or experience related to the brief. Before carrying out this research, a list of questions are formed to structure the conversation. Students should be encouraged to listen actively and to ask new questions if they arise. Data is captured in the form of hand-written notes and where possible, audio recording.
- Surveys are another way of collecting data from people related to the design brief. Surveys can be carried out in person or they can be distributed online. Data is captured in the form of responses to the questions.
- *Desk-based research* involves reviewing research, literature, videos of talks, podcasts and existing solutions related to the brief. This form of research enables the learner to gain an understanding of what is known and unknown. Typically, research is carried out online and in the library.
- *Bodystorming* involves physically experiencing or acting out a situation in order to gain empathy and a deeper understanding of the situation. Data is captured in the form of photographs, video and hand-written notes.
- Prototyping and testing involves creating and testing early prototypes in order to gather feedback and iterate upon the design, where necessary. Data is captured from testing in the form of handwritten notes or audio/video recordings.

As learners conduct their research, you should provide opportunities for them to share and make sense of it as they proceed. By encouraging them to reflect on their work they can be supported to understand the value and impact of their research and identify areas for improvement.

Holistic engagement with the unique qualities of every distinct situation is at the heart of good design practice. As a teacher, you provide a scaffolding and structure within which an issue is presented, unpacked and addressed. The nature of the issue, situation or problem can range from an environmental situation (e.g. how best can we arrange the furniture in this room to accommodate two disabled people and a baby) to a product design (a food dispenser for a pet who can only eat certain foods) to a social problem (how might this school be reshaped to allow for students of different religious beliefs and none, to feel equally valued).

Task 8.5 Sensemaking

Sensemaking is an important aspect of designing. Skills of analysis and synthesis are developed and these provide the students with a clear understanding of their design challenge. Sensemaking involves more than just summarising the research, it involves organising, analysing and interpreting it in order to generate insights.

The following techniques can be used:

- *Organising data* involves gathering and sorting all data gathered from various forms of research. Data can take the form of notes, sketches, photos, video and audio recording.
- *Analysis* involves unpacking and breaking apart data to extract key quotes, surprising findings and other relevant information. When working in groups, story sharing is an effective way of doing this. Learners take it in turns to share their research while their peers capture notes on post-it notes which are put on a vertical surface. Photos, observation sketches and other imagery should also be shared.
- *Synthesis* involves moving around and grouping the pieces of information to identify common themes and patterns. Once groupings have emerged, they should be labelled, identifying themes.
- *Framing insights* involves creating clear and actionable statements which capture the key insights to guide idea generation. An insight, something surprising or remarkable that has been discovered through analysing research, is often the deeper meaning attached to the finding. Ask the students to discuss comments or findings that are surprising or interesting to them. The students should frame insight statements that will guide their idea generation.

GENERIC QUALITIES OF DESIGN EDUCATION

Designerly thinking develops many of those generic attributes so frequently referenced as essential in the contemporary world, often termed 21st century skills, key skills or core competences. The fostering of these skills is an essential component of developing citizenship, at local, national and global levels. Among those qualities and competences explicitly addressed by design education are autonomy, agency, confidence and collaboration.

Student *autonomy* is fostered through engagement in design by the challenge of contributing personal views and perceptions of a given situation. In the traditional mode of schooling, many students are accustomed to accept norms and procedures given to them, with no room or encouragement to question or contribute. Design requires individual students to formulate and present their own views, however incoherent and tentative.

Task 8.6 Idea Generation and Development

Idea generation is more than just coming up with random ideas, it involves thinking creatively, critically and collaboratively in order to generate a wide range of ideas in response to the insights.
You might use the following techniques:

- *Mindmapping* – a mapping of thoughts, ideas and sketches that stem from a central insight or statement.
- *Brainstorming* – rapid idea generation, done individually or collaboratively. Learners generate as many ideas as possible, both pragmatic and

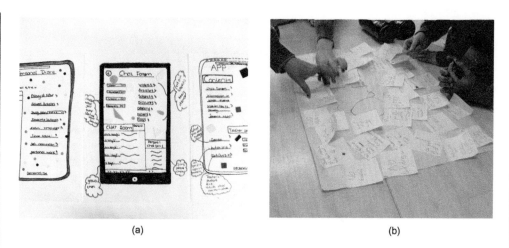

(a)   (b)

Figure 8.2 Idea generation.

speculative. They should be encouraged to be visual and to defer judgement on their own and others' ideas.

- *Sketching* – a distinctive form of drawing which is rough and quickly executed. Sketches are used to propose, explore, develop and communicate ideas.
- *Design critique or crit* involves learners communicating their ideas to their teacher and peers for constructive feedback. This provides an opportunity for evaluating the strengths and weaknesses of ideas, and identifying next steps for iteration and development (Figure 8.2).

Student *agency*, meaning the capacity to act upon an issue and to have an impact on a situation, is fostered through the design challenge or brief that drives the process. All students will experience the sense of relative success and failure that comes with any mission to innovate.

Student *confidence* in expressing their views and in contributing to solutions is constantly supported through the design process. This applies as much to the shy and reticent young person as it does to the voluble and extrovert pupil.

Collaboration is inherent to designing. Working in groups, young people learn how to listen, how to negotiate and how to influence the process. They also learn to respect the views of others and to appreciate the different strengths and attributes that everybody brings to the group.

Underpinning all these 'soft skills' is the core value of *empathy*, the capacity to understand and relate to how another person feels and thinks.

Task 8.7 Focus on the Needs of the Users

Good design is inclusive and equitable, placing the needs of the user and society to the fore. Students must try to understand and empathise with the challenges faced by the user or society. To support students to explore the diversity of needs, students can create *Personas* and *Empathy Maps*.

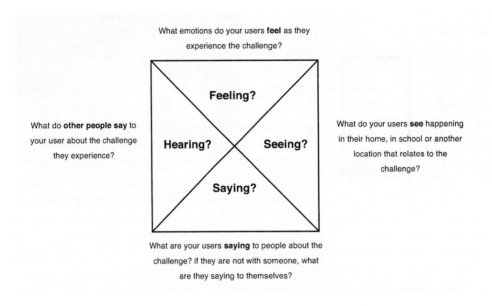

What emotions do your users **feel** as they experience the challenge?

What do **other people say** to your user about the challenge they experience?

Feeling?

Hearing?   **Seeing?**

Saying?

What do your users **see** happening in their home, in school or another location that relates to the challenge?

What are your users **saying** to people about the challenge? if they are not with someone, what are they saying to themselves?

Figure 8.3 Focus on the needs of users – Persona, empathy map.

- A *Persona* is an archetype of the user which is created using research. In creating a *Persona* students might decide on a fictitious name, age profile, demographic and employment and lifestyle status.
- An *Empathy Map* might explore what their *Persona* sees and feels when they engage with the problem and what others around them feel and say when they see the *Persona* experiencing these challenges.

Both strategies can be repeated and refined as more research is discovered and both strategies help students to relate and connect to the problem, motivating them to progress through the design process to a solution (Figure 8.3).

The ambiguity and risk of Art and Design education, with its open-ended and imprecise assessment criteria, has never inspired the confidence and certainty that policy-makers, funders, parents, teachers and pupils have sought. Now, however, these qualities which are at the heart of creativity are increasingly appreciated by educationists and policy-makers as essential to constructive learning (Biesta, 2016; OECD, 2019). It is significant that one of the most powerful instruments of international education comparison and measurement – the Programme for International Student Assessment (PISA) – is now addressing the challenge of how to assess creativity as an outcome of education. The PISA programme consists of tests carried out with 15-year olds across a range of participating countries. Up to now, the tests have focused on reading, maths and science. The resulting league tables of national performance are often cited as points of comparison between the quality of different countries' education systems.

In 2024, for the first time, PISA includes tests for Creative Thinking. For PISA, Creative Thinking means 'the competence to engage productively in the generation, evaluation and improvement of ideas that can result in original and effective solutions, advances in knowledge and impactful expressions of imagination' (OECD, 2022). The PISA creative thinking assessment is focused on two broad thematic content areas:

- Creative expression involves communicating one's inner world to others. This thematic content area is further divided into the domains of 'written expression' and 'visual expression'.
- Knowledge creation and creative problem solving is related to the investigation of open questions or wicked problems. This thematic content area incorporates scientific problem solving and social problem solving (OECD, 2022).

Clearly, the PISA Creative Thinking model closely resembles the designerly thinking model presented in this chapter, especially in problem solving in both scientific and social issues.

Task 8.8 Learning through Making

While making might be considered as the final stage within a design project, it is in fact a key feature in moving an idea from initial conception to final outcome. Alongside sketching, storyboards and diagrams, students should be encouraged to think through their ideas by making.

Students can work with readily available materials and tools such as paper, cardboard, lollipop sticks, pipe cleaners, plasticine, modelling foam, velcro, cable ties, string, rubber bands, wooden dowel, tape, glue, scissors and scalpels.

Some examples of prototyping:

- *Paper* is used to mock-up screen-based ideas. Students can create and sketch elements of an interface on pieces of paper, post-it notes or card.
- *Physical modelling* is done with card, lollipop sticks, pipe cleaners, plasticine or any basic materials that will allow the students to create a 3D representation of their idea.
- *Video* can be used to demonstrate a form of technology that is not possible to physically build.
- *Story-boarding* can be used to model ideas that are intangible, for example an experience or a system. A series of sketches can be used to tell the story of how something would work (Figure 8.4).

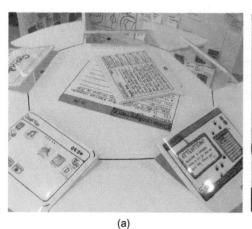

(a)   (b)

Figure 8.4 Learning through making.

SUMMARY

Designerly thinking is a powerful platform for fostering creativity and critical awareness. As a teacher of Art and Design you are in a unique position to utilise this approach to teaching and learning. By increasing the role of design education in your teaching programme, you can augment the fine art dimension of your course by providing your students with a rich and rewarding experience that extends from problem identification and analysis through collaborative engagement to provisional solution. A strong design component in your teaching promotes Art and Design education in speaking directly to the educational priorities of the contemporary world.

This chapter has suggested ways you can cultivate designerly thinking in your Art and Design teaching. By doing so, you can improve the quality of your students' experience in Art and Design, prepare them for the wicked problems of life in the 21st century and contribute to their wider education as global citizens in an unpredictable world.

NOTE

1. The term 'design thinking' is often used but recent critical debate has proposed 'designerly thinking' as a more appropriate term, involving a conscious, reflective methodology of engagement with the specifics of every situation rather than the crude and pragmatic imposition of a poorly-understood model upon other conventional practices (see Laursen and Haase, 2019).

RESOURCES

The Design Council's ten step guide to running a design workshop in secondary schools. https://www.designcouncil.org.uk/our-work/skills-learning/resources/ten-step-guide-running-design-workshop-secondary-schools/

Design for Change (DFC) offers a framework for implementing design projects within schools.

https://dfcworld.org/SITE/Toolkit

The *Design and Technology Association* (DATA) provides a range of teaching and learning support for design at second level. https://www.data.org.uk/

Fixperts for Schools is a flexible, free design learning programme for use within secondary schools. https://fixperts.org/register/startersecondaryschools/

The *World's Largest Lesson* is a bank of resources developed to promote the use of the Sustainable Development Goals (SDGs) in education. These are useful for framing a design project. https://worldslargestlesson.globalgoals.org/

BIBLIOGRAPHY

Biesta, G. (2016) *The Beautiful Risk of Education*. Routledge: New York/Oxford.

Buchanan, R. (1992) 'Wicked problems in design thinking', *Design Issues*, 17(4), pp. 3–23.

Cross, N. (2001) 'Designerly ways of knowing: Design discipline versus design science', *Design Issues*, 17(3), pp. 49–55.

Granville, G. (2019) Design in the secondary curriculum, in R. Hickman, J. Baldacchino, K. Freedman, E. Hall and N. Meager (eds.) *The International Encyclopedia of Art and Design Education*. Wiley: New Jersey. https://doi.org/10.1002/9781118978061.ead104

Hoffman Davis, J. (2008) *Why Our Schools Need the Arts.* Teachers College Press: New York.

James, S.J., Houston, A., Newton, L., Daniels, S., Morgan, N., Coho, W., Ruck, A., and Lucas, B. (2019) *Durham Commission on Creativity and Education,* Project Report. Arts Council UK.

Kimbell, R., and Stables, K. (2008) *Researching Design Learning: Issues and Findings from Two Decades of Research and Development.* Springer Netherlands: Dordecht.

Laursen, L., and Møller Haase, L. (2019) 'The shortcomings of design thinking when compared to designerly thinking', *The Design Journal,* 22(6), pp. 813–832.

Murray-Tiedge, D. (2015) Does design belong in visual arts education?, in S. Schonmann (ed.) *International Yearbook for Research in Arts Education,* Vol. 3. Waxmann Verlag: Munster and New York, pp. 196–202.

OECD. (2019) *Fostering Students' Creativity and Critical Thinking.* OECD: Paris.

OECD. (2022) *PISA 2022 Creative Thinking.* OECD: Paris. www.oecd.org

Papanek, V. (1971) *Design for the Real World.* Van Nostrand: New York.

Robinson, K. (2011) *Out of Our Minds: Learning to Be Creative.* Capstone: Chichester.

Robinson, K., and Aronica, L. (2015) *Creative Schools: The Grassroots Revolution That's Transforming Education.* Viking: New York.

Chapter 9   Adventurous Teaching-Learning with Assessment

Bayley Morris

INTRODUCTION

Adventurous teaching-learning thinks through and beyond 'school art' practices (Downing, 2005), orthodox curriculums, prescriptive methods, skills-based activity, familiar routines (Jeffers & Parth, 1996) learning outcomes and mastery, and the close relationship of these to assessment. It advocates instead for wriggle room, open-endedness, immanence, and surprise in teaching-learning. This is experienced by both 'teacher' and 'learner', as subjects that are attentive to and emerge through human and non-human (material) entanglements. Deep learning can be enabled for the creative and cultural producers of the future. This chapter leaps off Atkinson's (2018) disobedient and pedagogical adventures and applies this thinking directly to planning and assessment procedures in the AC&D classroom. The question of how to assess novel teaching-learning processes is addressed, as are the tensions in doing so. Approaches that can venture with adventure will be offered to you as will the invitation to w(o/a)nder.

OBJECTIVES:

By the end of this chapter, you should be able to:

- Puzzle out adventurous teaching-learning.
- Advocate as to how and why it matters.
- Expand curricula planning, imbuing it with adventurous potential.
- Identify some, and further conceive of approaches to assessment that can venture with adventure.

PUZZLING OUT ADVENTUROUS TEACHING-LEARNING

Adventure is associated with daring, unusual, surprising, exciting, and serendipitous experiences and a stimulating quest that takes you elsewhere or where the unknown permeates a thrilling journey. Adventure is a slippery term, alive in its subjectivity.

DOI: 10.4324/9781003377429-12

Task 9.1 Articulating Your Own Understanding of 'Adventure'

Write about the last time you experienced an adventure or adventurous moment. Consider:

- What happened;
- Why it was adventurous;
- The choices you made;
- The role that uncertainty or surprise played;
- How you felt;
- What you discovered.

You are encouraged to venture beyond and reimagine the traditional, the known, and the expected in teaching-learning practices (Irwin & O'Donoghue, 2012: 230) and invite the new and unexpected.

Atkinson (2018) advocates for the adventure of pedagogy through and beyond art. He views art practice as disobedient to established ways of thinking, making, seeing, and being. He also associates disobedience with real learning (Atkinson, 2018), in its capacity to incite complex and uncertain adventures in questing beyond the human for the different ways in which we come to know. Inspired by the work of Buck-Morss (2013), Atkinson states that, "Real learning is conceived as a leap into a new or modified ontological state whose affects, and relations produce an expansion of acting and thinking" (2018: 2). It embraces the unknown and the suddenly possible and educes thinking-being-doing otherwise. Deep knowing does not centre on accumulating bodies of knowledge or skills alone as encouraged by traditional instrumentalist pedagogic approaches. Atkinson suggests that we move through what pupils *should learn* and consider *how* they learn. Teachers-learners should thus be care-full to support each *how* of every pupil. This is an invitation to look out and feel for surprising and serendipitous encounters in which the suddenly possible expands and excites our notions of what teaching and learning can be.

Atkinson (2018) stresses that this is an experimental process, open to creative exploration in which we need to remain curiously optimistic that positives will emerge from different lines of becoming even though the outcomes are unclear.

> Real learning in the sense of experimentation has no prescriptive force, it is restless, disobedient and awaits subjects-yet-to arrive. Real learning is a deterritorialization, a disobedient force opening up potentials for new or modified ways of doing, making, seeing, thinking, feeling; a potential to generate new peoples.
>
> (Atkinson, 2018: 60)

Secondary AC&D is the ideal subject for such disobedience as art practice demands an exploration of ideas and experimentation with processes, media, materials, and techniques. It also has the capacity to challenge and move us. Deep knowings are cognitive, affective, and tacit. There is much scope for adventurous teaching-learning, particularly at KS3 where curriculum content is often highly prescribed, sequential, and objective-based, with experimentation safely ring-fenced in favour of measurable approaches. This can lead to superficiality and shallow understandings (Hickman, 2010: 14).

WHY ADVENTUROUS TEACHING-LEARNING MATTERS

Wild (2011: 423) summarises Downing's (2005) observations as 'school art orthodoxy' in which AC&D education is didactic, with too great an emphasis on formalism at the expense of content, too narrow a selection of artists studied through pastiche. Addison and Burgess (2003) refer to 'perceptualist orthodoxy' in the Secondary AC&D curriculum in which the two-dimensional picture and formalist techniques are privileged. Individual progress is emphasised over collaborative or relational activity, and this runs through from KS3 to KS5. However, these orthodox symptoms are most keenly felt at KS3, and this is also the stage of study in which pupils' ideas and values on our subject are especially shaped. Curriculum content is largely technical and grounded in building competency to demonstrate the visual elements and principles. There are limited opportunities to explore issues through, with, as art, although broader opportunities emerge at KS4 (Downing, 2005). The prevalence of painting and drawing, artistic references from the early 20th century, and male, European artists are highly perceptible (Addison & Burgess, 2003; Downing, 2005; Hickman, 2010).

When focusing largely on the 20th century modernist painters, skills, techniques, modelling, representation, accuracy, and even the colour wheel become linchpins for content. These have discernible histories and uses but have become pervasive phenomena (Addison & Burgess, 2003). Despite having rich and varied disciplinary biographies and inspirations, we may uncritically adopt such linchpins as if they were *shoulds* set in stone. When we see others employing these methods, we believe them to be prerequisites of effective AC&D education. This perpetuates transmission models of teaching, particularly at KS3 in which pupils are often teacher-led and dependent and have limited opportunities for autonomy (Addison & Burgess, 2007).

There are more opportunities for teacher agency than we might think or observe. As artists, designers, and makers, we recognise the not-known dimensions of our practice, the moments that take us beyond. We also understand the enthusing breadth of AC&D in concepts, creativity, processes, and application and how this differs over time and periods. We owe it to our pupils and the future advancement of AC&D education to provide relevant openings for adventure and encounters with the not-yet-known.

VENTURING WITH ADVENTURE

Task 9.2 Paired Activity: Implementing Adventurous Learning

In pairs, respond to the following questions:

- In what ways might we create these openings for adventure?
- How can we put these ideas to work?

Task 9.3 Group Activity: Creating a Krauss Teaching-Learning Activity

In small groups, co-create a teaching-learning activity inspired by Annette Krauss' 'Hidden Curriculum' project (2012). Experiment together to trial and error participatory and performative modes in and outside the space of the AC&D classroom.

To venture beyond the expected, consider how to incorporate neglected areas of AC&D into the curriculum. This may include but is not limited to contemporary practices such as animation, socially engaged art, performance art, installation, and video. Such approaches will likely support attainment for pupils who dislike or lack confidence in skill-based 2D activities. Lack of space, resources, and IT equipment may inhibit these choices. And yet we can improve access to and engagement with contemporary art through simple means, be it creating animations on PowerPoint or by tasking pupils to move classroom furniture to make room for performances.

Decide with care as to what pupils will encounter, how it may be experienced, to what context it applies and critically consider its value in *why* it should be incorporated into the curriculum. Challenge yourself in putting adventurous ideas to work at KS3. Openings for collaboration and relationality can be embedded which move away from prevalent individualism. Explore and think through the work of a broad range of artists with your pupils, addressing meanings, concepts, intentions, and applications as well as processes. Deep learning can be achieved when historical and cultural connections are made to artists and pupils might even determine the artists, makers, designers, and architects chosen. As teachers-learners we can foster intrinsic motivation, interest, and independence by trusting students to make choices. Bounding pupil choice to artists exhibiting today can narrow this and move inspiration away from basic image banks like Pinterest.

Grant (2020) puts forward ideas for preferable futures and suggests that secondary AC&D education might flourish through a newfound association with societal needs and issues. This will likely challenge 'thought to think' (Atkinson, 2018: 7) and may introduce new connections and exciting destabilisations that you cannot preconceive. Teaching-learning becomes issue-based and conceptually driven as opposed to skill-based. This does not have to be an either/or in terms of learning catalysts. Knowledges and practices can be hosted and shared rather than hoarded (Wenger et al., 2002).

Atkinson (2018) insists that it is a pedagogical imperative to initiate learning encounters which allow learners to be disobedient to invent their own ways of learning. We can relax prescription and work attentively to validate the matterings of pupils. With greater autonomy, pupils may take different learning routes and arrive at different destinations (Mulholland, 2019). Learning becomes non-linear, distributed, and differentiated. It can be awkward and daunting to allow adventure and invite pupil choice and this can develop over time. Some classes may require greater guidance and scaffolding than others. Nonetheless, a speculative and experimental approach to planning-teaching-learning can be embraced, as can the desire to find wriggle room amongst the orthodoxies. Purposefully creating openings for adventurous ways of thinking-being-doing in AC&D can expand pupil experiences and increase the relevancy of learning for pupils. After all, who is the curriculum for if not them?

AN ADVENTUROUS CURRICULUM

The National Curriculum for Art and Design for Key Stages 1-3 (Department for Education, 2014) is slim in content and limited in ambition and depth (Atkinson, 2018; Payne & Hall, 2018). This guidance is also non-statutory in the UK for academy schools which are publicly funded but managed independently from local authorities. As teachers-learners there is much room to exercise creativity and welcome adventure within our schemes of work and lesson plans. This may incite transformation, but not always. Deleuze and Guattari (2004) put forward the notion of 'lines of flight' for when difference and unpredictability is encountered.

Task 9.4 Individual Activity: Adapting KS3 Planning for the Principles of Adventurous Learning

Review and adapt a current KS3 lesson plan/scheme of work:

- How is deep knowing prompted? Does the lesson plan/scheme of work go beyond opinions on the works of artists and skills-based activity?
- Why does this content matter? Think beyond art here.
- What room is there for adventure and/or student personalisation?
- In what ways do your lesson objectives close or open opportunities for adventurous learning?
- What lines of flight might emerge?

Gude's thinking (in Addison & Burgess, 2013) is presented in Box 9.1 to support you in crafting adventurous plans.

BOX 9.1

- Playing – as pleasurable investigation and as a means to connect deeply personal, unarticulated, idiosyncratic aspects of one's being;
- Forming Self – using art to understand the self as a constructed, complex, and evolving entity;
- Investigating Community Themes – identifying and inquiring into the problems and potentials of particular times and places;
- Encountering Others – understanding and being ourselves re-shaped and transformed through encounters with other ways of conceiving the world;
- Attentive Living – in the natural and human-constructed environment;
- Empowered Experiencing and Empowered Making – understanding and enacting the many meaning-making strategies of artists and other cultural workers;
- Deconstructing Culture – using an array of artistic and theoretical tools to perceive and analyse the cultural construction of meanings;
- Reconstructing Social Spaces – forming and participating in physical, virtual, and discursive spaces for social interaction;
- Not knowing – accepting the open-endedness of complex thinking, not enforcing premature closure because of anxiety when experiencing the uncertainty, liminity, and fluidity of contemporary life.

(Gude in Addison & Burgess, 2013, pp. 40–41. Reproduced with permission of the Licensor through PLSclear)

Now see Box 9.2 for an example of a lesson in which adventurous teaching-learning is in play. This will help you to envisage how the ideas and principles in this chapter can be put into context.

BOX 9.2
A lesson example

1. Identify a diverse range of artists who explore contemporary societal issues or concerns in their practice. Do this mindfully in choosing from the East as well as the West and in choosing artists from different specialisms, working with different techniques, materials, and objects, or even performatively. Select some key examples to show your pupils.
2. Allow pupils to play art detectives and encourage them to question and think on the works. This can be done as an individual or collaborative exercise. Provide some differentiated questions to scaffold this process.
3. Through their feedback, help them to question and identify how and why these artists have responded to contemporary concerns. This can also support a discussion on the force of art and why it matters.
4. Split pupils into small groups and provide collections of objects/materials/textures. Ask them to create an artwork that explores a problem/issue. Throw in an adventurous and open-ended prompt such as 'the artwork must move'. This might be excitingly interpreted in different ways. Pupils can use their bodies (but not their voices) as well as the objects provided. They need to carefully consider the agency of the objects that they are working with, listening to what they say when juxtaposed with something else or placed in different positions. Communicate the time available and the fact that they will be asked to show/perform the work.
5. Now request that the groups show/perform the works one by one. Pupils can discuss one another's performances, perhaps even guessing the problem/concern in play before this gets revealed. Students can be prompted to consider how their ideas matter, how their objects perform, the struggles that they encountered, and what they might do differently. This may provoke conversation on art's role to communicate, or not.
6. Ask the groups to come up with the objectives for this lesson.
7. Bonus task: One object and one pupil move to a different group. Consider how you might best manage this. Sticking with the original problem or concern of the group, the 'moving' work must be reimagined and performed anew. Transformation, creativity, problem solving, and open-endedness is in play. The work is always in process. The groups can then be asked to analyse, compare, and contrast their two performances, discussing how they might define the success criteria and how they consider to what degree their work meets it. The success criterion put forward by students may inform the summative assessment criterion by which you mark a range of works in this scheme.

It is challenging to account for the not-yet-known in frameworks that frequently require the teacher to foreground what will be taught, when and how. Atkinson (2018) suggests that we relax prescriptive parameters and respond in the moment with pupils when differences in learning processes occur. A pedagogy *without criteria*. How then should curriculum plans be crafted?

Planning is a process through which to explore intent, experimentation, and reinvention. Be innovative with the content. Gaps may purposefully be included in lessons to invite the unknown and embrace divergence. Instead of a gap, you could write an activity as multiple choice. You could make the choice in the moment of delivery or put the options to pupils for a vote. You could give time to addressing a broad and enticing question which opens a fluid space of debate. Different material stations could be set up in a lesson and you could choreograph pupils' movement between these. You could allow for open-endedness by questioning what happens when... or what if... with pupils. Final outcomes of a project need not be the same with pupils taking ownership for planning these as per their individual learning pathways. Learning objectives could be broad to account for expansions in understanding or divergent surprises, or they might be personalised by pupils.

Task 9.5 Adapting KS3 Planning for Adventurous Learning in Detail

Choose one of your KS3 schemes of work. Delete the plans for the lessons towards the end of this scheme of work, usually dedicated to the production of a final piece. Rework this section of the scheme of work to make room for one/ some or all the following:

- Open-endedness
- Individual mattering
- Collaboration
- Playfulness
- Performativity
- An artist red herring
- A rogue material
- An opening to the next scheme of work
- Different spaces

What does your plan look like now? How do you feel about this? If you could design a whole scheme of work adventurously, what would you do?

MATERIAL ENTANGLEMENTS

Another way to imbue curriculum planning with adventurous potential is to value material entanglements. This is a move away from skills, aesthetics, and representation.

In AC&D education, materials/things/objects are traditionally seen as passive, ready to be formed by the trained hand of the maker (Ingold, 2013: 21) to represent and/or convey meaning. An adventurous and materialist approach sees the presence and being of things. Bennett (2010) stresses that things have agency, 'thing-power'. This invites us to think differently about how and why we interact with materials. We might think through them and with them, whilst also attuning to what they have to say.

It is important to note that some art practices do not have nor produce art objects. And yet these practices also reframe the relationship between the artist and the work and demand a rethinking of the meaning of mastery.

Barrett and Bolt (2012) argue that 'making' is a 'co-collaboration' in which matter as much as the human has responsibility for the emergence of art. This is an affective, relational, and multi-sensory way of being with things. This is experienced by both 'teacher' and 'learner', as subjects that are attentive to and emerge through human and non-human (material) entanglements.

Task 9.6 Planning through Material

Play and experiment with materials/objects. Allow process and discovery to lead you rather than intent and design.

- What are these things saying to you?
- What do they tempt you to do?
- What might it be like to be these things?
- What have they taught you?

You are invited to further w(o/a)nder with this. Consider how 'thing-power' supports sustainability and how it might inform and be experienced in teaching-learning. How might modelling be impacted for example?

TEACHER-LEARNER

Throughout this chapter, the term *teacher-learner* is used to describe us as AC&D educators. When learning is distributed between teacher and pupils and teacher-pupils-things, the educator is a learner, continually being taught by other agents in the classroom.

This is rooted in Freire's (1996) student-teacher-student-teacher continuum in which the teacher teaches but is also taught by their students. This occurs through dialogue, and they share responsibility for cultivating an environment in which all grow. Difference must be embraced as part of the learning process in jointly moving away from knowns.

In acknowledging the agency of things/materials and how learning happens through and beyond dialogue, educators become "relational elements or gears in a more widely distributed pedagogical machine" (Rousell & Fell, 2018: 17). When embracing adventurous pedagogical strategies as teachers-learners, we are subjects-yet-to-come (Atkinson, 2018) whereby our understanding of AC&D is always open to expansion.

ASSESSMENT

Summative assessment is the assessment *of* learning, occurring typically at the end of a unit of work in looking at past achievements/outcomes. Summative assessment frameworks that foreground skill-based activities are more prevalent in the Secondary AC&D classroom than other forms as technical ability is easier to quantify.

Atkinson (2018) acknowledges a 'contrast of values' between disobedient pedagogies and many current modes of summative assessment and the tensions between adventure and evaluation are acknowledged in this chapter. How might a teacher-learner pre-empt the success criteria for a task that is open to immanence and the unknown? By what criterion can adventurous practices be graded?

It is important to stress that summative assessment of adventurous learning is possible, and it is a creative challenge to design success criterion that complements adventure and complexity. You must trust in your own judgement to assess learning which falls outside 'the black box' (Black & William, 1998) of orthodoxies and fixed outputs. You are encouraged to "think critically about which approaches to assessment, learning and therefore Assessment *for* Learning, really satisfy... personal, professional, long-term and holistic purposes for young people's [AC&D] education" (Hargreaves, 2005: 19). This is an empowering and ongoing opportunity to innovate high quality subject-specific assessment practices.

> **Task 9.7 Creating Your Own Success Criteria**
>
> Using the example in Box 9.2, write your own summative success criteria to assess individual progress.
> Consider:
>
> - What qualities/behaviours/skills to look out for;
> - How these may be evidenced.

Assessment *for* learning or formative assessment is the ongoing "process of seeking and interpreting evidence for use by learners and their teachers to decide where the learners are in their learning, where they need to go and how best to get there" (Assessment Reform Group, 2002: 2). It is carried out formally and informally with and for pupils during the learning process to aid progress, offer support, address misunderstandings, and modify teaching content. This is critical when relaxing prescription and responding to individual mattering.

Effective and meaningful assessment in AC&D is "based on dialogue between teachers and students during lessons, together with detailed, constructive marking that... [makes] pupils reflect independently on their own work" (Ofsted, 2008–2011: 43). A balance of formative and summative assessment is essential, as is the notion of assessment as dialogue (Ash, Schofield & Steers in Addison & Burgess, 2007). We may unconsciously inhibit pupil agency, and so it is important to evoke thoughtful reflection and allow pupils to 'think out their own answers' and express their ideas (Black & William, 1998: 10). You may even wish to ask beguiling questions or make unorthodox suggestions to open new doors in their thinking:

> The question is not: is it true? But: does it work? What new thoughts does it make possible to think? What new emotions does it make it possible to feel? What new sensations and perceptions does it open to the body?
> (Massumi in Deleuze & Guattari, 2004, pp. xv–xvi)

GCSE criterion can support you with KS3 assessment, as can the NSEAD Framework for Progression, planning for Learning, Assessment, Recording and Reporting (2014). The language and criteria from this framework have been utilised in Box 9.3. Question stems are presented in the context of the lesson example in Box 9.2. These stems can aid pupil self-assessment formatively but can also be used to inform summative assessment data.

BOX 9.3
A lesson example

Generating Ideas	What idea did you scrap and why?
	What changed from performance 1 to performance 2 and why?
	How did you and your group arrange and organise the objects to present a moving and meaningful response?
Making	How have the objects guided you? What did they say and how do they feel now?
	How do your performances capture or explore a problem or concern?
	What were the ideas behind…?
Evaluating	Which performance did you consider to be the most successful and why?
	How did your performances speak to your original intentions?
	In what ways might this work be reimagined again and what might it say next time?
Knowledge	If you had to compare this work to one of the artists, which one would it be and why?
	What was your favourite object to work with and how did this inform the performance?
	Why might artists explore societal issues in their work?

Some starting points for thinking assessment at KS3 with adventurous teaching-learning include:

- Assessing background, context, ideas, and thoughts behind a work or works and the articulation of this. How do the intentions marry with the articulation? This enables consideration of meaning and evaluation of conceptual depth.
- Creative thinking might be assessed, and this can be evidenced in outcome, pupil evaluations, or behaviours demonstrated in both individual and collaborative activities.
- Process is important, as well as or instead of the result in contemporary art. This may demand that assessment occurs holistically in a project of articulations demonstrated and behaviours witnessed. Summative assessment therefore happens over time.
- Asking colleagues in the Drama department how they assess performance works and observing this practice. This will be especially helpful in assessing performance art and creative behaviours.
- Facilitate open dialogue with pupils about what they consider to be the success criterion. This can work well in peer assessment exercises.

- You might look for how the unknown entered the learning process and how this was handled with autonomy.
- Skills are not absent from adventurous learning. What skills might you assess?
- Emphasis and context are important. that is, when assessing a collaborative installation piece but grading individuals you can focus on how well they worked in their team, how well they used the space, how well the piece articulates their intentions or conveys meaning, how they overcame problems, how innovative and appropriate their choice of materials/things were, how they engaged with the work of artists, etc.

These starting points invite critique on the duality of summative/formative assessment or of learning/for learning. In adventurous teaching-learning, they begin to collapse into one another as practices that are no longer fixed or opposite. To value collaboration, process, and open-endedness, formative practices and feedback may be used as summative data. Deep knowing is co-constructed, and adventurous assessment practices become fluid (Hargreaves, 2005). This can be taken further when we see materials/objects/things as agential. Assessment is viewed as human and non-human dialogue in which we remain attentive to how matter has spoken.

Whole school assessment measures will only go so far; the conversation must be stretched to accommodate exciting subject specific openings and shaped for individual learners.

SUMMARY AND AN INVITATION TO W(O/A)NDER

Within this chapter, we have puzzled out adventurous teaching-learning and explored how and why it matters. You now understand how these practices depart from 'school art' orthodoxies and with this understanding, you can advocate instead for wriggle room and open-endedness in teaching-learning. Established knowledge and practice frameworks are critiqued but not entirely dismissed as openings for difference are invited, allowing for transcendence in well-known ways of being, thinking, and doing.

This chapter helps to bridge the gap between current school art practices and Atkinson's (2018) disobedience. This middle ground is ripe with tension, but it can be w(o/a)ndered for the benefit of your pupils. It is a generative space of experimental and creative potential. This chapter also presents conjectural approaches to assessment which you can adapt to specific contexts, experiment with, and extend. Adventurous teaching-learning is a speculative and reflective practice which must be iteratively practised.

You have had a go at expanding your curricula planning, imbuing it with adventurous potential and have received some recommendations regarding curriculum content. Approaches to assessment have also been conceived in the context of an adventurous KS3 lesson.

Deep learning can be facilitated for autonomous, imaginative, and cultural producers of the future who are sensitively attuned to the more than human. To empower cultural producers as teachers-learners, you must become producers yourselves, acting adventurously as 'agents of change' (Addison & Burgess, 2003: 163) with the appetite to expand AC&D education.

RESOURCES

Addison, N. & Burgess, L. (2003) *Issues in art and design teaching*. London: Routledge Falmer.

Addison, N. & Burgess, L. (2013) *Debates in art and design education*. Abingdon, Oxon: Routledge.

Atkinson, D. (2018) *Art, disobedience, and ethics: The adventure of pedagogy*. Palgrave Macmillan.

NSEAD Curriculum Writing Group. (2014) The National Curriculum for Art and Design Guidance: Secondary KS3-4. A Framework for Progression, planning for Learning, Assessment, Recording and Reporting. https://www.nsead.org/files/ea96b489c63e0f01f79f4db5d1c8bc19.pdf

BIBLIOGRAPHY

Addison, N. & Burgess, L. (2003) *Issues in art and design teaching*. London: Routledge Falmer.

Addison, N. & Burgess, L. (2007) *Learning to teach art and design in the secondary school: A companion to school experience*. Florence: Taylor & Francis Group.

Addison, N. & Burgess, L. (2013) *Debates in art and design education*. Abingdon, Oxon: Routledge.

Assessment Reform Group. (2002) *Assessment for learning: 10 principles*. London: Assessment Reform Group.

Atkinson, D. (2008) Pedagogy against the state. *The International Journal of Art & Design Education*, 27(3), 226–240.

Atkinson, D. (2018) *Art, disobedience, and ethics: The adventure of pedagogy*. Cham: Palgrave Macmillan.

Bennett, J. (2010) *Vibrant matter a political ecology of things*. Durham: Duke University Press.

Black, P. & William, D. (1998) *Inside the black box*. London: King's College.

Barrett, E. & Bolt, B. (2012) *Carnal knowledge: Towards a 'new materialism' through the arts*. London: I.B. Tauris.

Buck-Morss, S. (2013) A commonist ethics. In S. Zizek (Ed.), *The idea of communism* 2 (pp. 57–75). London/New York: Verso.

Deleuze, G. & Guattari, F. (2004) *A thousand plateaus: Capitalism and schizophrenia* (Trans. B. Massumi). London: Continuum.

Department for Education. (2014) The national curriculum in England: Key Stages 3 and 4 framework document. Available at: https://www.gov.uk/government/publications/national-curriculum-in-england-secondary-curriculum (Accessed: 1st March 2022).

Downing, D. (2005) School art – What's in it? *The International Journal of Art & Design Education*, 24(3), 269–276.

Freire, P. (1996) *Pedagogy of the oppressed*. 20th anniversary ed. London: Penguin.

Grant, W. (2020) Liberal ideals, postmodern practice: A working paradox for the future of secondary school art education in England? *The International Journal of Art & Design Education*, 39(1), 56–68.

Hargreaves, E. (2005) Assessment for learning? Thinking outside the (black) box. *Cambridge Journal of Education*, 35(2), 213–224.

Hickman, R. (2010) *Why we make art: And why it is taught*. Bristol: Intellect Books.

Ingold, T. (2013) *Making: Anthropology, archaeology, art and architecture*. Abingdon, Oxon: Routledge.

Irwin, R. L. & O'Donoghue, D. (2012) Encountering pedagogy through relational art practices. *The International Journal of Art & Design Education*, 31(3), 221–236.

Jeffers, C. S. & Parth, P. (1996) Relating controversial contemporary art and school art: A problem-position. *National Art Education Association*, 38(1), 21–33.

Mulholland, N. (2019) *Re-imagining the art school paragogy and artistic learning.* 1st ed. Cham: Springer International Publishing.

NSEAD Curriculum Writing Group. (2014) The national curriculum for art and design guidance: Secondary KS3-4. A Framework for Progression, planning for Learning, Assessment, Recording and Reporting. https://www.nsead.org/files/ea96b489c63e0f01f79f4db5d1c8bc19.pdf

Ofsted. (2008–2011) Making a mark: Art, craft and design education. https://assets.publishing.service.gov.uk/government/uploads/system/uploads/attachment_data/file/413330/Making_a_mark_-_art_craft_and_design_education_2008-11.pdf

Payne, R. & Hall, E. (2018) The NSEAD survey report 2015–16: Political reflections from two art and design educators. *The International Journal of Art & Design Education*, 37(2), 167–176.

Rousell, D. & Fell, F. (2018) Becoming a work of art: Collaboration, materiality and posthumanism in visual arts education. *International Journal of Education Through Art*, [Online] 14(1), 91–110.

Wenger, E. et al. (2002) *Cultivating communities of practice: A guide to managing knowledge.* Boston, MA: Harvard Business Press.

Wild, C. (2011) Making creative spaces: The art and design classroom as a site of performativity. *The International Journal of Art & Design Education*, 30(3), 423–432.

Chapter 10   Photography and Pedagogy: Reflecting on Initial Teacher Education Practice with a Camera

Jo Fursman

INTRODUCTION

Photography and the camera have an important role in the research and development of education practices and pedagogy. As early as the 1870s, the use of photography to record school experience has been a unique and crucial tool in telling stories of education, reflecting on its past and influencing future policy (Chappel, Chappel and Margolis, 2011). The valuable work photographers as artist practitioners and researchers have achieved with young people and their educators in primary and secondary schools in England has enabled a critical space to develop between what is known about education, the school and pedagogy. This chapter explores some of the real experiences of those who work and study in schools and develops tasks based on the research of education, photopedagogy and photographic therapy, where the photographer (you) can employ a camera to document and explore pedagogies and new identities as you move through your teaching practice. Artists' approaches, photographers' practice and how these can be used in developing your own photography practice are explored, knowing how lens-based technologies can be another kind of teacher that can contribute to your developing pedagogy.

This chapter moves a critical eye over what lens-based practice affords initial teacher education, asking you to explore lens-based practice and the taking of photographs as a tool to investigate and reflect upon important transitions as you move through during teaching practice.

The wider decisions around what kind of educator you desire to become and how you will shape your pedagogical approaches can be examined and recorded via photography. The practice of documenting through photography can contribute to reflective practice in sketchbooks to build a collection of images telling the story of your development. The exercises, themes and practical suggestions in this chapter can be shared and adapted to schemes of work and workshops and used in school projects.

DOI: 10.4324/9781003377429-13

OBJECTIVES:

By the end of this chapter you should be able to:

- Use lens-based practices as a method of observation;
- Use photographic images to examine key transitions you move through during your Post Graduate Certificate in Education (PGCE) Art and Design practice and early career;
- Use lens-based skills including digital practices;
- Use photographic images you capture to develop your reflective practice;
- Reflect on the impact of lens-based practice in education;
- Know how photographers, artists and researchers have used lens-based practice to examine education.

PHOTOGRAPHY, PEDAGOGY AND EDUCATION

At the beginning of your initial teacher education, you will be asked to gather observational evidence which can be achieved effectively with photographs. Photographic images of student work and outcomes, exhibitions, your art skills and school projects are highly useful records of your own progress in the first stages of teaching. Photography, pedagogy and education have a beneficial and complex relationship, the camera technology can be part of your education practice as another kind of teacher enabling you to develop new pedagogies. This point in your training is important, it asks you to approach the artroom as a critical space in school. For example, an artroom can have its own identities; as a space for educating about art, but also for making, exhibition, meeting and examining. Art education pedagogies shape the artroom, documenting your first impressions at this stage can help you to establish what kinds of spaces you want to develop during your career.

THE SCHOOL PHOTOGRAPH

The camera in school is commonly used to take a school photograph. This requires young people to pose in particular ways, unintentionally producing schooled identities. According to Burke and Riberio de Castro (2007), these images make important links between school, home and family but perform the body of the school child in fixed ways. As an imaged-based research, Prosser employs in-school photography to decipher how school is structured, its high and low status relationships, critical moments and significant sequences (1999:86). Mitchel and Weber's research examines school photography as a 'phenomenon and method' (1998:175) and found it is often 'outsiders – those outside the teaching profession, notably school photographers, who construct and maintain certain images of schooling' (1998:176). Historical school photographs researched by Chappell, Chappell and Margolis (2011) demonstrate how school photographs define and bind school rituals. For pupils captured in school photographs, rituals in organising the image 'perform particular narratives which can have wider effects on constructions of values and belief about themselves in wider society' (2010:56). If going to school for pupils is only about learning, these images reproduce and confirm that. But, if school is also regarded as about becoming a *citizen* (Babad, 2009), there is more space for these kinds of images to be explored critically. Furthermore, how these images construct and reproduce the body of the teacher and teacher identity is overlooked, teachers either don't appear in the images or are absorbed into the vernacular of the school photo. This indicates how pedagogy, classroom organisation or even the teacher's role itself may play a part in helping to set up the structure of the image, but the focus remains solely on the pupil.

Negotiating the unique and dual experience of being a learner and an educator during PGCE study will prompt you to remember how you experienced your own education (Mitchel and Weber, 2009). As this will undoubtedly have some impact on how you move through the transition towards art educator, the tasks in this chapter examine what this transition can look like from beyond the normalising gaze of the school portrait genre, requiring you to interrogate your teaching practice more visibly through lens-based practice.

PHOTOGRAPHS MADE IN SCHOOL

Deciphering how images might depict the complexity of becoming and being an educator is important for your critical reflection and investigating how teachers have been depicted through lens-based practice is a useful place to begin. The photo stills reproduced in Darcey Lange's *Studies in Four Oxfordshire Schools* (1977) Figures 10.1 and 10.2 depict unique learning relationships that develop between art teachers, pupils and the artwork they produce. Lange's work demonstrates how cameras can capture pedagogic events and depict the unexpected and incidental moments and events occurring in education spaces. The images demonstrate the different ways pedagogy functions in art lessons, how art teachers use the classroom space and the function of objects in art lessons. Using photography during your teacher education focuses on the 'becoming-educator', reflecting an emerging teacher practice and the distinct relationships between educators and pupils.

Classroom Portraits (2004–2015) by Julian Germaine describes how classrooms and students can look when not asked to perform themselves as students. In Figures 10.3 and 10.4, in contrast to school portraits, some students look indifferent or bored. They stare out of the image, confronting the viewer and reflecting a more realistic experience of school for some students. In these images, the art teacher is not present, but Germaine takes the place of the teacher, reflecting the unique perspective an educator position has in the artroom.

Figure 10.1 Darcy Lange, 'Studies of Teaching in Four Oxfordshire Schools' 1977. Charles Mussett, Art Teacher, Radley College, Class Study. Courtesy the Darcy Lange Estate and Govett Brewster Art Gallery.

Figure 10.2 Darcy Lange, from 'Studies of Teaching in Four Oxfordshire Schools' 1977. Eric Spencer, art class, Cheney Upper School. Courtesy the Darcy Lange Estate and Govett Brewster Art Gallery.

Figure 10.3 Cavendish School, Eastbourne, UK. Year 7, Art, 2015. From the series Classroom Portraits 2004-2015 by Julian Germain.

Figure 10.4 Rhodesway School, Bradford, UK. Year 7, Art. 2004. From the series Classroom Portraits 2004-2015 by Julian Germain.

Figure 10.5 Assisted Self-Portrait of Natalia Tokarska from Construct (2018–2022)
by Anthony Luvera.

This part of the chapter asks you to think about how lens-based images can be achieved and developed. The tasks are designed to be explored in the university and in your training contexts. They offer a balance between exercises that can be made alone or can build towards workshops you can use with other trainees, mentors and students. The tasks reflect the different stages you will move through during your 'becoming-educator' and link to aspects of the Teachers' Standards (Department for Education, 2021) and the Core Content Framework for Initial Teacher Training (Department for Education, 2019). The tasks also connect to the aspects of 'becoming-educator', interlinking experiences you bring with you to your teacher education practice and described by Buffington, Williams, Ogier and Rouatt as 'early experiences and family, school art experiences, mentors, identity and young adult experiences' (2016:329) (Figure 10.5).

EQUIPMENT

The tasks are designed to be made with technologies available to you and can be explored by those both new to and used to using lens-based media. The tasks can be made with phone cameras, tablets or digital single lens reflex (SLR) cameras or more experimental or analogue equipment. Tripods can be useful, but cameras can also be placed carefully on stable surfaces. As you get used to handling equipment, the spontaneity of capturing an unexpected image can be just as rewarding as carefully planning and composing your intentions. To stretch its limits, the technology can be adapted and experimented with. Consider what images look like with and without using a flash, indoors with lights or outdoors in natural light. How you maximise the lighting opportunities in the places and spaces you capture images in and how you adapt to what is available to you can often lead to intriguing results and further experimentation.

ETHICS

Using lens-based equipment and making images in school or university contexts must be approached ethically. If you capture images of young people, educators and other trainee teachers, permission must be gained using informed consent using a consent letter clearly explaining what the images are for and why you are taking them. To work ethically, images you produce in these contexts should be made on, or later stored on a password-protected device and deleted when you have finished with them.

Reading safeguarding policies and communicating your intentions with your mentor will ensure you follow school guidelines when taking images. As discussed earlier, photographs are employed in education in many different ways, but you are likely to teach young people who must not be photographed in any way. In contrast, your mentor might publish images of their students and their artwork on school social media platforms. Capturing images from the back of a classroom, or from different points of view and scales can make it impossible to identify the young people in the photograph.

Task 10.1 Warm Up: Taking a Camera for a Walk

This exercise encourages you to familiarise yourself with the education environments you study and practice in. They can be made in your university or in school contexts, with a partner, group or on your own.

Use a phone camera, tablet or a digital camera, program the device so you can see the image on its screen. Hold it in comfortably in front of you and position the lens so it is parallel with the surface of the ground. Walk for five minutes and take an image every thirty steps.

Discussion

- Where do you go? What do you capture in the images? What kinds of surfaces, spaces and objects are recorded as you walk? What do the images tell you about where you are?
- How do you move and shape yourself around the school space you are in? How does the camera shape these movements?
- Repeat the task and experiment with the zoom and wide functions on the device. What happens when images are close-up or wide?
- Try out the task when you are moving between different spaces or around the artroom. How do you move through and around where you are and what you encounter?

FOCUSSED OBSERVATION

Darcy Lange's school studies and Julian Germain's school portraits can help you to reflect on what you have found during the warm-up task. Objects in the artroom and around the school help to produce narratives useful for eliciting key useful information in teacher education. Alongside gathering contextual information, the lens-based images provide insight into how art lessons and rooms are organised and managed. Use the images from the task below to share your experiences in the early stages of your teaching practice. Capture where you take up your space in the artroom as a trainee and how the teachers you work with move around and work with their students, equipment, materials, and other adults. Document materials, objects, organisation, spaces the teachers and students use, where they are and if these overlap.

Task 10.2 Using Photography for Focussed Observation

Discussion. What questions can you ask about an artroom with a photograph?
  Equipment. Digital camera or device that has a camera function.
  Activity: Capture images of the artrooms in your school placement to describe:

- How it appears from your point(s) of view as a training teacher;
- How the artroom appears from the point of view of the mentor;
- How the artroom appears from the point of view of the pupil;
- Describe the artroom through images before and after lessons, at the beginning and end of the school day;
- Use photographs to compare different artrooms or spaces art is taught in during your training practice.

Discussion: Using the images you have produced to ask; how do you know it is an artroom?

- What defines the room as an artroom? What is the artroom and the art department called? What language is used to describe it and the staff who work there?
- What are the interesting or special features it has?
- What furniture and objects make it unique in comparison to other class-rooms in the school?
- What have you included or excluded and why?
- What key issues about teaching and training do your photographs present or make visible to you?
- Using your own search for historical and contemporary examples of artrooms or school photos, how do these compare with your images in this task?

USING THE CAMERA AND THE PHOTOGRAPH IN REFLECTIVE PRACTICE

Reflection-in-action is theorised by Donald Schön (1991) as a method of reflecting deeply on the event and complexity of learning in the moment. Schön defines reflection-in-action by describing how basket-ball players or jazz musicians get a 'feel for' when playing (1991:55) and when the play is refined through 'on the spot adjustments' (ibid). In teaching practice, this 'feel for' could be experienced through ongoing reflection while you are teaching. This allows you to build upon what is effective, developing, readjusting and discarding and what is not useful in the moment of practice and described by Prentice:

As a reflective teacher you come to recognise the problematic nature of teaching Art and Design and systematically reflect upon your practice in order to improve it. In so doing you simultaneously become engaged in teaching and learning; a relationship that echoes the quality of creative activity in art, craft design.

(2000:14)

USING PHOTOGRAPHY IN REFLECTION-IN-ACTION

This problem highlighted by Prentice describes the simultaneous pull between art practitioner and educator which is sometimes difficult to describe. The unique usefulness and reproducibility of the photographic image in the role of speaking, discussion and describing was recognised earlier by Benjamin (2008), meaning that the camera function could help images 'keep pace with speech' (2008:4).

This usefulness and reproducibility give the photographic process and image its 'quickness'; an ability to use camera technology to 'examine ourselves looking back at ourselves'. Being an art educator and artist in the same moment can be captured in the process of reflection-in-action, the camera mirrors speech, giving the photographer a way to image experience. This is demonstrated in the photovoice methods of Graziano and Litton who (citing Booth and Booth, 2007) explain 'photovoice involves giving people cameras and using the pictures they take to amplify their place in and experience of the world' (2003:9).

Employing reflection-in-action to explore, your transition towards educator can be achieved by examining practices of phototherapy and community photography. Phototherapy became prominent in the 1970s as a tool in psychotherapeutic practices, (Weiser, 1993). Self-portrait photography is a key part of the phototherapeutic process, helping the image maker to identify and image the self. As a tool in documenting the self, phototherapy helps the photographer or client develop in relation to new contexts and circumstances. Impressions of the self-emerge in the image as new positions within contexts are sought. Craig also explores this as a process to help draw new perspectives on experience describing; 'Whilst the content in the image stays the same, the person does not' (2009:16).

SELF-PORTRAIT PHOTOGRAPHY

The self-portrait and community photography in England has an important role in helping people to position themselves visibly in the places and communities where they live and belong (Luvera, 2019). Demonstrated in Anthony Luvera's photography practice, what he terms 'assisted self-portraits' are achieved with people experiencing homelessness in *Frequently Asked Questions* (2014–ongoing) and *Residency* (2006–2007) (Figure 10.6). The participants direct, produce and select their own images, results move beyond self-portraiture to give the sitters new perspectives on their lives.

DOCUMENTING THE TEACHER SELF

The emergence of the teacher-self presents key revelations but also moments of uncertainty. Assisted self-portraits can capture these important moments and

Figure 10.6 Documentation of the making of Assisted Self-Portrait of Natalia Tokarska from Construct (2018–2022) by Anthony Luvera.

experiences. Teacher education can be an emotional and challenging time that with careful reflection reveals your strengths and new insights. This transition has been identified as stages of concern by Maynard and Furlong (1993) (cited by Capel, 2010) which appear and overlap as experience develops. These concerns include, 'early idealism', 'survival', 'recognising difficulties', 'hitting the plateau' and 'moving on' (1993:248) and can occur continuously as you move through different moments of experience and learning.

Taking self-portraits can help to visibly decipher the different stages you transition through during your training. As a reflective practice, it is invaluable in recognising strengths, leading to reflection and a profound understanding of development. Useful in producing images of the self, giving control to the sitter helps to retain authorship of their own image and all aspects of what the image contains (Craig, 2009).

The task below invites you to explore your developing teacher-self through an exploration of photographic self-portraits. These can be done during workshop-led practice and on teaching placements with help from a partner.

Task 10.3 Using Photography for Reflection-in-Action

Discussion: What instances in your training can you identify where you know you have been using reflection-in-action?

Self-assisted portraits. Equipment: Cameras, memory cards, tripods or a firm surface for the camera. Memory card reader. Computer and printer/photocopier.

- Decide where you want to take the images;
- Fix the camera to a tripod or place it on a firm surface;
- Find and program the shutter timer release setting on the camera. A partner can assist you in focussing the lens. Stand in front of the camera and wait for the shutter to release. Review and re-take;
- Test the portraits in different settings, with different backgrounds and positions. Consider how to take close-up images or capture your whole body;
- Upload and print thumbnails of your images to share during a discussion, referring to Maynard and Furlong's stages of *concerns*

Discussion:

- What did you talk or think about and feel when you were taking the images?
- Where did you choose to take the images and what was involved in those choices?
- Describe the backgrounds and backdrops you decided were important to include.

Write fifty words about how the images reflect on the phases and practice in the teacher training process. Develop a discussion around where you started in your training (early idealism) and where you want to move towards (moving on). Repeat this task when you begin and reach the end of different stages in your training.

BUILDING LEARNING RELATIONSHIPS USING PHOTOGRAPHY

The tasks and discussions above demonstrate how unique learning relationships can be established in your transition from trainee to qualified art educator. This section asks you to address important learning relationships between educators and pupils through photography. The relationships between educators, students, school and classroom reflect the important social experiences a young person has outside the family and home (Babad, 2009). Using the camera in this complex in-school space allows a practicing or new teacher to reflect on and develop useful and positive relationships. These beneficial relationships between young people and photographers, student and educators are described by Ewald and Lightfoot:

> Photography can create moments of authentic collaboration between teachers and students, moments when a deeper understanding of the lives of others emerge

(2001:119)

The presence of the camera can change unbalanced power relationships in the artroom and support positive dialogue and unique thinking. The camera can also be another kind of teacher, developing new pedagogies between the educator and student. Using lens-based technology in the artroom means you might need to move differently or 'become an amateur' to demonstrate how to learn skills, sharing a parallel experience of the technology and its possibilities. The 'side by side positioning of teachers' and learners' bodies could provide the opportunity for talk, and equally for silent reflection' (Kraftl, 2015:172).

Speech and silent reflection can establish equal and respectful learning relationships. Earlier in this chapter, I discussed how the camera can re-formulate the objectivity of the schooled body, how pupils appear and are heard. Forrest describes the quest for perfect photographic image as the 'doings' of the photographer (2013:105) and how photography is a 'physical business' (ibid:106). This insight into the embodied process of making photographic images sees photographers stretch, contort, crouch or laying down, meaning the camera technology and body coincide and work together. Using the camera means the bodies of the educator and schoolchild look different in the complex and unique space of the school. For Elo;

> ...image, body and thinking relate to each other in a circular way: both body and thinking make use of images, both images and bodies think, and both thinking and images involve a body.
>
> (2013:90)

The space between an image, the maker and the viewer is also key in developing positive learning relationships. Bringing the senses and photography together, the impact of the photographic image on the experiences of people of colour is examined by Tina Campt (2017). She describes how these photographs can help to examine the self differently than just seeing; 'listening to images' (2017:5) gives deeper insight into the 'forgotten histories of diasporic memory that these images transmit' (2017:6). Resonating for both educators and pupils connected to the global majority; deeply listening to pupils through their lens-based images and knowing what they communicate can be profoundly useful in knowing the multiplicity of contexts on which photographs can draw upon.

Investigations with lens-based technologies can help pupils establish themselves in the community and environment of their school. Seeing themselves in a photograph or on a digital screen becomes a different way for pupils to understand themselves as learners and where they are positioned in the unique space of school (Fursman, 2020) (Figure 10.7).

This is where the eye of the body and the eye of the lens work together to process compositions and intimate moments of reflection on the school context. Making and looking at photographs can lead to different kinds of relationships, this is demonstrated in the practice of Wendy Ewald who makes work with young people in their schools and homes and with their families. Giving the control of the camera and photographic images to the young people she works with:

> they learn to look closely at visual images and think more consciously about what they see, about the various elements that go into making a photograph, about how images can communicate an idea.
>
> (Ewald, 2001:17)

Figure 10.7 Possible School (2017). Inside Looking Outside; students taking photos of students taking photos. Joanna Fursman.

Figure 10.8 Wendy working with Celeste. Towards a Promised Land. Wendy Ewald. Photograph courtesy of Peter Mauney.

In *'Towards a Promised Land'* (2003–2006) Ewald worked with twenty young people who were new to living in England, who all lived in Margate with their families. The powerful images demonstrate the relationships that developed through using the camera, but also how the images illicit conversation and dialogue recorded with and on the photographs. The images were exhibited publicly in Margate, referencing its unique position as a place that has received refugees since the First World War (Ewald and Neri, 2006) (Figure 10.8).

The task below uses Ewald's approach and Campt's listening process to develop photographic work with young people. The task requires you to examine and reflect on the learning relationships you develop with pupils. For pupils, this task asks them to reflect on relationships that are important to them when they are at school. If pupils do not wish to or are unable to make images of themselves, other possibilities are suggested.

Task 10.4 Using Photography to Reflect on the Educator and Learner Relationship

Discussion: (in a training setting) What is important about the educator and pupil learning relationship? Identify where and how it appears in the Teachers' Standards and ITT Core Content Framework and how you develop this in your pedagogical practice.

Question: (With pupils) What kinds of relationships are important to them when they are at school?

- Begin by exploring a wider context: examine examples of photography that describe relationships. For example, this could be relationships between people, between important objects, between objects and people, between human and non-human or a connection between school and home;
- Experiment and demonstration; using digital SLR, phone cameras or Ipads, test three different ways to make images of relationships described above;
- Experiment with lighting, space, backdrops and backgrounds;
- Print out your images and, using a photovoice method, speak about the different kinds of relationships in them using the reflection and discussion below;
- Reflection: how do the images communicate your ideas about relationships? How did you decide on the composition of the photographs?

Discussion and listening reflection with pupils: Who and what are featured in the images? Can you listen to what the images express? What do they help you say about the relationships? If you have made images with people in them, how do they appear? If you have included objects in the images, how do the objects describe relationships you have with them and to others?

SUMMARY

The discussions and tasks in this chapter have asked you to appear and become more visible in the process of learning and developing as an art educator through using lens-based practice. It recognises the key relationships, events, skills and objects you might encounter as you move through this transition, using the photographic image to help you to reflect on and mark that time. Working with a camera in a school context inside and outside a classroom can draw attention to your presence, but it allows critical and active reflection to happen in the contexts in which you practice.

The tasks ask you to explore different education contexts. This reverses the school gaze and does what Ivinson describes as 'embodied knowing' (2012:491) asking you and students to look and move differently, guided by intentions and the lens-based technology you use. Lens-based technology can be an important second teacher and can help you to notice and understand unexpected aspects of your transition to art educator. Lens-based images tell you more about yourself, help you to notice key moments for reflection and carefully document your transition to successful art educator.

RESOURCES

Anthony Luvera's guide to working with self-portraits in the National Portrait Gallery. http://www.luvera.com/young-peoples-guide-self-portraiture/

Artangel Website, documentation and discussion around Steve McQueen's *Year 3* https://www.artangel.org.uk/project/year-3/

Grain Photography Hub. Examples of author's photography practice in school. https://grainphotographyhub.co.uk/portfolio-type/joanna-fursman/

Julian Germaine. https://www.juliangermain.com/projects/classroom-portraits-uk

Photographers Gallery. https://www.juliangermain.com/projects/classroom-portraits-uk

Photography for Whom website. https://photographyforwhom.com/product/photography-for-whom-issue-1

Thomas Tallis School Photography website. https://www.photopedagogy.com

Wendy Ewald *Towards a Promised Land*. https://wendyewald.com/portfolio/margate-towards-a-promised-land/

BIBLIOGRAPHY

Babad, Elisha. (2009) *The Social Psychology of the Classroom*. New York and Abingdon: Routledge.

Benjamin, Walter. (2008) *The Work of Art in the Age of Mechanical Reproduction*. London: Penguin.

Buffington, Melanie L., Williams, Amy E., Ogier, Erika and Rouatt, Lauren. (2016) Telling Our Tales: Becoming Art Educators. *National Art Education Association Studies in Art Education: A Journal of Issues and Research* 57(4), pp. 329–340.

Burke, Catherine and Ribeiro de Castro, Miriam. (2007) The School Photograph: Portraiture and the Art of Assembling the Body of the Schoolchild. *History of Education* 36(2), pp. 213–226.

Campt, Tina. (2017) *Listening to Images*. Durham: Duke University Press.

Capel, Susan. (2010) Secondary Students' Development as Teachers over the Course of a PGCE Year. *Educational Research* 43(3), pp. 247–261.

Craig, Claire. (2009) *Exploring the Self Through Photography. Activities for Use in Group Work*. London: Jessica Kingsley Publishers.

Chappell, Drew, Chappell, Sharon and Margolis, Eric. (2011) School as Ceremony and Ritual: How Photography Illuminates Performances of Ideological Transfer. *Qualitative Inquiry* 17(1), pp. 51–67.

Department for Education (2019) *ITT Core Content Framework*. Gov.uk.

Department for Education (2021) *Teacher's Standards. Guidance for School Leaders, School Staff and Governing Bodies*. Gov.uk.

Elo, Mika. (2013) The New Technological Environment of Photography and Shifting Conditions of Embodiment. In Rubenstein, Daniel, Golding, Johnny and Fisher, Andy (Eds) *On the Verge of Photography, Imaging beyond Representation*. Birmingham: Article Press, pp. 89–104.

Ewald, Wendy and Lightfoot, Alexandra (2001). *Wanna Take Me a Picture. Teaching Writing and Photography to Children*. Boston, MA: Beacon Press.

Ewald, Wendy and Neri, Louise. (2006) *Towards a Promised Land*. Göttingen: Steidl.

Forrest, Eve. (2013) Between Bodies and Machine: *Photographers with Camera, Photographers on Computers*. In Rubenstein, Daniel, Golding, Johnny and Fisher, Andy (Eds) *On the Verge of Photography, Imaging beyond Representation*. Birmingham: Article Press, pp. 105–122.

Fursman, Joanna (2020) Chasing pedagogy: Searching for a new school portrait, or can this be a school if it doesn't look like one? International Journal of Education through Art. 16 (2), pp. 197-207.

Graziano, Kevin J. and Litton, Edmundo F. (2007) *Issues in Teacher Education* 16(1), pp. 7–19.

Ivinson, Gabrielle. (2012) The Body and Pedagogy: Beyond Absent, Moving Bodies in Pedagogic Practice. *British Journal of Sociology of Education* 33(4), pp. 489–506.

Kraftl, Peter. (2015) *Geographies of Alternative Education. Diverse Learning Spaces for Children and Young People.* University of Bristol and University of Cambridge. Bristol: Policy Press.

Luvera, Anthony. (2019) Then with Now. In Luvera, Anthony (Ed) *Photography for Whom?* Photographyforwhom.com. pp. 5–8.

McDonald, Lawrence. (2008) Exacting Reproduction: Darcy Lange's Work Studies in Schools. In Vincente, Mercedes (Ed) *Darcy Lange: Study of an Artist at Work.* Ikon/Govett Brewster Gallery. Manchester: Cornerhouse, pp. 115–141.

Maynard, John and Furlong, Trisha. (1993) Learning to Teach and Models of Mentoring. In McIntyre, D., Hagger, H. and Wilkon, M. (Eds) *Mentoring: Perspectives on School-Based Teacher Education.* London: Kogan Page, pp. 69–85.

Mitchel, Claudia and Weber, Sandra. (2009) Picture This! Class Line-Ups, Vernacular Portraits and Lasting Impressions of School. In Prosser, Jon (Ed) *Image-Based Research: A Sourcebook for Qualitative Researchers.* London: Falmer Press, pp. 175–189.

Prosser, John. (Ed) (1999) *School Culture.* London: Sage.

Schön, Donald. (1991) *The Reflective Practitioner: How Professionals Think in Action.* London: Ashgate.

Weiser, Judy. (1993) *Phototherapy Techniques: Exploring the Secrets of Personal Snapshots and Family Albums.* Vancouver: Phototherapy Centre.

Chapter 11 Encouraging Critical Awareness Through Art and Design Education

Will Grant

INTRODUCTION

Why make art? The answer is perennially difficult to provide, complicated (and indeed enriched) as it is by a lack of disciplinary consensus. Aesthetes have long argued for art as autotelic – idealistically produced outside of moral or political purpose – and art as *ends* is a rationale still championed by many who teach our subject (Cary, 2011). If this represents the extent of your professional purpose, skip this chapter!

Here I want instead to explore the practical potential for Art and Design education as *means*, and for that meaning to be, specifically, the activation of pupils' agency on the issues of social equity. Art and Design education's potentially catalytic connection to critical awareness is not a novel concern (Addison, 2010) but I would argue it a timely relationship to explore. Against a background of increasing global connectivity and popular youth movements centred on the issues of environmental, economic and social justice, student teachers and school pupils demonstrate an increasing interest in a critical Art and Design education.

The idea of introducing critical content into the educative institution disquiets many conscientious teachers. Potential concerns include (i) accurately introducing nuanced issues of social morality, inoffensively, and (ii) the prospective accusation of having stepped beyond professionally suitable ground in the classroom. The British government's recent introduction of guidance on 'safeguarding political impartiality' (Department for Education, 2022) in the English classroom raises these stakes. Resultantly, even student teachers who aspire to critical pedagogy often drop this ambition prematurely. I hope here, instead, to inspire you to practice critical Art and Design pedagogies despite the challenges of doing so in the neoliberal school.

OBJECTIVES:

By the end of this chapter, you should be able to:

- Justify Art and Design education's place in exploring issues of social equity and pupil agency;
- Take inspiration from Art and Design projects explicitly rooted in social justice, from within secondary school settings and beyond;

DOI: 10.4324/9781003377429-14

- Understand how the processes, or pedagogies, you employ might be oriented to implicitly tackle the issues of equity;
- Explain the importance of contextual relevance when critically engaging with the issues of social inequity and have the tools to consider this need for your own pupils.

JUSTIFYING CRITICAL ART AND DESIGN PEDAGOGIES

It is typical today to measure educational success in employment statistics and starting salaries, but as Adams writes such 'rhetoric of vocation and entrepreneurialism' sidesteps 'questions of social justice' (2013, p. 243). For many Art and Design educators, we enter the classroom with hopes more closely aligned to Dewey's humanist rationale: 'to set free and develop the capacities of human individuals without respect to race, sex, class' (1957, p. 186).

Asking a pupil to formulate an emotive opinion or allowing them agency in putting paintbrush to paper empowers them to author their own story. However, I would argue the potency of Art and Design education as pathway to freedom might go further: through reference to socially minded contemporary art practice (Adams, 2010), making purposeful connection between art and your pupils' lives, or indeed in existentially equipping pupils to 'exist well…with the world' (Biesta, 2019, p. 4) through new modes of perception. This does not so easily come about in mathematics or Modern Foreign Languages.

In a context of increasingly technocratic measurement and top-down policy, the Art and Design classroom requires concerted defence to remain a space where democratic, critical, socially aware pedagogy can facilitate creative dialogue. I hope the below provides some practical means to undertake this process in your classroom – if you so wish.

CRITICAL CONTENT

Here I introduce some thinking around content – starting with two prompts oriented to the substantive *what* of your classroom – and then two that consider the *who*.

Artmaking: Projects of Provocation

Encouraging a critical awareness in the Art and Design classroom does not involve you, the teacher, expressing political opinion. Indeed, mandating pupils to undertake activity with a particular political bias would be inherently uncritical. It would not ignite a pupil's own analytical reflection, nor their artistic agency. Instead, these prompts ask pupils to connect artmaking with their expression of authentic value positions.

(a) **Text and Slogan**. There is a long history of visual accompaniment to language designed for social control. From the frontispiece of Henry VIII's *Great Bible* of 1539, where the unmistakable figure of the king above the title confirms his position as God's agent on earth – through to the digitally warped physiognomy of models employed to advertise the 21st century cosmetics. More recently, artists have employed the word *as* artform with intent to challenge orthodoxies of control. Examples might be seen in subversive aesthetic imitation of the applied arts (Barbara Kruger), through conceptual poetic commentary (Fiona Banner), or indeed in direct confrontation with political powers (Bob and Roberta Smith).

Given their critique of social norms, introducing Kruger or Banner's artworks might represent opportunity to build critical content into your classroom. Kruger's iconic tritone collages confront cultural constructions of power and consumerism in a critical tradition. Banner has printed texts from war films onto the gallery wall and most noticeably into her publication *NAM* (1997) which questions the social consequences of our disproportionate fictionalisation of historical conflict. Asking pupils to learn from these works and apply their own language to the excesses or asymmetry of modern society could prove critically engaging.

Perhaps most immediately of all, we can see critical potential in Bob and Roberta Smith's use of text. His signage is overtly political; the message contained within typically a progressive plea for the power of art in the lives of young people to be recognised politically. The following activity offers one way to weld artmaking to the critical act of public statement, drawing directly on the aesthetic of Bob and Roberta Smith.

Task 11.1 Case Study: The Placard

Here, pupils create their own 'placard', to be actively displayed or paraded around the school. Pupils should think carefully about the slogan they want to publicise – a positive reinforcement or promotion of something important to them – and then render this text with drop shadow in Smith's trademark showman type. 'If you were in charge, how do you want the world to change – what would you say to those around you?'

The display of this work is important. Too often, 'school art' is produced only for the audience of an assessor rather than a public, which only acts to reinforce pupils' sense of education's purposelessness and therefore their own lack of power. Instead, this work comes alive in performance, ideally carried around the public grounds of the school in mock protest or parade on in the least displayed in a shared space.

Consider: Would you feel self-conscious organising an artistic 'performance' with pupils? Why? Did you undertake any similar activity in your own education, and how did it make you feel? What might the dangers of expecting pupils to act publicly include? What might this do for the reputation and visibility of the Art and Design department among colleagues?

(b) **Transgressing institutional policy**. The institution of school, which Foucault convincingly suggested has conceptual kinship with the prison in its 'regular chronologies, forced labour, its authorities of surveillance and registration...' (1977, p. 228), is not an obvious environment for authentic artistic activity (Cary, 2011). There is an inherent friction – arguably one which has led to 'school art' as a distinct, enervated discipline detached from contemporary practice (Efland, 1976) – when one tries to engender innovation in an environment demanding imitation.

What might a transgressive Art and Design pedagogy involve in practice? We can perhaps see an example of it, in the simplest sense, when your pupils walk the school grounds independently to draw en plein air. Interrupting typical institutional expectations of surveillance and control, such action subverts this dynamic – pupils turn their gaze on the institution. Trust required of the teacher arguably upends the power dynamic of the closed classroom.

In a project popular with pupils, I once scanned and enlarged the page within their A6 'diaries' which laid out behaviour expectations. This page was well known to pupils – as young people tend towards a concern for accuracy in the way their misdemeanours are policed. Therefore, when pupils were presented with this well-known page, they were immediately engaged in debating the aspects of control they felt unfairly infringed their autonomy. The project that followed is detailed below.

Task 11.2 Case Study: Appropriating Policy for Satirical Ends

After receiving photocopied behaviour policies, the class looked to the work of Tom Philips. Philips' altered Victorian novel *A Humument* (1966) is a post-modern publication that disrupts ideas of authorship and originality through partial erasure. Bringing these two sources together, I invited pupils to 'erase'

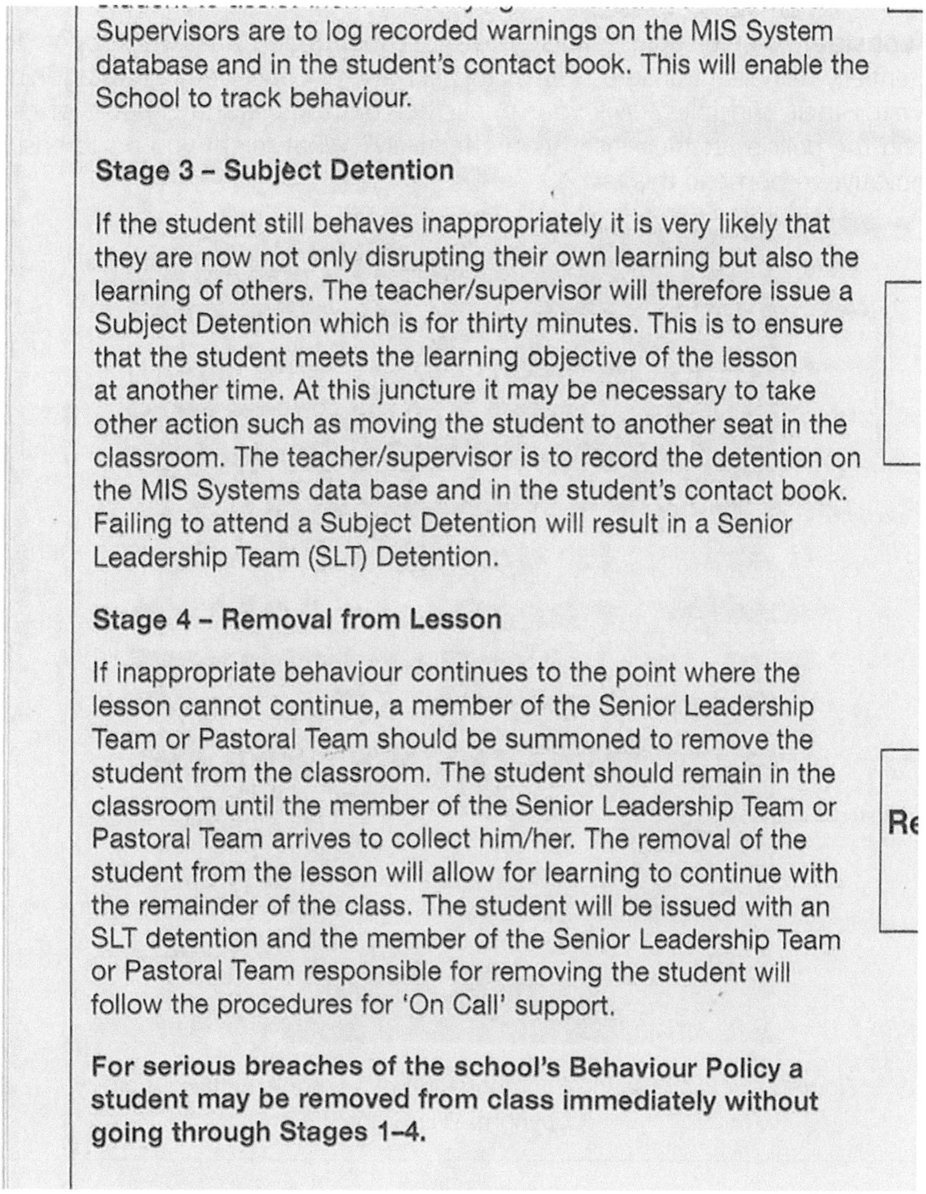

Supervisors are to log recorded warnings on the MIS System database and in the student's contact book. This will enable the School to track behaviour.

Stage 3 – Subject Detention

If the student still behaves inappropriately it is very likely that they are now not only disrupting their own learning but also the learning of others. The teacher/supervisor will therefore issue a Subject Detention which is for thirty minutes. This is to ensure that the student meets the learning objective of the lesson at another time. At this juncture it may be necessary to take other action such as moving the student to another seat in the classroom. The teacher/supervisor is to record the detention on the MIS Systems data base and in the student's contact book. Failing to attend a Subject Detention will result in a Senior Leadership Team (SLT) Detention.

Stage 4 – Removal from Lesson

If inappropriate behaviour continues to the point where the lesson cannot continue, a member of the Senior Leadership Team or Pastoral Team should be summoned to remove the student from the classroom. The student should remain in the classroom until the member of the Senior Leadership Team or Pastoral Team arrives to collect him/her. The removal of the student from the lesson will allow for learning to continue with the remainder of the class. The student will be issued with an SLT detention and the member of the Senior Leadership Team or Pastoral Team responsible for removing the student will follow the procedures for 'On Call' support.

For serious breaches of the school's Behaviour Policy a student may be removed from class immediately without going through Stages 1–4.

Figure 11.1 Original extract from a school's behaviour policy document.
Copyright: Will Grant.

parts of their behaviour policy, collaging or painting on top of some sections, while selectively leaving words to produce an inverted message. Many gleefully took this opportunity to upend their codified rules of behaviour – creating phrases that condemned authority figures, suggested reward for certain crimes, and parodied the original document in novel ways (Figures 11.1 and 11.2).

This creative act of defiance was powerful not because it effected change, but because it reminds pupils that they might play with power for cathartic, and collective, enjoyment. An 'authorised' transgression of this nature might be argued as subservient to the institution it pretends to challenge; however, I believe this view self-defeating. It ignores the value in reminding pupils that rules, laws, or codes are socially constructed and therefore open to critique. As Brown writes: 'art and humor [sic] are the irreverent ways in which children can frame reconstructive action' (2003, p. 289).

Consider: Would senior leaders in your school understand and support the potentially cathartic transgression of this activity, or conceive it as antagonistic towards their principles? Will your pupils be comfortable and capable of critiquing the policies of their institution effectively? What might you do to ensure innovative response in this task?

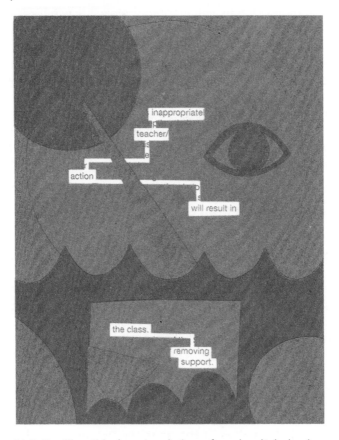

Figure 11.2 Pupil's satirical appropriation of a school's behaviour policy.
Copyright: Will Grant.

In this section, I have suggested that critical content might include opportunity for pupils to practically engage with (i) public display of their personal views and (ii) careful critical commentary on the power structures within the school itself.

Contextual Studies: Representation

This section extends consideration of content– but with specific concern for the artworks and artists you embed in your classroom curriculum. In comparison to the *what* of the previous section, here I am concerned with the substantive issue of *who* your pupils encounter in their Art and Design education.

(c) **DAMP HEMs.** Richard Hickman's acronym DAMP HEMs (2019, p. 3) is relatively well known, a derogatory description of contextual studies reinforced through the unambitious expectations of the National Curriculum:

Dead **A**rtists, **M**ostly **P**ainters – **H**eteronormative, **E**uropean, and **M**ale

Inequity is enacted when narrowly defined privileged sections of a society are promoted and celebrated at the expense of minority or oppressed groups. Put simply, to push back against this paradigmatic inequity, the critical Art and Design teacher is beholden to produce an authentically diverse curriculum. The traditional bias lampooned by Hickman might be redressed through the explicit inclusion of living, multi-modal, queer, global, and female artists and designers in the classroom. This recalibration should be expanded to consider artists of colour too.

To be clear, this process is not one of equating relative value to all artistic production, as critiques of critical contextual studies (who claim positive discrimination) might imply. Clearly, Frieda Kahlo, Keith Haring, Amy Sherald, or the Singh Twins are important, successful and inspirational artists in their own right whose work might excite and educate your pupils alongside, or just as effectively, as Vincent Van Gogh, Henri Matisse, or Pablo Picasso.

Can you audit your curriculum to see how it intersects with the issues of gender, sexuality, nationality, and ethnicity, as well as charting how many contemporary practitioners feature in your teaching? You might choose to compare this audit to data on your pupil demographic – will pupils see themselves in your curriculum? Will pupils see and understand the lived experience of others, too?

Task 11.3 Example: Julie Mehretu's *Mogamma* (2012)

If you are looking to diversify your contextual studies curriculum, the celebrated contemporary artist Julie Mehretu is a worthy 'anti-DAMP HEM' for study (although she does paint, alongside the use of other media). You might, for example, look to Mehretu's Mogamma (2012) series of monumental, yet delicate ink and acrylic drawings. Here, she overlaps abstracted architectural details of the Mogamma – an administrative building in Tahir Square, Cairo, often the site of civil protest and unrest – with other politically febrile locations across the world. In so doing, she seeks to deny the viewer pictorial clarity and instead a maelstrom of dynamic lines towers above them, in imitation of the complex, domineering power relations typified by authoritarian architectural forms. As she writes:

> I think architecture reflects the machinations of politics, and that's why I am interested in it as a metaphor for those institutions. I don't think of architectural language as just a metaphor about space, but about spaces of power, about ideas of power.

(Mehretu in Dillon & Young, 2009, p. 29)

> Can your pupils record architectural details from around your school and collectively transfer fragments of these forms to a large format drawing, overlapping one another's marks to produce a similarly complex web of impenetrable detail?
>
> **Consider**: How might the technical processes of recording and developing a project such as this be diversified? Perhaps the use of digital technologies to construct composition, tracing paper to model the relationship between overlapping drawings, or photographic projections to accurately imitate Mehretu's orthographic imagery?

(d) **Stories of Art.** To offer a diverse curriculum while ignoring the reality of structures that have perpetuated social inequity, such as the narrow Western canon of art, would arguably still limit classroom criticality.

The most widely read, popular art historical text is E. H. Gombrich's *Story of Art*, first published in 1950. Never out of print, the work is archetypal of Western-centric, linear conceptions of artistic development – if you have not read it, your understanding of the canon will still likely have been shaped by this author's editorial decisions. It is a brilliant book – ambitious, but accessible – but a deeply flawed root from which to draw an accurate sense of artistic history. Contextual studies in Art and Design must, for purposes not limited to issues of social equity, move beyond this selective modernist history. To begin, Gombrich mentions only a *single* (!) female artist within his 650-page book – the German printmaker Kathe Kollwitz. He is open about the inherently partial nature of his selection, but despite this transparency the consensual erasure of female, and (largely) artists of colour, from an authoritative narrative cannot be acceptable to a critical art and design teacher.

Therefore, I might advocate for discussion around the perspective and context of works such as Gombrich's. When he writes: 'Many tribes have special ceremonies in which they wear masks with the features of these animals...as if children played at pirates or detectives' (2006, p. 41), could we discuss and debate what might make us uncomfortable: his analogous comparison of 'tribes' and children, for example. Is this typical of 20th century thinking? Is it still typical? Is such comparison innocent, knowing, or malevolent? In this discussion, we reveal historical mechanisms of oppression, and as Hausman et al. write: 'curricula that embody critical thinking about the dynamics of power in culture and society are key factors for transformative education' (2010, p. 371).

An excellent companion piece to Gombrich, with great value as a critical educative tool, is James Elkins' *Stories of Art* (2002). Here the author's students are asked to produce their own 'maps of art history' revealing their plurality of interests in place of Gombrich's own.

CRITICAL PROCESS

The last section looked to the examples of critical Art and Design content. Here I introduce prompts loosely collected against two processes, through which your pupils might critique social inequity. To put simply, this is the *how* of your classroom – the activity, or embodied way of engaging artistic process for critical social improvement.

(e) **Agentic Activity.** Too frequently, products of the Art and Design classroom remain invisible. The work of pupils has no audience beyond a moderator, or marker, and in turn is banally divorced from the reality of the world. Instead, I challenge you to consider how your pupils might produce artwork with genuine purpose, and wider visibility.

One inspirational example of an active pedagogy is the global *Empty Bowls* project. In this initiative, not only do pupils publicly display their works, the vessels they create are used to serve food to paying guests – who then keep the bowl and provide charitable donation towards combating hunger. There are multiple benefits to such an endeavour, not least pupils enjoying the gratification of observing their artwork in use. Naturally, one would want to make sure (especially with examination groups) that pupils' work had been evidenced before gifting, but educative activities such as *Empty Bowls* exceed academia. As John Hartom, one of the teachers who first conceived of *Empty Bowls* comments, 'the empty bowl has become a metaphor for the power people feel when they help erase world hunger' – a socially-minded artistic project with genuine human impact.

For another example of Art and Design education encouraging pupils' agentic sovereignty, we can look to Room 13, a network of pupil-run art studios in schools. In contrast to the teacher-led, or teacher-owned, Art and Design classroom the ethos of Room 13 encourages pupils to take complete ownership of a space in their school and run it as a commercial art studio. This radical agency was, astoundingly, first enacted by a group of Scottish primary school pupils, who not only persuaded their school to provide independent art studio space (Room 13) but formed a committee and opened a bank account to manage their finances.

Room 13 is arguably more provocative than Empty Bowls in its paradigmatic challenge to educative power dynamics. It is the philosophy of communal ownership and creative freedom unburdened by scholastic bureaucracy that critically confronts the limitations of traditional schooling. While it may be difficult in many contexts to envisage an autonomous Room 13, anyone can practically employ some aspect of this programme;

- You might seek part of your department – a store cupboard – which can be handed to pupils to use habitually, as they please, for artmaking purposes;
- You might gift classes curational agency in the display of their exhibitions;
- You might look to elevate your 'art club' to organise commercial events, reinvesting the proceeds in materials or resources for their future use;
- You might collaborate with pupils in planning a cultural visit;
- You might allocate some part of your classroom display space for pupils' own use.

While a genuine attempt to establish a 'Room 13' in any school should rightly be a pupil-led endeavour, any of the above borrows from the democratic spirit of the original project and challenges typical structures of subordination in the institution of the school. If a pupil can identify as an active participant in the construction of their Art and Design education, then this might result in an agentic awareness of collective action in other aspects of civil society.

Task 11.4 Case Study: The Not-School Student-Centred Gallery Display

In this suggested activity, you might follow in the example set by Room 13 and dedicate a portion of your classroom display space to a student group. To begin, suggest to an extra-curricular Art and Design club, if you run one, that they create some work to display in this space. Ideally, move towards this wall being reserved for artwork conceived and created without *any* institutional involvement – artwork that has no directed intent but instead is made to be displayed against pupils' own initiatives.

To ensure this is effectively managed, you may want to establish a set of principles and organise pupils with responsibilities for maintaining the space – with the hope that you can then step out from management altogether, such that the endeavour is entirely pupil operated.

Consider: Are there already pupils in your department who feel some ownership of this space? Might they be interested in genuine curatorial ownership of some part of the department? Have pupils proactively brought you artwork completed at home, independently? Might these pupils be excited by the display of these works?

(g) **Dialogue.** Artmaking is an inherently dialogic act, as artist communicates with their experiences, and materials, in an iterative cycle of construction. Therefore, as argued earlier in this chapter, any art-rich curriculum will promote pupils' critical awareness to some extent – their observant, reactant, integration with their surroundings.

As a critical teacher, we might ask how dialogue can be actively situated at the very core of the classroom – and what benefit this brings? First, pupils must be given the space to make artistic choices, both spontaneous and recursive. This is their dialogue with the world, and any lesson objective or success criteria that you choose to impose, any predefined exemplar that you share, speaks for them. Unless genuine space for pupils' ideation can be accommodated within your curriculum then our discipline's dialogic nature is suppressed by the didacticism that defines a deficit model of education.

Perhaps the most prominent proponent of critical pedagogy, Paulo Freire, was absolutely clear – conceptualising your pupils as empty vessels to fill with knowledge, is reductive, dehumanising, and an oppressive concept of educative dynamics. As he writes:

> …for students, the more simply and docilely they receive the contents with which their teachers "fill" them in the name of knowledge, the less they are able to think and the more they become merely repetitive.
>
> (Freire, 2013, p. 109)

The alternative? A move towards student-centred, dialogic classroom practice, which positions your knowledge alongside that of your pupils, constructing new understanding through comparison and creativity. What might this ask of you in practice?

- You might form a student advisory panel to help adjust or amend your curriculum.

- You might look to rebalance your lesson planning to include more debate, discussion, and conversation and less instructional, demonstrative, or directive language.
- You might co-construct success criteria or objectives with your pupils
- You might introduce an anonymous suggestions box into the department, into which pupils can slip ideas for future lessons
- You might promote meaningful self and peer assessment over repetitive use of teacher feedback
- You might commit to ensuring every pupil's voice is heard in classroom discussion
- You might look to the lived experience of your pupils to reposition your curriculum as directly relevant to them and their community (see below)

Briefly, I would augment advocacy of classroom dialogue with that of collective or communal artistic activity – an arguably inherently critical act. Working collaboratively necessitates empathetic consideration of others, exposing systemic inequities, and simultaneously offers a meaningful challenge to the conceptual acceptance of education as individualistic competition.

Given that much contemporary artistic practice is undertaken by collective, partnership, or community, I might suggest it anachronistic that so many pupils today encounter the stereotypical modernist principal of the lone, wunderkind, artist through their own education. Due to the requirement placed upon us to measure, compare, and ultimately grade an individual's progress, within a wider framework of competitive educational markets, asking pupils to make work individually remains standard practice.

To counter a culture of individuality, might pupils work in productive pairing, as is typical of the copyrighter and creative director in the advertising industry? Could they iteratively add to a shared canvas, as Warhol and Basquiat once did, or might one produce a costume for another's performative dance, following the Dada works of Arp and Taeuber-Arp?

In this section, I have suggested prompts to illustrate three guiding principles of critical Art and Design pedagogy: agency, dialogue, and collaboration.

THE CONTEXTUAL RELEVANCE OF THE LIVES OF YOUNG PEOPLE TO A CRITICAL ART AND DESIGN PEDAGOGY

To this point, I have looked to introduce practical examples of critical Art and Design activities that you might echo in your own classroom. There is a caveat.

Before mimicking any of the above in your own classroom, consider *your* pupils. What challenges and barriers do they face in their lives? What excites and infuriates them? Might autonomy be dangerous in the hands of some, or unimaginable for others?

Let me give you an example of critical art pedagogy gone wrong. In 2013 two Israeli teachers ran a research project where they asked Palestinian pupils to make artwork to nurture their 'ethno-cultural awareness and identity' (Markovich & Rapoport, 2013, p. 9). As part of their well-intentioned plan, they provided their impoverished participants with expensive canvas and oil paint to 'integrate' them into artistic 'high culture' – the idea: that to provide the 'master's tools' would empower these young artists' own sense of self-worth. Every single pupil refused to participate. The teachers mistake was to assume that the oppressed wanted to adopt the very artistic materials symbolically associated with the hegemonic cultural exclusion of them and their peers. On reflection it was clear – the pupils considered such artmaking elitist – that it 'did not belong in their world' (2013, p. 14).

How will you make sure that your transformative Art and Design pedagogy is rooted in the lived experience of the pupils you are trying to empower, rather than asking them to adapt who they are to fit *your* interest in critical awareness?

SUMMARY

The two sections above introduced prompts through which you might awaken critical consciousness in your Art and Design pupils. Practical suggestions were made, including consideration of the *what*, *who* and *how* of your curriculum and classroom. All of these ideas have some connection to the writing of Paulo Freire – who spent his life promoting the transformational potential of education to address issues of social inequity, and I would advocate for further engagement with his work if the above appeals to you. These Freirean connections are visible through the value ascribed to autonomy, resourcefulness, empowerment, diversity, agency, collaboration, sensitivity, and dialogue in the collected activities. If you can place these qualities at the heart of your classroom, you are a practicing critical Art and Design teacher.

I hope now that you might feel able to:

- Confidently justify Art and Design education as a legitimate space for exploring the issues of social equity and pupil agency;
- Consider projects explicitly rooted in social justice;
- Understand how the classroom pedagogies you employ might be geared towards tackling issues of social equity;
- Take account of your own pupils' contexts to engage then effectively in a critical Art and Design education.

A critical awareness seeks to make visible the hidden and in turn upset the asymmetrical networks of power that rely on conformity, fatalistic thinking, and the false assumptions of a neutral educative act. As Freire wrote, 'those who talk of neutrality are precisely those who are afraid of losing their right to use neutrality to their own advantage' (2013, p. 131). What you do in the Art and Design classroom either embeds the status quo or challenges it: which do you choose?

RESOURCES

UK Scrapstore Directory: https://www.reusefuluk.org/scrapstores-directory
You may be connected to local businesses or organisations who can provide your department with recycled sculptural, collage, or construction materials. If not, do search the UK Scrapstore Directory to see if your pupils might benefit from a sustainable approach to artmaking.
Guerrilla Girls Resources: https://www.guerrillagirls.com/
If you are interested in redressing gender inequity in the public display of artwork with your pupils, then the Guerrilla Girls resources are an excellent starting point. Be warned, not all resources are age appropriate for the secondary school.
ARTiculation Prize: https://www.nationalgallery.org.uk/learning/secondary-schools/articulation/articulation-prize
The ARTiculation prize has, for over a decade, allowed many hundreds of pupils the opportunity to speak publicly about their opinions on artworks that inspire

them. While not all of your pupils will be immediately confident in sharing their opinions in this forum, it provides a valuable resource of pupils' talking about art.

James Elkins' Stories of Art Video Resource: https://www.youtube.com/playlist?list=PLJp6WIMKaI7zrpqYofh8CskCzxw90s2XB

When pushing back against a narrow orthodoxy of art history, do review the large resource of videos that the author Elkins has produced. This might guide your reconceptualisation of curricula towards inclusivity and diversity.

Barbara Kruger: https://spruethmagers.com/artists/barbara-kruger/

Fiona Banner: http://www.fionabanner.com/index.htm

Bob and Roberta Smith: http://bobandrobertasmith.co.uk/

Olafur Eliasson: https://olafureliasson.net/archive/artwork/WEK109190/ice-watch

Gavin Turk: http://gavinturk.com/

Michelangelo Pistoletto: https://www.tate.org.uk/art/artworks/pistoletto-venus-of-the-rags-t12200

Tim Noble and Sue Webster: http://www.timnobleandsuewebster.com/

Guerra De La Paz: http://guerradelapaz.com/gdlpwp/

Tom Philips: https://www.tomphillips.co.uk/humument

Julie Mehretu: https://www.mariangoodman.com/artists/51-julie-mehretu/

Dora Maar: https://www.tate.org.uk/whats-on/tate-modern/dora-maar

Empty Bowls: https://emptybowls.com/

Room 13: http://room13international.org/

BIBLIOGRAPHY

Acuff, J. B. (2018). 'Being' a critical multicultural pedagogue in the art education classroom. *Critical Studies in Education*, 59(1), 35–53. https://doi.org/10.1080/17508487.2016.1176063

Adams, J. (2010). Risky choices: The dilemmas of introducing contemporary art practices into schools. *British Journal of Sociology of Education*, 31(6), 683–701.

Adams, J. (2013). The artful dodger: Creative resistance to neoliberalism in education. *Review of Education, Pedagogy, and Cultural Studies*, 35(4), 242–255. https://doi.org/10.1080/10714413.2013.819726

Addison, N. (2010). Critical pedagogy. In N. Addison, L. Burgess, J. Steers, & J. Trowell (Eds.), *Understanding Art Education*. Routledge.

Biesta, G. (2019). What if? Art education beyond expression and creativity. In R. Hickman (Ed.), *The International Encyclopedia of Art and Design Education*. John Wiley.

Brown, N. C. (2003). Are we entering a post-critical age in visual arts education? *Studies in Art Education*, 44(3), 283–289. https://doi.org/10.1080/00393541.2003.11651744

Cary, R. (2011). *Critical Art Pedagogy: Foundations for Postmodern Art Education*. Routledge.

Department for Education. (2022). *Political Impartiality in Schools*.

Dewey, J. (1957). *Reconstruction in Philosophy*. Beacon.

Dillon, B., & Young, J. (2009). *Julie Mehretu: Grey Area Exhibition Catalogue*. Deutsche Guggenheim.

Efland, A. (1976). The school art style: A functional analysis. *Studies in Art Education*, 17(2), 37–44.

Elkins, J. (2002). *Stories of Art*. Routledge.

Foucault, M. (1977). *Discipline and Punish*. Pantheon Books.

Freire, P. (2013). *Education for Critical Consciousness*. Bloomsbury.

Gombrich, E. (2006). *The Story of Art, Pocket Edition* (13th ed.). Phaidon.

Hausman, J., Ploof, J., Duignan, J., Brown, W. K., & Hostert, N. (2010). The condition of art education: Critical visual art education [CVAE] club, Winter 2010. *Studies in Art Education, 51*(4), 368–374. https://doi.org/10.1080/00393541.2010.11518814

Hickman, R. (2019). Teaching and learning critical studies. In R. Hickman (Ed.), *The International Encyclopedia of Art and Design Education.* John Wiley.

Markovich, D. Y., & Rapoport, T. (2013). Creating art, creating identity: Under-privileged pupils in art education challenge critical pedagogy practices. *International Journal of Education Through Art, 9*(1), 7–22. https://doi.org/10.1386/eta.9.1.7_1

Chapter 12

Privacy versus Public: Teenagers' Self Expression through Digital Photography in Social Networking Sites

Teresa Torres de Eça and Ângela Saldanha

INTRODUCTION

Identity as a negotiated and socially constructed concept is one of the major concerns of the adolescent growing up process. In their attempt to define identities, adolescents try to assert their individuality, while also joining others within specific social groupings. For such purposes teenagers often use visual narratives conveyed through digital media in public networking spaces on the World Wide Web. A phenomenon associated with this is the 'selfie', which is a temporary, contextually specific, changeable, situated as well as durable and stable digital image of the individual (Cruz & Thornham, 2015). As in any other type of communication, the media used influences the message, which in the case of the selfie has potential benefits and risks for both producers and audiences. The selfie can serve as a form of documentation and communication with others, as well as a source of empowerment. For many, selfies enable a gaining in self-confidence and for the receiving of acknowledgement and so when handled positively are a way of increasing personal agency and visibility. Taking into account the importance of selfies in adolescents' social channels, educators and teachers in the field of Art and Design can integrate this phenomenon into curriculum content by including the critical appraisal of digital self-portraits in their teaching. Image creation and manipulation can be contextualized and critiqued in Art and Design lessons as part of a positive educative process.

OBJECTIVES:

By the end of this chapter you should be able to:

- Recognize the visual, media and legal literacies aspects of young peoples' self-representation in public networking spaces.
- Identify approaches to digital and visual literacies in the Art and Design classroom.
- Know about the Erasmus+ European Union Project #NarcissusMeetsPandora (https://narcissusmeetspandora.eu/).
- Understand the #NarcissusMeetsPandora conceptual framework.

DOI: 10.4324/9781003377429-15

TEACHING VISUAL ARTS IN OUR TIMES

Alongside advances in technology and science, in recent years we have seen profound societal challenges; an increasing flux of migrations, social and political conflict, the closing of frontiers, intolerance and a lack of control over the environmental crisis. As a consequence of the 'exploitation and devastation that has controlled and regulated human and non-human existence' (Atkinson, 2022), we have put at risk the survival of human rights, humanity itself and the living planet (2022 UNESCO report on education, 20).

This is the world teachers face, and in which we work with children, young people and adults who are all affected by all these conditions. Concurrently with this, large numbers of people are familiar with the sharing of global virtual cultures and connections via digital social channels, and with phenomena such as edutainment and gamification. Additionally, many are used to having their profiles exposed on the internet in private or public groups. However, in the face of these universal globalizing trends, teachers are frequently bound by locally fragmented curriculums, standards, goals and core competencies. These do not always specifically promote a space for the development of critical agency about the widespread visual production of social media, and the impact on young peoples' daily lives of their use of images, including self-images, in this overwhelming global digital environment.

Task 12.1 Social Channels

Talk with your students:

- Ask them what their preferred applications for social channels are.
- Ask them what kind of images they share in social channels.
- Ask them if they feel protected in social channels.

Although teachers are bound by outdated curriculums (Steers, 2004), many will feel an educational imperative to figure out ways of developing their students' agency in a global digital environment that will motivate the students to grow as responsible planetary citizens. One way that Art and Design teachers can do this is by using methods for positive understandings of the self and other imagery in visual media. Art and Design teachers are uniquely placed though their knowledge of art history, architecture, design, film, photography, painting, sculpture and so on, to pass on the concepts, contextual narratives, art and design theoretical knowledges and the elements and principles of visual language. In implementing this knowledge with the specific intent to help students in constructing their identities in an unstable but globally linked world, teachers will be working in line with drivers such as UNESCO's Global Citizenship Education (UNESCO, 2015)[1] which aims to empower learners of all ages to assume active roles, both locally and globally, in building more peaceful, tolerant, inclusive and secure societies (Figure 12.1).

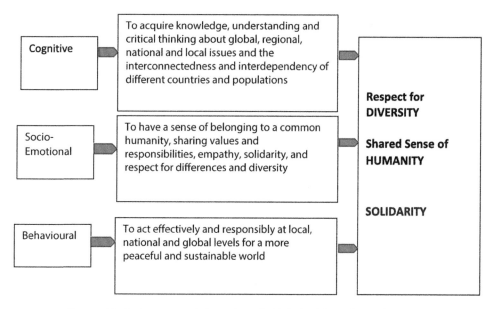

Figure 12.1 Conceptual domains of Global Citizenship Education.
Diagram adapted from UNESCO Report (2018).

TEACHING IN A DIGITAL ERA

Children and young people in many parts of the world have never experienced a world without online digital technologies. Complex systems of connectivity through mobile and wireless networks include more and more producers, distributors and consumers in new virtual territories that have diluted physical boundaries. For many children and young people, identity references are made through co-constructed standards in digital environments with a logic of action that has no regard for the point on the planet where they live (Prensky, 2009). At the same time, the knowledge and digital competences put into play by the use of these means are intuitively acquired in the great majority of cases and developed in peer and self-learning virtual situations, in which young people act as both consumers and producers of information (Duncum, 2011). In this context, Art and Design teachers must examine their position and the kinds of knowledge, methods and processes we are using to work with today's young people. How are we, as Art and Design teachers, supporting our students' responsible identity development, how are we promoting healthy self-reflection and the exploration of visual information; values and social behaviours?

All educators and teachers who are committed to the UNESCO Sustainable Development Goals can agree with the need to address the three domains of learning (Figure 12.2) – cognitive, socio-emotional and behavioural (UNESCO, 2015). Of these, the cognitive dimension considers knowledge and thinking skills as necessary to better understand the world and its complexities. Art and Design teachers know how much learning in our subject can increase divergent and convergent thinking. In relation to socio-emotional dimensions, we agree that through arts we address values, attitudes and social skills helping students to develop affectively, psychosocially and physically, and we create learning situations through arts thinking and arts making that enable learners to live together with others respectfully and peacefully. Finally in terms of the behavioural dimension: the arts enable performance, practical application and engagement.

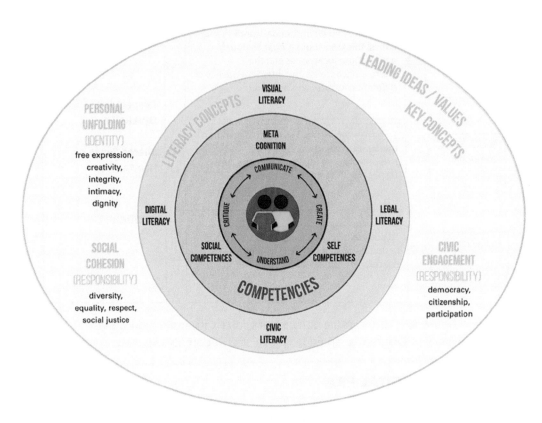

Figure 12.2 Transdisciplinary model to help educators and teachers to work digital self-representation with young people.

Source: Project #NarcissusMeetsPandora (2022).

But are we as Art and Design teachers engaging with the Sustainable Development Goals through our subject? In the sciences, there are voices claiming less directive teaching as a method for promoting more practical and engaging learning tasks using digitally based strategies. For example, 'Tinkering and Making' movements in the European School Academy[2] online courses for teachers make claims for play-based exploration and experimentation in learning, fostering purposeful exploration and making, often through, trial and error. For them, making adds a technological aspect to the creative process, combining physical objects and technology (hardware and software). Makers learn through experimentation, by taking technology apart and trying to create something new. Tinkering and Making focuses on building a creative learning environment in which students learn by doing, fostering problem-solving skills, creativity, innovative thinking and resilience; essential skills for learning to learn through game-based learning and gamification. Tinkering and Making supports students' development in creativity, computational thinking and

---

Task 12.2 Tinkering and Making

Tinkering and Making strategies are very close to creativity and design methodologies. You can try Tinkering and Making in your classroom by following these basic steps:

Tinker phase: Teachers help the students to decide on a topic worthy to be explored and then develop one or more provocation or polemic questions that will support the students in thinking creatively about how they relate to the topic at a local level.

Make phase/building skills and knowledge: In the Make phase, the teacher identifies what skills and knowledge students will need to develop their ideas. Teachers may invite experts from other fields to the classroom to engage students in learning activities to develop the necessary skills and knowledge that they will need to put their ideas to work in the Innovate phase.

Innovation phase: Demonstrating skills and knowledge through a problem-solving project:

- **Mind mapping**: Students are asked to create a solution to the problem they identified. Mind mapping activities help students to broaden perspectives, for example by using Post-its, collage and drawing they are encouraged to identify as many ideas as possible in a short period of time. Following this, students take the different ideas from the Mind mapping phase and sort them into thematic groups;
- **Plussing:** Group conversations and sharing ideas in sharing sessions to present each phase of their production to peers including story ideas, scripts, storyboards and more will help the class to construct shared knowledge through positive feedback;
- **Ideate and Prototype:** students elaborate ideas, make revisions to their ideas and start building the prototypes. Group conversations at this point can help the students as well as the teacher;

Publication or Authentic Presentation: Presentations to the public, including mentors and experts, in a real-world situation, whether it is an exhibit of the project in a gallery or museum or a showcase of the project at a local community event. This allows for students to gain visibility and public feedback.

Adapted from: http://www.learningisopen.org/toolkit/tinkering-making

Suggestion 1: Elaborate 1 provocation question about the topic 'Privacy Versus Public'.

Suggestion 2: Elaborate a group or individual mind map using collage of text and images related with your provocation question.

programming skills that are essential in digital environments (Albani et al., 2019). As Art and Design teachers, we should also be exploring in our teaching issues of visual literacy; legal literacy; ethics and aesthetics related to the digital environment. Critical thinking through arts understanding and making has always been one of the core skills developed in the arts curriculum (Duncum, 1997; Efland et al., 1996; Steers, 2003), which can now be extended into the digital environment.

CRITICAL THINKING

Art and Design curriculum developers are used to addressing critical thinking related to the capacity to read images and the understanding of their contexts. Visual Culture education, for example, was one of the rationales that influenced Art and Design teachers to foster a critical understanding of a full range of images from the media and the arts. However, we now live in a society that differs from previous generations in terms of who produces the images that are consumed, how mass media is distributed and how public visual information and arts production is processed. As referred to at the beginning of this text, different approaches to teaching and learning are required to address the current permeability between disciplines, the diverse systems of multiple production, distribution and consumption and the porosity of virtual territories. In this context, teachers, and parents, cannot take it for granted that students will learn autonomously how to manipulate digital environments with positive agency. This being the case, more is required of Art and Design teachers than to simply deliver art content, art history and cultural awareness through art production. In response to this need, learning though relational aesthetics, dialogic learning and making together are appearing in many Art and Design classes. Especially after the effects of the 2019–2021 COVID 19 pandemic, there is a need to foster socio-emotional affect, psychosociality and the physicality skills that were sidelined by the necessity for widespread online learning during the pandemic (UNESCO, 2020). Different approaches, based on joint learning, conversation and caring are needed to respond to our times. Education is not anymore viewed as a field separate from institutional efforts in health, law, sustainability, peace and social justice. It is at this cross point that a critical pedagogy approach to education in the arts can be put into action.

CRITICAL PEDAGOGY

Critical education voices, such as Paulo Freire, clearly articulated ways in which educational practices and policies continue to reproduce inequalities in society and advocated for an emancipatory pedagogy exploring democratic, dialogic and counter-hegemonic educational strategies (Freire, 1972). Such counter-hegemonic practitioners claimed that through critical reflection, learners can become aware of and explore the existing social and political order in a dialogic way. By the end of the 20th century, dialogic practices were specially promoted by media literacy education; cultural education and visual culture education that advocated for a top-down role for educators who would help students to understand the dynamics of power and be able to act critically (e.g. New London Group, 1996). Today, Art and Design teachers often use dialogical practices in their teaching strategies because it is an effective approach to the design of critical pedagogies. It enables students to be an active participant in their learning and establishes collaborative processes for critical reflection about images and media, including in digital environments.

DIGITAL ENVIRONMENTS

By digital environments, we mean the variety of information and communication technologies, which include the internet, digital networks, databases, content, services as well as mobile and associated technologies and devices. Children, young people and young adults spend many hours immersed in social media and video games, these being the digital environments that can influence their identity development by suppressing or supporting certain developmental processes such as the intrapersonal factors which operate within individuals and lead them to build a life story. To address this within the context of education for the purpose of supporting young people's development of a purposeful and integrated life story, a recent Erasmus+ project called 'Narcissus Meet Pandora'[3] brought together researchers, artists and educators from across Europe to explore the way adolescents use digital environments. The project found that adolescents are very conscious of how social media and digital games can foster collaborative relationships, exercise agency and be used negatively or positively in their identity development. It became apparent that, for the participants in the project the integration of critical approaches to digital environments that they encounter in their Art and Design learning will enhance this consciousness. For example, visual arts education curriculums can be used to address issues such as visual self-representation on social media.

Since young people's thinking is being more and more influenced by images it is important to use imagery exploration in their favor, namely by promoting one of the most important features in adolescence: critical thinking. To do so, it is essential to allow and help young people to critically analyze the social and political contexts that surround them. This competence is inextricably related to well-being and social justice in the sense that individuals are encouraged to question and challenge dominant points of view.

Narcisus Meets Pandora. (2022)

#NARCISSUSMEETSPANDORA[4]: CONCEPTUAL FRAMEWORK AND EDUCATORS' GUIDELINES

Erasmus+ Project #NarcissusMeetsPandora identified a lack of capacity to address in the field of young peoples' education, digital competences around the production and analysis of socially inclusive visual media. To address this lack of capacity, the project aimed to develop young peoples' digital skills and social engagement in an innovative way by providing high-quality skills for stimulating reflection and creative expression. The project worked directly with young peoples' digital portraits in the development of a critically effective pedagogical experience. To help the teachers and educators participating in the project to implement workshops about digital self-representation and social media, the project coordinators created a conceptual framework and educators' guidelines. The framework was very useful in the definition of levels of literacies; metacognition and dynamic skills when working with young peoples' social media and digital self-representation. Identity, as a negotiated and socially constructed concept, is one of the major concerns of the adolescent developmental process. In their attempt to define identities, adolescents try to assert their individuality, while also joining others within a specific social group. For such purposes, teenagers often use visual narratives conveyed through digital media in public networking spaces. It is important to bring this type of visual narrative to the Art and Design classroom, where teachers and students can engage in dialogue about the differing aspects of its creation and publication.

The framework to help the production of the educators' guidelines was constructed by researchers involved in the project, specialists in art education and visual literacy, pedagogues and psychologists. Figure 12.2 is the diagram encapsulating the work of the team during the first stage of the project.

The diagram shows the different layers of educational dimension and how these interconnect literacies, skills and individual and social competences to create learning situations that explore self-representation in digital media, for example, in 'selfies'. Visual literacy, digital literacy and legal literacy are treated together because they are equally important in the process of creating and publishing the 'selfie' in the public space. The creators of selfies need to understand the technical and aesthetic aspects of doing this as well as the legal aspects of authorship, image rights and the rights of people represented in the images. These understandings reveal concerns about the intra-personal aspects of identity, creativity, artistic expression, privacy and self-realization. Other, interpersonal aspects of the selfie relate to social cohesion, the ability to cooperate with others, the respect for others' opinions and lifestyles, the openness to diversity and a sense of equality and social justice.

The framework that grew out of Project #NarcissusMeetsPandora is intended to help curriculum developers in any educational context. Its transdisciplinary approach enables its use in the design of a large-scale school project, a single lesson plan or an intermediate set of activities in your classroom. In #Narcissus MeetsPandora, teachers engaged in the activities themselves before implementing them with students so that they could experience the lack of neutrality in digital environments, that they expose spaces for both negative and positive social behaviours. In TASK 12.3, you will find a self-reflection activity you can do with colleagues before planning a Project #NarcissusMeetsPandora learning experience.

Task 12.3 Reflection Activity

Discuss with your colleagues:

- What do I know/what have I experienced regarding taking and editing pictures?
- What are my thoughts on the ethics of manipulating images?
- Which messages do I think are the most important to transmit?
- How can I properly engage with young people and motivate them to explore these issues?

Critical agency was an important aspect of Project #NarcissusMeetsPandora. Social media platforms offer opportunities for meaningful dialogue between disconnected social groups as well as allowing for the maintenance of contacts between friends in distant networks. Young people have the possibility to communicate with people from different cultures, thus allowing them to improve their own intercultural awareness and competences. Furthermore, social media can facilitate collective activism (Tufekci & Wilson, 2012; Velasquez & LaRose, 2015). Even so, addressing social issues through social media does not always mean effective commitment to a cause (Deally & Dixit, 2021). Involving students in discussion and reflection is a good strategy for addressing with them the issues of cultural democracy and civic engagement. TASK 12.4 describes how a #NarcissusMeetsPandora workshop explored collective activism.

Task 12.4 Activism in Social Media

This workshop deals with activism on the internet and the idea of the common good. It aims to establish collaborations and connections between team members and engagement with a local community. It reinforces the notion of empathy and tolerance and the internet as a place to look for the other rather than as a narcissistic place only. This workshop promotes discussion and working in pairs to create a poster for a campaign. Introductory questions can help the students to reflect, such as:

- Have you ever used your pictures to raise awareness about a relevant and common issue for people in your local community?
- How can your portrait be a voice for a broader audience?
- What are your ideas about performative activism?

Suggestion: Discuss the topic 'Privacy versus Public' with your colleagues. Work in pairs to create an e-poster or e-flyer for a campaign about Students' Digital Responsibilities and Online Safety.

(*Source:* Project #NarcissusMeetsPandora, Educators Guide, 2022.)

SELFIES

In digital environments, the selfie can serve as a form of documentation and communication with others, as well as a source of empowerment. For many, the selfie allows them to gain confidence in themselves and to receive acknowledgement as a way of increasing one's own sense of agency and visibility (Cruz & Thornham, 2015). In Art and Design education, self-portraits as personal narrative are a common exercise through a range of media and techniques such as drawing, painting and sculpture and through the analysis of self-portraits by artists such as Rembrandt, Goya, Courbet and others. Selfies being so popular with young people, it would be unusual for the Art and Design teacher to let this important part of online self-presentation that is related to identity issues and peer relations (Boursier & Manna, 2018, p.2) which is go unnoticed in the art classroom. The selfie as a social process with self-actualization purposes that can be understood in terms of a balance between opportunity and risk (Giddens, 1991, p.78) can be connected by Art and Design teachers with the tradition of self-portraits in visual art. Through this, Art and Design teachers can motivate their students and also develop transdisciplinary competencies and skills by letting students bring the selfie to the classroom as an image to be produced and discussed within the framework of critical thinking. Young people often manipulate the selfie using augmented reality, filters and all sorts of applications that distort, remix and create new meanings in the photographs. When placed in the context of critical education, such processes become a means to understand the power of images in communication and to discuss the possibility of critiquing presumed identities and realities for constructive purposes.

PRIVACY VERSUS PUBLIC

Selves are constituted through interaction with others and for today's teenagers, self-actualization increasingly includes a careful negotiation between opportunities (for identity, intimacy and sociability) and risks (invasion of privacy, misunderstanding and abuse) afforded by internet-mediated communication (Livingstone, 2008). Bringing issues of public knowledge, open access information and an individual's copyrights, should be common in schools, and perhaps specially in the arts subjects. This is because through making in the arts subjects, we come to understand through practice how to create meaning through remixing and manipulating visual, textural and aural information. Arts learning situations can help young people to be more aware of their rights and responsibilities in seeking, receiving and imparting information freely through social media. It can also enable greater understanding of pernicious phenomena such as fake news and how one can unintentionally become a 'fake news agent' oneself. By tackling these themes through Art and Design activities, teachers can offer guidance on what one needs to consider when creating, seeking and disseminating visual information. In the #NarcissusMeetsPandora educators' guidelines, researchers explored the need for educators and teachers to make arts-based activities that explore privacy and data protection issues (see Task 12.5). It is not always easy for young people to understand the full extent of the right to privacy online which includes the right to be forgotten and have some of their publications removed permanently from the Internet. Raising issues about freedom from surveillance, the right to use encryption and anonymity and the right to data protection (control over personal data collection, retention, processing, disposal and disclosure) can be a part of discussion in the Art and Design classroom. Young people have the right to be free and safe online and to feel that this is the case. There is a need for an awareness that behaviours such as digital bullying and coercion are a violation of their human rights, and for young people be able to recognize and act on these. Bringing to the Art and Design classroom questions about private and public content as human rights issues can be approached by teachers and students as part of the contextual analysis of images produced by themselves and others, and in the remixing or production of new images.

Task 12.5 Public or Private

- When you make a selfie, do you think about whether it's going to be a public or private image?

Suggestion: Work in pairs to create one private selfie and a public selfie. Discuss with a larger group the process of doing this and the effectiveness of the results.

(*Source:* Project #NarcissusMeetsPandora, Educators Guide, 2022.)

SUMMARY

In our educational mission, to help teenagers deal with all the ethical, legal and visual technological issues in the production of personal images for digital environments; as teachers we need to test, together with our students, the experience of connecting with the digital environment. Gaining an understanding with them of their and our vulnerability in social networks can help them to use their visual narratives with reduced risk, in a responsible and active way that guarantees a fairer representation of the self and the possibilities for positive political agency. Critical pedagogy can be an effective approach to this, acknowledging that teachers need to create spaces of care (Atkinson, 2022), in which both the teacher and the learner in ways that acknowledge the different levels of responsibility in the teacher/learner relationship engage in a collaborative journey, a joint experimentation that does not necessarily have a clear view of what the outcome of the process will be. This permanent journey or 'pedagogy of the unknowable' (Ellsworth, 1989) defines the role of the teacher as someone who challenges, provokes and creates learning situations by respecting contexts and expectations that better deal with the societal challenges of our times (UNESCO, 2015).

NOTES

1 https://en.unesco.org/themes/gced
2 https://www.europeanschoolnetacademy.eu/courses/course-v1:EDURegio+ DigitallyCompetent+2020/courseware/52d675e198dd4c00bde4251a07698... 2/2
3 https://narcissusmeetspandora.eu/
4 #NarcissusMeetsPandora is an INNOVATIVE ARTS-BASED PRACTICE THAT TAKES UP DIGITAL TECHNOLOGIES AS TOOLS FOR YOUTH TO CRITICALLY AND SOCIALLY ENGAGE IN THE SOCIAL MEDIA CONTENTS PRODUCTION. Founded by the European Commission

RESOURCES

European Network for Visual Literacy. http://envil.eu/
The European Network for Visual Literacy (ENViL) is an informal network of more than 120 art teachers, researchers, specialists of didactics, curriculum developers and teacher trainers from 25 countries. It is open for everybody working in the field of visual education.

#NarcissusMeetsPandora Project. https://narcissusmeetspandora.eu/
#NarcissusMeetsPandora webpage provides open source documents created during the project, such as The educators Guidelines and Digital ToolKit.

COPPA (Children's Online Privacy Protection Rule). https://www.ftc.gov/enforcement/rules/rulemaking-regulatory-reform-proceedings/childrens-online-privacy-protection-rule
Here, you can find information on parental consent, confidentiality and security, safe harbour provisions etc.

UNESCO handbook: 'Personal Data and Privacy Protection in Online Learning: Guidance for Students, Teachers and Parents'. https://iite.unesco.org/wp-content/uploads/2020/06/Personal-Data-and-Privacy-Protection-in-Online-Learning-Guidance-for-Students-Teachers-and-Parents-V1.0.pdf
The Handbook is based on the 'Personal Data Security Technical Guide for Online Education Platforms', which was launched by the UNESCO IITE and Tsinghua University earlier. Both the Handbook and Technical Guide complement each other to promote personal data and privacy protection for teachers, students and parents in online learning.

Conceptual domains of Global Citizenship Education GCE. Source: Adapted from UNESCO. 2015. *Global Citizenship Education: Topics and Learning Objectives*, p. 15 and UNESCO. 2018. *Global Citizenship Education: Taking it Local*, p. 9.

BIBLIOGRAPHY

Albani, L., Marcolini, P., Catoni, S., Faes, L., & Pacenza, G. (2019). *Tinkering Coding Making Volume Teorico*. Trento: Fondazione Mondo Digitale.

Atkinson, D. (2022). Practice, Interstices, Otherness and Taking Care. *Revista Imaginar, 66,* 4–18.

Boursier, V. & Manna, V. (2018). Selfie Expectancies among Adolescents: Construction and Validation of an Instrument to Assess Expectancies toward Selfies among Boys and Girls. *Frontiers in Psychology,* 2–21. https://www.frontiersin.org/articles/10.3389/fpsyg.2018.00839/full

Cruz, E. G., & Thornham, H. (2015). Selfies Beyond Self-Representation: The (Theoretical) F(r)ictions of a Practice. *Journal of Aesthetics & Culture, 7*(1), 1–10. doi: 10.3402/jac.v7.28073

Deally, O., & Dixit, A. (2021). How to Avoid Performative Activism on Social Media. *Parachute.* https://www.theparachutemedia.com/culture-entertainment/deconstructing-performative-activism

Duncum, P. (1997). Art Education for New Times. *Studies in Art Education, 38*(2), 69–79.

Duncum, P. (2011). Youth on YouTube: Prosumers in a Peer-to-Peer Participatory Culture. In JAE9.2 ○C NTAEC 2011. https://ed.arte.gov.tw/uploadfile/periodical/3052_9-2-p.24-39.pdf.

Efland, A., Freedman, K., & Stuhr, P. (1996). *Postmodern Art Education: An Approach to Curriculum*. Reston, VA: NAEA.

Ellsworth, E. (1989). Why Doesn't This Feel Empowering? Working Through the Repressive Myths of Critical Pedagogy. *Harvard Educational Review, 59*(3), 297–324.

Freire, P. (1972). *Pedagogy of the Oppressed.* Harmondsworth: Penguin.

Giddens, A. (1991). *Modernity and Self-Identity: Self and Society in the Late Modern Age.* Cambridge: Polity Press.

Livingstone, S. (2008). Taking Risky Opportunities in Youthful Content Creation: Teenagers' Use of Social Networking Sites for Intimacy, Privacy and Self-Expression. *New Media & Society, 10*(3), 393–411. doi: 10.1177/1461444808089415

Narcissus Meets Pandora. (2022). *Framework for Educators.* To be published at https://narcissusmeetspandora.eu/

New London Group. (1996). A Pedagogy of Multiliteracies: Designing Social Futures. *Harvard Educational Review, 66*(1). http://www.sfu.ca/~decaste/new-london.htm

Prensky, M. (2009). H. Sapiens Digital: From Digital Immigrants and Digital Natives to Digital Wisdom. *Innovate: Journal of Online Education, 5*(3). https://www.learntechlib.org/p/104264/.

Steers, J. (2003). Art and Design. In: White, J. (Ed.) *Rethinking the School Curriculum: Values, Aims and Purposes.* London: RoutledgeFalmer.

Steers, J. (2004). Orthodoxy, Creativity and Opportunity. *International Journal of Arts Education, 2*, 24–38.

Tufekci, Z., & Wilson, C. (2012). Social Media and the Decision to Participate in Political Protest: Observations from Tahrir Square. *Journal of Communication, 62*, 363–379. doi: 10.1111/j.1460-2466.2012.01629.x

UNESCO International Commission on the Futures of Education. (2015). Sustainable Development Goals http://en.unesco.org/sdgsUNESCO International Commission on the Futures of Education. (2018). *Global Citizenship Education: Taking It Local.* Paris, UNESCO. https://unesdoc.unesco.org/ark:/48223/pf0000265456.

UNESCO International Commission on the Futures of Education. (2020). *Education in a Post-COVID World: Nine Ideas for Public Action.* https://en.unesco.org/sites/default/files/education_in_a_post-covid_world-nine_ideas_for_public_action.pdf

UNESCO International Commission on the Futures of Education. (2022). *Reimagining Our Futures Together: A New Social Contract for Education.* https://unesdoc.unesco.org/ark:/48223/pf0000379707

Velasquez, A., & LaRose, R. (2015). Youth Collective Activism Through Social Media: The Role of Collective Efficacy. *New Media & Society, 17*(6), 899–918. doi: 10.1177/1461444813518391

Wagner, E., & Schönau, D. (2016). *Common European Framework of Reference for Visual Literacy–Prototype.* Münster/New York: Waxmann.

Chapter 13   Art History in the Art and Design Curriculum

Neil Walton

INTRODUCTION

The purpose of this chapter is to discuss rationales and strategies for teaching art history as part of the Art and Design curriculum and to prompt reflection on some common classroom practices, asking why we do them and whether we should do them differently. What do you understand by the term art history? Perhaps it has featured in your own studies, either centrally or as a supplement to studio practice. If the latter, did art history inform your practice? Directly or indirectly? Did it provide a source of ideas and exemplars to embrace, modify or reject? Or did it provide a contrasting activity, a space to gain some reflective distance from studio work?

Art history is an important discipline, valued for the mind-broadening and empathy-building virtues of studying a range of periods and cultures, and for developing skills of close observation, interpretation and judgment. The claim made in this chapter is that art historical awareness should also be recognised as central to the study of Art and Design because the fundamental categories 'art', 'craft' and 'design' have changed and shifted so radically over time. The resulting complexity and plurality should be reflected in what and *how* we teach. To convey the notion of art history at work here means questioning some common perceptions of it, for example, as involving the teaching of a linear chronology of great artists, or as a purely written add-on to practice. The view presented in this chapter is of art history as a field of debate in which students encounter diverse exemplars and work out their own commitments.

OBJECTIVES:

At the end of this chapter, you should be able to:

- Understand different rationales for the inclusion of art history in the Art and Design curriculum.
- Explore the practical ways in which art history can underpin decisions about curriculum and pedagogy in Art and Design.
- Understand the possibilities and limitations of familiar classroom practices related to art history.

DOI: 10.4324/9781003377429-16

Perhaps you have come across the justly celebrated, and probably most famous, art history book, E. H. Gombrich's *The Story of Art* (Gombrich 2007). A classic chronological survey, it has sold over eight million copies around the world since its first publication in 1950. The central narrative it relates mainly follows the development of European art with a few forays into other cultures, notably in Persia and China. Although its brilliantly concise storytelling is a large part of its success, this narrow approach is no longer really representative of scholarship in the field. Nevertheless, it has firmly established the idea of art history as a linear chronological development. It is a powerful idea and hard to move beyond, but more recently the art historian James Elkins has written an interesting critical response called *Stories of Art* (Elkins 2002), which highlights the contingency of both the particular story that Gombrich told, built around the evolution of realistic representation, and also of the very idea of a linear narrative. Opening the book, Elkins describes how he gets his students to complete a simple exercise, a thought experiment, to draw a loose and informal map of art history as it exists for them at a personal level. The aim is not to guess at an accurate timeline but to find an imaginative shape or system for art, showing individual preferences, attachments and chance encounters. You could try this out for yourself. Your history of art could be imagined as a field of stars, or as a coastline, as a flow chart or as a schematic transport map with criss-crossing lines and interchanges (the artist Simon Patterson did something like this in his 1992 work *The Great Bear* which appropriates the London Underground map, and it has frequently been adapted). It could highlight other relationships besides geography and chronological sequence – whatever seems most important to you. For example, it could show up the complex, fluctuating relationship between ideas of 'art', 'craft' and 'design' in European and other contexts (see Shiner 2001), or the received cultural hierarchies between fashion, cinema, pop music and video games. It could chart the use of particular themes or materials. It could point out where architects and designers have looped back to earlier ideas in history or have drawn on disparate sources such as climate science and religion, psychology or folk art. It could be broad and eclectic, or very focused in a particular area of personal interest.

Task 13.1 A Personal Map of Art History

- Draw a loose and informal map or chart showing a personal view of art history.
- Avoid using a simple timeline and freely include a variety of elements and dimensions, such as high art and popular culture, personal preferences and chance connections.

Although art, craft and design are essentially practical and have their primary home in studio practice, they are closely related to, both described and shaped by, the theoretical disciplines of art history, aesthetics and art criticism. The character of these relationships is the focus of this chapter. To critically reflect on the possible structures of the Art and Design curriculum, it will be helpful for you to know something of the long-running debates about the disciplinary bases of art education (see Hickman 2005). After a long period of relative neglect, the place of art history in Art and Design is currently undergoing renewed interest, in part due to Ofsted's focus on knowledge in the curriculum and related research (Young 2008; Spielman 2017; Green 2021). In the 1980s and 1990s, there were vigorous exchanges about the role and purpose of art history, notably in the pages of the

Journal of Art and Design Education (Dyson 1982; Garb 1984; Kindler 1992). These exchanges were part of a broader discussion about the domains that comprise art education and the disciplines that feed into it, prompted by developments in educational thinking on both sides of the Atlantic (Field 1970; Eisner 1972). Drawing on research at Stanford University, Elliot Eisner specified the realms or domains of artistic learning as the productive, the critical and the historical. In America this subject-centred line of thinking led to a comprehensively worked out approach called discipline-based art education (DBAE), which drew on the four professional fields of art history, art criticism, philosophical aesthetics and art practice. The discipline-based approach never really gained traction in Britain. Important related work was done under the heading of critical studies (Rod Taylor's 1986 book *Educating for Art* is an excellent example), but DBAE as such was more often criticised for its perceived narrowness and elitism (Swift 1993).

These debates were aired some time ago; however, they remain relevant. It is important for you as a newly emerging art educator to be aware of recent controversies in our subject. This is a healthy exercise to avoid the narrow temporal focus that can result from the constant churn of educational policy: a collective professional amnesia. Moreover, the argument presented here is that there are compelling reasons to revisit the discipline-based approach to Art and Design. One is that in the past few years new and persuasive theories have been advanced about knowledge and the curriculum. The sociologist Michael Young has written about the powerful knowledge that emerges from a strong relationship between disciplines and school subjects (Young et al. 2014). Christine Counsell has argued that the substantive content of what we teach in the classroom should lead students onto, or at the very least make them aware of, the much larger disciplinary 'hinterland' that is the active field of practice and scholarship in which new ideas are generated and revised (Counsell 2018). Jan Derry draws on inferential role semantics to show how subject-specific knowledge depends on a rich web of conceptual relations which allow us to represent the world (Derry 2018).

The second, related, reason is that the relevant disciplines, notably art history and philosophical aesthetics, have significantly changed in the intervening years and have substantially addressed the charges of narrowness and elitism that were often levelled at DBAE. Already in 1984, the art historian Tamar Garb could point to substantial critiques of her discipline from Marxist, feminist and poststructuralist perspectives (Garb 1984), and such critical moves have continued with work on queer, anti-ableist, postcolonial, critical race and decolonising theory (Grant and Price 2020). In parallel with this, philosophical aesthetics has similarly developed broader, more inclusive perspectives (Brand 2000). As a result of these changes, the disciplinary bases of art education are now well placed to critically influence and energise where there is unreflective orthodoxy in school practice.

Task 13.2 Discussing Knowledge, Domains and Disciplines

- What role do you think knowledge should have within Art and Design?
- What is the relative importance of the following disciplines to Art and Design education: art practice, aesthetics, art criticism, art history? Also try substituting craft or design across this range of terms.
- Is it helpful to consider Art and Design education in terms of domains, such as the productive, critical and historical?
- Are there other possible domains you would suggest, perhaps the perceptual or the imaginative?

The purpose of the conceptual mapping exercise above was to highlight the complexity and contingency of the stories that we tell about art. In a field as complex as art history any narrative, any conceptual mapping, will impose a partial and selective shape. Although it is important that students gain a secure knowledge base to support their learning and personal development in art and design, including detailed, warranted historical and material facts, it is only through using some shared system of concepts, judgements, inferences and norms that we can begin to represent facts and connect meaningfully to the world. It is only when learners are engaged in the activities of making judgements and giving and asking for reasons within a specific conceptual framework that understanding can develop (Derry 2018). Moving learners in and out of their existing, relatively limited personal frame of reference and through richer, more complexly interlinked and specialised ones is the difficult task of pedagogy. In Art and Design, we can be playful and creative with this process, but a prerequisite is that you as the teacher have a strong and accurate knowledge base yourself to support this flexibility, including an understanding of art's contingent histories. Karl Popper once claimed that the best place for any beginning seeker after knowledge to go is where the disagreements are (Samuels 1985). The disagreements and controversies are part of what we should be teaching.

Task 13.3 Self-Assessment

- How would you assess your own knowledge of art, craft and design history?
- What areas are you strong on and where might you extend and deepen your knowledge, for example, design history?

Any Art and Design curriculum is bound to be partial and selective. As Christine Counsell writes, 'Decisions about what knowledge to teach are an exercise of power and therefore a weighty ethical responsibility' (Counsell 2018). This presents us with a dilemma. On the one hand, students are entitled to a comprehensive overview of art, craft and design through the key years of their school education. On the other hand, given the sheer breadth and diversity of things which are taken as art now, acquiring that cumulative sufficiency is no easy task (Fordham 2017). Though painting, sculpture, drawing and printmaking are still central art forms, they have been joined by photography, performance, installation, digital and time-based media, and of course art has a close relationship with design and craft in graphics, typography, textiles, ceramics and other areas of making. Most art teaching uses a familiar range of materials, techniques and themes, but the range of things that show up as art today is very wide. Art could be a warehouse-sized installation or a marble statue, a pen and ink drawing or a pile of blankets, and many other modest or spectacular items. This array can be bewildering, especially for those with less cultural capital. Some accessible way to convey the confusing and fractured state of affairs is needed.

To ensure that the current scope and plurality of art is represented in the curriculum, I suggest using a schematic historical conceptual scheme. Using this framework to inform curriculum planning not only ensures that a wide range of work is featured, but it also offers opportunities to highlight the field's complex and contested character. This is a powerful means of making students active participants in their learning (for a precursor of this taxonomy, see de Duve 1999) (Figure 13.1).

A R T   C   O   N   C   E   P   T   S

TRADITIONAL	MODERN	CONTEMPORARY
CONVENTION Artists use forms, genres, themes and meanings that are passed on from generation to generation	**ORIGINALITY** An artist is an individual who creates something new and personal without relying on previous work	**COLLABORATION** Art is a social process in which people work together, sharing ideas and allowing new forms to emerge
CRAFT Art uses skilful techniques that can be taught and which produce reliable, already known outcomes	**MEDIUM** Art uses media like painting, drawing and sculpture. A medium combines materials and conventions. It can be discovered and explored	**PRACTICE** Art can't be confined to established forms, media and materials. Anything can become art. Art and life are blurred
IMITATION Artists copy the work of their predecessors. Copying is a way of showing respect and approval	**EXPERIMENTATION** Artists try out unexpected moves and test them directly against experience, finding new standards of success	**DECONSTRUCTION** Art breaks down familiar boundaries. It raises questions and challenges all established ideas and conventions

Figure 13.1 Art concepts adpated from de Duve 1999.

The contention of this framework is that several conceptions or paradigms of art are in circulation. New views of art have emerged over time to challenge the old, complicating though not erasing what has gone before. For shorthand, let us call these the traditional, the modern and the contemporary. Each of these conceptions has its distinctive values, characteristics and different educational approach. For traditional art, continuity across generations and socially shared understandings are what lend its forms and meanings resonance. To teach art traditionally is to transmit the inheritances of a culture: its skills, practices and concerns. By contrast, and in response, the modern idea of art rejects established practices and instead values originality, experimentation and expression. The force of the modern idea of art depends on the sincerity and perceptiveness of the individual artist, or of a community recognising each other's artistic autonomy. In the modern conception, to teach art is to facilitate experimentation and discovery, to break down the habits and conventions that overlay the sources of art, variously defined. The contemporary idea of art radicalises the modern challenge to tradition. Its force is in destabilising and deconstructing every aspect of art: its media, conventions of production and reception, the boundary between art and everyday life and the distinction between artist and viewer. This idea of art is the most radical in its pedagogy, questioning all institutional framings. Democratising and merging the roles of teacher and learner, it conceives of education as a non-hierarchical, collaborative process.

Some key ingredients of these different conceptions are set out in the table given here. This layout highlights how different and contradictory the ideas in each column can be. Each idea of art has its defenders and its critics, but here they are presented without prejudice or preference. Although these paradigms of art emerged over time, they are all still available today. The purpose of introducing this framework to learners is to encourage a critical, questioning attitude in students as they look at and think about a range of artworks and other cultural items, and as they reflect on the way that they are encountering various practices. It should encourage learners to position themselves, drawing on their own emerging ideas and intuitions.

Task 13.4 Locating Yourself within Different Conceptions of Art

- Which of the three categories in the above table do you find most appealing?
- Which of these approaches to teaching have you experienced and found helpful or unhelpful?
- Are there other conceptions or paradigms of art you could suggest to add to or replace the given ones?

Notice how this conceptual framework not only sets out different ideas of art but also different approaches to teaching. As art educators we can demonstrate the big historical ideas underlying practice through the ways we teach. Embedding historical references in pedagogical approaches in this way avoids art history being merely a superficial supplement to practice. For example, a common practice in many school art departments is copying, transcription or visual analysis of the work of a chosen or designated artist. With some good justification copying has been criticised as a superficial, decontextualised orthodoxy (Hughes 1989; Addison 2015). Certainly, it would be incongruous to learn about a Barbara Kruger billboard by making a painstaking pencil sketch of it, and it is not usual to see this kind of practice in classrooms. But in its proper place copying plays a powerful role. For example, learning through the kind of traditional Chinese painting exemplified by the Manual of the Mustard Seed Garden (Sze 1977), a student apprentice must closely observe model works before rehearsing marks and figures precisely and repeatedly until they become almost automatic. It is a hallmark of all kinds of traditional art that copying the work of predecessors is both a pedagogical tool and simultaneously a way of demonstrating respect. By enacting that process of careful imitation, students learn something of importance about these cultural practices and underlying philosophy. We can also teach students about the historical reception of such practices that often misrepresents certain cultures as essentially static and unchanging (Said 1978).

By contrast, to convey an understanding of the modern idea of art calls for a pedagogy that foregrounds experimentation and discovery, an exploration of materials and the dynamics of visual form and the effects and meanings they can produce through the development of an individual style. All too often schools run a Year 7 project introducing line, tone, colour and shape as 'formal elements' but without either the discoveries in visual experience or the cultural context that give these exercises their powerful significance, notably, the innovative pedagogy of Johannes Itten at the Bauhaus in the 1920s. Itten's aim was to liberate creative forces in the student as part of his holistic vision, a broad and ambitious spiritual and practical programme to replace bourgeois society (Wick 2000; Sturgis 2020). These larger ideas are almost always left out of the formal elements project, and yet we should be putting them right up front.

Traditional and modern practices invoke very different and often incompatible values and ideas. The contentious character of art today is a great opportunity to foster debate. It should be clear from the foregoing that art history in the Art and Design curriculum need not be relegated to marginal activities such as the occasional homework to research an artist reference or adding some written annotations in the pages of a sketchbook. Art history is usually conceived of as various forms of reading, writing and speaking about art, craft and design, but the argument of this chapter is that art historical thinking should underpin both curriculum and pedagogy in the subject. It should be grounded in careful looking, judgement and interpretation but also debate and discussion about the big ideas, values and commitments that art embodies.

All too often school art projects feature only one or two brief contextual references which are passed over quickly *en route* to a sequence of entirely practical lessons. Where students are required to produce writing about an artist or artwork it is often as a sidebar to practice and as a separate standalone activity. It is hardly surprising if the resultant writing tends to be either a flat description or list of disconnected facts when students are set a task with no clear rationale or motivation. Careful looking and its translation into words are more than merely registering and recording sense data. To look is to do something more than just seeing. Looking involves an active structuring of experience, that is, a discursive, concept-using activity that is continuous with the distinctively human practices of language and of giving and asking for reasons (Brandom 2011). To write about an artwork is to make claims about it, and that involves a student engaging with different kinds of authority and responsibility. There is the authority of the work itself, which demands commitment and fidelity to its presence and specificity. At the same time, in making claims about the artwork the student is experimenting with taking on responsibility and authority, in that she now becomes responsible for the claims she is making and is open to being asked for reasons for her claims. Note also how these engaged forms of looking, writing and discussing, by stressing ownership and production, complement the creative work of making art, craft and design.

Common school practice seldom recognises how important it is that students get to see and discuss a great many different and contrasting examples of artworks as well as other cultural artefacts. Research about artistic and cultural references is often done by students individually, rather than as part of a live and ongoing classroom exchange. And yet there are ways of engaging students with a rich field of visual images. Perhaps we need to be both more playful and simultaneously more serious in our pursuit of this. Some great examples can be found on artpedagogy.com, an online resource created by two inspirational teachers, Chris Francis and Jon Nicholls (Francis and Nicholls 2022). In one particular exercise on the Artpedagogy website called 'conversations', two randomly selected works are placed side by side and accompanied by the questions: 'Which words might you place in the middle of the two works to act as a bridge and form a connection?' and 'What happens if a word is chosen at random and placed between the two images – can this still influence our interpretations?'. This playful, inventive exercise recalls some older precedents in art historical scholarship. The art historian Heinrich Wölfflin pioneered a comparative technique using two slide projectors with images shown side by side. He analysed artworks in terms of formal oppositions such as linear and painterly, open and closed, plane and recession, multiplicity and unity and so on (Wolfflin 2015). The filter of Wölfflin's oppositions set up a dialectic between his pre-existing descriptive scheme and responsiveness to the artworks he addressed. It is vital always to recognise the specificity of cultural artefacts, not because artworks exist beyond the discursive but because every attempt at description, even the most faithful, produces something new.

> ## Task 13.5 Devising a Framework for Observing and Analysing a Cultural Artefact
>
> Various writing frames have been put forward to support students' analysis of works. A popular example is to use the headings, Form, Content, Context, Mood (Taylor 1989).
>
> - What do you think are the strengths and shortcomings of this frame?
> - Are there any artworks or cultural artefacts that it would be unsuitable for?
> - What other aspects could be included?

Another precedent for exploring the relationships between images can be found in the work of the art historian, Aby Warburg, in his *Mnemosyne Atlas*. During the 1920s, Warburg created a series of sixty-three large panels featuring hundreds of reproductions of images. On these panels, Warburg mapped unexpected, deeply researched links between a wide range of sources, for example, artworks and manuscript pages alongside modern images drawn from newspapers and magazines. He referred to these complex, dynamic constellations as a 'denkraum', a thought-space (Warburg Institute 2022). Creating something like this on the walls of a classroom, with students adding, moving, linking, discussing and revising elements would be more valuable than using the narrow timeline of periods and movements that is often equated with art history.

> ## Task 13.6 Map the Stories of Art That Are Featured in a Departmental Curriculum
>
> Revisit the initial art history mapping exercise to help you reflect on learnings from this chapter. If possible, do this for your current art department.
>
> - Audit the curriculum in your department with regard to the art histories it might be telling, either implicitly or explicitly. Take into account displays and the sequence of projects.
> - Consider where there are significant gaps or omissions.
> - Work with students to create your own 'culture atlas/denkraum' display where unusual connections are made between contemporary and historical art, between fine art, craft and design in fashion, computer games or films.

Art historical learning is not merely writing down dates or biographical facts about artists. It is learning about meanings and interpretations, materials and processes, journeys and connections across time and location, as well as political stories of omission and oppression. It can be particularly helpful to flag up links between contemporary and historical artworks and design practices. Many contemporary artists, from Ai Wei Wei and Fred Wilson to Cathie Pilkington and Yinka Shonibare, explore links to predecessors in a historically informed way (see links below).

SUMMARY

In this chapter, we have seen how art history in the Art and Design curriculum does not need to conform to the standard models of a linear chronological story of, mainly Western, art. By better reflecting the current state of disciplinary thinking in art history, we can bring students as active participants into a field of debate. The fractured and contentious nature of art, craft and design today is a great opportunity to foster debate and we should be placing greater emphasis on this. One way of thinking about the purpose of art education is to say that we would like students to become increasingly authoritative about aspects of the field, to take on commitments and a sense of ownership. This sense of acquired authority and ownership can be manifested in a variety of roles. One version of this might be the authority of the artist over, and responsibility to, their own work, but we can also consider a range of other roles: the art critic, the curator, theorist, designer, craft maker, the illustrator and the art historian.

RESOURCES

Ai Weiwei (2010) Sunflower Seeds. https://www.tate.org.uk/art/artworks/ai-sunflower-seeds-t13408

Art history in Schools – This is an organisation that works to increase the engagement of young people in primary and secondary schools with art history. Recognising that the subject is most often taught in independent schools, Art History in Schools emphasises that all students, regardless of background should have access to this entitlement.

Artpedagogy – A model of creative curriculum thinking, this website shares a portfolio of ideas that link to diverse, visually and conceptually exciting examples of artworks, providing the multi-layered contextual reference that all art and design students should benefit from. These are accompanied by intelligent commentary, inventive juxtapositions, prompts and suggestions as well as thought-provoking questions and practical suggestions for the classroom.

Barbara Kruger. https://www.tate.org.uk/art/artists/barbara-kruger-1443#:~:text=Kruger's%20artistic%20mediums%20include%20photography,of%20the%20Arts%20and%20Architecture.

Cathie Pilkington and Alison Wilding (2020) The Ancestors. https://www.royalacademy.org.uk/exhibition/the-ancestors

Fred Wilson (1993) Grey Area. https://www.tate.org.uk/art/artworks/wilson-grey-area-t13632

James Elkins (2002) *Stories of art*. London: Routledge. – This slim and accessible volume is a re-imagining of E. H. Gombrich's classic art history textbook. It is playful but has a serious message and intent. It shows how art history can be reconfigured in many different ways, revealing different global viewpoints, and showing that there is no end to the invention and reinvention of art's stories.

Simon Patterson (1992) The Great Bear. https://www.tate.org.uk/art/artworks/patterson-the-great-bear-p77880

Yinka Shonibare (2001) The Swing (after Fragonard). https://www.tate.org.uk/art/artworks/shonibare-the-swing-after-fragonard-t07952

BIBLIOGRAPHY

Addison, Nicholas (2015) Critical studies. In Addison, N. & Burgess, L. (eds.) *Learning to teach art and design in the secondary school*. London: Routledge.

Brand, Peg Z. (2000) Glaring omissions in traditional theories of art. In Carroll, N. (ed.) *Theories of art today*. Madison: University of Wisconsin Press.

Brandom, Robert (2011) *Perspectives on pragmatism: classical, recent and contemporary*. Cambridge, MA and London: Harvard University Press.

Counsell, Christine (2018) Taking curriculum seriously. *Impact: Journal of the Chartered College of Teaching*. Issue 4, 6–9, September.

De Duve, Thierry (1999) When form has become attitude and beyond. In Foster, S. & de Ville, N. (eds.) *The artist and the academy*. Southampton: John Hansard Gallery.

Derry, Jan (2018) *Knowledge in education: why philosophy matters*. London: UCL Institute of Education.

Dyson, Anthony (1982) Art history in schools: a comprehensive approach. *Journal of Art and Design Education*. 1:1, 123–134.

Eisner, Elliot (1972) *Educating artistic vision*. New York: Macmillan.

Elkins, James (2002) *Stories of art*. London: Routledge.

Field, Dick (1970) *Change in art education*. London: Routledge and Kegan Paul.

Fordham, Michael (2017) https://clioetcetera.com/2017/01/05/knowledge-inde pendently-necessary-or-collectively-sufficient/

Francis, Chris & Nicholls, Jon (2022) https://www.artpedagogy.com/couch-to-artist-task1.html

Garb, Tamar (1984) New methodologies in art history: implications for school teaching. *Journal of Art and Design Education*. 3:3, 347–356.

Gombrich, Ernst (2007) *The story of art*. London: Phaidon.

Grant, Catherine & Price, Dorothy (2020) Decolonizing art history: questionnaire. *Art History*. 43:1, 8–66.

Green, Bridget (2021) Revisiting the conceptual domain: educational knowledge and the visual arts. *International Journal of Art and Design Education*. 40:2, 436–448.

Hickman, Richard (2005) *Critical studies in art and design education*. Bristol: Intellect.

Hughes, Arthur (1989) The copy, the parody and the pastiche: observations on practical approaches to critical studies. In Thistlewood, D. (ed.) *Critical studies in art and design education*. Harlow: Longman.

Kindler, Anna (1992) Discipline-based art education in schools: a possible approach. *Journal of Art and Design Education*. 11:3, 345–356.

Popper, Karl (1963) *Conjectures and refutations*. London: Routledge and Kegan Paul.

Said, Edward (1978) *Orientalism*. London: Routledge.

Samuels, Andrew (1985) *Jung and the post-jungians*. London: Routledge.

Shiner, Larry (2001) *The invention of art*. Chicago, IL: University of Chicago Press.

Spielman, Amanda (2017) Speech at the festival of education. https://www.gov.uk/ government/speeches/amanda-spielmans-speech-at-the-festival-of-education

Sturgis, Daniel (2020) Bauhaus: to turn away from normality. *Art, Design & Communication in Higher Education*. 19:1, 9–18.

Swift, John (1993) Critical studies: a Trojan horse for an alternative cultural agenda. *Journal of Art and Design Education*. 12:3, 291–304.

Sze, Mai-mai (1977) *The manual of the mustard seed garden*. Princeton, NJ: Princeton University Press.

Taylor, Rod (1986) *Educating for art*. London: Longman.

Taylor, Rod (1989) Critical studies in art and design education: passing fashion or the missing element? In Thistlewood, D. (ed.) *Critical studies in art and design education*. Harlow: Longman.

Warburg Institute (2022) https://warburg.sas.ac.uk/virtual-tour-between-cosmos
-and-pathos-berlin-works-aby-warburgs-mnemosyne-atlas-exhibition
Wick, Rainer K. (2000) *Teaching at the Bauhaus*. Stuttgart: Hatje Cantz.
Wolfflin, Heinrich (2015) *The principles of art history: the problem of the development of style in early modern art.* Los Angeles, CA: Getty Publications.
Young, Michael (2008) *Bringing knowledge back in: from social constructivism to social realism in the sociology of education.* London: Routledge.
Young, Michael & Lambert, David (2014) *Knowledge and the future school: curriculum and social justice.* London: Bloomsbury.

Chapter 14 The Pupil-Curator: Curating in/as Collaborative Learning

Andy Ash and Marquard Smith

INTRODUCTION

In this chapter, we argue for, (1) the significant benefits of the implementation of 'curating' in education/learning in general, and specifically, (2) for curating as a collaborative activity for Art and Design pupils in the context of schools/the secondary classroom, and also in learning beyond the classroom (Bentley 1998) in museums/galleries. We propose that curating is, (a) a radical pedagogical activity (Ash and Smith 2022) that functions to facilitate learning collaboratively, (b) a co-constructing of knowledges (Bruner 1977; Hein 1998) that generates new ways of doing/seeing/knowing/being, and, (c) is thus empowering for students and pupils, a means by which they are enabled to develop a breadth of understanding of possible Art and Design practices and find and amplify their voices (Flutter and Rudduck 2004). We promote the idea of the curator-practitioner, a means by which Art and Design students learn that to be responsible for organising and presenting their work, and that of others, is integral to their practice. The curator-practitioner can be modified and adapted for the context of Art and Design learning in secondary schools to the *pupil-curator*.

These ideas underpin conceptually and are put into 'real-world' practice by a module taught on the MA Museums & Galleries in Education programme at UCL Institute of Education entitled 'Curating and Educating'. We will draw here on this module as a case study of good and better practice, as a resource to be re-purposed and utilised in schools by Art and Design teachers and pupils as a generative and affirmative, as well as fun, way of 'learning through doing' (Dewey 1966).

The module's aims and objectives, its assignment and assessment, and especially its collaborative spirit, can be utilised by Art and Design teachers to facilitate learning, both in the context of schools and in non-school learning environments such as museums, galleries, and heritage sites. It is also a way to embed, implicitly and explicitly, the idea of 'research' into secondary school learning, where research is praxis, and praxis is research, which is beneficial for pupils personally, academically, and professionally.

DOI: 10.4324/9781003377429-17

OBJECTIVES

At the end of this chapter, you should be able to:

- Define and understand the terms curating and collaboration;
- Justify introducing curating and collaboration in Art and Design education;
- Take inspiration from the case studies and see what might be applicable in your context;
- Recognise and want to deploy the possibilities of empowering pupils by developing curation and collaboration in the art and design curriculum.

CURATING AND COLLABORATION

We start by giving some background and outline curation and education as converging fields of inquiry and practice, along with the possibilities for repurposing them in schools. Firstly, we highlight:

1. *curating education,* which is to say learning in museums, galleries, and heritage, and also;
2. curating *as* education, as a critical pedagogical praxis *by* educators, artist-educators, and curators, *in* (and beyond) galleries/museums/heritage, and *for* audiences.

In the module, which is ripe for re-purposing, we foreground four key questions/ dimensions of curation and education and suggest that you consider the following as starting points in your own teaching.

Task 14.1 Curating

- Curation and education: how and why is 'curating' central to our understanding of what museums, galleries, and heritage sites 'do' when they 'do' education, learning, and pedagogy?
- Curating and educating/curating education: consider contemporary practices, and also historical trajectories or convergences of curating and educating in galleries, museums, and heritage sites. Discuss with your colleagues how education/learning programmes have been developed/delivered by curators/educators/artist-educators working in or with museums, galleries, and heritage sites.
- The curatorial turn/the educational turn (see Resources): how have recent 'turns' in (i) academic debates (in Curatorial Studies, Museum Education, Radical Pedagogy, Exhibition Studies, and Artistic Research) (ii) the practices of artists, designers, and architects, and (iii) art/museum/gallery/heritage sector professionals and educators transformed the relations between curating and education within galleries, museums, and heritage site (and beyond them also)?
- Curation *as* education: how can we understand curating *as* learning? What 'forms' does curating take *as* education (this might include the idea of an exhibition as an educational proposition; education/learning 'on site' and the opportunities this affords; programming (for instance for/with children,

---

young people, families, SEND, refugees, LGBTQ+ communities, older adults etc.) that is itself a curatorial activity whose development, forms/formats, and delivery might be born of radical pedagogical impulses, participation, co-production, and so forth? What radical and critical possibilities emerge from such collaborating between practitioners, scholars, educators, audiences, and researchers?

Together, these questions/dimensions provide you with an academic framework for understanding and engaging critically with the figure of the curator, curatorial praxis, curating as education, cultural institutions, and environments for learning. Furthermore, the curating *of* education, as well as curating *as* education in museums/galleries/heritage sites, can alert your pupil-curators to many of the professional skills necessary to develop their own curatorial practice as future educators, artist-educators, learning professionals in the art/museum/gallery/ heritage sectors, and critical thinkers in general.

What we are advocating for is pupil-curators learning about the 'practice' of 'doing' curating and educating ('learning through doing', as we noted earlier), as well as some engagement with the histories/theories around them. During the 'Curating and Educating' module in the MA Museums & Galleries in Education programme at UCL IoE, our students not just became familiar with diverse histories/genealogies/geographies of curating/educating, but also learnt about *ways of working together*, the true nature of collaboration, and how they might and can and should work together (in their differences from one another).

In the outworking of the module, collaboration itself became a methodology. In order to establish this, we advocate that you first work with your pupil-curators on a 'social contract' (see Task 14.2) that they develop together – defining the conditions under which they are willing/obliged to work together and be accountable to one another.

Task 14.2 Terms of Engagement/A Social Contract

How we do things matters as much as *what* we do! We encourage pupil-curators to think carefully – individually and collectively – about their 'ways of working together'. Using the materials below, develop a social contract with your pupils. Ask the pupils in small groups to create their own one-page social contract for a collaborative exhibition project you set them (a social contract is a designed agreement for a set of values, behaviours, and social norms including the consequences if the contract is broken). Using the following points ask them to prepare to share their findings:

- discuss agreed values for working collaboratively;
- discuss agreed behaviours for working collaboratively;
- discuss agreed expectations for working collaboratively;
- how would someone be held accountable if they broke the agreed social contract?

You may want to get the groups to present their different social contracts and either vote on the most appropriate or workable contract that the whole class could use, or they could take sections from different contracts to make a combined contract. The key is to get a democratic agreement on a social contract they can all work with and abide by (see Resources for examples of social contracts).

GROUP WORK

To develop meaningful group work, the Terms of Engagement/Social Contract (see Task 14.2) draws on social contracts from the 17th and 18th centuries and more recent social contracts inspired by feminist hacks and critical race theory. The drafting of the pupil-curators' own 'Social Contracts' a way for the groups to get to know one another, to discuss their ways of working together (the 'how' of what they were going to do), as well as the project itself (the 'what' they were going to do), with regard to their agreed values for working collaboratively, their responsibilities towards one another, their accountability, and so on. As teachers we should try to establish collaborative ways of working that will embed collaborative skills/competences that will be of long-term benefit for the pupils personally, academically, and professionally (Vygotsky 1978).

MEANING MAKING

In thinking about how you might repurpose the practical activities of the 'Curating and Educating' module at UCL IoE for your Art and Design pupils, it will be useful to ponder the etymology of the key words we are using in this chapter. Etymologies often provide insights into terms we are familiar with, yet the full richness and meaning of which we might be unaware.

Collaboration is a key word in this undertaking. The origin of the word derives from the Latin verb *collabōrāre*. The prefix col- is a variant of com-, meaning 'together'. At the heart of the word is 'labora' labour, meaning 'work'. To collaborate, then, is to be together, and to do together.

Likewise, our other key word, 'curation', has an etymological relationship to *care* (as well as *curiosity*); in classical Latin, to take care of the health and well-being of bodies of others; in Medieval Latin, to take care ecclesiastically of the souls of others; and more recently in English, 'curating' is about caring (by way of conservation and preservation, management, and guardianship) for objects in museum collections; and even more recently and more widely to 'curate' one's social media in the consumer culture of late capitalism. In this chapter, we develop this to embed, embody, and articulate a curatorial practice that is attentive to, that cares for minds, bodies, and spirits in the context of education. This strikes us particularly pertinent to schools, and society more generally, living in the wake of Covid, in times in which more thought and consideration needs to be afforded to aspects of care of pupils and their care for one another.

Curating in/as collaborative learning is manifest, then, through the UCL IoE module, which culminated in the students in groups developing and realising a 'real-world' exhibition at Candid Arts Trust in Islington, London. This project afforded the students the opportunity to 'put into practice' everything they'd read, discussed and explored in practice around both (1) collaborating with others (i.e.

working together and the challenges and benefits of this) and (2) collaborating with diverse groups and audiences, which both bring to the fore the need for (and benefits of) co-production, co-creation (Bruner 1977) and co-curation in establishing a 'community of practice' (Wenger 1998) around shared concerns and passions.

Task 14.3 Your Exhibition/Collaboration – 'Putting Ideas into Practice'

Find a space/place for the pupils to develop their own 'real-world' exhibition, think as big or as small as you can facilitate. You might approach a local gallery or museum (education departments are often looking for projects with local schools), you might have a space in your school or a feeder school, or you might take part in a local festival (many cities/boroughs/towns have open houses, open studios, or community events). Reach out to organisations that can include pupils in local events, maybe a starting point would be to seek out areas of your community that focus on 'care'? The key is to generate an opportunity for collaboration, to co-produce – with pupils, between pupils and with publics to establish meaningful, embedded, communities of practice.

This is your school 'Culture Centre', which can be as permanent, temporary, real, or virtual as resources allow (See Resources for how this was conducted by Smith at UCL IoE).

Currently, curating is the word used to characterise the majority of learning/education labour done in the museums, galleries, and heritage sectors. A role in the past such as Education Officer is now more likely to be known, for instance, as Curator of Learning. Similarly, teachers and museum/gallery staff are less likely to talk about delivering education for audiences, but are more likely to talk about 'curating learning opportunities', and other similar terminology. Many artist-educators will be employed by galleries and museums to 'curate' learning programmes for pupils (Pringle 2009), young people, older adults, etc. It is appropriate therefore that we introduce pupils to this contemporary discourse early on in their secondary Art and Design curriculum so that the future artists and designers among them become familiar with a fuller range of the roles and responsibilities that are available and will be available to them, across creative sectors.

Academics/educators and professionals often collaborate with diverse audiences including children, young people, students with a SEND, LGBTQ+ communities, refugees, and older adults. There are ways to become versed in (and deploy) numerous teaching and learning methods that facilitate co-production and co-learning: student-led learning, blended learning (Bonk and Graham 2005), workshopping, flipped learning (Bergmann and Sams 2012), technology-based learning, as well as seminars, tutorials, and on-site learning (Hooper-Greenhill 1999) (museums, galleries, heritage sites, etc., further diversify the modes and locations of delivery.) As a part of your project you may want to consider these approaches and their pedagogical implications (see Resources section), how they work for individual pupils, groups and collaborative audiences (real or imagined/hypothetical) as you look to craft these communities of practice (Wenger 1998). Consider in your context the pedagogic benefits in terms of knowledge/skills/behaviour progression – of group projects and group assessment. Additionally, consider what role there might be for example for pupil self-assessment, peer-assessment, and self-reflexive journals (Ash et al. 2014).

THE COLLABORATIVE RESEARCH PROJECT

The IoE assignment was framed as a research project. We explained to the students that the projects were opportunities to produce a collaborative research project on 'radical institution making' (Ash and Smith 2022). In addition to reading materials from Museum Studies and Museum Education, Curation, Exhibition Studies, Radical Pedagogy, and so on, we also supplied the students with, (1) a 'hypothetical case study' and, (2) four thematic briefs, from which the students could choose the research project they wanted to do.

In the context of the secondary school, to help your pupil–curators start their collaborative planning, we suggest you use a 'hypothetical case study' which relates to a real 'piece of work' (conducted by Smith, see Resources) on the idea of establishing a school Culture Centre. This is a civic placemaking initiative that would bring together assets, resources, and expertise, centring these for pupils, parents, and staff and sharing what is in the institution's care with wider communities locally, nationally, and internationally. You then guide them to refer to the hypothetical case study often in their discussions (in terms of their vision, direction, scope, etc.) as they develop and realise their own research projects. For pupils of Art and Design, within the context of the school classroom or learning beyond the classroom, you as the teacher scale this accordingly.

In Task 14.4, there are four briefs. Although originally written for MA students, these can be re-purposed/tailored by Art and Design teachers for (and with) secondary school pupils, to be developed/realised on-site in schools or off-site in collaboration with local cultural institutions, communities of interest, stakeholders, etc. The briefs are wholly relevant thematically, conceptually, pedagogically, and politically/ethically in terms of benefits for the pupils, the teachers and the school, and diverse communities/audiences with which they might collaborate. Each brief can be undertaken as a separate project or as one of a number of briefs for group work within one larger project. Adaptations can be made to suit the context of any school or educational setting.

Task 14.4 Case Studies Briefs

Using the four briefs as models, select one or several that you feel may be appropriate for your context and learners. Reflect on the project's intentions, the issues it covers and the questions it raises. Re-write these for your pupils so that they can 'put it into practice' as an exhibition, project, public programme, or other form of manifestation or presentation.

The material in the four briefs, as well as the 'hypothetical case study', are intentionally fluid, designed to avoid predetermining outcomes, and to allow the pupil-curators' projects to unfold based on discussions within the groups, and with the Art and Design teachers and any external stakeholders.

You will need to clarify with the pupil-curators that each group:

- must meet together regularly to discuss the project, allocate tasks, review progress, etc.;
- must deliver a 10-minute group presentation (when best to do this can be decided by the teacher) allowing time for a further 10 minutes to take feedback, and integrate the presentation and feedback into the final project;
- To deliver a project report (format to be decided by the teacher), which includes:

- A SWOT analysis of the project (see, for example: https://www.mind-tools.com/pages/article/newTMC_05.htm);
- Relevant/indicative images;
- A bibliography (including books, articles, websites, organisations, criticism, etc., on the most interesting/innovative discussion of the issue, and a précis of these issues);
- A draft budget if applicable;

The Briefs:

Box 14.1
Object Based Learning as Social Responsibility

Background

Object Based Learning (OBL) (Kador and Chatterjee 2021) begins from the object/artefact, facilitates pupil-or visitor-centred learning, and often involves learning through doing, handling and touch-based activities, and ultimately new tactile/haptic epistemologies (Marks 2000), including through virtual or augmented realities. At the same time, OBL captures the imagination for museums, galleries, and heritage sites as they strive to realise their commitments to social and civic justice.
  Key issues/questions to consider here are:

- Which objects/artefacts could be utilised in OBL in the school's hypothetical Culture Centre to foreground social justice and counter explicit and implicit classism, racism, gender bias, able-ism, and age-ism?
- What is the nature (the qualities, the materiality, and the affordances) of objects/artefacts that enable them to be deployed to this end?
- How might these objects/artefacts be made into a museum-like 'collection' to be deployed to these ends?

OBL's commitment to social justice is all the more challenging in the wake of Covid-19. OBL in museums/galleries/heritage thus calls for a post-digital vision in which we must think the material, physical object *and* the digital object simultaneously.

Practical Framework

For this brief, to meet the challenges and opportunities posed by OBL, ask the pupil-curators to devise a public programme (exhibition, events, participation, training, screenings, etc. length to be decided by the teacher) that serves a diverse inter-generational audience. Your audience might include the school staff, families, and other adult learners, including older adults.

Collecting Differently/Collective Knowledge Production

Background

As curator and academic Caroline Rito writes in 'what is the Curatorial Doing?' (Rito 2020), her contribution to the edited collection *Institute as Praxis*, '[m]useums have long been perceived as sites where knowledge is produced.' This, she goes on, 'is usually attributed to the collections they hold and the expertise they gather around their material and immaterial archives'. The epistemic function of cultural institutions is changing, as more traditional ways of thinking and working are giving way to 'new modalities of knowledge production', as Rito calls them.

Key issues/questions to consider here are:

– What might such 'speculative and experimental' approaches to programming, curation, and research be?
– What might these approaches look like, and what might they do?
– How can such cultural activities generate enquiries differently, ask different questions, offer different answers, and produce knowledge differently and produce different knowledges?

Practical Framework

The pupil-curators are asked to take this philosophy/praxis as a starting point and devise an exhibition programme (duration to be decided by the teacher), drawing on the school's Culture Centre's (in the 'hypothetical case study', see Resources) existing collections/archives and utilising them in ways different to how they are used currently, This should be to not simply stage exhibitions that require passive viewing, but to regard the exhibition programme as an interactive research/pedagogical proposition for the visitors to the Centre.

The pupil-curators are asked to:

– craft a critical engagement with the relevant sector practice, and literature;
– inclusive of an Introduction, contextualisation, and conclusion;
– write a Visitor Guide containing an introduction, contextualisation of the exhibition, critical review of the displayed objects/artefacts/films/etc., and a conclusion;
– devise the schedule for the programme, the blurbs for each exhibition, contributors, etc.

Kids in Museums

Background

Museums and galleries and heritage sites are not classrooms. New and unexpected kinds of learning, and ways of learning, as noted above, become possible in the environment of a cultural institution that is configured differently – in terms of its architecture, interior design, accompanying paraphernalia (from desks and chairs to paintings and plinths), etc., and what these make possible. Key issues/questions to consider here are:

For this sector, at stake are three stark issues: (1) learning in cultural institutions should be fundamentally different from learning in classrooms for reasons that include the learning environment and the power dynamics therein: (2) pupils can be un-invested in, or made to feel dis-invested in culture by the museum, gallery, and heritage sectors, albeit for different reasons, and: (3) policy makers, academics, and industry professionals all say that learning and education should be at the heart of museum, gallery, and heritage practice, although this is actually rarely the case, a point made all the more cruelly during and in the wake of the Covid-19 pandemic.

Practical Framework

The pupil-curators consider some or all of the following in how/what provision for school-aged children/young people 'in' the Culture Centre can and should be. Keep in mind issues such as:

- access, inclusion, and diversity; neurodiversity, SEND, and mental health;
- a re-definition of outreach 'beyond the museum/gallery/heritage';
- roles for kids, take-overs, mentoring; costs, financing, sponsorship, philanthropy. What would the pupils want?;
- schools/communities; co-production/co-curating/participation;
- play and fun and curiosity and wonder and joy;
- the role of the digital and the post-digital in (and in the wake of) the Covid-19 pandemic.

The pupil-curators are asked to create a strategy (how long to be decided by the teacher) for the provision of school-aged children/young adults in the Centre, inclusive of the following:

- vision and mission;
- engagement strategy;
- evaluation;
- recommendation for types of provision;
- review of a few other Culture Centres for a comparative analysis.

Accessibility, Inclusiveness, and Diversification

Background

In *The Participatory Museum*, Nina Simon writes that '[c]o-creative projects originate in partnership with participants rather than based solely on institutional goals' (Simon 2010). She writes about the reasons cultural institutions engage in co-creative projects:

> 1) to give voice and be responsive to the needs and interests of local community members, 2) to provide a place for community engagement and dialogue, and 3) to help participants develop skills that will support their own individual community goals.

Simon quotes Julian Spaulding, founder of the Glasgow Open Museum, who envisaged that the institution would 'deliver what people wanted rather than what the museum thought they wanted or thought they ought to want'.

Practical Framework

Taking this philosophy/praxis as a starting point, guide the pupil-curators towards co-creating with other groups/institutions outside of the school, an education programme (duration of this to be decided by the teacher). The education programme will draw on the school's hypothetical Culture Centre's' (in the 'hypothetical case study', see Resources) existing collections/archives. In their project, the pupil-curators should include details of the programme itself (the schedule, the blurbs for each session, contributors, etc.), plus a critical engagement with current museum/gallery practice and literature. This should include their thoughts on the challenges and possibilities afforded by co-creative projects, and the care necessary to establish truly reciprocal relations between 'communities of interest/practice' and the Culture Centre.

THE ASSIGNMENT OUTCOMES

A festival staged at Candid Arts Trust in Angel, Islington was organised to host and showcase the exhibitions that were together entitled 'A Murmuration'. For their module/assignment, the MA students developed/realised four exhibitions, public programming, workshops with primary and secondary school children (including children with special educational needs and disabilities), an artist-in-residency programme, and more events in the service of social and civic justice; accessibility, inclusivity, and diversification; engaging communities, and social change.

What follows are our students' responses to the four briefs. These can be used with your pupil-curators as exemplars of exciting and inspiring practice.

The four briefs/themes/zones/outcomes were:

Brief 1 – OBL as Social Responsibility, through research & development, became 'Her Stories'.

OBL as Social Justice was developed by the students into 'Her Stories'. 'Her Stories' was an exhibition on gender inequity in China, and for Chinese women living outside China. Through art, visual and material culture, archival documents, and oral history, the exhibition showed how inequality is exposed through various objects and the stories women share about them. It highlighted how drawing attention to and rejecting such inequality can lead to different realities and possibilities. Working with two artists from the University of the Arts, London, contemporary objects and historical documents, along with interviews (doing 'oral history'), the students encouraged visitors to participate in reflecting on and sharing ideas, via a mirror, and posting comments using sticky notes.

Brief 2 – 'Collecting Differently/Collective Knowledge Production' became 'Taking Refuge: Being Here and Not Being There'

'Taking Refuge' was an exhibition centred around the ongoing refugee crises globally, engaging local communities and Islington borough's 'temporary residents' on what it means to 'be here' and 'not be there'. It included commissions and propositions by artists, designers, and architects; film screenings; an exhibition by school pupils within the exhibition; panel discussions; and an artist-in-residence leading weaving workshops for children, families, and local residents as occasions for collective story telling.

Brief 3 – Kids in Museums was transformed by the students into 'Creating Senses: Kids in Galleries'

Museums and galleries can be unwelcoming to children. To counter this, the exhibition utilised multisensory experience for kids, including those with SEND, and was accompanied by multisensory workshops. The visiting school pupils were encouraged to take over the gallery space, to have multi-sensory encounters, to explore through making and generally have fun in the exhibition.

Brief 4 – 'Accessibility, Inclusiveness, Diversification' was manifested by the students as 'Wish you were here'

This exhibition was a living archive constituted by reminiscences sourced from those who work locally in Angel – the key workers, transport workers, supermarket staff, and those in the hospitality industry. It used postcards to share their experience of working/not working in the neighbourhood during lockdown, and in the wake of Covid-19. Visitors were invited to read and engage actively by adding to the post card display, sharing their own thoughts and experiences (Figure 14.1).

You can find out more about the 'A Murmuration' exhibitions/programmes in the resources section.

(a)   (b)

Figure 14.1 'Wish you were here' exhibition in 'A Murmuration'.

SUMMARY

In this chapter, we have introduced the concepts of curation and collaboration as a viable art curriculum development for Art and Design teachers, and the benefits of the idea of curating in/as collaborative learning for your pupils. By redesigning the tasks and briefs from our module, these 'real-world' briefs and case studies can remake with your pupils the collaborative spirit underpinning and articulated by the UCL IoE students' festival, 'A Murmuration'.

'A Murmuration' was a collaborative project that was itself also about the experience of collaborating, the process and challenges and benefits of working together. It was a manifestation and an articulation of a collaborative sensibility, indicative of how ingredients and the work involved in creating conditions for inter-dependence, openness, transparency, honesty, trust, sharing, generosity, care, responsibility, and working together towards a common purpose can manifest in exhibitions, public programming, workshops, and other activities. This collaboration was born of, and also enabled meaningful forms of participation, co-creation, and co-curation – between students, and between students and diverse audiences.

RESOURCES

Link to A Murmuration instagram site: https://www.instagram.com/ucl.amurmuration/

The Social Contract additional information:

Live Art Development Agency, 'How We Work' (with artists, with others, Braver Spaces Policy, Access, Equality, Finance and Fundraising: https://www.thisis-liveart.co.uk/about-lada/how-we-work/

Tate ('Investigating the Geographies of Partnership Between Galleries and Youth Organisations', by Nicola Sim: file:///Users/marquardsmith/Downloads/circuit_natural_allies_or_uneasy_bedfellows_-_nicola_sim.pdf)

Gasworks, Participation (evaluation): https://www.gasworks.org.uk/participation/

Centre for Possible Studies/Serpentine Gallery/Edgware Road: https://centreforpossiblestudies.wordpress.com/

The Showroom, Communal Knowledge:

https://www.theshowroom.org/programmes/communal-knowledge

Feminist/activist perspectives on social contract theory (which includes sections on 'arguing from care' and the 'race-conscious argument': https://www.iep.utm.edu/soc-cont/

UNESCO, on a more 'inclusive' social contract: https://en.unesco.org/inclusive-policylab/sites/default/files/publication/document/2017/2/Group%20ine-quality%20intersectionality.pdf

The Racial Contract (https://en.wikipedia.org/wiki/The_Racial_Contract)

Some other resources available on curation

Cashia, Amanda, Disability, Curating and the Educational Turn File

Curating and the Educational Turn File

Sumaya Kassim, The Museum is The Master's House File

Pringle, Emily, The Practitioner-Researcher File

Texts to consider:

Clover and Williamson. (2019). 'The Feminist Museum Hack as an Aesthetic Practice of Possibility', *RELA: European Journal for Research on the Education and Learning of Adults*, 10.2, pp. 143–159.

Janna Graham, Ballerai Graziano, and Susan Kelly. (2016). 'The Educational Turn in Art: Rewriting the Hidden Curriculum', *Performance Research*, 21.6, pp. 29–35.

Modest, W. (2020). 'Museums Are Investments in Critical Discomfort', in Oswald and Tinius, *Across Anthropology: Troubling Colonial Legacies, Museums, and the Curatorial*, Leuven: Leuven University Press, pp. 65–75.

BIBLIOGRAPHY

Ash, A., et al. (2014). Assessment and Examinations in Art And Design. *Learning to Teach Art and Design in the Secondary School*. N. Addison and L. Burgess. London, Routledge: 18.

Ash, A. and M. Smith (2022). *Lecture MA Museum & Galleries in Education, 'Collaboration'*. IOE UCL.

Bentley, T. (1998). *Learning Beyond the Classroom: Education for a Changing World*. London: Routledge (and Demos).

Bergmann, J. and A. Sams (2012). *Flip Your Classroom: Reach Every Student in Every Class Every Day*. Washington, International Society for Technology in Education.

Bonk, C. J. and C. R. Graham (2005). *The Handbook of Blended Learning Environments: Global Perspectives, Local Design*. San Francisco, Jossey-Bass/Pfeiffer.

Bruner, J. S. (1977). *The Process of Education*. Cambridge, USA, Harvard University Press.

Dewey, J. (1966). *Democracy and Education: An Introduction to the Philosophy of Education*. New York, The Free Press.

Flutter, J. and J. Rudduck (2004). *Consulting Pupils: What's in It for Schools?* London, Routledge.

Hein, G. E. (1998). *Learning in the Museum*. London, Routledge.

Hooper-Greenhill, E., Ed. (1999). *The Educational Role of the Museum*. London, Routledge.

Kador, T. and H. Chatterjee (2021). *Object Based Learning and Well-Being:Exploring Material Connections*. London, Routledge.

Marks, L. U. (2000). *The Skin of the Film: Intercultural Cinema, Embodiment and the Senses*. Durham, USA, Duke University Press.

Pringle, E. (2009). The Artist as Educator: Examining Relationships between Art Practice and Pedagogy in the Gallery Context. *Tate Papers*: 11.

Rito, C. (2020). What Is the Curatorial Doing? *Institute as Praxis*. C. Rito and B. Balaskas. Berlin, Sternberg Press: 44–61.

Simon, N. (2010). *The Participatory Museum*. Sant Cruz, CA, Museum 2.0.

Vygotsky, L. S. (1978). *Mind in Society: The Development of Higher Psychological Processes*. Cambridge, MA, Harvard University Press.

Wenger, E. (1998). *Communities of Practice: Learning, Meaning, and Identity*. Cambridge, Cambridge University Press.

PART 3

CRITICAL CURIOSITY IN THE ART AND DESIGN CLASSROOM

Chapter 15 Personalising Decolonisation

Marlene Wylie

INTRODUCTION

This chapter deals with the concept and process of decolonisation of the art, craft and design (ACD) curriculum from the personal perspective of an art educator who describes themselves as Black British cisgender female of Afro-Caribbean descent whose own educational experience was set in the UK during the period when the 'West Indian' child was made educationally sub-normal in the British school system (Coard, 1971). Recognising that the pedagogy and subject knowledge is shaped and determined by ACD teachers' experience of education, it is important to share, highlight and promote anti-racist art education resources, research and theory through the lens of lived experience and personal reflection.

To decolonise our minds and in turn our teaching practices we must review, through questioning, reflection and research our personal learning journeys and identities. This process models what we will need to undertake for our professional development as committed anti-racist art educators. We will use key questions and personal reflections from the NSEAD, Anti-Racist Art Education Action (ARAEA) checklists to discuss, challenge and explore historical and contemporary issues around colonial histories, race, and identity. By developing our racial literacy, we will raise our confidence to challenge racist thinking and question colonial narratives with humility and insight.

OBJECTIVES:

Using a series of key questions found in the NSEAD Anti-racist Art Educator toolkit, you will be able to:

- Understand the importance of decolonising art education;
- Understand your own role as a teacher in the decolonisation process;
- Know how to apply the ARAEA checklist in the classroom.

Put simply, decolonisation can be defined as the process of reviewing the canon (the standard by which we judge and appreciate art and art practice), or of questioning its ability to include different, non-canonical voices or perspectives. As

DOI: 10.4324/9781003377429-19

a process, decolonisation unmasks the ways in which the peoples, cultures, histories, and knowledges of global majority populations have been systematically misrepresented, marginalised, and misunderstood; and how the peoples, cultures, histories, and knowledges of White Europeans are considered as the normal, the natural and correct. 'No education', bell hooks reminds us, 'is politically neutral' (hooks, 1994, p. 37).

It is important to note however that decolonisation is not the same as diversification in the curriculum (Akel, 2020). Martin Johnson and Melissa Mouthaan have argued that 'in many instances, programmes for teachers' continuous professional development opt for politically safe, strategy-based instruction, or issues of race in linguistic terms relating indirectly to "diversity"'. In line with this we need to critically interrogate 'the biases and assumptions that underpin current education arrangements'. (Johnson & Mouthaan, 2021) rather than adopt the approach which simply seeks to add a more diverse range of artists to our curriculums.

The issue of decolonisation could not be more urgent and important as we seek to solve many of the issues that thwart us in the 21st century pluralist society. Britain's colonial legacy and history also continues to impact every corner of our society – in our workplaces, educational institutions, streets and cities, galleries, museums and political institutions (see the Independent Report in resources). In art education the data shows that although students from Black and minority ethnic backgrounds participate at higher-than-average rates in the visual arts in secondary school, making up 40% of those studying A-level art and design, this dramatically drops at degree-level study to 16% (Department for Education, 2021). The Runnymede Trust postulates that an issue behind this is 'the selection of the curriculum, the selection of practices and cultural movements studied, and the teaching methods and approaches used' (Runnymede & Freelands, 2021, p. 10).

In the classroom, the legacies of colonisation express themselves in a variety of ways; the predominance of White artists in the curriculum; a flattening of the art histories of non-western countries; a 'colourblind' approach to art, or a failure to recognise our student's cultural and intergenerational knowledges. One common example of this is the teaching of subject matter such as "African ritual masks", or "Australian Aboriginal" dot paintings. Not only does this practice erase the diversity of cultures within the African and Australian continents, but the cultural and historical contexts and even the artists behind these artworks are rarely acknowledged.

Confronting the journey that lies before us is a daunting task and may even appear to be an impossible one, but as Clare Stanhope writes, 'it is also liberating. This is a journey fraught with inconsistencies and injustices that constantly raises questions of our own knowledge base' (Stanhope, 2021, p. 15). Decolonisation is not something to be done and then done with, but an ongoing process of self-reflection, questioning and re-orientation. A diversified and decolonised Art and Design curriculum is not only useful for Black, Asian and other ethnically diverse students, it is also important in truthfully representing to everyone the world, its histories, cultures, and arts with all of their complexities.

Task 15.1 Self-Reflection

Reflect on your understanding of the decolonisation process from the perspective of your own lived experience, whatever your own cultural background. How does doing this reflection make you feel? What are the issues you want to research and explore further?

UNPACKING LIVED EXPERIENCE

The decolonisation journey recognises that everyone comes to this process with baggage. We are all products of our histories, so it is therefore important to recognise that to reflect on how we have developed our thinking in the arts is crucial to effectively engage in the review of our curriculum and teaching. Our cultural heritage and family background will dictate the level of confidence we feel about discussing and exploring issues of race, racism, and colonial legacy. In *The Lived Curriculum: Experiences of Jamaican Teachers*, Carmal Roofe writes that using one's own educational experiences is a critical means of encountering and shaping the curriculum that you teach (Roofe, 2022, pp. 25–26). There is often a tendency for us to 'fix' what we may recognise as a narrow curriculum by jumping to quick solutions. Roofe reminds us however that the process of decolonisation first starts with self-reflection, as well as a consideration of how we might play a role in propping up racist and colonialist ideologies. It is therefore vital that our reflections inform our racial literacy and continue throughout our teaching career. This method for educators and learners to undertake reflection on curriculum encounters resonates deeply with me and serves as a helpful framework for this chapter.

I sought to pursue a career in the visual arts because for me it is the oxygen I need for wellness and self-fulfilment even though barriers created by migration, colonialism, minoritisation, assimilation and racism have been present throughout my lived experience. Despite these challenges I have found a creative path that was made possible by educationalists who understood the landscape and the need to facilitate equity. I am deeply grateful for the committed teachers, lecturers, and colleagues who have been part of my journey and who travailed the extra mile to mitigate against all the deficits along the way. I am grateful that art education has given me life and purpose, despite many challenges I can testify to divine intervention and the power of community to fulfil what I regard as a right for every student to have an opportunity to achieve.

My parents arrived in Hackney, East London in the early 1960s with British passports as part of the tail end of the Windrush era. Born in Britain, I was raised by my Jamaican parents with strong allegiance to what they perceived to be the mother country, Britain. Jamaica gained independence in 1962 and at that time was therefore a nation still drenched in colonial thinking and allegiance. The image below of my class photo in the mid-1970s has become the starting point for a series of deep reflections around my lived experience and my professional journey as an artist, designer and educator of colour. My own experience as a school student has shaped my journey in decolonisation and the teaching practice which has emerged from this. I was one of only two pupils of colour in the school photo. I find it rather symbolic that we appear to be both quite literally marginalised – placed on the edges of the group (Figure 15.1).

My own teaching experience and professional life as an art educator over the years has been undeniably shaped by my PGCE tutor Paul Dash, a celebrated artist whose work has made an important contribution to the Caribbean Arts Movement. In his book *Foreday Morning*, Paul Dash candidly shares the personal experiences of his life as a black boy and man in Britain: from his arrival in 1957 from Barbados through to his career as an educator, writer and artist committed to multi-cultural and anti-racist art education. In his autobiographical writing and research into African Caribbean pupils' art education experiences, Paul Dash authoritatively examines the challenges of race, coloniality and modern Britain (Dash, 2021).

Rightly, at the start of my teaching career twenty-five years ago the view I carried then was that I had much to learn to develop subject expertise. I still hold

Figure 15.1 Primary school Photograph, 1975, Marlene Wylie.

this view many years later although I now also discover the wealth of unlearning I need to engage in alongside the learning I have achieved. To make way for constructive critical professional development I reflect and explore the gaps and omissions in much of my Euro-centric educational and lived experience. With this perceived deficit comes the recognition that the conditioning that has led to my regard for the Western canon as the pinnacle of knowledge and expertise in art education, and on the face of it I can now name as White supremacy. This theme is explored in texts such as the Theuri/Gillborn interview (Theuri, 2015) in which she demonstrates the rich learning that she acquired in her exploration of critical race theory and it's relationship to art education.

In Debates in Art and Design Education, Jane Trowell as a White art educator explores her own 'unmasking' (Trowell, 2020). Trowell offers challenging and important reflections for White educators, particularly around the concept of allyship. Her study of George Yancy's concept of 'ambush' is especially sobering. Yancy writes:

> The moment that a white person claims to have 'arrived', to be self-sufficient or self-grounded in their anti-racism, she often undergoes a surprise attack, a form of attack that points to how whiteness insidiously returns, how it ensnares, and how it is an iterative process that indicates the reality of white racist relational processes that exceed the white self.
>
> (Yancy, 2014, p. xiii)

Jane Trowell believes that there is no point of arrival on this journey, only a path with many ambuses that arrest action. She highlights Yancy's exhortation for 'White' people to remain 'unsutured', and that 'to be unsutured, is to be linked to losing one's way, [it] is dispositional and aspirational' (Yancy, 2014, p. xvi).

Though some of us may feel more comfortable with the meanings and importance of this process of decolonisation, others may view the term with suspicion. In her powerful collection of essays *Teaching to Transgress, Education as the Practise of Freedom*, bell hooks acknowledges that learning about colonial and White supremacist structures can bring about discomfort. However, this discomfort can also be an important starting point from which we can interrogate our institutions and begin the process of re-learning (hooks, 1994, p. 43). She writes that in the positive transformation of institutions we:

must take into consideration the fears teachers have when asked to shift their paradigms. There must be training sites where teachers have the opportunity to express these concerns while also learning to create ways to approach the multicultural classroom and curriculum.

(hooks, 1994, p. 36)

FORMATION OF THE NATIONAL SOCIETY OF EDUCATION IN ART AND DESIGN ANTI-RACIST ART EDUCATION ACTION CHECKLIST

NSEAD has been committed to improving ACD education for everyone since 1888. With the changing demographics of society, the mission is multifaceted. By their admission, the NSEAD, with social justice at its core, has recognised that as a learned society their work around equity, diversity and inclusion is urgent and beneficial for all and requires constant research and renewal. The instigation of the NSEAD ARAEA in July 2020 brought into being the task force behind the development of a series of resource materials, articles and events to support reflections around race and ethnic identities. The group contributed a combination of expertise and lived voice to create three Anti-Racist Art Education Checklists to support ACD educators and partner organisations in the review of their curriculums, publications and resources.

Although NSEAD have used the term 'checklist', Stanhope writes:

…they are to be considered more a tool to open up conversation, support questioning and review current provision. The intention is that the support materials are not created as a linear 'to-do' list, rather a means by which one can actively engage in the process of critically reviewing one's decision-making, actions, and language.

(Stanhope, 2021)

The philosophy and recommendations on how to use the checklists are provided by NSEAD through a specially designated area on their website. Much of the philosophy for the development of the checklist is taken from bell hooks 'A Pedagogy of Hope' (hooks, 2003) and are threaded throughout this chapter.

Task 15.2 Teaching Community: A Pedagogy of Hope

Read bell hooks *Teaching Community: A Pedagogy of Hope* (hooks, 1994). The book offers a powerful vision of education as a tool for personal and social transformation and provides a roadmap for teachers who are committed to creating a more just and equitable world. Create a chart of hooks key points and your interpretation of its philosophy. You might want to focus on aspects that resonate with you and your teaching around:

- Community and social responsibility;
- Creating inclusive and equitable learning environment that addresses issues of power, privilege, and oppression;
- Engaging in critical thinking and self-reflection to identify and challenge their own biases and assumptions;
- Pedagogy should be viewed as a collaborative process that involves both the teacher and the student in the creation of knowledge and meaning;

The expectation is that these NSEAD support materials will evolve over time as the journey of learning and unlearning progresses. The NSEAD ARAEA Group believe that it is only through constant reflection, questioning, feedback and collaboration that the decolonisation process can take place.

Task 15.3 National Society of Education in Art and Design ARAEA Curriculum

Download the NSEAD ARAEA Curriculum (see link in resources).

Read the sections and key questions presented on the checklists. Which of the areas shown (Cultural Capital, Intersectionality, Colonial Legacy, Context & Terminology, Criticality, Unconscious Bias, and Diversity & Belonging) do you feel directly relate to what has been explored in this chapter? Which areas would you like to research further? Why is this? In your context and setting, what other questions need to be asked?

In building a strong foundation to my personal decolonisation journey, I have naturally found an insatiable appetite to carry out research, learn and unlearn about colonisation and the role that Britain has played in this and previous eras. This research, learning and unlearning was and continues to be an important process for me. I have learnt that to gain new knowledge and understanding we need to turn to a diverse range of perspectives and voices, particularly of those who have lived within colonised countries. This requires both commitment and an open mindset.

Using the ARAEA checklist map, create key questions that best fit the reflections that relate to your lived and art education experience. As mentioned earlier, these reflections can help foster a deeper and more personalised understanding of decolonisation in the classroom. A series of five reflections are given as exemplars in the following tasks to help with your own exploration.

Task 15.4

Key Question	Diversity & Belonging
Is there any reference in your curriculum to artists, makers and designers from your local community	Britain has had many waves of different **peoples** moving into and across Britain. How is the impact of this in your locality covered in your curriculum?

A visit to the *Life Between Islands* Exhibition at the Tate Britain in 2022 highlighted for me a number of artists whose work centres on the rich creative practice that could be mapped very closely to my lived experience and that of my parents. It was deeply engaging to have a focus on aspects of the art curriculum that speak directly and powerfully to a lived experience.

Another example of an equally formative experience is the William Morris Gallery's 2022 exhibition 'Colour is Mine'. The William Morris Gallery is situated in Walthamstow, East London and serves as the local gallery from my childhood days. In 2022, in collaboration with Liberty of London, the gallery hosted the first

Althea McNish retrospective named 'Colour is Mine'. Althea McNish (1924–2020) was a pioneering designer of Caribbean descent who produced culturally exciting and highly impactful textile art. As a child I was never taken to the gallery, only now as an adult am I able to make profound connections between the well documented work of William Morris and a designer like Althea McNish with cultural roots in the Caribbean. Seeing the work of these two designers in the same space was for me a formal recognition of McNish's rightful place in the chronology of British textiles. On a very personal level I have been very emotionally affected and empowered by the easy access I now have to artists and designers who in previous years have been obscured and certainly not given the prominence we are now seeing in the 2020s.

'I just want to be an artist/designer' were the words I dared to mutter as a sixth-form student in the 1980s. On reflection I realise that I had no expectation of seeing global majority artists, designers and makers in the world of the arts. In fact, I didn't know that they existed. For me the reality of minoritisation meant I would always expect to be in the margins, peripheral. Art and Design teachers cannot underestimate the significance of the visibility of Black, Asian Ethnic Minority artists, makers and designers to the young people within our classrooms. I have no doubt that it would have been very empowering for me to know more about the successes of Althea McNish during my early years and to have studied the Caribbean influences on her work. It would have created a sense of belonging and reassured me that my cultural heritage was indeed a worthy and valuable source of artistic expression.

Figure 15.2 A poster from a sketchbook, Marlene Wylie 1983.

I have vague memories of being introduced to this exhibition (Figure 15.2) by a teacher in my school in the 80s who was keen to diversify what I was being exposed to through the school curriculum and extra curricular activities. Reflecting on this now I am grateful that I was given an opportunity to explore this important response to the then art.

The Black Art Movement is an important area of study now as it was then. Find out more about this movement by researching the book 'What is Black Art?' Edited by Alice Correia. She gives voice to these artists through interviews, exhibition catalogues essays and reviews. As a counter narrative, read what Eddie Chambers has to say about the fetishization of the BAM in the media and gallery retrospectives in *World is Africa: writings on Diaspora Art* (Chambers, 2021, pp. 13–36).

Task 15.5

Key Question	Cultural Capital
How do you address cultural capital in your Art and Design curriculum?	Do you draw on the cultural and intergenerational knowledge of your students, their friends, carers, families and communities?

'Cultural Capital' (Bourdieu, 1973), here I describe as cultural intergenerational knowledge the 'Pedagogy of the Home, Familia'. Working on the Hackney Education Diverse Curriculum resource provided an opportunity to explore cultural capital relevant to my lived experience and home life. Through the work of artist Veronica Ryan (Figure 15.3) whose public art represents the contribution and presence of the Windrush generation in Hackney. My contribution to the development of resources for the Hackney Diverse Curriculum art commission involved research, exploration and cultivating an understanding of the rich thinking behind the artist's sculpture. It is this experience that gave recognition to the deficits or gaps in my knowledge on the merits of the cultural foods that were on offer at home as part of our childhood diet.

Through her large-scale marble and bronze depictions of fruits of the Caribbean – the soursop, custard apple and breadfruit in marble and bronze, Veronica Ryan explores themes relating to her life and childhood, migration and memory. These fruit were all staples that could be found on her frequent trips to Riley Road market with her mother. Ryan explains her artistic rationale for what she calls the 'human scale' of these sculptures:

[A] soursop, a breadfruit and a custard apple aren't monumental in any way; and this puts the sculpture on a kind of domestic human scale. Kids can sit on them, and the idea is that there won't be any separation between the public and the sculpture, so I also see them as works that will have an ongoing conversation with the public.

(Ryan, 2021, p. 9)

Having taken trips to Ridley Road Market myself as a child, it was both empowering and validating to have a work in the national gaze that was directly linked to my race and identity. The Hackney Windrush Artwork Commission writes that this artwork brings together 'a personal and shared narrative, embodying the

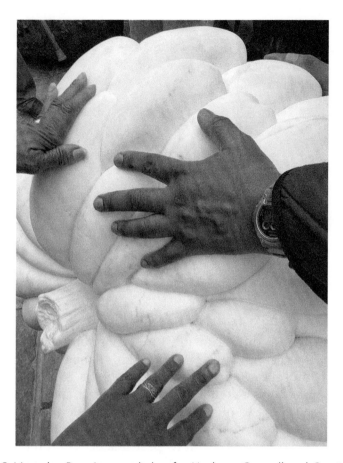

Figure 15.3 Veronica Ryan's commission for Hackney Council and Create London. Winner of the Turner Prize 2022.

alienation and adversity in navigating a new place and making it home' (Hackney Windrush Artwork Commission, 2021). I had an experience of the deep level of engagement that connecting with the cultural background of my parents allowed. I felt compelled to respond to the 'Please *do* touch!' invitation by the artist.

Task 15.6	
Key Question	**Criticality**
How does your curriculum provide opportunities to discuss, question and explore historical and contemporary issues around race and ethnic identities?	Do the cultures you study promote these debates and challenge the colonial narratives of 'other'? What references are you using in your curriculum? What opportunities are you providing to visit galleries & museum which create space to actively discuss issues facing society?

In 2021, I was fortunate to spend several days in the Pitt Rivers Museum Oxford (see resource link) considering objects in collaboration with Melanie Rowntree the Learning Officer. Our focus on secondary aged young people was to consider objects that would give students an opportunity to reflect, both emotionally and ethically as artists. The intention was for each object to not only elicit a creative

(a)   (b)

Figure 15.4 Research the work of the Pitt Rivers Museum – 'Labelling matters'.
Copyright Pitt Rivers Museum, University of Oxford.

response but also a decolonising question. My trip into this contested space was profound. Personally, and professionally, I found myself in deep reflection about the potential for rich learning, unlearning and critical analysis (Figure 15.4).

The history of UK museums and many of their objects are closely tied to British Imperial expansion and the colonial mandate to collect and classify objects from the world over. The processes of colonial collecting were often violent and inequitable towards those peoples being colonised. This difficult history has led some museums to engage more closely with its past practices and the nature of its collections, display and interpretation and the effects these continue to have today. While such questions are being posed in museums across the sector, the nature of Pitt Rivers' history, collections and displays (its historic labels including racist and derogatory language, commonly used at the time), makes these questions particularly pressing and especially challenging.

You can encourage students to engage critically when visiting museum collections by developing worksheets that prompt students to question displays. They might think about how the museum could begin to address the issues, and student could offer ideas for a plan to decolonise the collection. This is an opportunity to think more broadly in challenging the colonial narrative, and to embrace hope, reconciliation and redress and focuses on co-curatorial approaches to bring new voices into the museum and ensure public engagement is led by socially engaged work with communities (see Ash & Smith chapter).

Task 15.7

Key Question	Colonial Legacy
In your curriculum planning is there an awareness of the impact of colonial civilisations?	When you refer to art, craft or design objects that are currently held in European museums that originate from other countries or civilisations, do you explore: How those objects came to be held there? How were the objects originally intended to be used? If the object should remain in the possession of a museum? What are the stories that these objects can tell?

Figure 15.5 Mbira, a musical instrument from Zimbabwe, Pitt Rivers Museum. Copyright Pitt Rivers Museum, University of Oxford.

For me, the legacy of Jamaica as a colony became very prominent in my thoughts as a result of an immersive experience whilst on an extended family trip to the island in 2018. This triggered deep reflections centred around the loss and gain of colonialisation (Figure 15.5). You can encourage students to research the effects of colonialism around the world and why there is a need to consider the importance of decolonisation by watching this video: www.prm.ox.ac.uk/mbira.

Object-based learning (Chatterjee et al., 2015) is a student-centred and experiential based learning approach. Objects are primary data that hold and embody information about the conscious and unconscious beliefs, values, ideas, attitudes, histories and assumptions of the creator, the owner and by association the society in which they were made. The objects provide a powerful and direct link to the past and can enhance students understanding of the topic/subject being studies. They nurture an appreciation of different cultures and they encourage the student to use all of their senses, but especially touch, sight, and smell.

Task 15.7

Key Question	Colonial Legacy
The terms 'African art' and 'African artist' conflate the many diverse and varied countries and communities with the continent. In your schemes of work and curriculum planning have you avoided such terminology?	What part of the African continent is the art from? Do you include North Africa (Egypt, Morocco, Ethiopia etc.) as well as sub-Saharan Africa? Note that the; inspiration, design, purpose, meaning, processes of manufacture, usage, and value of masks in Nigeria are very different from those 2000 miles away in Mozambique.

During my time at school, I don't believe we were ever introduced to an artist of colour, and I don't remember being encouraged to produce issues-based work around identity. I do however vividly remember someone asking why I didn't produce 'African art'. This threw me because my Afro-Caribbean heritage and colonial imperialist experience and assimilation has left me feeling very disconnected from my African ancestry. Research looking into the learning of African Caribbean pupils in art and design classrooms by Paul Dash (2021) is an important read exploring issues relating to this.

Being stripped of cultural heritage only to later be told to produce artwork that refers to my cultural heritage felt very confusing to me. As the former Jamaican Prime Minster Michael Manley has written, post-colonial society must 'rediscover the validity of their own culture, retrace the steps that led them through history to that point and establish within a frame of reality, the culture which colonialism imposed upon them' (Manley, 1975, p. 163). Manley's views suggest that colonialism erased the natural schema of the people and replaced it with the schema of the colonisers.

The ARAEA Checklists seeks to support you on your journey of becoming an anti-racist art educator. Used as a tool or audit it aids conversation, supports questioning and provides an opportunity to personalise your approach.

> **Task 15.9 National Society of Education in Art and Design ARAEA checklist**
>
> With reference to the ARAEA checklists, what would decolonisation look like within the context of your classroom? What positive changes could be made in the range and presentation of Black, Asian and ethnically diverse artists? What particular challenges do you anticipate? How could you overcome them?

SUMMARY

My view is that when we engage in deep reflection on the decolonisation of the Art and Design curriculum, we naturally personalise the process. Personalisation in this sense refers to the internal work that must be carried out to arrive at an appreciation that there is an emotional response that is required to meaningfully explore social justice issues and power dynamics with integrity. Doing this will preclude an etherisation of the process, for example by ticking boxes in an institutionally administered form followed by a return to business as usual.

As the ACD teacher it is your responsibility to decolonise the curriculum for your pupils. Decolonising the curriculum means creating space and resources for a continuing dialogue among staff and students, and also within ourselves. As ACD teachers we not only challenge the dominance of the western canon of dead White male artists, we also seek to uncover and transform racialised injustices through our ongoing personal reflection. We identify the complex and contested nature of the current colonial and Eurocentric curriculum and seek to provide an alternative ACD curriculum that recognises the diversity of our students by way of auditing and reviewing our provision. We educate our students on how to imagine and envision all cultures and knowledge systems in the ACD curriculum, respectfully and critically examining what is being taught and how it frames the world.

RESOURCES

Black Lives Matter Charter: https://www.cultureand.org/news/black-lives-matter-charter-for-the-uk-heritage-sector/

Dash, P. and Addison, N. (2015). 'Towards a plural curriculum', in Addison, N. and Burgess, L. (eds.) *Learning to Teach Art and Design in the Secondary School*. 3rd ed. Abingdon: Routledge, pp. 200–225.

Correia, A. (2022). *What Is Black Art?: Writings on African, Asian and Caribbean Art in Britain, 1981–1989*. Milton Penguin Books.

Independent Report: The report of the Commission on Race and Ethnic Disparities (2021): https://www.gov.uk/government/publications/the-report-of-the-commission-on-race-and-ethnic-disparities

Minnicucci, D. Decolonising and diversifying the art curriculum: https://www.nsead.org/files/92a9838e0f65e74138d71de0a006df13.pdf

NSEAD ARAEA Curriculum Checklists: https://www.nsead.org/resources/anti-racist-art-education/

PDF: https://www.nsead.org/files/d9fbea0329b715b73d7e88eba3247dbd.pdf

Pitt Rivers Museum: https://www.prm.ox.ac.uk/critical-changes

The Black Curriculum: https://theblackcurriculum.com

UAL Decolonising Arts Institute: https://www.arts.ac.uk/ual-decolonising-arts-institute

BIBLIOGRAPHY

Akel, S. (2020). *What Decolonising the Curriculum Really Means*. Available at: https://eachother.org.uk/decolonising-the-curriculum-what-it-really-means/ (Accessed: 8 December 2022).

Bourdieu, P. (1973). 'Cultural reproduction and social reproduction', in Brown, R. (ed.) Knowledge, Education, and Cultural Change. London: Routledge.

Chambers, E. (2021). *World is Africa: Writings on Diaspora Art*. London, Bloomsbury.

Chatterjee, H.J., Hannan, L. and Thomson, L. (2015). 'An introduction to object-based learning and multisensory engagement', in Chatterjee, H.J. and Hannan, L. (eds.) *Engaging the Senses: Object-Based Learning in Higher Education*. Farnham, Surrey: Ashgate Publishing, pp. 1–20.

Coard, B. (1971). *How the West Indian Child Is Made Educationally Sub-Normal in the British School System*. London: Villiers.

Dash, P. (2021). *Foreday Morning: Revised Edition*. London: Bogle L'Ouverture Publications.

Great Britain, Department for Education. (2021). *Statistics: GCSEs (Key Stage 4)*. Available at: www.gov.uk/government/collections/statistics-gcses-key-stage-4 (Accessed: 8 December 2022).

Hackney Windrush Art Commission. (2021). Available at: https://www.hackney-windrush.com/news/hackney-windrush-artwork-commission (Accessed: 8 December 2022).

HESA. (2020). *Table 24 – UK Domiciled Undergraduate Students of Known Ethnicity by Subject Area and Ethnicity 2014/15 to 2018/19*. Available at: https://www.hesa.ac.uk/data-and-analysis/students/table-24 (Accessed: 16 December 2022).

hooks, b. (1994). *Teaching to Transgress: Education as the Practice of Freedom*. Abingdon: Routledge.

hooks, b. (2003). *Teaching Community: A Pedagogy of Hope*. Abingdon: Routledge.

Johnson, M. and Mouthaan, M. (2021). *Decolonising the Curriculum: The Importance of Teacher Training and Development*. Runnymede Trust. Available at: https://

www.runnymedetrust.org/blog/decolonising-the-curriculum-the-importance-of-teacher-training-and-development (Accessed 12 December 2022).

Manley, M. (1975). *The Politics of Change: A Jamaican Testament*. Washington: Howard University Press.

Roofe, C. (2022). *The Lived Curriculum Experiences of Jamaican Teachers: Currere and Decolonising Intentions*. Cham: Palgrave Macmillan.

Runnymede Trust & Freelands Foundation. (2021). *Visualise: Race & Inclusion in Art Education: Call for Evidence*. Available at: https://assets.website-files.com/6148 8e50132da098d2dd729b/62c6bf3339659acfccfb61c2_Visualise-Race%20and%20 Inclusion%20in%20Art%20Education.pdf (Accessed: 8 December 2022).

Ryan, V. (2021). *'In Conversation with Veronica Ryan'*. Interviewed by the Freelands Foundation. *Focus*.

Stanhope, C. (2021). 'An anti-racist 'pedagogy of hope'. *AD Magazine*, 32, p. 15.

Theuri, S. (2015). 'Critical race theory and its relationship to art education', in Hatton, K. (ed.) *Towards an Inclusive Arts Education*. Stoke-on-Trent: Institute of Education Press.

Trowell, J. (2020). 'Closer to the skin: Whiteness and coloniality in 'white' art educators', in Addison, N. and Burgess, L. (eds.) *Debates in Art and Design Education*. Abingdon: Routledge, pp. 123–140.

Yancy, G. (2014). *White Self-Criticality beyond Anti-Racism: How Does It Feel to Be a White Problem?* London: Lexington Books.

Chapter 16

Queering the Art Classroom: A Practical Guide for Art and Design Teachers

Tabitha V.P. Millett

INTRODUCTION

Increasingly, museums and galleries are archiving and assembling art histories relating to lesbian, gay, bisexual, transgender, questioning/queer, intersex, asexual subjects and the cultural figuration of those who are more generally gender/sexuality non-conforming (LGBTQIA+)[1] (Millett, 2021). From the art of classical times up to our present day, artworks and visual cultures that include imagery of non-heteronormativity are being explored through the lens of queer visibility/advocacy. This is also true at the popular level in television, film and music.

This chapter is a practical guide to queering the secondary school Art and Design classroom by applying a queer theoretical lens to artwork that explicitly references LGBTQIA+ subjects, and also applies the same lens to artwork that has no association with LGBTQIA+, or gender and sexuality. This is done with the aim of engendering queerer explorations across the full range of art subject matter in Art and Design.

As such, this chapter offers practical approaches for trainee Art and Design teachers to investigate in the Art and Design curriculum, gender and sexuality and LGBTQIA+ artwork/subjects. An argument throughout this chapter is that the process of making can enable students and teachers to come into dialogue differently with subjects such as gender and sexuality and the world more generally, through the fundamental materiality and process nature of learning in Art and Design (Biesta, 2017, p. 66; Millett, 2021). This is done to move beyond assimilatory LGBTQ+ inclusion discourses prevalent in schools, towards a pedagogy that challenges norms and identity categories through art practice itself.

OBJECTIVES

At the end of this chapter, you will:

- Have the tools to address and discuss LGBTQIA+ artwork with students;
- Understand what queering is and how to approach queer art practice and artwork;
- Be familiar with a practical exercise centred on exploring queering gender and sexuality with your students.

DOI: 10.4324/9781003377429-20

WHAT IS QUEER?

Before we discuss ways of queering the Art and Design classroom, it is imperative to understand that queer as a concept has diverse roots from a range of academic and cultural fields such as feminism, race theory, the gay and lesbian liberation movement, reactions to the AIDS crisis, sadomasochistic culture, postcolonialism, transgender studies and poststructuralism, to cite just a few (Hall and Jagose, 2013; Millett, 2021). Amongst these the gay liberation movement of the 1960s–1980s was a key origin for queer because it was in reaction to this movement that queer broke away from the assimilatory politics embedded within it (Millett, 2021). At that time, homophobic governments ignored the AIDS crisis globally, which led gay rights activists to present a collectively conservative assimilist gay identity to appeal for support with HIV/AIDS policies and gain recognition in public life (Millett, 2021). This assimilation was a privileging of those gay identities that conformed to heterosexual norms/ideals – also called 'homonormative'[2] identities (Bersani, 1987; Gray, 2016; Millett, 2021), that led to the exclusion of less conventional gay identities. Therefore, one of the foundations of queer is to provide a critical theory, often called 'queer theory', that is anti-assimilatory, to challenge norms and identity categories that can lead to exclusionary essentialism as seen in the gay rights movements of the 1960–1980s (Millett, 2021). For example, gay and lesbian essentialism is the belief that all gay and lesbian people share a common trait or norm that is predetermined biologically – for example, all lesbians are butch and are born that way (Millett, 2021). However, queer theory aims to challenge essentialist categories of identity, seeing these as restrictive, instead arguing for multiple ways of being inside and outside of these categories. Queer views identities as not biologically determined or inherent but continually being created or to use Gilles Deleuze's (1988) language, in a state of 'becoming' (Millett, 2021). This radical stance led to the conclusion, especially in the early 1990s, that having an anti-identity stance, through its failure to reproduce essentialist identities could reorder social conventions.

Another key origin of queer theory is poststructuralism, a body of theory that focuses on how the human subject is constituted through political power, language and discourse. Poststructuralism allows for the interrogation of norms-producing discourses and subjects, this interrogation being a dominant theme in queer theory (Millett, 2021). For example, heterosexuality is conceived of as a normative matrix that privileges, naturalises and reproduces the heterosexual subject, known as 'heteronormativity', for example, it is a given that women are feminine, and men are masculine, whilst viewing anything outside of this matrix as abnormal or abhorrent (Butler, 1990; Rubin, 1993; Millett, 2021). Based on this, queer aims to interrogate and subvert the heteronormative matrix (Butler, 1990; Sedgwick, 2008; Millett, 2021).

In the light of the two origins of queer theory that I have highlighted, I argue that queer's purpose is to constantly interrogate our surroundings by teaching us not to accept the repressive structures we face within society, and to instead push for new ways of being (Millett, 2021). In other words, Millett (2021):

> queer should be regarded as a process or a method for questioning what is around us – a doing rather than a being.
>
> (p. 71)

For the next section, we will put the 'doing' into action in Art and Design education, through questioning what could be queered within secondary school art practice.

QUEERING ART PRACTICE IN THE ART AND DESIGN CLASSROOM

Arguably, Art and Design in some UK schools remains dominated by school art orthodoxies while other ways of art making remain unaddressed within the Art and Design curriculum. When queering the art classroom, we aim to disrupt these school art norms. One avenue for disrupting norms within the Art and Design classroom is to build on art's inherently experimental functionality. By engaging students in the role of 'not knowing', as is required in the art making process, outcome-driven pedagogies can be challenged (Fortnum, 2013; Millett, 2021). I argue that learning through art in a more experimental fashion is 'akin to queer theoretical ideas of identity construction being an unstable process and always in a state of becoming' (Millett, 2021, p. 15). In terms of art education, a focusing with the students on the unpredictability of material processes and experimentation instead of, for example, pastiching known works, may offer avenues other than a skills-focused, formalist and outcome-orientated pedagogy. Equally this may offer new ways of exploring all subject matter in the Art and Design curriculum including gender and sexuality. Therein, when queering the classroom, a holistic process that focuses on both content (including LGBTQIA+/gender and sexuality themes – discussed further below) and on pedagogy (how we teach) must be implemented. In other words, queering should aim to reorientate learning away from just 'what' is learnt towards 'how' it is learnt through creating art.

In Art and Design education, there has been much advocacy for exploring LGBTQIA+ themed artwork[3] and art projects, to incentivise greater inclusion and stimulate critical thinking skills amongst students (Check, 1992; Addison, 2005, 2007, 2012; Dittman and Meecham, 2006; Ashburn, 2007; Chung, 2007; Stanley, 2007; Walker, 2007; Lampela, 2010; Gubes Vaz and Sanders, 2014; Millett, 2019, 2021). 'Identity' is a favoured topic for art projects in schools, which suggests that there is a space to explore LGBTQIA+ subjects with students in Art and Design. Yet identity projects in Art and Design tend to have only superficial explorations of the issue. For example, identity themed projects can focus on portraiture as the main signifier of identity through replicating the formal elements to represent a human face, while bypassing any critical discussions about identity, including identity fluidity (Addison, 2005). Simply including LGBTQIA+ themed art into projects like 'Identity', without any queer engagement with the context and meaning of the artworks can run the risk of perpetuating school art norms and essentialist discourses. This risk could occur because LGBTQIA+ artworks often present very specific representations of some LGBTQIA+ people, which need to be addressed from a queer perspective to fully understand them – in this way troubling the knowledge presented.

In this section, I have suggested how focusing more on art processes and less on formalist skill and outcomes can begin to queer school art norms. The next section discusses the current approaches to LGBTQIA+ subjects in schools to set the context for how we might approach these differently in Art and Design.

LGBTQIA+ ART

Since the early 19th century in Western societies, LGBTQIA+ people have fought for recognition, as traditionally in these societies they have been excluded from the cultures' histories, institutions and politics (Millett, 2021) (Figure 16.1). Recently, this fight for identity affirmation has been reflected by LGBTQIA+ artists whose artwork has consisted of clearly LGBTQIA+ imagery to present a unified LGBTQIA+

Figure 16.1 Sade Lee. The Actresses 2008. Courtesy of the artist.

identity (Millett, 2021) and approaches to same sex relations (Hall, 2013; Getsy, 2015; Millett, 2019, 2021) (see Figures 16.2 and 16.3). Even so, it can be problematic to present artwork with visible LGBTQIA+ identities because examples of this could lead to tokenism/essentialism as they do not always account for identities in a state of flux (Millett, 2019, 2021). Not to mention the problematic grouping and restrictive naming of 'LGBTQIA+ artwork', leaving students with stereotypical and narrow understandings of LGBTQIA+ artists and their contributions.

One avenue for exploring artwork that contains LGBTQIA+ subject matter with students while avoiding tokenism or essentialism is through 'queering' the context of the work's production by challenging notions of a fixed identity or histories and knowledges (Luhmann, 1998; Nelson, 1999, 2002). This queering can take place through critical class discussions in which teachers explore with students how knowledge itself is produced (Luhmann, 1998; Nelson, 1999, 2002). In other words, queering is not about learning the 'correct' knowledges/information on LGBTQIA+ subjects/artworks, as there is not one specific knowledge/experience that all LGBTQIA+ people share. When queering is applied as a pedagogical method, it is possible to question whether what is presented is the only available knowledge, when a plurality of knowledges is potentially available.

In this section, we have discussed how there is a space for exploring LGBTQIA+ subjects in the Art and Design classroom, and yet how the inclusion of LGBTQIA+ art can still perpetuate essentialisms. In the next section, we explore how LGBTQIA+ artwork could be explored with your students in practical and meaningful ways through queering your pedagogy as well as your curriculum content.

Figure 16.2 Cassils. Pin up from the magazine lady face man body, No 3, 2011 photo:
Cassils with Robin Black. Courtesy of the artist.

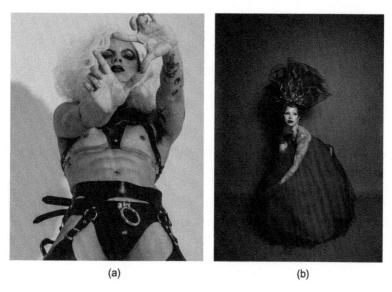

(a)   (b)

Figure 16.3 Alexandre Berton. Untitled (left) and Untitled (right). Courtesy of the artist.

225

HOW ART AND DESIGN TEACHERS COULD APPROACH LGBTQIA+ ARTWORK WITH THEIR STUDENTS

As mentioned at the beginning of this chapter, there are many different historical trajectories that can be drawn on with regards to artworks that refer to LGBTQIA+ themes in their content. There are noteworthy LGBTQIA+ historical resources that scholars have suggested to explore in the school context. Most notably, the first century AD Roman silverware piece known as the Warren Cup which features imagery of two male lovers (See Resources) (Frost, 2007). Such an object could generate discussions with age-appropriate students with regards to ideas of masculinity, consent, power and changing societal values, which will question the permanence of social structures and knowledge (Frost, 2007). However, in this section, I will focus on contemporary artwork because of the very far-reaching subject matter that this provides (Figures 16.4 and 16.5).

Task 16.1 LGBTQIA+ Work

Below are some questions, adapted for the Art and Design classroom Kumashiro, K. (2002), that you could explore with your students when presenting LGBTQIA+ work.

- What is important in this artwork?
- Do some of these identities appear more 'normal' than others? Why? What does 'normal' mean? What does 'abnormal' mean?
- Do these images reinforce or challenge stereotypes of LGBTQIA+ people?
- Is it possible to generalise a group of people? Why might this be done?
- Are there other aspects of identity on show in these images? Race? Class?
- Why would representation in this way be important for some LGBTQIA+ people?
- What is LGBTQIA+ art? Do you have to be LGBTQIA+ to make it? Does it have to have LGBTQIA+ content?
- Why do you think somebody would want to present in a more masculine manner if they are born female, and visa versa?
- Do you think this artwork is suitable for discussion in an Art and Design lesson?

Here you can begin to demonstrate to your age-appropriate students that there are no final truths regarding sexuality and gender, in the sense for example of there being only one way to be lesbian. Instead, questions of what is perceived as true may be raised. This can begin to destabilise the artwork that is being presented as stable knowledge, and disrupt prior student knowledges by introducing notions of fluidity. By applying these questions to some current artwork, you can start to deconstruct and make visible the hegemonic structures that support the legitimisation of heteronormativity and homonormativity in society. Additionally, investigating identity in this manner can access for students that sexuality is only one dimension of our identities and that there are other intersecting identities that shape and reshape us. If students are taught that identity is constructed and is therefore contextual and processual, they may infer that they are in control of their own destinies and can create their own meanings for apparent norms that could be challenged (Dittman and Meecham, 2006; Addison, 2007; Millett, 2021).

(a)   (b)

Figure 16.4 Gabriel Garcia Roman. Carlos and Fernando 2016 (left) and Kathy 2014 (right).
Courtesy of the artist.

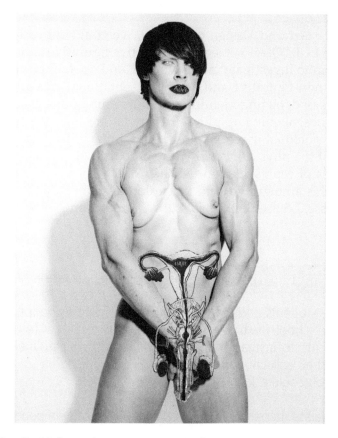

Figure 16.5 Cassils. Disfigured Image: Anatomically Correct, 2013 collage: photo paper,
marker, gouache, razor etching 17x11in. Courtesy of the artist.

In this section, we have discussed how LGBTQIA+ artwork might be discussed with students to avoid essentialist discourses. In the next section, we explore another avenue, a queerer one that uses the art classroom's greatest strengths. Instead of focusing on how we explore these subjects through discussion, we begin to explore issues of fluidity and new knowledge in non-representational ways that allow for art's materiality and process to take the lead investigative role. This allows us through teaching queerly to even more authoritatively break free of reproducing with our students representations of existing knowledge.

QUEERING ARTWORK

Gender and sexuality are complex and fluid, capturing this in the representationally sophisticated way that the subject deserves can be difficult for students. Furthermore, having gender and sexuality represented in recognisable and explicit depictions, such as the LGBTQIA+ artworks mentioned previously can limit such explorations to bodily representations which can lead to essentialism in categories of recognition (Getsy and Simmons, 2015). By way of extension, identities that are made recognisable through the human body are also easily placed in binaries; male/female, gay/straight and White/Black (Millett, 2021). So, to explore gender and sexuality in a queerer manner, the aim must be to refuse these limiting identifications/representations that can lead to essentialism by creating artworks that avoid recognisable representations through which society can be regulated and individuals marginalised (Getsy and Simmons, 2015; Millett, 2019, 2021).

To queer in the Art and Design classroom, we could subvert essentialist discourses that hold LGBTQIA+ subjects to restrictive figurative and representational artwork and begin to investigate more dynamic and open interpretations (Millett, 2021). Arguably, non-figurative and non-representational artwork engenders less determined ways of depicting identities, as more ambiguous visual work can disrupt figural binaries, opening up plural interpretations (Getsy, 2015; Millett, 2021). There is political potential in refusing representation whilst opening new avenues for exploration of the physical world with students that surpasses the previously known categories of representation (Millett, 2021). There are many examples of artwork where this ambiguity could be explored with students, for instance artwork by Eva Hesse, Louise Bourgeois, Lucy Orta, to name a few.

Task 16.2 Queering Artwork

As homework, students could research abstract artworks/sculptures and bring the images into school. (If students do not have the resources for this, you could ask your students to instead make a digital collection via OneDrive and you could present their collection in class).
Questions you could ask:

- Can you relate these sculptures to the idea of fluidity in gender and sexuality? How? Why?
- Can you relate the artwork's/sculpture's texture, shape, function or form to gender and sexuality? If so which genders and sexualities?
- Do you think the artists intended to relate their work to gender and sexuality?
- Why are we relating gender and sexuality to artworks instead of human bodies?
- Can you relate these sculptures to the idea of representing fluidity of meaning in the world in general?

So, the aim of queering the Art and Design classroom is twofold, firstly we can use art making to trouble LGBTQIA+ essentialism when addressing LGBTQIA+ imagery in the curriculum, and secondly, we can trouble school art orthodoxies by having students experiment with making outside of formalist, representational, outcome-focussed and pastiche agendas. I am arguing here that the making processes of art, if explored in an experimental and non-representational manner, are akin to understandings of a fluid identity as both rest on experimentation, process, movement, flux and becoming.

In this section, I have suggested how we could look to artwork outside of the figure or representationalism to offer new avenues to explore fluidity in knowledge itself, in addition to looking at gender and sexuality with students. In the next section, I suggest how this could be practically explored in the art classroom.

HOW ART TEACHERS COULD QUEER THE ART AND DESIGN CLASSROOM THROUGH ART PRACTICE

The aim of this chapter is to enable your students to research gender and sexuality outside of the representational trapping of the figure in the hope of evoking the complexities of subjectivity instead of a singular representational subject/sign – as seen in some LGBTQ+ artwork. The Art and Design teacher can do this by scaffolding their students' explorations of heteronormativity in the everyday, outside of the figure/human, through focusing on objects. For instance, ask students to bring in from home everyday objects that may have gender and sexuality associations. Typical objects the students might bring into class could be perfume bottles, lipsticks and toy trucks, then explore with them how an object's texture/form/smell/sound/material/mechanism could represent gender and sexuality. These initial stages are vital as teachers can then think through with their students, ways of disrupting those normative representations through making. Thus, thinking becomes making, allowing students to study in more liberated ways gender and sexuality and the idea of fixed knowledge generally. This provides the students with more creative freedom than representational sign/human figure/formalist/outcomes (Millett, 2021).

Task 16.3 Objects

Over several lessons, ask students to bring in objects that *they* think might relate to gender and sexuality. For example, a red house brick might be conventionally associated with masculinity, due to its rough texture or rectangle shape and socially stereotypical associations (men build things). Through interrogating the material and making processes of the object, students could disrupt these connotations through practical ways. For example, the brick could be broken or carved into something previously unrecognisable – the brick becomes something else – hence, symbolically it changes its associations and obscures the original gender and sexuality representation. The original object (brick) and gender and sexuality the students associated with it, cannot now be easily read or depicted due to the change in its form, leaving more complex readings and explorations through texture, movements, materials and process-making (Millett, 2021).

Possible questions for discussion:

- How do objects relate to gender and sexuality? Why?
- Can you relate your object's texture, shape, function or form to gender and sexuality? If so which genders and sexualities?
- Why are we relating gender and sexuality to objects instead of human bodies?

Once you have discussed the objects with your students, ask your students to produce shadow drawings (on cardboard) in groups from their objects. Shadow drawing is a great way to scaffold students to think in abstract ways. Therein, ask the students to overlap the objects and make the shadows as large as possible to obscure the object, making its shadow unrecognisable. Ask your students:

- Why are we using shadow drawings?
- Why are we obscuring the object through shadow drawing?
- Is there significance in obscuring the object, including when thinking about fluidity in gender and sexuality?

Once students have created their shadow drawings, they could make a collaborative maquette sculpture through cutting out the shadow drawings from cardboard. This maquette will scaffold their making/thinking of an abstract sculpture.

However, there are multiple avenues for making/using the shadow drawing exercise. The students could further make a shadow drawing of the maquette itself, and in the spirit of queer, add the shadow drawings of the maquette, to the maquette, in an ongoing state of flux. Here, you could discuss fluidity and becoming.

Below are student responses, which provide examples of the teacher scaffolding an investigation into fluidity and new meaning in an accessible way by students working in groups to create shadow drawings from their home objects in a bid to 'break' or 'disrupt' representation. Gender and sexuality associations or the physical form of the object are interrogated to produce an abstract piece of work (Figure 16.8).

(a)

(b)

Figure 16.8 Student responses.

As seen in Figures 16.6 and 16.7, the form of the object is obscured by a focus on the shadow – rendering it ambiguous and hard to read. What new meanings can be seen in the shadows when this fluid approach to image making is adopted? Leading on from this, ask your students to respond through making to their discussions regarding

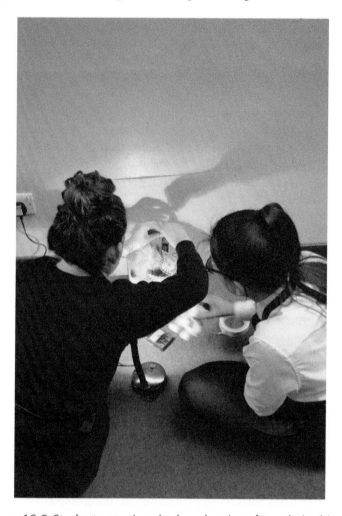

Figure 16.6 Students creating shadow drawings from their objects.

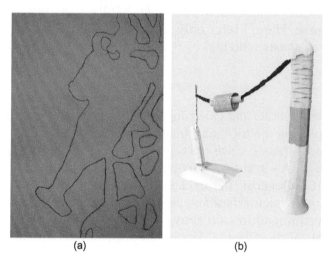

(a)   (b)

Figure 16.7 Shadow drawing and collaborative maquette.

reading gender and sexuality into objects and the shadow drawings. Figure 16.8 (on page 230) is some student work produced through this way of teaching (for more responses from students see Millett, 2019, 2021).

SUMMARY

In this chapter, we have explored how you could queer your art classroom. We have discussed what it means to queer and what could be queered with regards to Art and Design practice and the current approaches to LGBTQIA+ subjects in schools. We have discussed how LGBTQIA+ artwork could be explored with students through questioning knowledge and how it is produced. We have then focused on how we might explore gender and sexuality more practically outside the figure, through working with non-representation to allow more open and fluid interpretations of, and practice, in the material world.

The key points to take away from this chapter are:

- When discussing/presenting LGBTQIA+ identities/artworks, it is important to not essentialise and homogenise these identities and question how knowledge is produced.
- To explore art practice outside of didactic, outcome-based and formalist/skill-centred approach.
- Making is thinking. Explore gender and sexuality with your students outside of representation through experimentation, to open different avenues to investigate these topics.
- These are only a few examples and should not be used as paramount – that would not be very queer. In the spirit of queer, we should all push for new ways of exploring new ideas.

NOTES

1 The LGBTQIA+ acronym is used due to much UK policy and research doing so. However, the problematic combining of complex issues and fluid gender and sexual identities into fixed groupings is recognised.
2 The term to describe homosexuals conforming to heterosexual ideals, 'homonormativity', was described by Lisa Duggan in 2003.
3 It is problematic to label artwork as LGBTQIA+, as this underpins essentialist discourse. Here, I refer only to artwork by artists who self-identify as LGBTQIA+ or artists who make artwork referencing LGBTQIA+ themes.

RESOURCES

Queeringtheartclassroom.com and Queeringtheartclassroom (Instagram) for updates on exhibitions exploring the topics addressed above.

IJADE (2007). *Special Issue: Lesbian and Gay Issues in Art, Design and Media Education.* Exploring LGBTQIA+ in the art curriculum.

Millett, T. V. P. (2019). Queering the art classroom: Queering matters. *The International Journal of Art and Design Education*, 38(4), 809–822. An article focusing on data from the intervention addressed above.

Getsy, D. J. (2015). *Abstract Bodies: Sixties Sculpture in the Expanded Field of Gender.* New Haven, CT: Yale University Press. For more examples of queering artwork, Getsy's book addressed queering non-representational artwork.

BIBLIOGRAPHY

Addison, N. (2005). Expressing the not-said: Art and design and the formation of sexual identities. *International Journal of Art and Design Education*, 24(1), 20–30.

Addison, N. (2007). Identity politics and the queering of art education: Inclusion and the confessional route to salvation. *International Journal of Art and Design Education*, 26(1), 10–20.

Addison, N. (2012). Fallen angel: Making a space for queer identities in schools. *International Journal of Inclusive Education*, 16(5–6), 535–550.

Ashburn, L. (2007). Photography in pink classrooms. *International Journal of Art and Design Education*, 26(1), 31–38.

Bersani, L. (1987). Is the rectum a grave? *October*, 43, 197–222.

Biesta, G. J. J. (2017). *Letting Art Teach* (L. Klaassen, Ed.). ArtEZ Press.

Bradlow, J., Bartram, F., April, G., and Jadva, V. (2017). *Stonewall School Report*. London: Stonewall. Retrieved from: https://www.stonewall.org.uk/school-report-2017 (Accessed 15th October 2020).

Butler, J. (1990). *Gender Trouble*. New York, Oxon: Routledge.

Check, E. (1992). Queers, art and education. *Marilyn Zurmuehlen Working Papers in Art Education*, 11(1), 98–102.

Chung, S. K. (2007). Media literacy art education: Deconstructing lesbian and gay stereotypes in the media. *International Journal of Art and Design Education*, 26(1), 98–107.

Deleuze, G., and Guattari, F. (1988). *A Thousand Plateaus*. London: Athlone.

DePalma, R., and Atkinson, E. (2009). 'No Outsiders': Moving beyond a discourse of tolerance to challenge heteronormativity in primary schools. *British Educational Research Journal*, 35(6), 837–855.

Department for Education (DfE). (2019). Primary school disruption over LGBT teaching relationships education. Retrieved from: https://www.gov.uk/government/publications/managing-issues-with-lgbt-teaching-advice-for-local-authorities/primary-school-disruption-over-lgbt-teachingrelationships-education (Accessed 15th October 2020).

Dittman, R., and Meecham, P. (2006). Transgender and art in the school curriculum. *Sex Education*, 6(4), 403–414.

Duggan, L. (2003). *The Twilight of Equality? Neoliberalism, Cultural Politics, and the Attack on Democracy*. Boston, MA: Beacon Press.

Educate and Celebrate. (n.d.). *Resources*. Retrieved from: http://www.educateandcelebrate.org/resources/ (Accessed 15th October 2020).

Ellis, V. (2007). Sexualities and schooling in England after section 28: Measuring and managing 'at-risk' identities. *Journal of Gay and Lesbian Issues in Education*, 4(3), 13–30.

Formby, E. (2015). Limitations of focussing on homophobic, biphobic and transphobic 'bullying' to understand and address LGBT young people's experiences within and beyond school. *Sex Education*, 15(6), 1–15.

Fortnum, R. (2013). Creative accounting: Not knowing in talking and making. In Fortnum, R., and Fisher, E. (Eds.), *On Not Knowing: How Artists Think* (pp. 70–87). London: Black Dog Publishing.

Frost, S. (2007). The Warren Cup: Highlighting hidden histories. *International Journal of Art and Design Education*, 26(1), 63–72.

Getsy, D. J. (2015). *Abstract Bodies: Sixties Sculpture in the Expanded Field of Gender*. New Haven, CT: Yale University Press.

Getsy, D.J., and Simmons, W.J., (2015). *Appearing Differently. Abstraction's Transgender and Queer Capacities*. Berlin: Sternberg Press.

233

Gray, J. (2016). Language and non-normative sexual identities. In Preece, S. (Ed.), *The Routledge Handbook of Language and Identity* (pp. 225–240). Abingdon: Routledge.

Gubes Vaz, T., and Sanders, J.H., (2014). *Dialogue on Queering Arts Education Across the Americas, Studies in Art Education, 55*(4): 328–341.

Hall, S. (Ed.). (1997). *Representation: Cultural Representations and Signifying Practices* (First Edition edition). London; Thousand Oaks, CA: SAGE Publications Ltd.

Hall, G. (2013). Object lessons: Thinking gender variance through minimalist sculpture. *Art Journal, 72*(4), 46–57.

Hall, D., and Jagose, A. (2013). Introduction. In Hall, D., Jagose, A., Bebell, A., and Potter. (Eds.), *The Routledge Queer Studies Reader* (pp. xv–xx). London; New York: Routledge.

Kumashiro, K. (2002). *Troubling Education: Queer Activism and Antioppressive Pedagogy*. New York; London: Routledge-Falmer.

Lampela, L. (2010). Expressing lesbian and queer identities in the works of three contemporary artists of New Mexico. *Art Education, 63*(1), 25–32.

Luhmann, S. (1998). *Queering/Querying Pedagogy? Or, Pedagogy Is a Pretty Queer Thing*. London: Routledge.

Marston, K. (2015). Beyond bullying: The limitations of homophobic and transphobic bullying Interventions for affirming lesbian, gay, bisexual and trans (LGBT) equality in education. *Pastoral Care in Education, 33*(3), 161–168.

Millett, T.V.P. (2019). Queering the art classroom: Queering matters. *The International Journal of Art and Design Education, 38*(4), 809–822.

Millett, T.V.P. (2021). *Queering the art classroom*. PhD. Thesis. University College London. Available at: https://discovery.ucl.ac.uk/id/eprint/10130350/1/Millett_10130350_Thesis_redacted.pdf (Accessed: 13th October 2022).

Nelson, C. (1999). Sexual identities in ESL: Queer theory and classroom inquiry. *TESOL Quarterly, 33*(3), 371–391.

Nelson, C. (2002). Why queer theory is useful in teaching: A perspective from English as a second language teaching. *Journal of Gay & Lesbian Social Services, 14*(2), 43–53.

Ofsted. (2020). Guidance inspecting teaching of the protected characteristics in schools. NH: Author. https://www.gov.uk/government/publications/inspecting-teaching-of-the-protected-characteristics-in-schools/inspecting-teaching-of-the-protected-characteristics-in-schools (Accessed 15th October 2020).

Pinar, W. (Ed.), (2003). *Queer Theory in Education* (pp. 141–155). Mahwah, NJ: Lawrence Erlbaum Associates.

Macintosh, L. (2007). Does anyone have a band-aid? Anti-homophobia discourses and pedagogical impossibilities. *Educational Studies: A Journal of the American Educational Studies Association, 41*(1), 33–43.

Marston, K. (2015). Beyond bullying: The limitations of homophobic and transphobic bullying Interventions for affirming lesbian, gay, bisexual and trans (LGBT) equality in education. *Pastoral Care in Education, 33*(3), 161–168.

Monk, D. (2011). Challenging homophobic bullying in schools: The politics of progress. *International Journal of Law in Context, 7*, 181–207.

Rubin, G. (1993). Thinking sex: Notes for a radical theory of the politics of sexuality. In Abelove, H., Barale, M. A., and Halperin, D. M. (Eds.), *The Lesbian and Gay Studies Reader* (pp. 3–44). London, New York: Routledge.

Sanders III, J. H., and Vas, T. G. (2014). Dialogue on queering arts education across the Americas. *Studies in Art Education, 55*(4), 328–341.

Schools Out. (2020). *Resources*. http://www.schools-out.org.uk/?page_id=159 (Accessed 15th October 2020).

Sedgwick, E. (2008). *Epistemology of the Closet*. Berkeley, CA: University of California Press.

Simmons, W. J., and Getsy, D. (2015). Appearing differently abstraction's transgender and queer capacities. In Erharter, C., Schwarzler, D., Sircar, R., and Scheirl, H. (Eds.), *Pink Labour in Golden Streets: Queer Art Practices* (pp. 39–55). Berlin: Sternberg Press and Vienna Fine Arts Academy.

Stanley, N. (2007). Preface: 'Anything you can do': Proposals for lesbian and gay education. *International Journal of Art and Design Education*, 26(1), 2–9.

Walker, D. (2007). Out there? Looking for lesbians in British art—Some preliminary observations. *International Journal of Art and Design Education*, 26(1), 89–97.

Chapter 17   Addressing Sustainability in Art and Design

Henrietta Patience

INTRODUCTION

How Do You Define Sustainability?

There are many emphases around sustainability but all would encompass the definition offered by the United Nations Brundtland Commission, 1987, 'meeting the needs of the present without compromising the ability of future generations to meet their own needs' (World Commission on Environment and Development (WCED), 1987).

This chapter will offer rationales, present ideas and encourage reflection on the place of Art and Design education in this conversation. In the past, education has taken a rather piecemeal and inconsistent approach to sustainability – we will look at the history of this in more detail further on in this chapter.

As concerns for the future grow and as international efforts to reduce carbon emissions to protect our planet increase, teachers must play a crucial role. This is evident in the recently published Department for Education policy paper 'Sustainability and Climate change: a strategy for the education and children's services systems' (DfE, 2022a). Several universities offer research-informed professional development resources to help initial teacher trainees and teachers incorporate climate change issues into their practice. See Further Resources for resources from University College London and University of Reading.

Where do you see the place of sustainability in the Art and Design curriculum?

During your training you will be able to consider, challenge and debate what a broad and balanced entitlement for your students should include. In schools, you will survey curriculum maps and consider where your ideas, skills and knowledge can be utilised. Where does sustainability sit within this for you? How confident do you feel to address environmental and ecological issues?

This chapter aims to support your own exploration of the role Art and Design can play in raising awareness, expressing concerns and empowering future generations. You will be introduced to a range of practical and thematic ideas.

DOI: 10.4324/9781003377429-21

OBJECTIVES

At the end of this chapter, you should be able to:

- Form a rationale for the inclusion of sustainable themes, practice and resources in Art and Design;
- Evaluate existing practice in art departments to be more environmentally conscious and sustainable;
- Understand the value of art and design in cross curricular approaches to sustainable education.
- Consider the power of art and design in exploring ecological and environmental issues and enabling students to express concerns;

THE ROLE OF EDUCATION IN PROMOTING SUSTAINABILITY

Historical Context

I hope that your experience of being in schools has been one where there is a value placed on sustainability as evident in curriculum planning, resourcing and student agency. 'For our prehistoric ancestors all learning was probably environmental and success was measured by survival' (Smyth, 1995, cited in Scott and Vare, 2021, p.7). Though it would be easy to think that promoting awareness of sustainable, ecological and environmental concerns are a new focus in education, these concepts have been evolving and growing in momentum over the last 60 years having originated in the 1960s as Environmental Education which was concerned with rural conservation. In the 1970s the United Nations (UN) started to push for international policies on environmental education. The 1980s saw the UN set up a commission to look at environmental issues, the Brundtland Report 'Our Common Future' (WCED, 1987) which is from where the earlier definition in the introduction to this chapter originates. The 1990s saw the establishment of the Sustainable Development Education Panel covering schools, further and higher education bodies. The Holland Report (Holland, 1998), which identified sustainable change as one of its seven key concepts (Figure 17.1), was ahead of its time in advocating a whole school approach across subjects and identifying learning outcomes linked to desirable knowledge, skills and values. In the revised National curriculum of 2000, Education for Sustainable Development (ESD) became a statutory requirement in the subjects of Geography, Science, Design and Technology and Citizenship, though opportunities to promote ESD were identified in all subjects across the curriculum. The role of education in promoting sustainability has been supported by the work of international organisations such as United Nations Educational, Scientific and Cultural Organisation (UNESCO) and United Nations Environment Programme (UNEP) (Gadsby and Bullivant, 2010; Adams, 2016; Scott and Vare, 2021).

Where Are We Today?

With the current National curriculum making limited reference to climate change (DfE, 2013) and its absence from Ofsted's new education inspection framework (Ofsted, 2022) the impression could be given that these issues are not a priority for education. However, at the 2021 Climate Change Conference, COP26 (Conference of the Parties to the United Nations Framework Convention on Climate Change),

Figure 17.1 The Holland Report 7 Key Concepts.

in Glasgow, the DfE led the conversation on how to fight climate change through education and acknowledged that they have an important role to play in all aspects of sustainability (DfE, 2022a). There was also a focus on preparing young people with green skills for green jobs and the green economy anticipated to touch every career. The then Secretary of State for Education, Nadhim Zahawi said:

> Learners need to know the truth about climate change – through knowledge-rich education. They must also be given the hope that they can be agents of change, through hands-on activity and, as they progress, through guidance and programmes allowing them to pursue a green career pathway in their chosen field.
>
> (DfE, 2022a)

What Role Can Art and Design Play?

'Debates in Education' (Addison and Burgess, 2021) devoted its first three chapters to sustainability. 'Undeniably, the most urgent questions to take centre-stage since the first edition of Debates (2013) are those around sustainability. The outbreak of the Covid-19 pandemic only adds to this urgency' (Addison and Burgess, 2021, p. 1). As you set out on your journey in Art and Design education you will be exploring all that the curriculum can be. Because the National curriculum for Art and Design and exam board criteria are appropriately broad, teachers can design schemes of work and lesson plans that best inspire and meet the needs of all their students – the possibilities are endless. Art and Design education can provide a platform for challenging important issues including social justice, equity, environment, sustainability, citizenship and diversity (Addison and Burgess, 2003; Downing and Watson, 2004; Gadsby and Bullivant, 2010; Trowell, 2010).

Art has always dealt with themes from the natural world, but recently art has been used to express concerns with environmental issues. In their opposition to mass industrial processes, William Morris and the Arts and Crafts movement of the late 19th century were early pioneers of this (Addison, 2010). Throughout the nineteenth century, a vein of pastoral mysticism (Blake, Palmer, Linnell) ran in parallel with mainstream currents and the Arts & Crafts movement of the later 19th, early 20th century inspired by the writings and design of William Morris, championed designer/makers against mass industrialised process. The weakness of their position was that their products were always too expensive for most people to own; the problem for us now as artists, designers and educators is to make outcomes that are sustainable, cheap and desirable (Figure 17.2).

A growing number of artists reflect environmental concerns and many galleries have a policy of incorporating this into their programming. Tate's exhibitions, talks and workshops with their focus on young people have embraced this. Olafur Eliasson's 'The Weather Project' filled the Turbine Hall at Tate in 2003 (see https://www.tate.org.uk/whats-on/tate-modern/unilever-series/unilever-series-olafur-eliasson-weather-project /). He used humidifiers to create a fine mist in the air, and a semi-circular disc made up of hundreds of monochromatic lamps which radiated yellow light. The ceiling of the hall was covered with a vast mirror, in which visitors could see themselves as tiny black shadows against a mass of orange light. The public often responded to this exhibition by lying on their backs and waving their hands and legs.

Figure 17.2 William Morris & Co. Bobbin Chair 1870s (designed by William Morris and Burne-Jones) Pimpernel fabric (modern printing of original William Morris).

Ai Weiwei often recycles materials to make political points. 'Souvenir from Shanghai' 2012 is a cube of concrete and brick rubble from the artist's studio demolished by the government, set within an antique carved doorframe (see https://arthive.com/artists/78922~Ai_Weiwei/works/544822~Souvenir_from_ Shanghai). At the Eden Project, Jenny Kendler's 40-foot-long sculpture displays a hundred reflective birds' eyes mounted on aluminium. The eyes belong to birds threatened by climate change (see https://www.edenproject.com/visit/ things-to-do/birds-watching).

Task 17.1 Produce a Rationale for the Place of Sustainability in Art and Design

- Reflecting on what you have read so far and your own experience of art education, produce a rationale that sets out your beliefs, ideas, views and vision for the place of sustainability in art and design. What might be done better?
- Create a poster that sets out your rationale to be displayed in your school.

Resources, Materials and Practice

In line with the UN's goals for the planet 'Transforming our world: the 2030 Agenda for Sustainable Development' (UN, 2015) and the DfE's longer term actions for sustainability and climate change in education set for 2030 (DfE, 2022a), schools have a responsibility to be thinking about their environmental footprint, making efforts to embrace sustainable practice and endorse responsibly resourced materials. Initiatives such as the Eco-Schools Green Flag accreditation (see Resources) teach students the importance of sustainable awareness and practice. It could be argued that many Art Departments are at the forefront of such practice due to their need to be hugely resourceful and imaginative in their use of materials, reclaiming, upcycling and recycling. In recent years, there has also been an expansion of responsibly resourced art materials available through school art suppliers including materials like recycled card and papers, water-based gouache paints and earth pens. Art suppliers such as GreatArt (see https://www.greatart.co.uk/ how-we-work/), ARTWAY (see https://artway.co.uk/recycled-art-materials/) and ARTdiscount (see https://artdiscount.co.uk/blogs/artdiscount/vegan-veg-etarian-and-eco-art) have options and solutions to support sustainability, including a paintbrush recycling service. Although these are positive steps, they can often be limited and costly. Scrap and recycling schemes exist all over the country (see https://www.reusefuluk.org/scrapstores-directory) and can offer a treasure trove of materials to be utilised in projects as can charity shops and jumble sales.

There is also the question of sustainable practice and wastage, how much paint gets poured down sinks at the end of lessons? What sort of paint and dyes are you using and what effect do these have on the waste systems? How much paper gets screwed up and thrown in bins? What quality of paper do you use? Are modelling materials re-usable, for instance plaster vs clay? How many times do you print out handouts that could instead be digital?

To be more innovative and resourceful you could create sketchbooks from recy-cled paper, save food tubs with lids for storage of paints, invest in pumps to place on glue and liquid paints to avoid huge amounts being dispensed. If you are fortunate enough to have technician support, options like making sketchbooks from recycled paper are even more viable.

Task 17.2 Audit Materials

- Working with your department complete an audit of materials. Make a checklist of those that are most sustainably sourced/environmentally friendly and those that might be harmful to the environment. Think about alternatives.
- Look at your suppliers and compare to see how eco conscious they are. How might you be more resourceful? Encourage students to think about how they can be more resourceful? Ask parents and colleagues if they can add to these ideas.
- Set three targets for improvements to be made.

Reclaiming, Upcycling and Recycling

Some of the most exciting and imaginative work produced by students in schools often comes from experimenting with materials previously deemed unwanted, broken or unusable. You could take inspiration from Picasso's creative play with everyday objects in his work Baboon and Young, 1951 with its breadbasket and toy cars (see https://www.pablopicasso.org/baboon-and-young.jsp).

> Guess how I made the bull's head? One day, in a pile of objects all jumbled up together, I found an old bicycle seat right next to a rusty set of handlebars. In a flash, they joined together in my head. The idea of the Bull's Head came to me before I had a chance to think. All I did was weld them together… [but] if you were only to see the bull's head and not the bicycle seat and handlebars that form it, the sculpture would lose some of its impact.
>
> (Brassaï, Todd and Miller, 2002, p. 61)

This comment says as much about the creative process allowing for instinctive reactions, as it does about the materials used.

With the world's growing throw-away culture and plastic pollution, some artists are using materials to create their work that might otherwise be in landfill. For instance, the artist and designer Hannah Toft creates works with plastic sea trash collected on the West Coast of Scotland (see https://hannahtofts.com).

Task 17.3 Recycling Scheme of Work

- Set your students homework to collect materials that might otherwise be thrown away, empty washed colourful plastic bottles and lids, packaging and carefully selected broken plastic gadgets and toys. What might these inspire?
- See if you can create a scheme of work to incorporate the use of these materials in an innovative way.

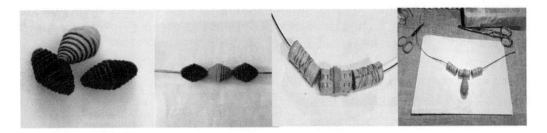

Figure 17.3 Exemplar beads using Scrap Store reclaimed felt and leftover cotton threads for a year 9 Textiles lesson. Images Courtesy of Kelly Bonathan-White.

Let's Not Neglect Craft and Design

With a re-evaluation being given to how we design and make art and objects, the design and craft elements of our subject should not be forgotten when we are considering innovative sustainable approaches. Burgess points out in 'Learning to Teach Art and Design in the Secondary School':

> Embedding sustainable design in your design education curriculum and pedagogy will invite pupils to become more reflective and self-aware about individual attitudes and responsibilities as inhabitants, and potentially as future practitioners, of a designed world.
>
> (Burgess, Schofield and Charman, 2015, p. 144)

Burgess suggests that craft is a too frequently neglected area of the 'art' curriculum. The Crafts Council does much to raise the profile of 'craft' in schools and support critical and contextual resources (Burgess, Schofield and Charman, 2015). Culturally 'crafts' have always been closer to a sustainable ethos than Fine Art. Traditional craft techniques and materials such as ceramics, collage, paper origami, knitting, weaving and textiles could allow students to engage with greener materials, techniques and processes (Figure 17.3).

BEYOND THE CLASSROOM

As well as championing sustainability in the classroom, you could consider the resources available outside. The often bureaucratic nature of trip planning is not always conducive to out of school activities but the benefits of students engaging with real life, real art, real nature, real environment and real activities are huge (Brophy, Marchant and Todd, 2019). There are many galleries and museums that are embracing sustainability in their programming of exhibitions. There is a longer-term focus with organisations such as the Climate Museum (see Resources), Wellcome Trust (see https://wellcome.org) and the Eden Project (see Resources) who all have a changing and accessible online presence. For those of you not wanting to stray too far afield you could take advantage of the school grounds or local parks. There is research to suggest that young people's connection with nature declines in their teens (The United Nations Children's Fund (UNICEF), 2015; Häggström, 2020). School grounds can provide a stimulating environment for students to interact, especially with regard to discovering and exploring local ecology (Figure 17.4).

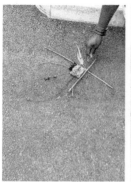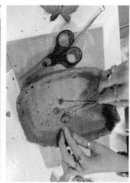

Figure 17.4 Land Art and Natural Forms Plaster Reliefs. Images Author's Own.

Task 17.4 Outdoor Art Activity

- Plan an art activity to happen outside.
- Where might this take place, for example, school grounds, a local park or a conservation area?
- How much time would you need to allow?
- Might as in the example this be something that happens as a club or enrichment activity?

Cross Curricular Approaches

Real life is not divided into individual subjects, it is interdisciplinary and complex and young people's understanding of the world comes through their ability to make connections (Gadsby and Bullivant, 2010; Trowell, 2010; Barnes, 2015; Scott and Twyman, 2018). We can open up opportunities for innovative exploration of sustainable, environmental and ecological themes through cross curricular approaches. Many artists combine disciplines in their work. For example, Invisible Dust (see Resources) brings together leading artists and scientists to create works of art that help people connect emotionally with climate change.

For those of you in schools with a STEAM curriculum (Science, Technology, English, Arts and Maths), there could be exciting opportunities to work within and across this cluster of subjects. STEAM, a development on STEM education, (Science, Technology, English and Maths), pioneered by Georgette Yakman, who recognised the value of creativity and innovation that Art brought to the cluster. There is also the potential to make sustainability interconnected and relevant, preparing students for green careers. The Cultural Alliance and NESTA in their STEAM briefing argue for the inclusion of the arts to develop skills that will be valuable for future work (seen at https://culturallearningalliance.org.uk/wp-content/uploads/2017/10/CD405-CLA-STEAM-Briefing-Teachers-Notes-08. pdf). This is echoed by the Durham Commission's research on creative education and its importance on economic growth, skills and social mobility (Durham Commission, 2021). Since the issues of climate change and sustainability are caused by and will affect all areas of our lives, it makes sense to cross pollinate our education (Figure 17.5).

Figure 17.5 Ecological Collaborative Artwork. Images Author's Own.

Task 17.5 Cross Curricular Scheme of Work

- Your task is to work with a colleague from another subject area to devise ideas for a scheme of work with a focus on sustainability.
- Where might subject knowledge meet?
- How might this reinforce student knowledge?
- Can you map shared languages and different understandings of the same terms?
- What might be the challenges for example, timetabling, logistics, attitudes/behaviours? How might these be overcome?

Student Agency

In a digital world, there is potential for an overload of information and possible anxiety from the culture of 'influencers' with their gospel of conspicuous consumption to doom-laden Eco-anxiety. Students will have a wide range of enthusiasms and anxieties, one of which might be the plight of their planet through climate change. The American Psychological Association has described 'a chronic fear of environmental doom' (Clayton, Manning, Krygsman and Speiser, 2017). This is a pressure that adds to worries about relationships, self-image, status, and all the other, often adolescent anxieties. The art department should be a space within which students can express their concerns and priorities in visual communication. Many of these concerns may seem trivial from an adult perspective or their solutions misguided but if we are to embrace the idea of student agency they should be part of the mix.

Whilst this chapter is concerned with bringing an awareness of sustainability to the art room, we must not forget that the subject is art, not environmental consciousness. Perhaps our teaching around the subject of environmentalism could

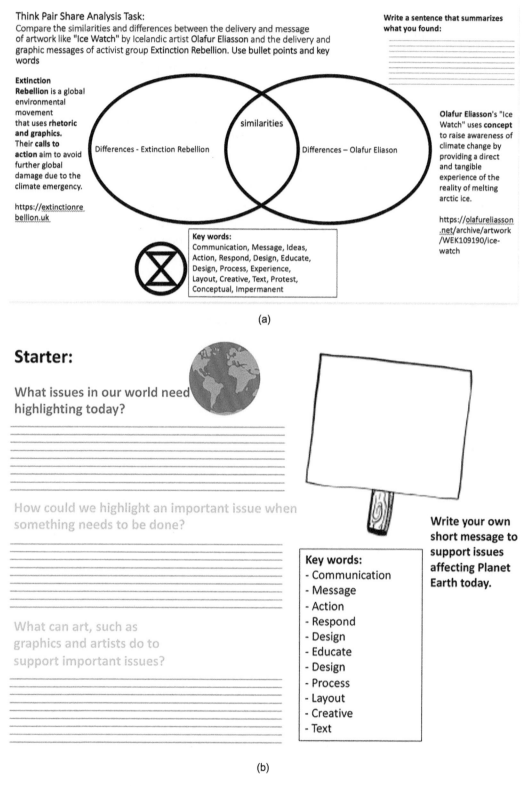

(a)

(b)

Figure 17.6 Worksheets to support student exploration of concepts and rhetoric in Contemporary Art and Graphic Design. Images courtesy of Charlotte Cousins.

be aimed at having a largely subliminal approach. Rather than make every project about sustainability, the subject of the piece of work might engage with a wide range of the students' interest and experience with the teacher then adding a layer of environmental awareness in ways of thinking and the materials used. This is where we need to be aware of the individuals' concerns. We might for instance introduce lessons about protest and creative activism citing Russian Revolutionary agit-prop or Extinction Rebellion's imaginative use of objects. The Climate Museum is a good place to start when looking for ideas and has links to a wide range of projects, protest movements, activists, creative activism campaigns and toolkits (see Resources).

It should always be borne in mind however that one of the great liberating strengths of Art and Design as a school subject and art in a wider social context is that it can take its subject and inspiration from the almost endless sum of human experience. Whilst as teachers we have a responsibility to debate and to some extent direct thought, this should be in order to expand not contract our students' thinking. It is important to point out the DfE's recent guidance for schools on political impartiality (DfE, 2022b), with regard to teachers not promoting any partisan political views. An important question for the teacher is how much you allow points of view with which you disagree and since you are teaching visual communication whether you judge the medium or the message (Figure 17.6).

Task 17.6 Discussing Environmental Issues

- Design your own starter task for a 10-minute activity that encourages student exploration of their own environmental and climate concerns.

SUMMARY

In this chapter, you have thought about what is meant by sustainability in education and how this might be developed in the context of the Art and Design classroom through the inclusion of sustainable themes, practice and resources. You will have gained an understanding of how art departments can be more environmentally conscious in their use of resources and materials inspiring schemes of work that utilise more sustainable practice. You have been introduced to ways that cross curricular approaches, including STEAM might be a more coherent and exciting way to teach sustainable, environmental and ecological knowledge and skills. Finally, you will have thought about the importance of art and design in promoting student agency to voice concerns and its liberating strengths in a wider social context.

RESOURCES

Climate Museum UK (https://climatemuseumuk.org)
An experimental museum that curates and gathers responses to the Earth crisis. A collective of creatives from across the UK, who organise activations to help people play, create and talk about the crisis. There is a range of collections with links to projects, activists, campaigns and toolkits on creative activism and protest movements that could be used in the classroom.
Eco-Schools (https://www.eco-schools.org.uk/)

This organisation works with schools and teachers supporting them to teach young people the skills and knowledge needed to benefit and improve our planet throughout their lifetimes. Their website showcases eco-project ideas for inspiration, so you could share your own projects and students work here.

Eden Project (https://www.edenproject.com/learn/schools)

Home to the world's largest rainforest in captivity, a unique resource for education and knowledge towards a sustainable future. You could plan a visit for students to explore the relationships between plants and people. There are also interactive virtual visit and teacher resource packs to support projects.

Invisible Dust (https://invisibledust.com)

Brings together artists and scientists to create exciting works of art with a focus on climate change. There are lots of exciting and innovative projects that might inspire cross curricular approaches.

University of Reading Climate Education Action Plan (https://www.reading. ac.uk/planet/climate-education/climate-education-plan)

In 2021, the University of Reading brought together young people, scientists, teachers and educationalists, policymakers and campaigners at a Climate Education Summit to create this action plan for better climate education in schools and colleges in the UK. This is to ensure all young people today and generations to come are equipped with the knowledge and understanding, and are empowered, to respond to and tackle the climate and ecological crisis facing our planet.

UCL Centre for Climate Change and Sustainability Education (https:// www.ucl.ac.uk/ioe/departments-and-centres/centres/ucl-centre-climate-change-and-sustainability-education).

Provide free research-informed professional development for teachers and school leaders across all phases, subjects and career stages.

BIBLIOGRAPHY

Adams, J. (2016) Sustainability in Arts Education. *International Journal of Art and Design Education*, 35(3), 294–295.

Addison, N. (2010) Art and Design in Education – Ruptures and Continuities. In: Addison, N., Burgess, L., Steers, J. and Trowell, J. (eds.) *Understanding Art Education: Engaging Reflexively with Practice.* London: Routledge.

Addison, N. and Burgess, L. (2003) *Issues in Art and Design Teaching*, London: Routledge Falmer.

Addison, N. and Burgess, L. (2015) Introduction. In: Addison, N. and Burgess, L. (eds.) *Learning to Teach Art and Design in the Secondary School: A Companion to School Experience.* Third edition. London: Routledge.

Addison, N. and Burgess, L. (eds.) (2021) *Debates in Art and Design Education.* Second edition. Abingdon, Oxon; New York: Routledge.

ARTdiscount, viewed 20 December 2022 from https://artdiscount.co.uk/blogs/artdiscount/vegan-vegetarian-and-eco-art

Art Hive, *Ai Wei Wei's Souvenir from Shanghai,* viewed 24 October 2022 from https://arthive.com/artists/78922~Ai_Weiwei/works/544822~Souvenir_from_Shanghai

Art UK, *Andy Goldsworthy,* viewed 30 October 2022 from https://artuk.org/learn/learning-resources/andy-goldsworthy-and-land-art

AQA. (2022) *GCSE Art and Design Specifications,* viewed 30 October 2022 from https://www.aqa.org.uk/subjects/art-and-design/gcse/art-and-design-8201-8206/specification-at-a-glance

ARTWAY, viewed 20 December 2022 from https://artway.co.uk/recycled-art-materials/

Barnes, J. (2015) *Cross-Curricular Learning* (pp. 3–14). Los Angeles, CA: Sage Publications Ltd.

Brassaï, Todd, J.M. and Miller, H. (2002) *Conversations with Picasso*. Pbk. ed. Chicago: University of Chicago Press.

Brophy, S., Marchant, E. and Todd, C. (2019) *Outdoor Learning Has Huge Benefits for Children and Teachers—So Why Isn't It Used in More Schools? [Online] The Conversation*, viewed 20 December 2022 from https://theconversation.com/outdoor-learning-has-huge-benefits-for-children-and-teachers-so-why-isnt-it-used-in-more-schools-118067

Burgess, L., Schofield, K. and Charman, H. (2015) Issues in Craft and Design Education. In: Addison, N. and Burgess, L. (eds.) *Learning to Teach Art and Design in the Secondary School: A Companion to School Experience*. Third edition. London: Routledge.

Clayton, S., Manning, C. M., Krygsman, K. and Speiser, M. (2017) *Mental Health and Our Changing Climate: Impacts, Implications, and Guidance*. Washington, DC: American Psychological Association, and Eco America.

Climate Museum UK, viewed 15 August 2022 from https://climatemuseumuk.org

DfE (Department for Education). (2013) *The National curriculum in England: Key Stages 3 and 4 Frame Work*, viewed 15 September from https://www.gov.uk/government/publications/national-curriculum-in-england-secondary-curriculum

DfE (Department for Education). (2022a) *Sustainability and Climate Change Strategy*, viewed 27 August 2022 from https://www.gov.uk/government/publications/sustainability-and-climate-change-strategy/sustainability-and-climate-change-a-strategy-for-the-education-and-childrens-services-sy

DfE (Department for Education). (2022b) *Political Impartiality in Schools*, viewed 09 August 2022 from https://www.gov.uk/government/publications/political-impartiality-in-schools/political-impartiality-in-schools

Downing, D., Watson, R. and National Foundation for Educational Research in England Wales. (2004) *School Art: What's in It?: Exploring Visual Arts in Secondary Schools*. Slough: National Foundation for Educational Research.

Durham Commission. (2021) *Durham Commission on Creativity and Education – second report 2021*, viewed 18 September 2022 from https://www.dur.ac.uk/resources/creativitycommission/DurhamCommissionsecondreport-21April.pdf

Eco-Schools, viewed 11 August 2022 from https://www.eco-schools.org.uk/

Eden Project, *Jenny Kendler's Birds Watching*, viewed 24 August 2022 from https://www.edenproject.com/visit/things-to-do/birds-watching

Gadsby, H. and Bullivant, A. (2010) *Teaching Contemporary Themes in Secondary Education: Global Learning and Sustainable Development*. London: Routledge.

GreatArt, viewed 20 August 2022 from https://www.greatart.co.uk/how-we-work/

Hannah Toft, viewed 24 August 2022 from https://hannahtofts.com

Holland, G. (1998) *The Holland Report*, viewed 24 September from https://www.tidegloballearning.net/files/uploads/Sustainable_Development_Education_Panel_Annual_Report_1998.pdf

Invisible Dust, viewed 11 August 2022 from https://invisibledust.com

Ofsted. (2022) *Guidance Education Inspection Framework*, viewed 19 September from https://www.gov.uk/government/publications/education-inspection-framework/education-inspection-framework

Pablo Picasso. *Picasso's Baboon and Young*, viewed 27 October from https://www.pablopicasso.org/baboon-and-young.jsp

People and Planet University League 2022/23, viewed 12 December 2022 from https://peopleandplanet.org/university-league

Richard Long, viewed 30 October 2022 from http://www.richardlong.org

Scott, T., and Twyman, T., (2018) Considering Visual Arts Practices at the Secondary Level: Extending Cross-Curricular Conversations Among Secondary Educators. *Art Education (Reston)*, 71(2), 16–20.

Scott, W. and Vare, P. (2021) *Learning, Environment and Sustainable Development: A History of Ideas*. Milton Park, Abingdon, Oxon; New York: Routledge.

TATE Gallery. *Olafur Eliasson's 'The Weather Project' Filled the Turbine Hall at Tate in 2003*, viewed 15 August from https://www.tate.org.uk/whats-on/tate-modern/unilever-series/unilever-series-olafur-eliasson-weather-project /

Tanya, S. and Twyman, T. (2018) Considering Visual Arts Practices at the Secondary Level: Extending Cross-Curricular Conversations Among Secondary Educators. *Art Education*, 71(2), 16–20.

The Cultural Learning Alliance. (2017) *Cultural Learning Alliance Briefing Paper No.1*, viewed 5 September 2022 from https://culturallearningalliance.org.uk/wp-content/uploads/2017/10/CD405-CLA-STEAM-Briefing-Teachers-Notes-08.pdf

The University of Reading. (2021) *National Climate Education Action Plan*, viewed 27 September 2022 from https://www.reading.ac.uk/planet/-/media/project/uor-main/uor-campaign/climate-for-change/climate-education-summit/climateeducationsummit-actionplan.pdf?la=en&hash=70A9DA27CDA84F375723D8C91F45B12F

Trowell, J. (2010), Collaborative Liberatory Practices for Global Citizenship. In: Addison, N. Burgess, L., Steers, J. and Trowell, J. (eds.) *Understanding Art Education: Engaging Reflexively with Practice.* London: Routledge.

UCL Centre for Climate Change and Sustainability Education, viewed 12 December 2022 from https://www.ucl.ac.uk/ioe/departments-and-centres/centres/ucl-centre-climate-change-and-sustainability-education

UN (United Nations). (2015) *Transforming Our World: The 2030 Agenda for Sustainable Development*, viewed 25 September from https://sustainabledevelopment.un.org/content/documents/21252030%20Agenda%20for%20Sustainable%20Development%20web.pdf

UNEP (United Nations Environment Programme), viewed 29 September 2022 from https://www.unep.org

UNESCO (United Nations Educational, Scientific and Cultural Organization), viewed25Septemberfromhttps://www.unesco.org/en/education/sustainable-development

UNICEF (The United Nations Children's Fund). (2015) *Children and the Changing Climate Taking Action to Save Lives*, viewed 30 September 2022 from https://www.unicef.org.uk/wp-content/uploads/2015/11/Unicef_2015childrenandclimatechange.pdf

Wellcome Trust, viewed 30 October 2022 from https://wellcome.org

World Commission on Environment and Development (WCED). (1987) *The Bruntland Report*, viewed 30 August 2022 from https://sustainabledevelopment.un.org/content/documents/5987our-common-future.pdf

Chapter 18   Advancing an Anti-Ableist Pedagogy in the Secondary Art and Design Curriculum

Claire Penketh and Sandra Hiett

INTRODUCTION

> a chief feature of an ableist viewpoint is a belief that impairment or disability (irrespective of 'type') is inherently negative and should the opportunity present itself, be ameliorated, cured or indeed eliminated.
>
> (Fiona Kumari Campbell, 2009, p.5)

An anti-ableist pedagogy (AaP) seeks to promote a deep engagement with disability, challenging a belief that it must always be equated with a diminished and negative experience. This chapter will build on your understanding of disability in order to promote an anti-ableist approach to art education. Here we consider this as a means of challenging everyday assumptions whilst valuing the presence of diverse bodies and minds in and beyond our art classrooms.

Ableism represents taken for granted beliefs about how we think, feel and come to know the world around us. It represents a set of assumptions about the ways so-called normal bodies and minds work. In educational terms, this might mean that we presume all learners can see and hear, work at a particular pace, develop improved coordination with age and have the capacity to concentrate for long periods of time. These taken for granted assumptions can create the ideal conditions for disablism, overt acts of discrimination, to grow (Goodley, 2014).

It is important to note from the outset that the language used in this chapter follows the British social model of disability. We use the term 'disabled person/ people' to indicate that whilst a person may experience impairment, they are disabled by social, cultural and attitudinal barriers. We encourage you to take a critical approach in reflecting on the relationship between disability and art education. We recognise the role that you, as an art teacher, can play in advancing an anti-ableist pedagogy that prioritises access whilst promoting a deeper understanding of the productive relationship between disability and art education, and this includes an engaging with disability arts.

DOI: 10.4324/9781003377429-22

OBJECTIVES

By the end of this chapter you should be able to:

- identify and challenge ableist assumptions in art education;
- explore opportunities to promote anti-ableist practice in your teaching;
- draw on contemporary work in disability arts to inform your personal/professional practice.

WHAT IS AN ANTI-ABLEIST APPROACH?

An anti-ableist art education is one that overtly challenges presumptions about what bodies and minds can be and do. It aims to question dominant ideas about disability as an individual problem but goes further to acknowledge and value the benefits that diverse bodies and minds can bring to creative and pedagogic practice.

Disability has been understood in different ways at different times and in differing social contexts. The ways we think about disability has a significant influence on the ways we approach the education of disabled children and young people. Within our current context, this is framed as a legal commitment to meet the needs of children and young people with so-called special educational needs and it is essential that all pupils have access to high quality experiences in art, craft and design. However, as an art teacher you also have a responsibility to challenge discriminatory attitudes, encouraging critical perspectives about disability at a curricula level and recognising the relevance of disability as a site for learning for disabled and non-disabled teachers and pupils.

Anti-ableism offers a direct challenge to everyday assumptions about ability helping us to develop our awareness of hidden bias, enabling us to imagine and value alternative ways of being. This idea has been introduced and developed by a number of disabled activists and scholars including Fiona Kumari Campbell in her influential book *Contours of Ableism* (Campbell, 2009). Being aware of ableism can enable us to challenge a deficit orientation towards disability, enabling us to improve access whilst creating a new space for critical explorations of disability within the curriculum. These two strands: *enabling access* and *curriculum innovation* are central to advancing AaP pedagogy (Figure 18.1).

DISABILITY STUDIES AND ANTI-ABLEISM IN ART EDUCATION

> disability studies offers a way to understand disability that stands quite apart from the scripts authored by special education.
>
> (Linda Ware, 2018, p.575)

Studies in ableism are rooted in disability studies, an interdisciplinary field that provides essential tools for disrupting dominant ideas about disability, including the absence of critical debates about special education. Teachers and academics working at the intersection of art education and disability studies have recognised

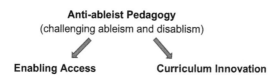

Figure 18.1 Components of AaP.

the benefits of the social model of disability for enhancing pedagogic practice. The social model of disability encourages us to recognise and remove social, attitudinal and physical barriers in education. In early work, the US art educator Doug Blandy called for art teachers to move away from negative ideas about disability. He rejected terms such as 'art brut' and 'outsider art' and called for disabled children and young people to be able to access art education without the prejudice brought by these associations. He also suggested that art teachers were well placed to promote an analytical approach to disability in the art classroom through a critical exploration of cultural representations of disability in art and film (Blandy, 1991). He argued that bringing disability into the realms of aesthetic education could offer a means of addressing prejudice by building an understanding of the ways that ideas about disability are socially constructed (Blandy, 1994). The importance of understanding and interrogating representations of disability in arts and culture has been recognised and applied across a range of disciplines, including education, through work in cultural disability studies (Bolt, 2018). Another US scholar, John Derby, has recognised the relationship between the arts and social justice, acknowledging art education as a site for critical social practice, and as a means of challenging discrimination. Derby argues that art education can learn from disability studies in order to promote a critical engagement that moves beyond the needs-based discourse of special education highlighting the reciprocal benefits of art education to work in disability studies (Derby, 2016). Both Blandy and Derby have advocated for a more critical approach to disability in art education, offering examples of the benefits of this for beginning teachers. Further examples of the application of an AaP in teacher education can also be found in work by Claire Penketh and Alice Wexler. Penketh introduces the idea of AaP as a 'vital' pedagogy whilst Wexler explores these ideas more particularly in relation to playful and provocative, collaborative drawing practices that are strengthened by the presence of non-normative bodies and minds (Penketh, 2020; Wexler, 2021). The authors, teachers and practitioners mentioned here are all committed to bringing critical perspectives to art education that are informed by disability studies, recognising its usefulness in theory and practice. Those keen to pursue a further introduction to disability studies could go to *Approaching Disability – critical issues and perspectives* (Mallett & Runswick-Cole, 2014). In this next section, we will begin by encouraging you to think about your own experiences and what disability means to you.

STARTING *WITH* DISABILITY

We cannot make any assumptions about you or your experiences of disability. You may or may not identify as being a disabled person but it is very likely that you have had some experience of disability, perhaps as a sibling, child, parent or carer. Positioning yourself in relation to disability is not only useful but some would argue is an essential starting point for any work in disability studies (O'Toole, 2013).

Task 18.1 Line, Dot Circle and Colour

- This first activity is designed to support your personal and professional reflections, encouraging you to consider your own positionality in relation to this topic by asking: *What is Your Relationship with Disability?*
- Use lines, dots, circles and colours to represent your relationship with disability. The information that follows should help you to think about this task.

For example, Claire is a non-disabled, white British academic working in the field of Disability Studies. She grew up in a family that was impacted quite significantly by her mother's illness and her experiences as a carer for her father who acquired vascular dementia. She taught art to disabled and non-disabled pupils in mainstream secondary schools in Liverpool, England.

Although we all have a relationship with disability, we are often presented with this as a one-way street – attending only to the so-called special needs of pupils. However, an inclusive school community must also acknowledge the experience of disabled teachers and adults in the school alongside its responsibility to challenge discrimination and educate children and young people about disability. This *line, dot, circle and colour* task is a quick and simple activity that asks you to represent your relationship to disability in a visual way by creating a diagram using only lines, dots, circles and colours. This can provide a coded starting point for you to reflect on what you understand by disability and the ways that this has influenced your personal and professional practice.

Sandra has used this *line, dot and circle* activity with her pre-service secondary art teachers, allowing her to facilitate discussions, opening a space for them to think about disability as a mutual experience with relevance for all, regardless of our direct or indirect experience.

Here are two examples of line, dot, circle and colour diagrams (Figure 18.2 and 18.3) produced by Sandra's pre-service secondary art teachers responding to the prompt: What is Your Relationship with Disability?

Having completed the dot, line, circle task, two trainee art teachers discussed how the activity gave them a fresh insight into their relationship with disability moving beyond what they already knew and providing a heightened awareness that was beneficial to their emerging classroom practice. Both trainees shared a partial decoding of their images (a partial decoding in that they disclosed some of what the image represented but not all). In Figure 18.2, Student A revealed how the parallel lines represent what she knows about disability and her relationship with it. She talked about where the lines failed to meet, running off the page, signifying what is unknown to her and stating that she 'still has a long way to go to break down those barriers'. In Figure 18.3. Student B locates herself as the big red circle with the dark blue dots near her representing those she teachers with similar learning difficulties and how she feels she can support them. On the right of these dots Student B drew a series of dotted lines that she is 'currently weaving' her 'way through' to understand the needs of all her pupils and how she can best support them in and through their art education.

Enabling Access

Access to art education is a right that all pupils should enjoy. The United Nations Convention on the Rights of the Child (UNICEF, 1989) asserts the right to education. Article 29.1 indicates that the education of a child should be directed to the 'development of the child's personality, talents and mental and physical abilities to their fullest potential'. Article 31 specifically sets out a child's right to participation in cultural life and arts. In order to ensure that all children can participate in art education we must be able to anticipate a broad range of abilities and experiences. The Equality Act (2010) and the Special Educational Needs Code of Practice (2015) outline a legal requirement to make **reasonable adjustments** to enable learners to access the curriculum. This access should be **anticipatory**, meaning that we need to address barriers before they create an issue for pupils, rather than working retroactively to address discrimination. Employing the principles of Universal Design

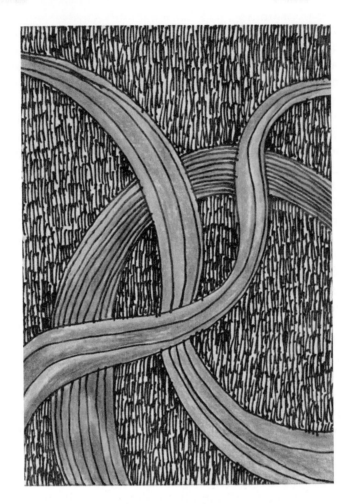

Figures 18.2 and 18.3 Student responses to the prompt, 'What is Your Relationship with Disability?'

for Learning (UDfL) can be useful in supporting a flexible approach to planning that anticipates diverse starting points for pupils and welcomes a range of possible outcomes. In contrast, a prescribed and inflexible approach limits our opportunities for access whilst also being counter-productive to the development of creative practice. An accessible curriculum in art education aligns with aspirations for the subject to promote individual aesthetic responses over prescriptive, predetermined or formulaic activities. The following principles may be useful to support your reflections on schemes of work or individual lessons.

The seven principles of UDfL are:

- Equitable use: Provides the same means of use for all pupils with diverse abilities and design which appeals to everyone;
- Flexibility in use: Design to accommodate a wider range of preferences and abilities;
- Simple and intuitive: Easy to understand and use regardless of the pupil's experiences, knowledge, language skills or current concentration level;
- Perceptible information: Communicates necessary information effectively, regardless of surrounding conditions or sensory abilities;
- Tolerance for error: Minimises hazards and adverse consequences of unintended actions;
- Low physical effort: Efficient and comfortable while minimising chance of fatigue;
- Size and space for approach and use: Design provides appropriate size and space, regardless of the pupil's body size, posture or mobility.

Revising Your Curriculum from an Anti-Ableist Position

You are now aware that we are promoting a reflective approach to realising the aims of AaP and we argue that critical reflection on ableist assumptions can offer a further starting point for planning and reviewing existing lessons or schemes of work. This will help you to think about different points of access to your lessons and help you move towards an anticipatory approach, supporting a proactive rather than reactive approach to the diverse needs of learners. In addition, it can promote an understanding of the benefits of an anticipatory approach to creative practice. Opening a lesson up in this way helps us to question habits of practice and established modes of working that may hold ableist assumptions (Figure 18.4).

Task 18.2 Ableist Assumptions

- Identify a lesson or scheme of work.
- Are there any ableist assumptions in this initial plan? For example, does the work rely solely on visual cues? Does the work presume typical levels of co-ordination and concentration? Do written instructions reflect assumptions regarding levels of literacy and cognition?
- If you have identified any ableist assumptions, you can begin to revise the project from an anti-ableist position. This might mean offering a range of multi-sensory starting points, a range of media and the segmenting of activities into shorter phases. This anti-ableist approach should enable you to identify the main focus of the project and to explore different ways of working.
- Reflect on your revisions. Can you identify any gains in terms of learning and teaching? Are there any benefits for creative practice?

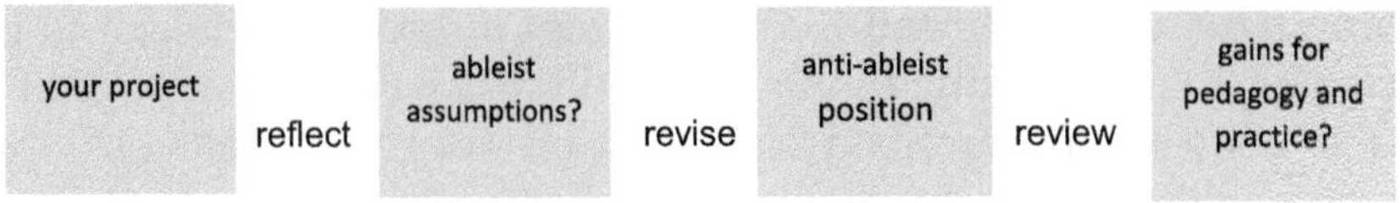

Figure 18.4 AaP: reflection as pedagogic practice.

EXAMPLE: CITYSCAPES

This example is given in more detail, and with illustrations, in the following publication: *Towards a Vital Pedagogy: Learning from Anti-Ableist Practice in Art Education* (Penketh, 2020).

The Project: Pupils were asked to make a drawn composition based on images of iconic buildings. All pupils worked on A3 in pencil to develop tonal drawings.

Reflect: What were the ableist assumptions? The project relied on all pupils working visually from images using the same media, 2B pencils, and for a prolonged period of time.

Revise from an anti-ableist position: A range of sensory starting points were offered including the sounds and sensations of the city, and drawing on pupil experiences of the environment. Pupils worked in groups, using their bodies to create architectural forms which were lit to cast shadows on the wall. Words and sounds were recorded to create a soundscape based on the ways that different bodies might move through the built environment.

Review gains for pedagogy and practice: There were benefits to moving beyond a singularly visual response. Pupils brought their differing experiences of the city to the project. A final display represented multimodal installation enabling connections with contemporary art practice.

ACCESS AND IMAGE DESCRIPTION

The pedagogic benefits of addressing access are evident in the example above and also become apparent in the use of another AaP methodology, image description. In this methodology, image descriptions or audio descriptions are created in order to support access requirements for people who are blind or visually impaired, image description has a further advantage of promoting a deep engagement with art, craft and design through collaborative exploration. Pupils can be taught the value of making their own images accessible to a wider audience, an idea that has particular relevance in sharing images through social media and web-based platforms. The use of alternative text (Alt Text), a short text description to support access, is a particular example of the ways that technology prompts us to make work available to a diverse audience. Image description, such as Alt Text, can also be a means of highlighting and engaging with ambiguity in images that we might assume can be easily read by others. Image description can be used to support pupils' understanding of the work of others but should also enable them to think about their own work and how that is being received.

The following activity is based on work by Georgina Kleege, a US-based academic who is visually impaired (Kleege & Wallin, 2015). She has actively promoted the use of image description for access but is clear on the pedagogic value that this can bring. This approach does not require pupils to imitate blindness. She explains that the following activity is not a simulation exercise, aware that imitating impairment can be reductive, simplifying and obscuring the reality of people's lived experiences. However, pupils are encouraged to view or turn away from the image. The presence of a teacher or a pupil who is blind or with a visual impairment is explored as a distinct advantage in this activity, rather than as a need for compensation.

Task 18.3 Image Descriptions

- Choose an image related to your topic or encourage pupils to work with one of their own images.
- Divide the class into small groups, A and B. Group A will describe the image whilst B turn away from the image and listen to the descriptions.
- The prompt 'where does your eye go first' offers a useful starting point for their descriptions and discussions of the image. Group A can offer a verbal or written description, picking out aspects that they think are most relevant and that they would want to share with the other group.
- When both groups turn back to the image, Group B can discuss their expectations and any points of departure or surprise. Following a discussion about this interpretation, both groups can collaborate on a written description and/or make a voice recording.

A central aim in presenting these activities so far has been to challenge an underlying assumption that disability represents a negative experience that requires compensation. There is no attempt here to minimise the effects of a person's impairment or their experiences of disablement. However, there is a growing awareness of the pedagogic and creative benefits of diversity and a recognition that experiences of disability and impairment can generate work that can increases awareness through visual and tactile arts. This first section has emphasised the importance of access. We will now move to the second component of an AaP, described here as *Curriculum Innovation.*

CURRICULUM INNOVATION

Whilst access is essential for enabling participation, innovations in curriculum content and design are vital for promoting a deeper understanding of disability. Curriculum is a powerful tool that can challenge or reinforce the status quo. Recent moves towards anti-racist art education and attempts to de-colonise the curriculum and reflect the power of the curriculum in creating greater awareness and in questioning and ultimately shifting social attitudes. Although disability has been widely represented in art works over time, representations of disabled people have not always been read and interpreted with the critical lens afforded to other marginalised groups. Encouraging an engagement with representations of disability is important as an initial move towards a more informed approach, particularly at a time when we have regular encounters with these representations through mainstream media such as social media, television and film. Work at the intersection of disability studies and art criticism offers useful insights into connecting histories of art with representations of disability. In particular, *Disability and Art History – Interdisciplinary Disability Studies* (Millet-Gallant & Howie, 2017) offers rich insights into the work of disabled and non-disabled artists. Whilst there is now a significant amount of material to engage with it is important to address the importance of positioning disability in the curriculum and to think about ways that this might be addressed. One particular approach is to address the absence of disability arts as a critical resource. In this next section, we address the absence of disability arts and offer suggestions for its inclusion in schools.

Putting Disability Arts into the Curriculum

An AaP presents opportunities to challenge negative stereotypes towards disability by building critical perspectives into the curriculum, specifically by drawing on work, made by disabled artists. Bringing disability arts into the art classroom enables us to engage with creative practice that is designed to promote and provoke a deeper engagement with experiences of disability, disablement and difference as a generative resource. Curriculum innovation, putting disability studies and disability arts into the curriculum, therefore enables us to shift the emphasis on individual deficit to a site for learning about identity through experiences that may have been previously marginalised (Ware, 2018). Disability arts have particular resonance as aesthetic work that is designed to provoke and challenge societal ideas about disability. It is work that is 'ready-made' to enable you to bring disability into the art classroom. This may take the form of a specific topic but can more likely inform a range of projects and approaches. Work relating to identity, for example, can incorporate perspectives about disability in a similar way to previously taboo or stigmatised identities such as those relating to LGBTQ+ (Addison, 2007). Projects relating to protest could draw on work by Liz Crow and Dolly Sen, both of whom have created art and performance to address the impact of social and economic policy on disabled people (see http:// www.roaring-girl.com/work/bedding-out/ and https://disabilityarts.online/ magazine/opinion/a-day-in-the-life-of-an-artist-dolly-sen/). Liz Crow's *Bedding Out* (2013), a durational performance where the artist brought attention to illness, energies and welfare changes could be used in dialogue with Tracy Emin's *My Bed* (1998), both pieces opening an opportunity to explore contemporary arts practice. A recent project, We Are Invisible, We Are Visible (WAIWAV), brought together 31 'invisible' disabled artists to create a series of interventions to celebrate the 102nd anniversary of the first international Dada art fair in Berlin, in 1920. This work offers a rich representation of contemporary practice in disability arts and can be accessed through the DAO weblink provided at the end of this chapter (see Resources). Whilst there is much work to draw on in the UK, it is important to recognise artists working at an international level. Christine Sun Kim draws on her experiences of deafness to produce drawings, videos, installations and performances bringing disruptions to conventional ways of thinking about sound and vision and their potential for creative practice (https://www. youtube.com/watch?v=2Euof4PnjDk).

There is a wealth of work to engage with. Organisations such as DASH and Disability Arts Online provide access and commentary on work made by disabled artists offering a rich resource that should challenge us and help us to explore disability through contemporary arts practice. In a 2022 issue of *AD*, the National Society for Education in Art and Design magazine, artist and teacher Paul Morrow connects contemporary art practice with AaP exploring their shared potential for embracing subjectivity and improvisation as a means of extending practice. Bringing disability arts into the curriculum can encourage us to explore 'points of departure' from orthodox practice (Morrow, 2022, p.14). Engaging with disability arts can therefore be central to enhancing the curriculum.

SUMMARY

This chapter has introduced AaP as a means of enabling access for pupils. It has acknowledged access to art education as a legal requirement and a human right. However, it has also given examples of the pedagogic benefits of an accessible art education and its alignment with approaches that move art education beyond orthodox practice, bringing new directions by engaging with critical perspectives in disability studies. Promoting and working with an AaP should reflect a process of trial and error, working with artists, designers, makers and pupils, as a form of creative practice in itself. In addition, the chapter has encouraged you to consider ways of bringing disability into the curriculum by engaging with work, made by disabled artists, to specifically address embodied and creative experiences of impairment and disability. Research has identified that teachers may feel underprepared to talk about disability or feel unsure of how we can bring disability into the classroom (Connor, 2020). Artists working in disability arts make work specifically using aesthetic tools in order to communicate, provoke and engage with their audience. We can all benefit by working with their practice. Lastly, the chapter has encouraged you to think about what disability means to you, not as a distant and separate category of learners described as having a special educational need or disability but as a feature of our shared humanity. An AaP promotes disability as an experience from which we can all learn.

RESOURCES

AD Magazine *Anti-ableist Takeover Issue* **(NSEAD) Autumn 2022 Issue 35**
AD is the National Society for Education in Art and Design magazine. This issue offers a collective response to anti-ableist practice with examples from artists, educators, pupils, activists, curators and academics. The work includes artist Sonia Boue who discusses her experiences of art education and art practice from a neurodivergent perspective and Sarah Graham's exploration of mental health and arts practice. The issue highlights a recent Disability Arts project *We Are Invisible, We Are Visible*.

Disability Arts Online https://disabilityarts.online/ **[accessed 18.10.2022]**
Edited by Colin Hambrook, Disability Arts Online, advances disability arts and culture, supporting the work of disabled artists and offering a platform for discussion. This is a fabulous resource that is regularly updated with examples of work across the arts including the visual arts and performance highlighting contemporary practice. DAO provides an opportunity for the wider arts sector to engage with disabled artists.

National Disability Arts Collection & Archive https://the-ndaca.org/ **[accessed 18.10.2022]**
This archive represents a collection of material from disability arts organisations and charts the history of the disabled people's movement and the role of the arts in disability activism. It includes interviews with artists as well as resources associated with the Disability Arts Movement and audio described essays on work by artists including Tanya Raabe-Webber and Tony Heaton.

Penketh, C. & Adams, J. (2019) The Biopolitics of Art Education: Special Issue *Journal of Literary and Cultural Disability Studies* 13(3), 247-253.
This Special Issue offers a number of articles by disabled and non-disabled artists and academics examining the relationship between art education and disability studies including an examination of so-called mad art, the rhetorics of inclusion, a discussion of role-playing disabled making, art history and low vision, art history, and the 'swinging identities of Dis/abilities'.

BIBLIOGRAPHY

Addison, N. (2007) 'Identity Politics and the Queering of Art Education: Inclusion and the Confessional Route to Salvation', *International Journal of Art and Design Education*, 26(1), 10–20.

Blandy, D. (1994) 'Assuming Responsibility: Disability Rights and the Preparation of Art Educators', *Studies in Art Education*, 35(3), 179–187.

Blandy, D. (1991) 'Conceptions of Disability: Toward a Sociopolitical Orientation Toward Disability for Art Education', *Studies in Art Education*, 32(3), 131–144.

Bolt, D. (2018) *Cultural Disability Studies in Education*, London: Routledge.

Campbell, F. K. (2009) *Contours of Ableism*, London: Palgrave.

Connor, D. J. (2020). "I don't like to be told that I view a student with a deficit mindset": Why it Matters that Disability Studies in Education Continues to Grow. *Canadian Journal of Disability Studies*, 9(5), 20–41.

Derby, J. (2016) 'Confronting Ableism: Disability Studies Pedagogy in Preservice Art Education', *Studies in Art Education*, 57(2), 102–119.

Derby, J. (2013) 'Nothing About Us Without Us: Art Educations Disservice to Disabled People', *Studies in Art Education*, 54(4), 376–380.

Derby, J. (2011) 'Disability Studies and Art Education', *Studies in Art Education*, 52(2), 94–111.

Goodley, D. (2014) *Dis/Ability Studies: Theorising Disablism and Ableism*, Oxon/New York: Routledge.

Kleege, G. & Wallin, S. (2015) 'Audio Description as a Pedagogic Tool', *Disability Studies Quarterly*, 35(2) [accessed online 25.10.2022].

Mallett, R. & Runswick-Cole, K. (2014) *Approaching Disability – Critical Issues and Perspectives*, London: Routledge.

Millet-Gallant, A. & Howie, E. (2017) *Disability and Art History – Interdisciplinary Disability Studies*, London/New York: Routledge.

Morrow, P. (2022) *Contemporary Art Practice and Anti-Ableist Pedagogy AD*. Issue 35, pp. 13–14. NSEAD.

O'Toole, J. C. (2013) 'Disclosing Our Relationships to Disability: An Invitation for Disability Studies Scholars', *Disability Studies Quarterly*, 33(2), n.p.

Penketh, C. (ed.) (2022) 'Anti-Ableist Takeover Issue', AD, The National Society for Education in Art and Design magazine. Issue 35.

Penketh, C. (2020) 'Towards A Vital Pedagogy: Learning from Anti-Ableist Practice in Art Education', *International Journal of Education Through Art*, 16(1), 13–27.

UNICEF (1989) *Convention on the Rights of the Child. Online 'unicef | for every child'* accessed 5.1.24 (https://www.unicef.org/child-rights-convention/convention-text).

Ware, L. (2018) 'Worlds Remade: Inclusion Through Engagement with Disability Art', *International Journal of Inclusive Education*, 12(5–6), 563–583.

Wexler, A. (2021) 'An Anti-Ableist Framework in Art Education', *Art Education*, 75(1), 30–35.

Chapter 19

Critical Perspectives and Teaching Strategies for Addressing Peace and Peacebuilding Issues in Art Education

Mousumi De and Ernst Wagner

INTRODUCTION

The goal of promoting peace through education and art has long been advocated by education philosophers and art educators. Policy mandates such as the *Seoul Agenda: Goals for the Development of Arts Education* (UNESCO, 2010) also suggest using art education to resolve social and cultural challenges. Goal 3 especially suggests using art education to support the reconstruction and restoration efforts of post-conflict societies to promote peace. As we witness emergent wars and conflicts, addressing peace and peacebuilding issues in art education remains important. To assist art educators in developing pedagogies that address issues of peace and peacebuilding effectively, a deeper understanding of these concepts and processes is imperative.

Peace is multidimensional in nature and its interpretations vary across different cultures and contexts. Eastern notions of peace connote harmony and balance achieved internally as a state of mind, while western concepts center on the absence of war and violence. Galtung (1969) proposed peace as being positive and negative; positive peace involves the active presence of justice, integration, and harmony, while negative peace refers to an absence of war, conflict, and injustice. Initially, he defined peace as the absence of direct, cultural, and structural violence. *Direct violence* refers to observable acts of harm inflicted by one party over another such as shooting, bombing, genocide, etc. *Cultural violence* refers to damage inflicted upon people that restricts their autonomy making them incapable of fulfilling their full potential. Examples include cultural systems that overtly or tacitly condone violence, such as gender inequality, racism, sexism, etc. *Structural violence* involves preventing people from fulfilling their human capital by dominant institutions and oppressive structural patterns, such as institutionalized racism, health and wealth inequality, repression of minority communities, and so on.

Galtung (1996) later conceptualized peace as what we have when creative conflict transformation can take place non-violently. A *conflict* occurs when two or more parties pursue incompatible goals while trying to stop the other from pursuing their goals. Galtung's definition embodies the characteristics of a *system*, whether a family, small group, or a society, that enables destructive or violent conflicts to be transformed through constructive and non-violent means. Other definitions of

DOI: 10.4324/9781003377429-23

peace have also been proposed. For example, Anderson (2004) defined peace as a *condition* that is experienced at different micro-and macro-levels that are interconnected. These include (1) *Personal Peace* experienced at inner level (within an individual) and interpersonal level (among individuals or groups); (2) *Cultural Peace* can be experienced at a local, civil (within a community), and a national level (within a nation); and finally, (3) *Global Peace* that can be experienced at an international level (among nations) and at an ecological level (i.e., with the natural world).

This chapter provides critical perspectives, strategies and activity examples for addressing peace and peacebuilding issues in art education.

OBJECTIVES:

By the end of the chapter, you will have an understanding of the following:

- Concepts and varied dimensions of peace, and the use of art in peace symbolism and anti-war art;
- Peacebuilding processes and how art interventions contribute toward specific goals in peacebuilding and reconciliation;
- The distinction between teaching art *about* peace and peacebuilding and art *for* peace and peacebuilding;
- The difference between art appropriation and cultural appropriation in using art and symbolism from diverse cultures.
- Critical perspectives and teaching strategies for addressing peace and peacebuilding issues through art.

The following activity provides an opportunity for learners and teachers to explore the sources and/or conditions that promote peace at different levels.

Task 19.1 Different Dimensions of Peace

Discuss, conceptualize, and illustrate, the different dimensions of peace:

- Task 19.1.1 *Personal peace (within self):* Consider what conditions or sources makes you feel at peace. Visually illustrate your understanding of peace, literally or metaphorically looking at the examples offered.
- Task 19.1.2 *Personal peace (with others):* Consider what conditions make you feel peaceful with others (e.g., family, friends). Visually illustrate your understanding of and/or a scenario depicting these literally or metaphorically looking at the examples offered.
- Task 19.1.3 *Cultural peace:* Consider what aspects or conditions bring peace within your community or country. Visually illustrate your understanding of and/or scenario literally or metaphorically.
- Task 19.1.4 *Global peace (internationally):* Consider a set of nations that are meaningful to you or the world as a whole and what aspects or conditions can bring peace between the nations or the world. Visually illustrate these literally or metaphorically.
- Task 19.1.5 *Global peace (ecologically):* Consider what conditions would bring peace in the ecology or the natural environment around you (within your city, country, or the world). Visually illustrate your understanding of and/or a scenario literally or metaphorically looking at the examples offered.

EXAMPLES – TASK 19.1: DIFFERENT DIMENSIONS OF PEACE

The following are two examples of *Cultural Peace* illustrated by young British Muslim girls in middle and high schools. Figure 19.1 titled *Coexistence* was co-created by two girls aged 11 and 15 years in the context of peace in the British community. It depicts a mosque at the center, juxtaposed with a dove and the Union Jack with verses of peace written in the Arabic language. It is a metaphoric representation of British Muslims and non-Muslims coexisting together in communal harmony. Figure 19.2 titled *Unity* was created by a 14-year-old girl. It shows individuals from diverse ethnic groups and sub-cultures holding hands around a ball in peace colours. It combines a literal and metaphoric representation of communal harmony in British society.

CRITICAL PERSPECTIVES AND TEACHING STRATEGIES

Scaffolding

Some learners might find concepts of peace, especially positive peace too abstract to visualize or illustrate in their art. Therefore, appropriate scaffolding processes might enable them to understand these concepts easily. Scaffolding involves processes that enable a learner to solve a problem or achieve a learning goal that they cannot achieve without (instructional) assistance. Some guiding questions to help learners understand and visualize peace might include, "what makes you happy or calm?" "What kinds of relations with others make you feel happy or calm?" To help learners understand cultural peace, some guiding questions might include, "What conditions in society are needed to promote social justice, equality, and integration? Or, "What actions might promote these goals?"

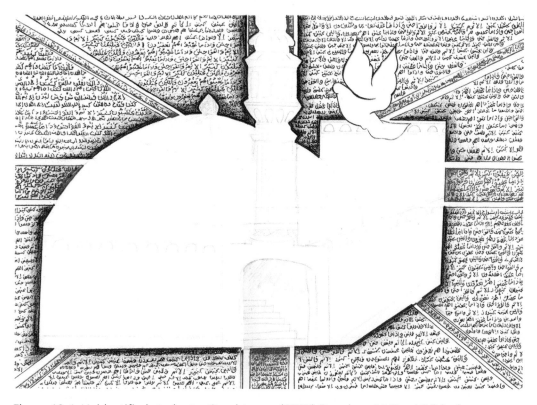

Figure 19.1 Unidentified students, *Coexistence*, (2005) Drawing, 11.7 × 16.5 inches.

Source: Courtesy of the artists.

Figure 19.2 Unidentified student, *Unity*, (2005) Painting, 11.7 × 16.5 inches.

Source: Courtesy of the artists.

Addressing Prior Religious and Cultural Notions of Peace

British classrooms, as in many countries, are culturally, religiously, linguistically, and ethnically diverse. Learners might have prior notions of peace based on their religious values or cultural beliefs. In Chinese culture, for example, peace is a combination of harmony and balance; in Japanese culture, it is a combination of harmony, simplicity, and quietness. In Arabic culture, the word "Islam" means peace and submission to God. For some learners, their cultural and religious notions of peace might seem all-encompassing and absolute. They may feel resistant to learning new or diverse peace concepts. These learners might benefit when their instructors are:

- Open to learners' religious or cultural notions of peace, and provide them opportunities to share them with others in the class;
- Provide diverse and multicultural concepts of peace and teach learners to be respectful of multiple viewpoints;
- Encourage learners to find shared values among diverse and multicultural concepts;
- Allow them to construct their own knowledge, meaning and understanding of peace.

ART AND PEACE

The arts have been used to symbolize peace throughout history. Some art forms represent attributes of positive peace such as harmony, while others document, or resist wars through anti-war imagery. The following provides an abbreviated version of these art forms that can be used as pedagogical resources for addressing issues of peace and peacebuilding in art education.

Peace Symbolism

Peace has multiple symbolic representations across different countries, cultures, religions, and organizations that work toward promoting peace. Each symbol has a contextual background and signifies a specific meaning. Overtime, some symbols have become universal and are used worldwide among different cultures and backgrounds. Two of these symbols are the Olive branch and the Dove. These symbols were historically used by Christians individually but have now been adopted as secular symbols of peace. Picasso's lithograph, *La Colombe* (The Dove) was adopted as the World Peace Council emblem in April 1949. The Dove symbol with an Olive branch combined was later adopted by several political committees

Figure 19.3 Mousumi De, *Om Symbol*, (2023) Mixed Media, 9.3 × 8.2 inches.

Source: Mousumi De.

Figure 19.4 Mousumi De, *CND Symbol*, (2023) Mixed Media, 9.3 × 8.2 inches.

Source: Mousumi De.

and used on currencies, namely The London Peace Society and the 18th-century American currency. Different cultures have their own unique symbols. For example, Indian Hindus signify the symbol Om as peace (*Shanti*). Figure 19.3 shows a reappropriated *Om* symbol. Over time, numerous symbols have evolved that include, among others, the White Poppy, the Broken Rifle, the Rainbow Flag and the Campaign for Nuclear Disarmament (CND) which has become a universal symbol for peace. Figure 19.4 shows a reappropriated CND symbol. The diversity of peace symbols is a reminder of the multifaceted nature of peace and learning about peace symbols from diverse cultures and contexts also contributes to multicultural and intercultural understanding through their shared notions of peace.

ANTI-WAR ART

Throughout history, artists have documented the devastating effects of war and the need for peace. In western art history, some examples, among many, are Callot's *Miseries of War*, Goya's *Disasters of War*, Sargent's *Gassed*, and Kollwitz's *Nie wieder Krieg*. One of the most influential works in contemporary times is Picasso's painting *Guernica* (1937) that depicts the destruction of the Basque town Guernica in Spain, which was bombed during the Spanish Civil War. Figure 19.5 shows a reappropriation of *Guernica* to illustrate the destruction of Kyiv in 2022. *Guernica* has long been the focus of political and anti-war activism. At Picasso's request, the painting remained in the Museum of Modern Art, New York until 1981. His conditions for its return to Spain included the restoration in Spain's of democratic institutions. In 1967, during the Vietnam war, 400 artists petitioned to withdraw *Guernica* from the United States for the duration of the war. A tapestry version of *Guernica* hangs at the UN headquarters in New York. In January 2003, the UN concealed the tapestry during former US Secretary of State Colin Powell's address, who made a case for America's war against Iraq that is antithetical to the message of the painting.

Another influential anti-war image is Nick Ut's photograph *The Terror of War*, famously known as the *Napalm Girl* taken during the Vietnam war. It shows a nine-year-old girl, Kim Phúc fleeing her village along with other children and Vietnamese soldiers after an attack. Ut's photograph amplified anti-war sentiments among Americans who were against US involvement in the war and the image remains iconic for documenting the devastating impact of war on children.

Figure 19.5 Mousumi De, *Guernica Revisited in Kyiv* (2022), Mixed Media, 22.2 × 8.3 inches.

Source: Mousumi De.

Task 19.2 Peace Symbolism and Peace Art

Conceptualize, illustrate, and discuss artworks that embody peace symbolism and peace art as mentioned below.

- Task 19.2.1 *Peace Symbolism:* Conceptualize an image that embodies two peace symbols avoiding cultural appropriation of either symbol. First, examine two peace symbols from diverse cultures individually, focusing on their meanings. Next, integrate the two into a single composition; both symbols should be recognizable individually while complementing the other.
- Task 19.2.2 *Peace Art:* Conceptualize an image that embodies positive peace between two cultures and/or countries in an open conflict. First, examine the open conflict and what negative and positive peace between them might involve. Next, using imagery that symbolizes the two cultures and/or countries and create an artwork showing peace between them, literally or metaphorically. Avoid only using anti-war imagery that shows an absence of conflict between them.

EXAMPLES – TASK 19.2: PEACE SYMBOLISM AND PEACE ART

The following are examples of *Peace Symbolism* and *Peace Art*. Figure 19.6 titled *As-salaam* was co-created by a 14-year-old British Muslim girl, with roots in Pakistan, and an Indian Hindu instructor. It integrates the Islamic peace symbol As-salaam written in Arabic with Henna patterns in the background in rainbow peace flag colors. Henna patterns are a part of both the Pakistani and Indian cultures. The artwork integrates an Arabic/Islamic symbol that is juxtaposed with a western symbol (rainbow peace flag colors). It was jointly created by individuals from diverse religious and cultural backgrounds that speaks to the unity of cultures through their shared visions of peace. Figure 19.7 titled *Togetherness* was created by a 15-year-old Indian girl in the context of the ongoing conflict between India and Pakistan. It shows two hands: the left in saffron representing the Indian flag and the right in dark green with a crescent representing the Pakistani flag.

Figure 19.6 Museret Imran and Mousumi De, *As-salaam*, (2005) Drawing, 11.7 × 16.5 inches.

Source: Courtesy of the artists.

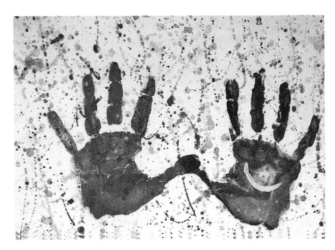

Figure 19.7 Unidentified student, *Togetherness*, (2005) Painting, 8.25 × 11.75 inches.

Source: Courtesy of the artists.

It symbolically depicts people from both sides living in harmony with each other, as an example of positive peace. The background represents the colors of the Indian festival *Holi*, which signifies the triumph of good over bad, and implies leaving the conflictual past behind and moving forward in peace.

CRITICAL PERSPECTIVES AND TEACHING STRATEGIES

Distinguishing Art Appropriation and Cultural Appropriation

When educating learners about peace symbols from diverse cultures and integrating them in art making (e.g., Task 19.2.1), it is important to educate them about the distinction between art appropriation and cultural appropriation. It is common practice in art education to appropriate images from one source, culture, or context to create a new composition with a new meaning. Appropriation in art involves the direct duplication, copying, or incorporation of an image by another artist, who represents it in a different context thereby altering its meaning and questioning notions of originality and authenticity. At the same time, appreciating and learning about another culture involves learning about their cultural objects such as artworks, artifacts as well as religious and peace symbols. It involves understanding the historical, sociocultural, and political meanings of these objects. Learners practice them by copying, duplicating, as well as appropriating them to create new images, new meanings, and expressions. Cultural learning and appreciation through such art practices should however steer away from cultural appropriation.

Cultural appropriation involves using a culture's symbols, traditional knowledge, intellectual property, and cultural objects like art, artifacts, music etc., by members of another culture without permission and making it their own. When people from a dominant culture use objects from another culture without respect of its contextual background, this can lead to stereotyping and can also be harmful when involved in the assimilation and exploitation of marginalized or colonized cultures. Cultural objects are important for the survival of such cultures and resistance to dominant cultures; these should not be commodified. When learners understand this distinction between art and cultural appropriation, they become critically aware of the implications of their art and avoid disrespecting and/or hurting the sentiments of another cultural group. This awareness is very important in art practice, especially when dealing with diverse religious and peace symbols (e.g., Task 19.2.1), and becomes critical in multicultural classrooms.

Distinguishing Anti-war Art and Peace Art

When educating learners about art and peace, it might be useful to address the difference between anti-war art and peace art. Anti-war imagery depicts the devastation of war, while peace art depicts positive and humanist imagery. Ranks (2008), a peace educator with extensive international experience in peace museums, explored the intersection of peace history and art history and found that there is more anti-war art than peace art. Many artists have created anti-war imagery, for example, Francisco Goya in relation to the Napoleonic Wars in Spain, George Grosz, and John Heartfield to the First World War, and Arnulf Rainer to the Hiroshima bombing, among others. Contemporary artists continue to create anti-war imagery through posters, photography, and other mixed media. Ranks (2008) suggests there is more anti-war art than peace art, perhaps because peace art is elusive in terms of definition. She suggests that to create a culture of peace, we must first imagine it, and the arts can help us do that. Therefore, encouraging the development of peace art pedagogies and peace art making can make an important contribution toward creating a culture of peace. These ideas also resonate with peace educators who suggest promoting concepts of positive peace that are action-centered and dynamic, which can inspire people in everyday life. Negative concepts that are couched in the language of opposites are passive and have no meaning other than by contrast to their corollary. Thus, along with learning about anti-war art, educators might also want to encourage learners to create peace art (e.g., Task 19.2.2).

PEACEBUILDING AND ITS PROCESSES

Peacebuilding is broadly defined as action to identify and support structures that will strengthen and solidify peace and avoid relapse of conflict. The central aim of peacebuilding processes is to create a sustainable environment for human security by enhancing society's capacity to manage conflict in a non-violent manner (Keating and Knight, 2004). Peacebuilding processes apply to pre- or latent conflicts (that have not yet erupted into violence) as well as post-violence conflicts that remain ongoing or hostile. Peacebuilding processes include a wide range of activities needed to prevent or recover from violence implemented through short-, medium-, and/or long-term operations. These include, among others, disarming warring parties, decommissioning, and destroying weapons, restoring judicial and political systems, reconstructing infrastructure, and rebuilding social and economic life. For avoiding a recurrence of violence, it is important to promote trust and cooperation between formerly conflicting parties and stabilize their relationships. Therefore, reconciliation is an integral part of peacebuilding, which focuses on transforming the attitudes, beliefs, and emotions of people involved in the conflict and promoting inclusion, and shared understanding based on common ground that can lead to sustainable and peaceful relations (Bar-Tal, 2000). Thus, peacebuilding has multidimensional processes involving the prevention of violence in ongoing conflicts and reconstruction and reconciliation in post-violence conflict situations.

ART IN PEACEBUILDING PROCESSES

The arts play an important role in peacebuilding processes by contributing to conflict resolution, activism, healing, and reconciliation. Peacebuilding practitioners and scholars suggest implementing strategic art-based interventions that are coordinated with specific peacebuilding processes that have distinct goals, with the long-term perspective of promoting social change (Shank and Schirch, 2008). The following are a few examples of how the arts are strategically implanted at different stages of the peacebuilding process.

ART INTERVENTIONS IN DISARMING PROCESSES

In post-violence conflict situations, disarming and destroying weapons are crucial steps toward peacebuilding. Weapons are decommissioned, destroyed, and then transformed into day-to-day utility or art objects. One compelling example is the *Transforming Arms into Tools project* (1995) implemented in Mozambique. Sixteen years of civil war had left millions of weapons hidden or buried in the country. The decommissioning of arms process encouraged people to hand over their weapons in exchange for tools like ploughs, bicycles, tractors, etc. A parallel project was implemented for remolding weapons into sculptures in 1998, during which 14 artists created 29 sculptures. Two of these sculptures include the *Tree of Life* made by four artists and the *Throne of Weapons* made by artist Kester, which was bought by the British Museum in 2001. Some of the artists were former child soldiers for whom the project provided a cathartic experience from the trauma of the war. Similar interventions have been undertaken in other conflict areas. For example, in Liberia, blacksmith Manfred Zbrzenzny collaborated with local youth to recycle munitions and contribute to the disarming process. In Mexico, the *Imagine and Disarm Project* (2012) by artist Pedro Reyes converted weapons seized by the Mexican Army into 50 musical instruments.

ART INTERVENTIONS FOR RECONCILIATION

Art is used in reconciliation processes in a variety of ways. Some interventions aim to change the belief systems and emotions of people engaged in the conflict, while others promote healing from trauma and violence. In different conflicts throughout the world, several small- and large-scale interventions have been implemented. One example of a small-scale intervention was posters created for a performance by the Serbian punk rock band, *Atheist Rap*. This was part of reconciliation efforts in the 1990s former Yugoslavian ethnic conflict. Ethnic groups included Serbs (Orthodox Christians), Croats (Catholics), Bosniaks (Muslims), and Albanians (Muslims). Since strong religious values were at the heart of the conflict, some artists and musicians in the newly formed States implemented music and theatre projects that made non-religious affiliations to foster reconciliation among people with strong religious differences.

One example of a large-scale intervention is the *Face 2 Face* (2007) photography project by artists JR and Marco in relation to the Israeli-Palestinian conflict. They photographed portraits of Israelis and Palestinians in the same profession living on either side of the dividing wall and pasted them beside each other on both sides of the wall. This allowed people on both sides to realize the similarities they share at a human level, which can contribute to reconciliatory efforts. The *Face 2 Face project* has been replicated in a variety of regions throughout the world involving community members in conflict with each other. Reconciliation is a long-term process that requires concerted and continuous efforts through such small-, medium-, and large-scale initiatives.

Task 19.3 Peacebuilding and/or Reconciliation: Research and Re-Create/ Design

Research (analyze, discover, and discuss) artworks and interventions, then Re-Create/Design (conceptualize, create, and share) artworks or interventions that contribute to Peacebuilding and/or Reconciliation processes.

- Task 19.3.1 *Research (analyze, discover, and discuss):* Works of art and art interventions that relate to peacebuilding or reconciliation from the examples below; discover and discuss artistic strategies, innovative aspects, intended audience, art media, materials, and processes (including time dimensions required in the creative process), and how these contribute to the peacebuilding or reconciliation efforts.
- Task 19.3.2 *Re-Create/Design (conceptualize, create, and share):* First, choose an ongoing or past conflict that is personally meaningful to you or relates to your community; consider the causes (whether these relate to direct, cultural, structural, or interpersonal violence) and the impact of the conflict (how it has affected people psychologically, socially, and emotionally). Next, apply the artistic strategies, innovative aspects, and art media/ materials and processes to your choice of conflict that can potentially contribute to peacebuilding or reconciliation. Consider the intended audience and places in the community where they can be seen or implemented. Share with peers how your work can potentially contribute to peacebuilding or reconciliation efforts to your choice of conflict.

The following are some examples of works of art or art interventions that contribute to peacebuilding and reconciliation processes in different conflicts throughout the world. Constructively engaging with the works through the research activity (Task 19.3.1) that will provide insights for developing your own art or design works through the Re-Create/Design activity (Task 19.3.2).

EXAMPLES – TASK 19.3.1: PEACEBUILDING AND/OR RECONCILIATION: RESEARCH

The following are some examples of artists, artworks, and art interventions using a variety of media that contribute to peacebuilding and reconciliation processes.

1. *Peace hare (Friedenshase)* by Joseph Beuys represents the transformation of symbols and creation of a new symbolic language in the public space that has the potential to create a sustainable impact on society.
2. *Birkenau series (Auschwitz)* by Gerhard Richter addresses grief, remembering, and honoring victims/survivors.
3. *Balkan Baroque* by Marina Abramovic represents processing and overcoming trauma.

4. *Your Golden Hair, Margarete–Your Ashen Hair,* Sulamith by Anselm Kiefer addresses grief, remembering, and overcoming trauma.
5. *Way of Human Rights* by Dani Karavan is a celebration of values and an appeal to society positioned in the public space.
6. *Non-Violence (The Knotted Gun)* by Carl Fredrik Reuterswärd outside UN headquarters, New York is a symbolic representation of and an appeal for non-violence and peace.
7. *Reconciliation (Reunion)* by Josefina de Vasconcellos representing reunion of people and nations after the World War II symbolizing hope and reconciliation
8. *The Hopeful Project* by Charlie Hewitt represents creation of a new symbolic language in the public space for hope and positive change in society
9. *Wrath and Reverence* by Al Farrow represents the relationship between religion and violence, peace and brutality, provoking dialogue and social and emotional transformation.
10. *The F Word Exhibition (The Forgiveness Project)* by Marina Cantacuzino represents rebuilding lives after overcoming hurt and trauma among victims/survivors.
11. *Calligraffiti* by El Saed represents symbolic language for bringing people, cultures, and generations together.
12. The Humans of New York Project (HONY) by Brandon Stanton addresses grief, remembering, and honoring victims/survivors for hope and positive change in society.

EXAMPLES – TASK 19.3.2: PEACEBUILDING AND/OR RECONCILIATION: RE-CREATE/DESIGN

The following are examples of art about *Peacebuilding* (Figure 19.8) and *Reconciliation processes* (Figure 19.9) in relation to the Indo-Pak conflict created by Indian high school girls, aged between 12 and 14 years. Figure 19.8 is a collage, titled *Education* co-created by three girls that metaphorically represents joint-educational programs, where youth from India and Pakistan can study together to build trust as part of the peacebuilding process. The two nationalities are symbolized by colors from their respective flags. Figure 19.9 titled *Dialogue* was co-created by two girls that symbolically depicts dialogue between people from both sides which promotes reconciliation through mutual understanding, compromise, and forgiveness.

Figure 19.8 Unidentified students, *Education*, (2012) Poster, 11.75 × 24.75 inches.
Source: Courtesy of the artists.

Figure 19.9 Unidentified students, *Dialogue*, (2012) Painting, 11.7 × 16.5 inches.

Source: Courtesy of the artists.

These artworks align with the goals of the campaign *Aman ki Asha* (*Hope for Peace*) implemented by media groups from both countries in 2010 to promote mutual peace, and diplomatic and cultural relations.

CRITICAL PERSPECTIVES AND TEACHING STRATEGIES

Addressing Contested and Culturally Sensitive Issues

Perceptions of peace and conflict are often influenced by learners' religious and political ideologies, beliefs, attitudes, experiences, knowledge received from family, friends, newsmedia, social media, as well as misinformation, cultural stereotypes, biases, and prejudice. Learners might have contested views regarding these issues that are culturally sensitive topics to address in the classroom. Some learners might feel inhibited from openly sharing their views that can limit authentic discussion, expression, and learning. Some teaching strategies to facilitate authentic discussion, engagement, and learning include:

- Providing non-partisan views and evidence-based knowledge following guidelines on maintaining *Political Impartiality in Schools* and teaching *Sensitive Political Issues* set forth by the Department of Education, UK Government (see Resources);
- Liaising with relevant departments/agencies in the school or community *prior* to approaching sensitive issues related to latent or open conflicts and developing art and design projects;
- Creating a psychologically safe class environment and assuring learners that divergent viewpoints are inherent in conflict situation;
- Encouraging tolerance, diversity and inclusion of others' viewpoints;
- Building trust between educators and students and amongst students and assuring them their views are independent of their grades.

Teaching Art 'about' – and 'for' – Peace and Peacebuilding

An important part of addressing issues of peace and peacebuilding in art education is understanding the distinction between teaching art *about* – and teaching art *for* peace /peacebuilding. Art *about* peace/peacebuilding involves teaching about the concepts of peace and peacebuilding processes, and how the arts are used in these domains. The primary goals of such pedagogy are to promote knowledge and cognitive and artistic skills in these domains. Art *for* peace/peacebuilding involves using art to transform learners in schools and people in communities who are directly or indirectly engaged in a conflict at the individual, interpersonal, cultural, or global level. Conflicts might include, among others, between Catholics and Protestants in Northern Ireland, between British Muslims and Non-Muslims, and people whose heritage is long established in the UK and more recent immigrants etc. Here the primary goal is to use art as a tool and medium for healing and therapy, transforming mentalities and stabilizing relationships to promote trust, tolerance, inclusion, that can contribute to the goals of peacebuilding and reconciliation processes. In a classroom situation, the primary goal is thus to promote transformational changes in addition to artistic skills and knowledge.

Using art *for* peace/peacebuilding requires educators to consciously examine their role in the peacebuilding process and make an intentional effort to design, implement, and evaluate curricula that can promote peace and reconciliation among learners. Such pedagogies must be developed and implemented under guidance and consultation with relevant departments in schools or agencies in the community that work for conflict resolution, trauma and healing, peacebuilding, and reconciliation.

RESOURCES

Agence VU: https://agencevu.com/en/serie/face-2-face-2007/
Aman ki Asha (Hope for Peace): https://en.wikipedia.org/wiki/Aman_ki_Asha
Atheist Rap: https://en.wikipedia.org/wiki/Atheist_Rap
Balkan Baroque: https://www.moma.org/audio/playlist/243/3126
Birkenau Series: https://www.smb.museum/en/exhibitions/detail/reflections-on-painting/
Calligraffiti by El Saed: https://eng.majalla.com/node/66211/el-seed-a-message-of-unity-drawn-in-%E2%80%98calligraffiti%E2%80%99
Face 2 Face: https://agencevu.com/en/serie/face-2-face-2007/
Imagine (psaltery) by Pedro Reyes: https://www.designboom.com/design/weapon-instruments-by-pedro-reyes-at-lisson-gallery/
Peace hereby: https://www.youtube.com/watch?v=t2j-579VznQ
Political impartiality in schools: https://www.gov.uk/government/publications/political-impartiality-in-schools/political-impartiality-in-schools
Reconciliation (Reunion): https://en.wikipedia.org/wiki/Reconciliation_(Josefina_de_Vasconcellos_sculpture
The F Word Exhibition (The Forgiveness Project): https://www.theforgivenessproject.com/
The Hopeful Project: https://ogunquitmuseum.org
The Humans of New York Project (HONY) by Brandon Stanton https://www.humansofnewyork.com/
The Tree of Life: https://britishmuseum.withgoogle.com/object/tree-of-life
The War of Terror by Nick Ut: https://www.nga.gov/collection/art-object-page.136637.html
Throne of Weapons: https://britishmuseum.withgoogle.com/object/throne-of-weapons
Way of Human Rights: https://en.wikipedia.org/wiki/Way_of_Human_Rights

Wrath and Reverence: https://www.21cmuseumhotels.com/museum/exhibit/
al-farrow-wrath-and-reverence/

Your Golden Hair, Margarete – Your Ashen Hair: https://www.metmuseum.org/art/
collection/search/490046

BIBLIOGRAPHY

Anderson, R. (2004). A definition of peace. *Peace and Conflict: Journal of Peace Psychology*, 10(2), 101.

Bar-Tal, D. (2000), *Shared beliefs in a society: Social psychological analysis.* Thousands Oaks, CA: Sage.

Galtung, J. (1969). Violence, peace, and peace research. *Journal of Peace Research*, 6(3), 167–191.

Galtung, J. (1996). *Peace by peaceful means: Peace and conflict, development, and civilization* (Vol. 14). London: Sage.

Keating, T. F., and Knight, W. A. (Eds.). (2004). Building sustainable peace. *Global Governance*, 11(1), 115–130.

Rank, C. (2008). Promoting peace through the arts. *Proceedings of the 2008 International Peace Research Association (IPRA) Conference*, IPRA 2008. 15–19 July 2008, Leuven, Belgium.

Shank, M., and Schirch, L. (2008). Strategic arts-based peacebuilding. *Peace & Change*, 33(2), 217–242.

UNESCO, (2010). Seoul Agenda: Goals for the Development of Arts Education, *World Conference on Arts Education*, 2nd ed., Seoul, Korea: R. Ministry of Culture, Sports and Tourism.

Chapter 20

Remapping the Curriculum: A Landscape Designed for the Future: Part 2. The National Society for Education in Art and Design 'Big Landscape': Mapping the Terrain of Art & Design

Andy Ash and Ged Gast

INTRODUCTION

This final chapter of the Practical Guide to Teaching Art and Design in the Secondary School aims to assist teachers in their curriculum understanding and planning. The chapter brings together ideas from previous chapters to explore the function of an art, craft and design (ACD) department in creating a contemporary curriculum pertinent to today's students' needs and interests. Through questions, we explore how the acquisition of knowledge, skills and understanding via experiential learning in ACD retains its essential position in supporting students' growth in current contexts.

To understand how to approach this, we consider why learning and teaching are not the same thing, before sharing our vision of the Big Landscape of Art and Design education. Referencing some other sections of *The Practical Guide to Teaching Art and Design in the Secondary School*, the chapter aligns these with the Big Landscape of the Art & Design Curriculum which is a new and evolving website created by the subject association for Art and Design, the NSEAD. We conclude by signposting resources to guide an Art and Design teaching team through collaborative curriculum planning, emphasising the importance of shared ownership and commitment to agreement on ethos, values and principles. The purpose of the Big Landscape is not to work as a checklist of things to be covered in a curriculum, but is rather to work as an aide-memoire for the Art and Design subject leader and teaching team of all the possible aspects of a curriculum that they can then plot their own unique pathway through to facilitate the personal and professional growth of their Art Department.

Links and QR codes support this exploration of the terrain with further activities and images taken from sections of the NSEAD Big Landscape.

OBJECTIVES:

By the end of this chapter, you should be able to:

- Use your understanding of curriculum breadth, scope and depth gained through earlier chapters to review your own curriculum and then specify the content you wish to prioritise for your drafting process;

DOI: 10.4324/9781003377429-24

- Determine how your values will underpin your approach to structuring learning and challenge for all abilities;
- Refine your curriculum planning approach based on the Big Landscape and where possible use this with colleagues to guide curriculum design in ways best suited to your students and community.

WHAT IS THE DIFFERENCE BETWEEN TEACHING AND LEARNING IN ART AND DESIGN, AND WHY CAN 'KNOWLEDGE' BE CONTENTIOUS FOR SOME ART AND DESIGN TEACHERS?

A strong curriculum that engenders learning requires breadth and depth in both content and pedagogy, and will reflect past and present cultural discourse through dialogic and applied practice, and will exploit organic/rhizomic curricular connections from the past and the present (Walton, Ch 13, this edition). ACD subject matter is defined by the substance of learning *in, about* and *through* the subject (Lindström 2012; Hickman 2005), the subject's contexts and stimuli draw upon the whole of life and human experience. The very nature of creative learning involves higher level critical thinking, fed by rich and diverse contexts, which, in turn, feed the imaginative connections that lead to innovation (Morris, Ch 9, Grant, Ch 11, this edition).

The antithesis of this is an orthodoxy of teaching (Addison and Burgess 2007) that results in the repetition of similar outcomes, following predictable and over-familiar learning structures that may engender *activity* but not necessarily *learning* (Wild, Ch 4, this edition). This results in a curriculum of known outcomes rather than the pursuit of an exciting learning journey without limits to the scope of the student's creativity. Many of the previous chapters have explored this issue (Wild, Ch 4, Morris, Ch 9, Fursman, Ch 10, Eça and Saldanha, Ch 12, Granville et al., Ch 8, Ash and Smith, Ch 14, Millett, Ch 16, this edition)

Task 20.1 Creative Process Stages/Steps

The following set of creative actions are typical stages that can be used as part of a creative process of learning in a Unit of Work/Project (Figure 20.1). Consider the following questions:

1. Are these creative process steps/stages familiar to you and reflect the essential process steps/stages that are taught in your department?
2. Starting with 'Research', is the order similar to the structure of the Units of Work/ projects that you plan for your students?
3. Or do the orange arrows represent something closer to the reality of creative activity? Why might that be?

Now create a set of cards labelled using these terms. Experiment with your colleagues, by rearranging these into differently ordered process steps or stages:

(a) Question and discuss how well a project organised in the different ways you devise would work?
(b) Consider the different learning process and outcomes that might result from each alternative process? Are any of these better suited to a specific gender/age/ability/student group, or particular area of activity?

(c)   Reflect on the value of reversing the order, starting with an outcome, or directly working with media and skills, before engaging with research, artists/designers and concluding with making a mode.

Now consider what constitutes a final outcome? If it is a summation of project learning, does it always have to be a substantial work? Could it, for example, be a collection of maquettes, models, something ephemeral or the presentation of a design folder for a site-specific commission? Consider how flexible you will be in future, varying the creative process steps/stages within taught projects.

NB. If you agree that the process is not linear, you might envisage a more dynamic process enabling movement iteratively between several process steps, for example, Draw, Experiment and Design (see orange arrows).

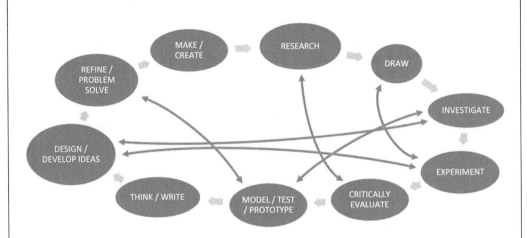

Figure 20.1 Typical Creative Stages in the Art and Design curriculum. Gast (2022).

ACD teachers may have differing views on the role of knowledge in our subject. Some limit it to the cultural and physical knowledge of artists and their work, while others seek greater emphasis on knowledge dimensions across the curriculum. In any case, in ACD not all knowledge is taught as facts, much is modelled, guided and built though making and doing, but still requires teachers to signpost, identify and communicate what that knowledge is and review the understanding gained following the learning activity (Pratt, Ch 3, this edition). Knowledge of design stages, processes and the way media and materials behave is scaffolded for the learners as understanding about materials, media and techniques (Granville et al., Ch 8, this edition). These are what inform a student's subsequent creative action, enabling them to improve their skills and creative decisions. Experiential and practical knowledge therefore becomes as highly regarded as the theoretical knowledge informing it (Thakara, Ch 6, this edition).

This kind of subject knowledge is 'powerful', enabling students to function confidently and successfully in subject specific ways (Wild, Ch 4, this edition). Powerful knowledge as promoted by Michael Young makes the case for 'specialised' knowledge as it functions within a subject (Young 2008). For example, knowledge of drawing media, paper surfaces, line and tonal qualities, shading techniques and the conscious (meta) control of our own mark-making abilities in applying these will surely contribute to better drawing outcomes, with deeper levels of engagement and understanding.

Knowledge Development

Practical, Theoretical & Disciplinary Knowledge is Powerful, informing art making, with the application of cultural understanding to enable creative action & skill building.

4 Knowledge Domains informing learning

- **EXPLICIT** - Know What (facts & theory)
- **TACIT** - Know How (experiential learning)
- **CONCEPTUAL** - Know About (critical & contextual, aesthetics, other cultures)
- **AFFECTIVE** - Know Self (self-perception, reflection, metacognition, motivation, feelings & emotions, making meaning)

Figure 20.2 Four knowledge domain model block (from the Big Landscape, Gast and NSEAD 2022).

The structure of ACD as a predominantly process driven and experiential subject, means that students acquire knowledge and learn mostly by making and doing. We believe a four 'domains of knowledge' model (Figure 20.2) for acquiring, building and applying knowledge matches the structure for how learning works best in our subject.

1. **Explicit Knowledge: Know What**

    Explicit knowledge is concerned with facts and theory gained through taught information and applied experience. This knowledge enables the learner to build understanding through applied processes and techniques, learning principles (rules) such as colour theory, composition or health and safety for safe practice. Explicit knowledge is also the factual information concerned with visual memory, critical and contextual information about artists, designers, movements, genres, periods, style, visual and contextual information about creative history and facts about works of ACD.

2. **Tacit Knowledge: Know How**

    Tacit knowledge draws on the experience gained through creative activity and enables the learner to access knowledge built and gained through experience and procedural knowledge informing skill development, knowledge of media, tools and materials, and how they interact and behave.

3. **Conceptual Knowledge: Know About**

   Conceptual knowledge enables the learner to engage in imaginative activity, abstraction and meaning making, acquiring contextual information through knowledge and concept building. Learners use this knowledge to imagine, conceive and develop new ideas, engage in visual speculation as they construct aesthetic models and evaluate their quality or relevance.

4. **Affective Knowledge: Know Self**

   Affective knowledge supports our self-reflective thinking, informing our creative decisions through knowledge of self, connecting our feelings and emotions to internal dialogue, drawing on our metacognitive reflection and informing meaning-making connections and personally expressive actions.

Task 20.2 Knowledge

What model of knowledge is central to your existing curriculum or teaching methodology?
Look either at existing department documentation and SoW/project/lesson planning or consider more broadly how you reference knowledge through your teaching.

- Can you identify broad types of knowledge or domains?
- Compare these with the model suggested here and consider whether:

(a) There is a strong correlation with the four domains?;
(b) There are areas of knowledge missing in your curriculum?;
(c) You have any additions/suggestions to the domains?;
(d) Having no planned approach to how knowledge is covered is sustainable.

Draft action points to review your teaching approach and make powerful knowledge explicit. Include this in learning critiques, seek evidence in sketchbooks, in evidence of making or self-evaluation following new teaching.

Skills are the practical application of knowledge needed to undertake the actions and functions required to ensure a successful outcome. Knowledge and skills are not interchangeable and do not mean the same thing. A skill is something you improve with practise and careful application of knowledge and experience. Revisiting skills reinforces learning, while revisiting in different contexts builds breadth and depth of experience (Cubbin, Ch 5, this edition). Transferable and soft skills, such as communication and problem solving, can be developed across areas of learning. Thinking skills, such as analysis and creative thinking, require practice and are best learned alongside practical skills (Eisner 1998). In practical and applied contexts, experientially acquired knowledge draws on critical understanding through the conceptual domain, making it important to apply knowledge and experience carefully to improve skills (Grant, Ch 11, this edition).

Knowledge and skills alone are not the only way to plan learning or assess characteristics and competencies. Attitudes and behaviours are increasingly regarded as central to learning because they determine the student's readiness to learn and mindset for taking in, processing and remembering what they learn (Gregson, Ch 7, Morris, Ch 9, Wylie, Ch 15, Millett, Ch 16, this edition) Attitudes and behaviours are also associated with transferability, supporting the flexibility of thinking needed for creative learning. Attitudes and behaviours are also essential in developing learning habits (Heaton, Ch 2, Ash and Smith, Ch 14, this edition), consolidating dispositions and building personal characteristics. Where skills are often specific to a process, media, technique or an approach, behaviours are by contrast attitudinal and transferable.

HOW DO WE KEEP A CURRICULUM RELEVANT TO THE CONTEMPORARY WORLD?

The curriculum should be relevant, meaningful and significant for students, connecting ACD and wider society (Ash and Smith, Ch 14, Wylie, Ch 15, Millett, Ch 16, Patience, Ch 17, Penketh and Hiett, Ch 18, De and Wagner, Ch 19, this edition). It must speak to the present time and the students' community whether this is local or global. Art reflects on human life while craft and design seek to enhance it (Granville et al., Ch 8, this edition). Teachers must consider age-appropriate subject matter and safeguarding when choosing topics, such as the ethical value of public monuments or buildings funded by slavery, for example. In this example, by learning about public sculpture, students can explore the issues around commissioning for public spaces and consider the Spiritual, Moral Social and Cultural (SMSC) dimensions of this, leading to students' visual work that examines historic events such as the toppling of the Colston statue or the social and moral agenda of an artist like Banksy. The potential scope for SMSC reference points is wide, but responsibility lies with the teacher in ensuring the curriculum is appropriate and relevant (Wylie, Ch 15, Millett, Ch 16, Patience, Ch 17, Penketh and Hiett, Ch 18, De and Wagner, Ch 19, this edition).

Teachers must select examples wisely and explore them without bias, encouraging students to form their own views and respond creatively (Gregson, Ch 7, this edition). The strongest curriculum promotes reflexive learning and enables students to think independently, investigate real-world issues and develop their own solutions. Teachers must consider relevance to context, age and maturity, promoting critical thinking approaches that enable students to accept feedback and investigate issues in a politically neutral curriculum. Higher-level thinking contexts referencing SMSC dimensions can be used to explore appropriate ethical and moral values for British children, along with decolonisation, personal perspectives and the application of powerful knowledge (Grant, Ch 11, this edition).

Task 20.3 Curriculum Relevance

By acknowledging the importance of avoiding a predominance of particular media, genres or defined style within selected artists and exemplars shown to students, teachers may wish to review the genres, periods, movements, types of media or art forms represented in their planned curriculum.

- How wide ranging and suitably relevant to our curriculum, are the artists, makers, designers and exemplars you use with students?
- Is my curriculum suitably:
  - respectful and decolonised to embrace racial and cultural diversity?
  - balanced and neutral regarding age, gender, disability, faith or belief?
  - representative of genres, periods, movements, styles and different times?

- representative of the many disciplines of ACD?
- spread across a range of media processes?
- respectful of contemporary and historic practices?
- diverse in referencing subject matter?

The terms 'art', 'art and design' and 'art, craft and design' are often used to refer to the scope of the National Curriculum in the four UK nations, and to local curricula. These terms define the emergence of groups of activity within higher education and in the professional career pipelines, with fine ACD all having distinctive historic differences. However, sustaining this breadth is challenging in the wake of post-modernist conceptual practices in HE and at the professional level, the digital revolution and the blurring of activity boundaries by new graduates from all fields of the visual arts and design (Morris, Ch 9, Fursman, Ch 10, Granville et al., Ch 8, Ash and Smith, Ch 14, Eça and Saldanha, Ch 12, this edition).

Even so, an expression of breadth and scope is helpful to both school-age children and their parents as well as senior leadership in schools in the definition of the need for specialist media, facilities, studios and teacher skills. Calling a subject simply 'Art' may diminish it in the minds of non-specialists, while referencing 'Craft and Design' in the title, underlines the need for specialist facilities and high quality and suitably equipped studio/classroom spaces.

Task 20.4 Breadth and Depth

- What is the breadth of your curriculum?
- Do all students have opportunity to gain experiences across the range of creative opportunity?
- Look either at existing department documentation and project/lesson planning, or consider more broadly how you reference knowledge through your teaching;
- Compare your knowledge model to the four-domain example set out here and consider whether each domain is suitably covered or over emphasised at the expense of another.

In response to this, you may choose to invest further research into knowledge domains or possibly redesign the way in which knowledge is planned and taught within your curriculum.

It is both helpful and common practice to create a curriculum plan/map that visually presents an overview of their curriculum content, which has three benefits:

1. A visual plan ensures blocks of learning, projects, examinations, assessments and all other annual and termly events avoid calendar clashes;
2. A visual overview enables checking, sequencing and continuity of experience, the progression of knowledge and skills, and identifies missing components and avoids repetition;
3. Assessment and examination dates are easily identified, with the scheduling of moderations, curriculum reviews, deadlines and management oversight.

The question of how content is set out can be a point of healthy discussion within an Art Department. A curriculum map provides an overview of the scheme of work (the What and the How), with essential learning (the Why) and adaptive teaching for each cohort, mapped across the year/terms (Cubbin, Ch 5, this edition). However, it cannot explain the wider contexts for learning, which require a full curriculum statement, including challenge and adaptive teaching for each project, themes, dimensions and any hidden curriculum elements.

HOW DO WE MAP THE TERRAIN AND PLAN FOR THE BIG LANDSCAPE OF AN ART AND DESIGN CURRICULUM?

The Big Landscape of the Art & Design Curriculum is a new and evolving website created by the NSEAD. It has been designed as a curriculum research and development tool for ACD teachers in support of their subject knowledge development and the evolution of the subject. It provides a visual classification and interactive interface for building understanding of the content, dimensions, scope and wider aspects of the ACD curriculum. To achieve this, it organises typical media, areas of creative activity, attitudes, aspects, themes and dimensions within a non-hierarchical taxonomy. It functions like an aide-memoire to support curriculum planning, review and research supported by exemplification. To aid their professional development, ACD teachers can use the Big Landscape for team discussion or review, as a prompt to planning a scheme of work, or by selecting whole blocks, phrases, headings or words, they can 'drill-down' to access description, explanations, link to exemplification, articles and research papers.

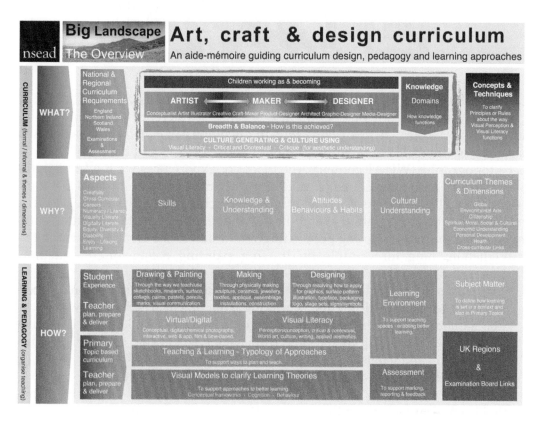

Figure 20.3 The Overview (Layer 2) of the *Big Landscape of the Art & Design Curriculum* (NSEAD 2023).

The Big Landscape also reminds us of the importance of determining the values and the ethos we set for learning in our subject. It helps the ACD teacher to select relevant knowledge, content and process learning to develop the most appropriate skills, habits, behaviours and attributes, enabling students to think critically, analyse, explore and express themselves in response to visual or other sensory stimuli, concepts, issues, themes and dimensions. It would be helpful for teachers to look at the Big Landscape at the same time as reading this section. Using the QR code below will enable you to see the features of the Big Landscape, the full interactivity of which is available through NSEAD membership (See Task 20.5).

Use this QR Code to see the website for the NSEAD Big Landscape.

We use the metaphor of a landscape because it references a learning journey across a terrain, in this case a terrain encompassing the whole scope and variation of the ACD curriculum. The Big Landscape sets out a map of the subject's topography (WHAT content), the places or experiences we might visit, the (WHY) these particular contexts might be of benefit to learning and personal growth as well as the breadth of learning approaches (HOW we will learn). The map enables the visualisation of an infinite number of different individual learning journeys or 'routes' young people might take across the creative learning terrain when learning, for example, by drawing, painting, collage or construction.

- **WHAT is the project about?** Content, knowledge and learning to be covered;
- **WHY are we learning this?** Thinking and practical skills/knowledge to be gained through critical and contextual references, building understanding whilst referencing themes and dimensions, to develop creative attitudes, behaviours and habits;
- **HOW will this be taught?** Teaching and learning approaches.

You will see from looking at the Content Poster of the Big Landscape using the QR code that blocks of information are grouped together under the What, Why and How bands as set out in Figure 20.4. These bands group the concepts, key

Figure 20.4 The Landing Page (Layer 1) of the *Big Landscape of the Art & Design Curriculum* (NSEAD 2023).

ideas and content related either to areas of learning in Art and Design, or provide information about themes, dimensions and pedagogy. Within the bands are blocks, each of which is designed to contain just enough information grouped together to encapsulate related content described by a word, statement, list or group of statements. The content in each block is not intended to be included in its entirety across a learning phase or Key stage, but rather as a suggestion of many possible options from which a teacher might select.

The blue Conceptual and Technical Development block (Figure 20.5), lists areas of conceptual and technical development, such as artistic elements, colour theory or compositional rules and a four functions of drawing model. Teachers may agree or disagree with some of this suggested content, such as compositional rules or types of perspective. Others may not agree that these are the best terms defining the functions of drawing. In ACD, we are unlikely to ever gain common agreement and it would be unhelpful to do so, as this would contribute to an orthodoxy of practice that we have argued against. The purpose of the Big Landscape is to list possible content and contexts, so a teacher can select and group together the most suitable content for a coherent curriculum and from this set out the learning intentions for each project/unit.

In the green Why Band, blocks group together Aspects of Learning, Curriculum Themes and Dimensions, as well as Cultural Developments and Creativity. One block, for example, provides links to guidance on more generic principles concerned with the development of attitudes, thinking skills, habits of mind, behaviour and critical thinking. Although generic in principle, these aspects are essential in developing creativity, critical thinking and practical skills (Figure 20.6).

There are two sections in the brown How Band. The upper blocks in the band detail how teaching approaches embrace these learning habits and behaviours. In

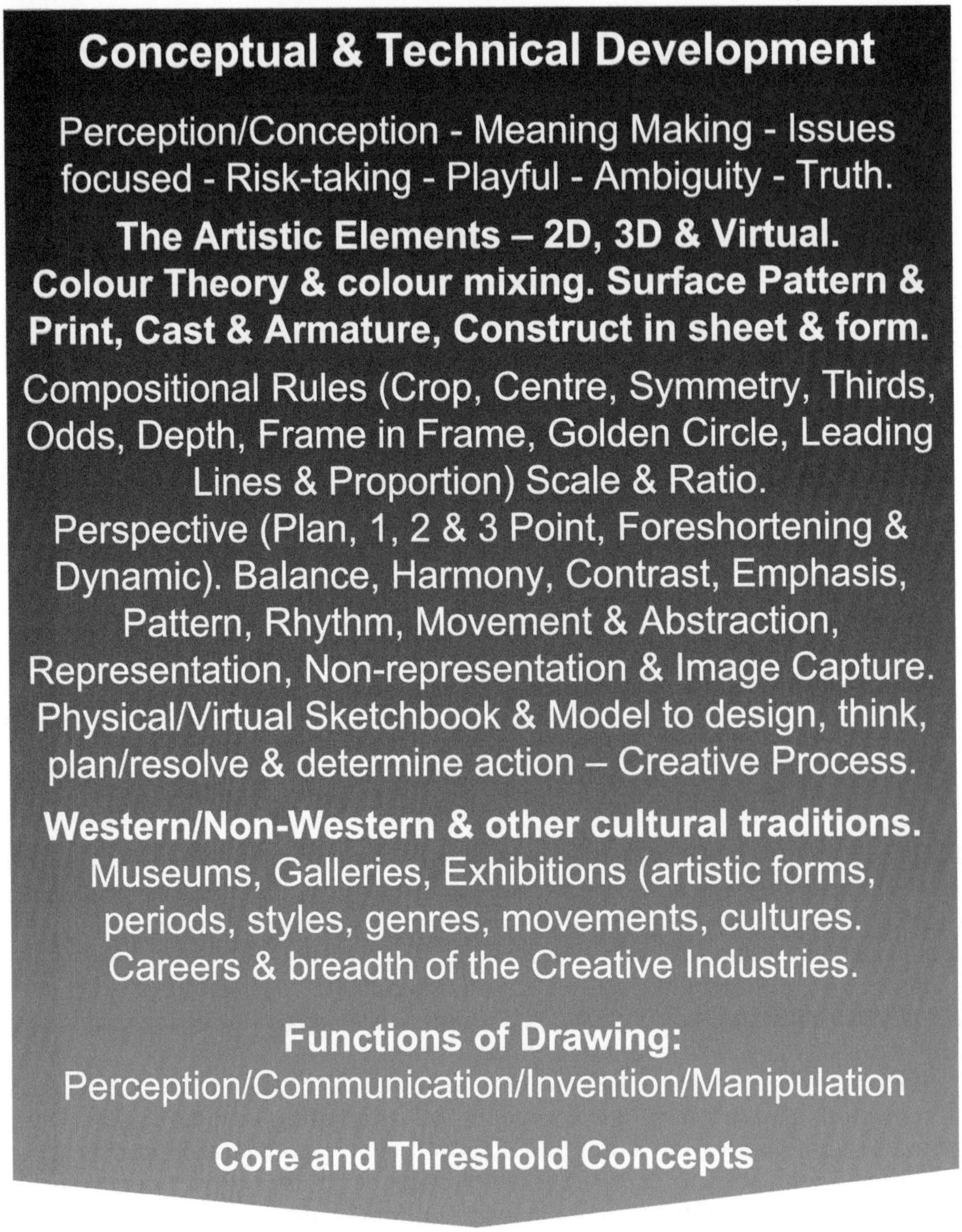

Conceptual & Technical Development

Perception/Conception - Meaning Making - Issues focused - Risk-taking - Playful - Ambiguity - Truth.

The Artistic Elements – 2D, 3D & Virtual.
Colour Theory & colour mixing. Surface Pattern & Print, Cast & Armature, Construct in sheet & form.

Compositional Rules (Crop, Centre, Symmetry, Thirds, Odds, Depth, Frame in Frame, Golden Circle, Leading Lines & Proportion) Scale & Ratio. Perspective (Plan, 1, 2 & 3 Point, Foreshortening & Dynamic). Balance, Harmony, Contrast, Emphasis, Pattern, Rhythm, Movement & Abstraction, Representation, Non-representation & Image Capture. Physical/Virtual Sketchbook & Model to design, think, plan/resolve & determine action – Creative Process.

Western/Non-Western & other cultural traditions.
Museums, Galleries, Exhibitions (artistic forms, periods, styles, genres, movements, cultures. Careers & breadth of the Creative Industries.

Functions of Drawing:
Perception/Communication/Invention/Manipulation

Core and Threshold Concepts

Figure 20.5 Conceptual and Technical Development Block (Layer 3) from the Big Landscape (NSEAD 2023).

the lower part of the band, you will be able to access information about pedagogical and conceptual models you may already know or use, but other examples of these might lead you to rethink the way you organise your teaching and learning to build concepts and ideas.

This is **NOT** an 'off-the-shelf' curriculum. Teacher's do not have to cover or teach all of this, but it should inform your professional development and give you easier access to information about concepts and approaches, when you want to

Figure 20.6 The green Why Band and Blocks (Layer 3) from the Big Landscape (NSEAD 2023).

Task 20.5 The Big Landscape

You can look at the Big Landscape online and view a public domain version. Compare this with your planning and use this to identify other areas or content you might wish to include in your curriculum;

- If you want access to the full and evolving version of the Big Landscape, you can do so as a member of the NSEAD https://www.nsead.org/membership/

learn more, or need a signpost to areas for further investigation. The Big Landscape is **NOT** fixed, it will promote a shared language and focus for debate, enabling regular updating and improvement as part of a living subject.

HOW DOES COLLABORATION AND PROFESSIONAL DIALOGUE LEAD TO A BETTER CURRICULUM?

A recognised key factor in a successful curriculum has always been shared ownership and some delegation of responsibility spread amongst the teaching team, to ensure the curriculum is current, relevant to the needs of the community and present cohorts, and that each teacher has personal investment (Dewey 1938). Similarly, the concept of co-creation and partnership between teachers and students is widely accepted and particularly powerful in ACD where there is greater flexibility and opportunity to specify content and define relevant learning objectives and outcomes.

In ACD, it is crucial for all members of the teaching team to engage with the planning of a curriculum, especially with the need to modify content regularly in response to opportunities as they arise, new colleagues' areas of expertise and student interests. Staff ownership builds interest, commitment and understanding, ensuring responsibility and willingness to adapt and evolve planning in response to different learning needs. Ofsted inspections highlight that members of the teaching team prefer to teach projects they have written or co-developed, rather than someone else's planning, leading to recognition and value for their contributions. Staff acceptance and commitment to all aspects of the curriculum are crucial for effective teaching.

Task 20.6 How Might We Audit Existing Provision before Drafting or Revising Your Curriculum?

Prior to writing any curriculum and as a part of the wider reading around good curriculum models and examples, teachers should carry out an audit of existing provision. There is an example of an Art and Design Audit Tool on the NSEAD website, developed by the Expert Subject Advisory Group as part of the revision to the English National Curriculum.

The Audit tool can be downloaded from:
https://www.nsead.org/resources/curriculum/art-and-design-expert-subject-advisory-group-resources/art-and-design-resources-for-teachers-and-learners/

Teachers might engage students in co-creating the curriculum to promote meta-cognition and foster independence. This approach empowers students to own their progress and learning experience (Dewey 1966), and it complements the concept of flipped classrooms (see Resources). Sharing curriculum direction and subject matter in advance with students allows for modification, personalisation and collaborative opportunities. Task 20.7 exemplifies a critical thinking approach that promotes team collaboration and idea-sharing, enhancing the ownership and effectiveness of curriculum planning in ACD.

Task 20.7 Team Task – Collaborative Key Stage 3 Curriculum Drafting Activity

These tasks take 2–3 hours, so may require a school training day or several department meetings with delegated tasks. Each team member should research, prepare, resource and lead team discussion on different sections. Outcomes should be documented to ensure shared ownership. Photographs of planning stages will share curriculum planning and encourage the team in the resolution of challenging curriculum issues.

The Collaborative Curriculum planning activity can be downloaded and printed from the QR code.

SUMMARY

In this chapter, we have mapped out some of the ground and steps to take when planning the ACD curriculum whilst advocating a more collaborative conversation to take place in schools. Through the metaphor of a Big Landscape, we have shared ways for teachers to orientate themselves or get their bearings for their own path within and through the curriculum. This chapter will empower teachers to choose and use the knowledge of their lived experiences in preference to 'off-the-shelf' models presently available widely. We have stressed the importance of not dictating or spoon-feeding pre-known outcomes, which can result in teachers becoming less familiar with the fundamental learning language of the terrain. Freire suggests the key to liberation is the awakening of critical awareness and the thinking process in the individual (Freire 2005), and a true partnership between the teacher, their students and the needs of the community. In contrast to this, many ACD teachers may be continuing to navigate a road well-travelled because they can confidently use this to build success and guarantee the achievement of examination targets, possibly at the cost of the kind of learning that Freire is referencing. The Big Landscape is designed to support teachers in overcoming this apparent dichotomy and become more autonomous, collaborative and self-reliant, while working as a part of a wider community of practice that continues to lead to success for their students. We want to encourage and give hope to ACD teachers, to encourage them to gain a confident perspective on the well-trodden path, to look up from the ground and to focus on their own pathway for the journey ahead and plan a curriculum fit for the future.

RESOURCES

TheFlippedLearningNetwork:http://flippedlearning.org/flexible_environment/
    flipped-learning-toolkit-from-edutopia/
NSEAD: https://www.nsead.org

BIBLIOGRAPHY

Addison, N. and Burgess, L. (2007). Introduction. *Learning to Teach Art and Design in the Secondary School: A Companion to School Experience*. N. Addison and L. Burgess. London, Routledge Falmer.

Bruner, J. (1960). *The Process of Education*. Cambridge, MA, Harvard University Press.

Dewey, J. (1938). *Experience & Education*. New York, Touchstone.

Dewey, J. (1966). *Democracy and Education: An Introduction to the Philosophy of Education*. New York, The Free Press.

Eisner, E. (1998). "What Do the Arts Teach?" *Improving Schools* **1**(3): 4.

Eisner, E. W. (2002). *The Arts and the Creation of Mind*. New Haven, CT, Yale University Press.

Freire, P. (2005). *Pedagogy of the Oppressed*. New York, Continuum.

Hickman, R. (2005). *Why We Make Art and Why It Is Taught*. Bristol, Intellect.

Kolb, D. A. (1984). *Experiential Learning: Experience as the Source of Learning and Development*. Englewood Cliffs, NJ, Prentice-Hall.

Lindström, L. (2012). "Aesthetic Learning About, In, With and Through the Arts: A Curriculum Study." *The International Journal of Art & Design Education* **31**(2): 166–179.

Young, M. F. D. (2008). *Bringing Knowledge Back In: From Social Constructivism to Social Realism in the Sociology of Education*. Oxford, Routledge.

Index

For Product Safety Concerns and Information please contact our EU
representative GPSR@taylorandfrancis.com Taylor & Francis Verlag GmbH,
Kaufingerstraße 24, 80331 München, Germany

Printed and bound by CPI Group (UK) Ltd, Croydon, CR0 4YY
08/06/2025
01897012-0003